American Legal Records – Volume 10

Edited for THE AMERICAN HISTORICAL ASSOCIATION by the
Committee on the Littleton-Griswold Fund

CRIMINAL PROCEEDINGS IN COLONIAL VIRGINIA

The Littleton-Griswold Fund of the American Historical Association
was established in 1927 by Mrs. Frank T. Griswold in memory of
William E. Littleton and Frank Tracy Griswold

American Legal Records – Volume 10

CRIMINAL PROCEEDINGS IN COLONIAL VIRGINIA

[Records of] Fines, Examination of Criminals,
Trials of Slaves, etc.,
from March 1710 [1711] to [1754]
[Richmond County, Virginia]

EDITED WITH AN INTRODUCTION BY
PETER CHARLES HOFFER
THE UNIVERSITY OF GEORGIA

EDITED AND TRANSCRIBED BY
WILLIAM B. SCOTT
KENYON COLLEGE

Published for
THE AMERICAN HISTORICAL ASSOCIATION
Washington, D.C.
by
THE UNIVERSITY OF GEORGIA PRESS
Athens, Georgia
1984

Library of Congress Cataloging in Publication Data

Main entry under title:

Criminal proceedings in colonial Virginia.

(American legal records; v. 10)
Includes bibliographical references and index.
1. Court records—Virginia—Richmond County.
2. Trials—Virginia—Richmond County.   3. Richmond
County (Va.)—History.   I. Hoffer, Peter C.   II. Scott,
William B., 1945–   III. American Historical
Association.   IV. Series.
KFV2916.R5A7   1710   345.755′05   84-161
ISBN 0-8203-0720-3 (alk. paper)   347.55055

TABLE OF CONTENTS

PREFACE

Publication of the Richmond County, Virginia, record of criminal fines, examinations, and trials (henceforth Richmond criminal proceedings, or *RCP*) has a dual purpose. The first is to make available to scholars, students, and the public a unique documentary account of law enforcement in early America. The *RCP* is the only southern colonial court record devoted solely to crime. Its detail and chronological span, featuring many verbatim transcriptions of witnesses' and suspects' testimony, are unparalleled among colonial court records. The second purpose of this publication goes beyond the intrinsic interest of the document. An extensive introduction traces the jurisprudential, social, and economic forces behind the operation of these courts. We encounter justices of the peace handling offenses ranging from illicit cohabitation to premeditated killing. In Richmond's courthouse are the roots of modern local justice—with one striking difference. The years 1711–54 covered in the *RCP* marked full deployment of a chattel slave system in the colony and a flood of black slaves into Richmond County. Local justice buckled under the strain. Gradually but inexorably, the chief burden of local justice turned from maintenance of social and moral order to ferreting out and suppressing serious crimes by slaves and their confederates. The *RCP* demonstrates the stiffening of a criminal justice system under economic and social pressure.

The editors would like to thank the scholars and institutions that have assisted us in this project. Harold Gill suggested the topic. Carol Berkin, Bradley Chapin, G. Melvin Herndon, N. E. H. Hull, Aubrey C. Land, and Kevin Kelly offered helpful criticisms. Philip Jordan and Reed Browning gave encouragement and support. The late Joseph H. Smith read, pruned, and perfected the entire work. Warren Billings, John Murrin, Gwenda Morgan, and Philip Schwarz permitted us to use unpublished papers. Michael Justus ably rechecked quotes and references. To Cary Carson and the staff of the research division of the Colonial Williamsburg Foundation, and Robert C. Anderson of the office of Research, University of Georgia, our debt is literal as well as figurative. Grants from the Colonial Williamsburg Foundation, the Office of Research, and the American Philosophical Society materially aided our efforts. The Virginia State Archives, under the direction of Louis Manarin, generously shared its microfilmed county records with us. We also thank the clerk of courts, Richmond County, and the staff at the new county courthouse, in Warsaw, Virginia, for their assistance. The University of Georgia Law Library, Erwin C. Surrency, librarian, made available its wealth of English and colonial law books. The deans and department chairmen at the Universities of Georgia and Notre Dame and the provost of Kenyon College provided secretarial services and released time, for which we are grateful. Finally the Littleton-Griswold Committee of the American Historical Association sponsored, nurtured, and brought this book into being. Herbert Johnson and Carol Berkin, for the Littleton-Griswold Committee, Jamil Zainaldin and Samuel Gammon, for the American Historical Association, and Charles East, Karen Orchard, and Malcolm Call at the University of Georgia Press all did wonders turning an untidy manuscript into a finished book. To all of them we are deeply grateful.

INTRODUCTION

THE RICHMOND COUNTY, VIRGINIA, CRIMINAL PROCEEDINGS RECORD

In 1710 the Virginia House of Burgesses informed the clerks of Virginia's county courts: "For the better and more regular prosecution and determination of all Causes in the said County Courts . . . and for the preservation of the Records thereof. . . . That all Proceedings and Judgments in Pleas of the Crown, for Fines and Forfeitures, and in other matters relating to Her Majesty's Revenues, be recorded in particular Books set apart for that purpose."[1] In Richmond County, as elsewhere before the statute, serious crimes against the person and against property had been set down in county court order books (ROB), sandwiched among far more voluminous entries of civil actions, probate administration, enumerations of taxable property, internal court business, and petty morals offenses.[2] Records of oyer and terminer tribunals called to try slaves accused of serious crime, according to the statute of 1692 (see below pp. xlv–xlvi), had been entered in the ROB as "memoranda" at the end of the regular county court records for the appropriate month.[3] Sessions of "examining courts" held to investigate felonies suspected of free persons (see pp. xxxv–xliv) were inserted in the ROB when they occurred. Examining court hearings were usually introduced with the phrase "A Court held at . . . for the examination of the prisoners apprehended."[4] In addition, before the 1710 statute some depositions in felony cases appeared in the "Miscellaneous Records" books.[5]

To Sir Marmaduke Beckwith, Baronet, English-born and educated clerk of all the courts in Richmond County, Virginia, the 1710 directive was plain.[6] From

---

1. William W. Hening, comp., *The Statutes at Large, Being a Collection of All the Laws of Virginia* . . . (Richmond, 1809–23), 3:511–12 (1710); hereafter cited as *Statutes at Large*.

2. The Richmond County Courts Order Books (ROB) (originals at the Richmond County Court House, Warsaw, Virginia, photocopies and microfilm at the Virginia State Library, Richmond [hereafter VSL]; microfilm copy at Colonial Williamsburg [hereafter CW]) cover the period from 1692 through the 1750s and beyond. The orders and judgments of the justices of the peace, the names of members of grand and petty juries and their presentments and verdicts, along with entries on wills, tithing, administrative matters, civil actions, and a number of petty offenses left out of the *RCP* after 1715 appear in those records.

3. For example, ROB, October 5, 1704.

4. ROB, April 5, 1719, a case of petty theft.

5. The "miscellaneous records" are published in a bound typescript edition, transcribed by Beverley Fleet, *Virginia Colonial Abstracts*, vols. 16 and 17: *Richmond County Records, 1692–1704* and *1704–1724* (Baltimore, 1961). They include testimony on the murder of John Newdall (16:84–91 [1702]), and the murder of unknown Englishmen (17:8 [1705]).

6. Beckwith (1687–1780) was born and reared in England and emigrated to Virginia. There he married the daughter of a leading planter and justice of the peace, William Brockenbrough. Beckwith served as deputy clerk to James Sherlock before his own elevation to the post. See George Harrison Sanford King, ed., *Marriages of Richmond County, Virginia, 1668–1853* (Fredericksburg, 1964), 13.

the March 1711 term of the county court until May 1754, he maintained a separate ledger of criminal offenses of varying severity. He was the only Virginia county court clerk to keep such a record.[7] At the end of regular sessions and special hearings, the clerk's notes, affidavits and depositions, warrants, orders, and other relevant papers were put in order and set down in a clean hand. Recognizances and sureties were also entered, for these might be forfeit to the crown.

The earliest portions of the *RCP* illustrate the breadth of the English concept of "pleas of the crown." The phrase, standard in common-law commentaries and manuals in use in Virginia, meant those offenses prosecuted by the crown rather than by a private citizen[8] (though—a standard exception—in certain *qui tam* actions, the informant split the convicted defendants' fine with the crown). These included misdemeanors, which ranged from petty offenses against the peace, sexual morality, and religious convention, to larcenies and woundings only slightly less serious than felony.[9] At one time, felonies were synonymous with capital offenses, but changes in English law weakened this association by the eighteenth century. In manuals and commentaries, homicides and treasons were sometimes classed as felonies and at other times listed separately.[10] The *RCP* includes homicides and a petty treason as well as other felonies.

Over the span of years from 1711 to 1730 the content of the *RCP* changed. More serious crimes were differentiated from immorality and violations of economic regulations, and the latter gradually dropped from the *RCP*. In 1714 the clerk relegated bastardy cases to the order books, with a few exceptions involving disorderly conduct as well as immorality. Absence from church, though a finable offense, was included only in the earliest years of the *RCP*. Violations of wine, cider, and beer licensing statutes were also soon omitted. This differentiation between some petty offenses and other crimes lay in the county clerk's distinc-

---

7. Other county clerks regularly entered criminal business at the end of the record for each session of the county court. Examining courts and oyer and terminer proceedings were entered between county court sessions, under the appropriate headings.

8. English legal writers presumed their educated readers' knowledge of this term; see, for example, the prefaces to Sir Matthew Hale's *Pleas of the Crown, a Methodical Summary* (London, 1678), and William Hawkins's two-volume *Treatise of Pleas of the Crown* (London, 1716). Both of these works were used in Virginia by justices of the peace.

9. Whatever the origin of "misdemeanor," acts very close to this description were commonly tried in the king's courts by his justices as early as the fourteenth century. See Theodore F. T. Plucknett, *A Concise History of the Common Law,* 5th ed. (Boston, 1956), 455–58.

10. The commentators agreed that felonies, homicides, and treasons were always viewed as the most serious of crimes. Edward Coke, in the *First Part of the Institutes of the Laws of England,* 4th ed. (London, 1669), 391, thought that the distinction between felony and lesser offenses arose from the "gall" or premeditated malice of the former. William Blackstone, *Commentaries on the Laws of England* (Cambridge, Eng., 1759–65), 4:95, disagreed, arguing that felonies were marked by forfeitures. Blackstone admitted that by the time he wrote, statutes had made some felonies less severe in penalty; *Commentaries,* 4:98. Parliament added a large number of offenses to the list of felonies during the eighteenth century in order to protect property against the rising anger of the displaced farm laborers; see E. P. Thompson, *Whigs and Hunters: The Origin of the Black Act* (New York, 1975). These crimes were *malum prohibitum,* acts which the law forbade, as opposed to *malum in se,* felonies of murder, treason, rape, burglary, and robbery. The conclusion the historian reaches from this evidence is that felonies were those offenses which, in the eyes of authorities, were most threatening to society and therefore required the most severe handling. Under this criterion murder and treason were felonies, although Hawkins, Blackstone, and others treated them in separate chapters before turning to the category of "felony."

tion between a deviation from social custom and an act dangerous to society. Drinking, fighting, swearing, and other violations of the peace were included in all but the last years of the *RCP* because they could lead to broader disorder, harm to persons, and destruction of property. Fornication, illegal cider selling, and nonchurchgoing were violations of law and violators were fined, but these offenses were entered in the ROB because they did not endanger society. The latter offenses fall into the category today called victimless crimes, whereas the former crimes have victims.[11]

In the 1730s, recordkeeping in the *RCP* moved further in the direction of exclusive concern with felonies. At the same time, the clerk presented far more detail in each of the cases. Long portions of testimony were regularly included. The *RCP* came to resemble a modern trial record, rather than the spare, terse outline characteristic of colonial courts. This tendency resulted in fewer and fewer cases recorded at greater and greater length. Without a legion of scribes, no colonial county clerk could continue such a project. By the end of the 1740s the record was restricted to felony cases. Every felony was recorded in the *RCP*; none appeared in the ROB. The few cases recorded for the period 1752–54 were all felonies. The project of keeping a full record of serious crimes ended in 1754.

The *RCP* demonstrates the dispatch and finality with which most criminal cases were handled in the locality, but the operation of criminal courts is never the abstract, impersonal, neutral mechanism for determining guilt and assigning penalties which bare records suggest.[12] Criminal court proceedings are social history as well as legal history. The perceptions and predispositions of judges and jurors toward persons and behaviors shaped criminal law enforcement and defined the contents of the official record. Criminal justice in Richmond County was not blind to the wealth, status, race, sex, and reputations of suspects and witnesses, and these affected the course and outcome of cases. The aspirations and debilities of suspects—part and parcel of the values and pressures of the society in which they lived—kept the courts busy, while the courts imposed curbs upon the range of social and economic behaviors.

James Willard Hurst has recently written that study of legal documents should "reach out" to wider aspects of history.[13] The *RCP* offers this opportunity. Social and legal history are inseparably bound in local courts. Judges and judged knew each other or at least each others' place in society. Individual status and reputation were flexible, but differences in standing at any one time were visible and understood. As Rhys Isaac has written, "correct observance of the rules governing status is the great imperative in such a system"; the justices expected deference, and the "lesser" classes extended it.[14] The justice of the peace sitting with

---

11. The distinction between crimes with victims and victimless crimes is central to modern criminology; see Sanford H. Kadish, "Overcriminalization," in Leon Radzinowicz and Marvin E. Wolfgang, eds., *Crime and Justice, I: The Criminal in Society* (New York, 1971), 56–71.

12. The effect of external influences upon criminal justice systems is discussed in Elmer H. Johnson, *Crime, Correction, and Society*, 4th ed. (Homewood, Ill., 1978), 99–100.

13. James Willard Hurst, "Legal Elements of United States History," *Perspectives in American History*, 5 (1971): 91.

14. Rhys Isaac, "Communication and Control, 'Family Government,' Law and the Feelings at Colonel Carter's Sabine Hall, 1752–1778: Soundings in a Diary," Shelby Cullom Davis Center Seminar Paper, February 2, 1982, 32; and see A. G. Roeber, *Faithful Magistrates and Republican Lawyers: Creators of Virginia Legal Culture, 1680–1810* (Chapel Hill, 1981), 73–80.

his colleagues in regular sessions or at special courts operated under informal local imperatives as well as the commissions, laws, and customs which officially conferred authority. Life in the county intruded into its courts.

RICHMOND COUNTY

In 1692, Rappahannock County was divided into two parts, the northern half of which was renamed Richmond County in honor of the Duke of Richmond.[15] Though carved from a portion of the Fairfax lands, this undulating, wooded strip of the "Northern Neck" never attained the historical prominence of neighboring counties on the Potomac. To be sure, in the next fifty years there was visible change in Richmond County's geographical boundaries, population composition, and landholding patterns. The "upper" or western part of the county was set off as King George County in 1721, reducing Richmond to a thirty-by-twenty-mile strip of Rappahannock riverside and a little more than half of its previous tithable population (see Map 1). Its white inhabitants were overwhelmingly English and Scottish. Slaves grew in number from a few to close to 50 percent of the population in the short span of time between 1700 and 1750.[16] Though by no means a backwater, Richmond's relative isolation and stability, combined with its shifting racial characteristics, render it suitable for a study of the social and economic context of colonial law enforcement.

The growth of population in eighteenth-century Richmond County was relatively slow. The increase in the county's tithables—free males and all servants and slaves over the age of sixteen—is only a rough guide to actual population figures but does permit comparison of the county with the entire colony.[17] From 1720 to 1754, the number of tithables rose 28 percent overall, or .86 percent per year.[18] The figures in Table 1 show how gradual this pace was.[19] The entire colony was growing at the rate of 4.6 percent per year from 1720 to 1750.[20]

While overall population in Richmond crept upward, racial composition changed dramatically. In this, the county and the colony were in close accord. At

---

15. Martha W. Hiden, *How Justice Grew, Virginia Counties: An Abstract of Their Formation* (Williamsburg, 1957), 19; *Statutes at Large,* 3:104–5 (1692).

16. Richmond County population figures from ROB, nos. 6–12, Richmond County Courthouse, Warsaw, Va.

17. On tithing and tithables, see Edmund S. Morgan, *American Slavery, American Freedom: The Ordeal of Colonial Virginia* (New York, 1975), 400–2. The relevant tithing statute appears in *Statutes at Large,* 3:258–61 (1705). Richmond County lies on the freshwater-saltwater estuary of the Rappahannock, the most unhealthy part of the river, which may account for the relatively slow population growth of the county. See Carville J. Earle, "Environment, Disease, and Mortality in Early Virginia," in Thad Tate and David L. Ammerman, eds., *The Chesapeake in the Seventeenth Century* (Chapel Hill, 1979), map at 124.

18. Richmond County tithables from ROB, nos. 6–12, originals in Richmond County Courthouse.

19. These figures, as noted on pages xiii–xiv below, do not include all those, in demographic terms, "at risk" to commit crimes, in particular free adult women. The tithable lists were not totally accurate, but severe penalties were prescribed by law and enforced in the counties to ensure that heads of households and sheriffs returned the correct information.

20. Robert V. Wells, *The Population of the British Colonies in America Before 1776* (Princeton, 1975), 260; Evarts B. Greene and Virginia D. Harrington, *American Population before the Federal Census of 1790* (1932; reprint, Gloucester, Mass., 1966), 150–51.

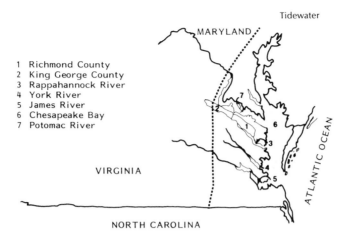

Map 1. Virginia in 1728

the opening of the century, Virginia was no more than 13 percent black,[21] and almost all of its Africans and Afro-Americans were slaves. These black men and women were highly visible to the British settlers, who viewed the color black and the behavior of slaves with trepidation.[22] At first, the slaves were dispersed over a large geographic area among a superior number of whites. By the middle of the century, this situation had changed. The tithable lists in Richmond for the year 1755 recorded 761 free adult white males and 1,263 adult male and female slaves. Over fifty years, this was an increase in the proportion of black tithables in excess of 200 percent. In Richmond County, Virginia, as throughout the Tidewater, at least 45 percent of the slaves were under the age of sixteen. The 1,263 tithable slaves in Richmond represented a total slave population of 2,060. The sex ratio among white families in the Tidewater was probably close to 1.03 males to one female.[23] Adding the adult white females and the underage free children to the tithable white population gives a total of 2,518. By 1750 black slaves thus comprised 45 percent of the inhabitants of the county.

Some portion of Richmond's increased population must be attributed to immigration of unattached free whites and European settlers. The slightly increasing frequency of Irish names in the ROB and *RCP* and the more numerous references to disorderly sailors and millhands as the years passed, as well as the detainment of runaway servants from other parts of the colony, testify to the continuous flow of people over the land. Many of the men and women were

---

21. Wells, *Population*, 161–62, gives the 13 percent figure. Wesley F. Craven, *White, Red and Black: The Seventeenth Century Virginians* (Charlottesville, 1971), 102, places the figure much lower. If Craven is correct, the rise in percentage of black population by mid-eighteenth century is all the more startling.

22. Winthrop Jordan, *White Over Black: American Views of the Negro, 1600–1815* (1968; reprint, Baltimore, 1969), 216–65; Morgan, *American Slavery*, 316–37.

23. Wells, *Population*, 152.

Table 1: Tithables, Richmond County, Three-year Averages, 1714–1750

Years	Tithables
1714–15 (1716 missing)	1,835
1717–19	1,889
1720–22 (King George County created)	1,555
1723–25	1,550
1726–28	1,613
1729–31	1,718
1732–34	1,696
1735–37	1,743
1738–40	1,762
1741–43	1,894
1744–46	1,906
1747–49	1,979

Source: ROB.

transients, for, unlike the Piedmont counties to the west, Richmond did not see massive incorporations of landless migrants into its yeomanry.[24]

Tobacco culture dominated the economy of eighteenth-century Richmond. Planters William Fauntleroy (or Fantleroy), Newman Brockenbrough, and William Glascock built warehouses for the staple on their lands, and Daniel Hornby and Landon Carter provided additional storage along the Rappahannock (see Map 2). These men, with Samuel Peachey, John Tayloe, Robert Tomlin, and others were gentlemen planters, esteemed and powerful in the community. Their extensive holdings in land and slaves, like their tastes in architecture, dress, and entertainment, were typical of their counterparts throughout the Tidewater.[25] As the century passed, the Richmond magnates increased their control of the land. The planter elite made up only a small part of the landholders in the county, but they held 49 percent of the taxable land in 1744.[26] The estates of lesser planters and the yeoman farmers were far smaller and less renumerative: only 15 percent of the parcels of land entered in the county tax records contained more than four hundred acres. If one had enough land, part of it could be rotated in fallow to maintain the fertility of the soil, but this option was not open to farmers with smaller holdings.[27]

The economic prosperity of the entire county depended in part upon the

24. Richard L. Morton, *Colonial Virginia* (Chapel Hill, 1960), 2:536–51; Jackson T. Main, *The Social Structure of Revolutionary America* (Princeton, 1965), 179–80. The process of consolidation of wealth was to continue through the end of the century. In 1800, Richmond led the Tidewater in concentration of wealth; see Norman K. Risjord, *Chesapeake Politics, 1781–1800* (New York, 1978), 22–23.

25. Elizabeth L. Ryland, *Richmond County, Virginia* (Warsaw, Va., 1976), 27, 29; Jack P. Greene, ed., *The Diary of Colonel Landon Carter of Sabine Hall, 1752–1778* (Charlottesville, 1965), 1:5–6; Joseph C. Robert, *The Story of Tobacco in America* (New York, 1949), 25.

26. Richmond County Tax Assessment Lists, 1744, ROB. The struggle of the yeomen freeholder to make his way in the early South was never easy; see Aubrey C. Land, "Economic Base and Social Structure: The Northern Chesapeake in the Eighteenth Century," *Journal of Economic History*, 25 (1965): 639–54.

27. Main, *Social Structure*, 180. On use of tobacco land, see Carville V. Earle, *The Evolution of a Tidewater Settlement System: All Hallows Parish, Maryland, 1650–1783* (Chicago, 1975), 24–30.

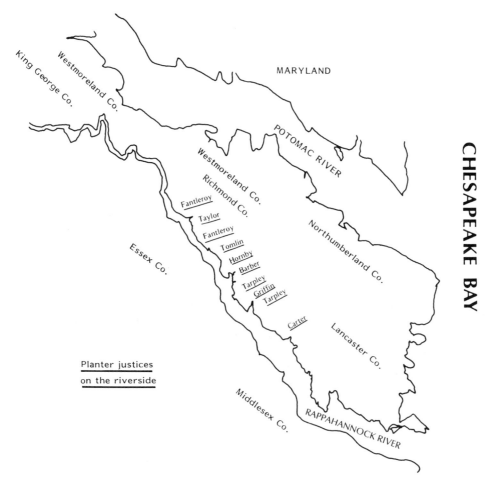

Map 2. Richmond County Planters in 1737. Derived from Lord Fairfax's Survey of the Northern Neck, 1737

export of tobacco to British markets. From Rappahannock river jetties, Richmond County cultivators shipped their crops to England and Scotland. The volume of their exports fluctuated, as Table 2 indicates. Tobacco production expanded in the region to which Richmond belonged as the numbers of blacks and use of slave labor increased.[28] The balance of trade between Great Britain and her tobacco colonies during these years lay on the side of the latter, but for the poorer planters, the margin between prosperity and ruin could be very small and might depend upon a slight fluctuation in price or productivity. These fluctuations were common and a constant irritant to the planters.[29]

28. Bernard Bailyn, "Politics and Social Structure in Virginia," in James Morton Smith, ed., *Seventeenth Century America; Essays in Colonial History* (Chapel Hill, 1959), 90–115; Stanley Elkins, *Slavery: A Problem in American Institutional and Intellectual Life* (New York, 1960), 41–48.

29. James F. Shepherd and Gary M. Walton, *Shipping, Maritime Trade, and the Economic Development of Colonial North America* (Cambridge, Eng., 1972), 165, and Appendix IV, Table 5, 225; Oscar T. Barck, Jr., and Hugh T. Lefler, *Colonial America* (New York, 1958), 367.

**Table 2: Volume of Exports of Tobacco
From the Rappahannock Counties, 1737–1750**

Year	Volume
1737	9,678
1738	7,073
1739	10,761
1740	10,141
1741	10,077
1742	12,403
1743	13,234
1744	10,886
1745	13,170
1750	15,937

Source: Jacob M. Price, *France and the Chesapeake: A History of the French Tobacco Monopoly 1674–1791, and of Its Relationship to the British and American Tobacco Trades*, 2 vols., (Ann Arbor, 1973), 1:669–70.

In many ways, Richmond was typical of Tidewater Virgina. Its planter aristocracy depended upon the production and export of tobacco. Its population mixture reflected the entrenchment of the chattel slave system alongside the fluidity of white migration—the ebb and flow of laborers seeking jobs and servants moving in and out of the marketplace. The social and psychological intangibles of this situation were common to the Tidewater. Anxiety about crop prices and dependence upon a staple system, the ever-present possibility of sudden recessions, and the rise of a "gut-wringing" slave system produced inducements to violent acts and property crimes on the one hand and a group of powerful and entrenched judges on the other.[30]

CRIMINAL JUSTICE IN THE COUNTY

Three types of criminal proceedings held in Richmond contributed to the record reproduced in this volume. Courts for the county met each month or less often if too few justices attended. The governor, in the name of the king, commissioned eight or more men of the county to hold these courts as "justices of the peace, and every one of them, from time to time and at all times, during their continuance in that office, as well out of court, as within, shall have power to maintain and keep the peace within their respective counties, in which, and in the hearing and determining all causes in court, according to the authority and power . . . granted to and vested in them."[31] Although more than 90 percent of the business that came before these county courts was civil—appointing administrators and executors of estates, determining the ages of tithables, hearing cases

---

30. Jordan, *White Over Black,* 111. The need for an escape from such pressures found expression in the gentry's love of balls and outings. See Carl Bridenbaugh, *Myths and Realities: Societies of the Colonial South* (New York, 1963), 21–28. The most recent historian of the county has found abundant evidence of these tensions; see Gwenda Morgan, "The Hegemony of the Laws: Richmond County, 1692–1776" (Ph.D. dissertation, Johns Hopkins University, 1980), 75, 138–39.

31. *Statutes at Large,* 3:508 (1710).

of debt, ejectment, and actions on the case of varying descriptions (unlike the English quarter sessions courts, which did not hear actions between private parties)—the justices were busy criminal magistrates as well.[32] In the county courts, judgment in lesser offenses was usually dispatched summarily, under the justices' commissions to hold court according to statutory or common-law guidelines on particular offenses. These infractions included public disturbances, violations of sexual, church, and licensing laws, and failure to perform civic duties. Trials upon charges of misdemeanor also took place here. Second, "called courts" or "examining courts" convened at the order of a justice to examine evidence when freemen and servants were suspected of committing a felony. Created in 1705, examining courts could dismiss charges, order a suspect tried in the county court for a misdemeanor, or bind over a suspect for trial at the General Court in the capital.[33] Frequently, the justices at the called court took a fourth course, not authorized in the legislation commissioning them to take evidence in felony cases: they reduced the offense to a misdemeanor, heard the case themselves, and punished the guilty party immediately. Finally, the criminal procedure act of 1692 empowered the governor to grant commissions of oyer and terminer to try slaves accused of felony, homicide, and treason. Past and present justices of the peace were ordinarily named in these commissions.[34] Slaves were not entitled to jury trials at the capital. Oyer and terminer judges in the county could acquit or convict and then punish slaves found guilty of serious crimes.

In theory, the local courts were subordinate to the central courts of the colony. The latter met, except for a brief period in mid-seventeenth century, only at Williamsburg. The General Court sat twice a year as a court of life and limb, hearing all capital offenses charged against free persons. Additional courts of oyer and terminer met at the capital twice a year after 1710. Grand juries and a portion of the trial juries were summoned for these courts from the capital area. The judges were the councillors and the governor or those under his special commission—though he rarely exercised this controversial prerogative.[35] Throughout the colonial era, the superior courts of criminal justice remained in the capital, despite repeated attempts to establish circuit superior courts.[36] Granting these central institutions' importance, the local courts also were imposing and effective organs of criminal justice for a number of reasons.

First, the vast majority of criminal cases and defendants from the county remained in the county. In the years 1711–49, for which the ROB and *RCP* are

---

32. Tabulation of the percentage of cases on the civil side of the county docket from the ROB, York County Order Books, 1717–32, microfilm, CW, and King George County Order Books, 1721–51, microfilm reels 22 and 23, VSL. All show that the massive preponderance of civil actions over criminal proceedings was universal.

33. *Statutes at Large*, 3:389–92 (1705).

34. *Statutes at Large*, 3:102–3 (1692).

35. Hugh F. Rankin, *Criminal Trial Proceedings in the General Court of Colonial Virginia* (Williamsburg, 1965), passim; Arthur P. Scott, *Criminal Law in Colonial Virginia* (Chicago, 1930), 45 ff.

36. St. George Tucker, ed., *Commentaries on Blackstone* (Philadelphia, 1803), 5:300. Local courts did hold their own against the centralizing tendencies (called by their advocates "reforms") of some governors. See, for example, Leonidas Dodson, *Alexander Spotswood, Governor of Colonial Virginia, 1710–1722* (Philadelphia, 1932), 120–21, and Roeber, *Faithful Magistrates*, 64–71.

complete, only 30 cases of serious crimes against the person or property out of 107 such crimes heard by county examining or oyer and terminer courts went on to the General Court in Williamsburg. If the various petty thefts, morals viola-tions, and offenses against the peace that were pressed in the county courts were included in the total number of criminal cases, the percentage of cases that ever were seen by a judge outside of Richmond County would shrink to 7 percent. Many serious crimes were handled entirely in the county. Unlike civil litigants who lost suits of £20 or more, men and women convicted of minor criminal offenses could not appeal to the courts of Williamsburg. The only criminal cases that left the county were suspected felonies by free persons. Even in this cate-gory, some charges brought to examining courts were reduced in severity and ended with corporal punishment in the county. This solution occurred, if the justices so willed, even when sufficient evidence was produced to send the sus-pect to the capital. Slave defendants in oyer and terminer trials never left the county. For all categories of crime, the accused were far more likely to face their fate in the county than in Williamsburg.[37]

Second, the personnel of the county court bench gave local justice legitimacy and continuity. In a system that depended upon the personal authority of the justices, the elevation of the influential planters to the local bench was sensible and expedient. To be sure, some of the justices in Virginia, as in England, were habitual absentees from the courts. Governor Francis Fauquier lamented in his 1763 report to the Board of Trade: "There is a court in every County which ought to sit once in every month, but is too frequently omitted on Account of the non-Attendance of the Members composing it, who are the Justices in the Commission of the Peace for the county."[38] Between 1714 and 1747 the average number of regular sessions of Richmond County courts (not counting courts continued from day to day) to hear criminal business was but seven per year. Finally, as if to prove Fauquier's point, a number of justices seem to have attended no more than one-fourth of the meetings of the court throughout their tenure as justices. Among these were Joseph Deeke, William Downman, Thomas Griffin, James Strother, Charles Grymes, and Gilbert Hamilton. The preponderance of evidence about the attendance of the justices in commission nevertheless dispels the charge that all of them were indolent and indifferent. A stable core of justices came to the sessions each year. In two-thirds of the years from 1714 to 1749, at least one of the justices in commission had a perfect attendance record for each year, and the regulars on the bench tended to remain fixtures from year to year. On the aver-age, more than two-thirds of the justices who attended more than half of one year's sessions attended more than half of the next year's sessions. This continuity was personified in Samuel Peachey, who sat from 1723 to 1752. Charles Barber attended regularly from 1711 to 1726, as did Moore Fauntleroy from 1714 to

---

37. Data from *RCP* and ROB.

38. Governor Francis Fauquier, "Answers to the Questions Sent to Me by the Rt. Honorable the Lords Commissioners for Trade and Plantations," January 30, 1763, Public Record Office, London, CO 5/1330, ff. 279–80, copy at CW. In England, justices of the peace were sometimes notorious for their absence from the sessions; see J. M. Beattie, "Towards a Study of Crime in Eighteenth-Century England: A Note on Indictments," in Paul Fritz and David Williams, eds., *The Triumph of Culture: Eighteenth Century Perspectives* (Toronto, 1972), 308.

1749, Joseph Belfield from 1721 to 1734, Thomas Wright Belfield from 1728 to 1740, and Anthony Sydnor, Daniel Hornby, and Thomas Barber during the 1730s and 1740s. All had nearly perfect attendance records. From long service on the bench and elsewhere in the community, these men knew the reputations of witnesses and suspects. For their part, defendant, witness, and victim knew that they would come across the judge's friends or family in the course of their day's activities in the county. If defendants returned to the court upon a second charge, they could be fairly sure that some of the judges who sat on their first case would still be there.

In addition to their long tenure on the local court, the justices held other posts. They were vestrymen, militia officers, sheriffs, surveyors, coroners, tobacco inspectors, and jurymen.[39] Tarpley later sat as the king's attorney, and when he returned to the county bench, his place was taken in the king's service by William Robinson, another Richmond County justice. Such men were the backbone of a governing elite. Wealthy and influential in their home counties, they manned legislative and judicial posts in Williamsburg as well. On the legislative side, through the years 1711–54, Richmond sent John Tarpley, William Thornton, William Robinson, William Woodbridge, Thomas Griffin, Charles Grymes, John Tayloe, John Woodbridge, William Fauntleroy, and Landon Carter to successive Houses of Burgesses. All were in commission as justices when they sat as burgesses for the county.[40] Perhaps more important, they did not fear or compete with a professional judicial cadre. The highest court in the colony was not composed of professional judges, as in some of the other colonies and, almost entirely, as in England. Instead, the council was directed by men from their own ranks, experienced planter-lawyers rather than full-time judges. The county bench did not function in the shadow of more learned and respected central courts, but labored alongside them in a two-track system of criminal justice. Typically of the county justices, John Tayloe and his son, John, Jr., sat in the colonial council and hence on the superior court of Virginia after both had served as Richmond justices.[41]

Although these men were more active magistrates and attorneys than contemplative legal scholars, Tarpley and his son, Travers Tarpley, as well as Samuel Peachey, Leroy Griffin, and Thomas Wright Belfield possessed substantial legal libraries. Their holdings in criminal law were as voluminous as those of some of the more celebrated legal scholars in the colony and included Michael Dalton's *Countrey Justice*, D'Anvers's and Sheppard's abridgments of the English laws, Keble's *Assistance to Justices of the Peace*, Nelson's manual for justices, and Wilkinson's *Treatise* on sheriffs and coroners. Close as the laws of the colony were to the statute and common law of England, these volumes were an ample guide to correct rulings in the courts. The justices supplemented manuals and commentaries with copies of the laws of Virginia and George Webb's *The Office and Authority of a Justice of Peace* (1736), published in Virginia. There is reason as well

---

39. H. R. McIlwaine ed., *Journals of the House of Burgesses of Virginia, 1702/3–1705, 1706, 1710–1712* (Richmond, 1912), 7, 143.

40. William G. Stannard and Mary N. Stannard, *The Colonial Virginia Register* (1902; reprint Baltimore, 1965), 47, 49, 93–102.

41. King, ed., *Marriages of Richmond County*, xvi.

to believe that the younger justices shared their books and pooled their learning, for the most recent census of law books in the colony shows almost no duplication of holdings among the members of the Richmond County bench.[42]

Third, law and custom gave the justices great discretionary power to sentence and punish offenders, a power fully grasped by independent local magnates such as Carter, Peachey, and Tayloe. As Landon Carter's diary suggests, the planter-magistrates took the moral and psychological burdens of judgment seriously. Whether on their own lands or in court, they coupled a belief in the rightness of the law (and of their own fitness to dispense it) with a willingness to follow its rules. Although the upper limits of corporal and financial penalties were defined by statute, the justices had great leeway in sentencing within these limits. Corporal punishment could mount to thirty-nine lashes. Imprisonment or custody could last for the period a defendant needed to raise money for court costs, usually a very short time, or continue for a set term, in Virginia, not to exceed a year. Fines went as high as £100 sterling. These penalties were often augmented by requirement of recognizances, bonds for good behavior or to keep the peace, secured by additional bonds from neighbors and friends. Fines for absence from jury duty and failure to appear when called as witnesses, against disturbers of the court, contemners of the justices, and sheriffs and their underofficers for failure to do their duty, letting a prisoner escape, or violating the laws themselves checked malfeasance and inefficiency within the criminal justice system.[43] To the suspect and all others present in the courtroom, judicial discretion in the county had realistic and immediate consequences.

Fourth, the place of the local hearings and trials had great impact upon the minds of Virginia colonists. Criminal courts met at the county courthouse. In Richmond, this was a small, square building at a crossroads two miles from the river. Administration of justice was a wholly public event. The courts' yards were open and crowded places, magnets for the commoner and the curious. Merchant, lawyer, and passerby mingled to do business, hear cases, and perhaps serve on a jury. The ceremonial of the courthouse, coupled with the colonists' interest in criminal cases involving neighbors, filled courthouses to overflowing when the justices sat to hear criminal offenses. The seating arrangement and placement of the bench in the courtroom gave visual emphasis to the power of the justices. The whipping post, to which many of the guilty were removed immediately after the justices had ruled, stood next to the courthouse. The gaol, with its yard, could be seen nearby. Whipping, branding, and pillory were public displays of the fruits of crime designed to warn the immoral. In a face-to-face society, public rituals of this nature strengthened the legitimacy of criminal proceedings.[44]

42. William H. Bryson, *Census of Law Books in Colonial Virginia* (Charlottesville, 1978), 46, 49, 52, 59, 66, 75, 80. On the perceptions of Carter and his milieu, see Greene, ed., Carter, *Diary*, 1: ff., 6, and Isaac, "Communication and Control," 11.

43. For examples of penalties for officers see discussion in introduction at n. 50. On the scope of discretion during the sitting of the court, see *Statutes at Large*, 3:509–16 (1710). In practice, the terms "bond for good behavior" and "recognizance for good behavior" were close in meaning; see George Webb, *The Office and Authority of a Justice of Peace* (Williamsburg, 1736), 263.

44. Rhys Isaac, *The Transformation of Virginia, 1740–1790* (Chapel Hill, 1982), 88–94; Roeber, *Faithful Magistrates*, 79–80.

The ultimate impact and effectiveness of local justice derived from its respon-
siveness to the realities of local status and class distinctions. Criminal law enforcement embodies social and moral understandings in matters of race, religion, sex,
wealth, and age. Criminal statutes and procedure may appear neutral, warning
potential offenders of all types, but the actual enforcement of law depends upon
relationships within a given society.[45] In Anglo-American courts, kinship, status,
and reputation were admissible evidence on the motives of suspected criminals.
English justices of the peace were told to inquire into family connections—advice
that gave protection to some suspects and denied it to others.[46] The same forces
worked in Richmond. In 1721, Gregory Glascock was brought before a Richmond County examining court to investigate the assistance he gave his father in
fleeing from a murder scene. The court was perhaps induced by the standing of
the Glascock family, one of the leading planter clans in the county, to believe that
Gregory had no criminal intent in aiding his father. Although the justices found
him "an accessory after the fact," "the principal not being in custody," they did
not proceed against him. He was permitted bail and asked to put up an additional bond for his good behavior.[47] In 1727, Thomas Livack was brought to trial
for counterfeiting. Testimony against him was given by Justice William Downman. When the court found Livack not guilty but ordered him to post a bond for
his behavior, Downman stepped forward as one of the sureties. The proceeding
reads as a warning to Livack to mend his ways from his friends on the court. On
occasion, grand jurymen complained that presentments of gentlemen for swearing and gaming were routinely ignored by the bench. Although cases of possible
favoritism were not typical of the mass of investigations and hearings, they do
remind us of the extralegal concerns that reached into the courtroom. As St.
George Tucker, later a Virginia supreme court judge, penned in his youth
under the title "Written in a County Courthouse": "Here Justice sits and holds
her scales: But ah! her balance often fails."[48]

The community as a whole conceded power and discretion to the justices.
Despite the unruliness of colonial society—evidence of which fills the *RCP*—both
high and low in Richmond bowed to the authority of the courts. In this, Richmond County was typical of premodern, rural Western society. Deference was
the rule, rebellion (though not disorder) the exception. The local criminal justice
system described here could not function without widespread community con-

---

45. The notion that criminal behavior is a socially defined boundary condition is discussed in Kai
T. Erikson, *Wayward Puritans: A Study in the Sociology of Deviance* (New York, 1966), 3–29, as well as in
Erikson and Robert A. Dentler, "The Functions of Deviance in Groups," *Social Problems*, 7 (Fall
1959): 98–107. A number of criminologists have embraced this doctrine, for example, Howard
Becker, ed., *The Other Side: Perspectives on Deviance* (New York, 1964), and Walter R. Gove, ed., *The
Labelling of Deviance* (New York, 1975).

46. William Lambard, *Eirenarcha* (London, 1588), 218; Richard Crompton (following Fitzher-
bert), *L'office et auctoritie de justices de peace* (London, 1583), 64–66. As late as 1769, "Persons of good
fame" charged with "inferior" felonies were always to be given bail, according to Blackstone, *Commentaries*, 4:296.

47. For Glascock's case, see *RCP*, 59–60 (1724).

48. On grand jury complaints, see Roeber, *Faithful Magistrates*, 140; and n. 68, below. Livack's case
appears in *RCP*, 103–4 (1727). For Tucker's rhyme, see William S. Prince, *Poems of St. George Tucker
of Williamsburg, Virginia, 1752–1827* (New York, 1977), 56.

sent. The legitimacy of the justices' discretion in defining the boundaries of illegal behavior in individual cases depended as much upon consensus in the county as upon written law. Justices of the peace could not call upon modern police forces to aid them in keeping order. To the extent that the justices could command local adherence to laws made in distant England or in Williamsburg and to the extent that they were accepted as punishers of wrongdoing by most of their neighbors, criminal law would be enforceable. Without community willingness to obey, criminal justice faltered.[49] In early eighteenth-century Virginia, all classes bowed to the discretion of their justices. This deferential attitude does not mean that there were no disturbances at "court day" or that crime was uncommon, but when disorder and crimes occurred, neighbors, witnesses, and even suspects cooperated with the courts. Court records document this consensus. The vast majority of suspects brought before the county court for minor infractions either pleaded guilty or put themselves upon the court, permitting the justices to determine guilt or innocence. The *RCP* and the ROB do not precisely inform the reader which of these courses suspects elected. The formula "the defendant had nothing material to say in his own defense" used in some entries may mean that the suspect had put himself upon the court. The justices were constrained by the same consensual sanctions. At the February 1723 sessions, Justice John Tarpley stepped down from the bench to bond himself for his good behavior after the grand jury had presented him for swearing. Other justices paid fines for failure to repair bridges and roads and for disturbing the peace.[50] Finally, those men and women held in the county gaol for failure to pay fines or put up bonds did not attempt to flee. Only two prisoners broke out of the flimsy Richmond County gaol in the forty-four years of these records; both were men accused of felony. With the consent of the community as a whole the courts functioned as guardians of order.

As the century progressed, the House of Burgesses recognized the effectiveness of the county's criminal courts and enlarged their powers. The failure of the vestrymen of the parish to curb morals offenses, tacitly admitted by statute in 1691, led the burgesses to turn to the county courts to perform this task.[51] The growing number and specificity of criminal statutes the burgesses ordered enforced in the county also showed that they were willing to place more complex social controls in the hands of the local justices (who included, of course, most of the burgesses among their numbers). New laws on the treatment of suspects, the handling of runaways, and the ferreting out of conspiracies among the blacks made the local courts progressively more intrusive instruments of public order. Governors did not use their pardoning power to interfere in local administration of justice, tacitly agreeing with the burgesses' assignment of criminal jurisdiction

---

49. See Richard Maxwell Brown, *The South Carolina Regulators* (Cambridge, Mass., 1963), 38–41, for an episode of local social disorders in which "Regulators" took justice into their own hands. "Giddy multitudes" had roamed Virginia in the 1680s; Morgan, *American Slavery*, 236 ff.

50. *RCP*, 48 (1723). In 1723, John Metcalf and Joseph Belfield (Belfeild in *RCP*) were fined 15s. for failure to keep bridges in good order. In 1727, a grand jury presented John Tayloe for disturbing the peace. He gave bond for good behavior; *RCP*, 49, 50 (1723), 97 (1727). But the magistrates did recognize status differences among themselves; Roeber, *Faithful Magistrates*, 82–83.

51. *Statutes at Large*, 3:71–75 (1691).

to the local courts.[52] As Benjamin Leigh was to declare in 1819, "As [the county court is] the most ancient, so it has ever been one of the most important of our institutions, not only in respect to the administration of justice, but for police and economy."[53]

Criminal Proceedings at the County Court

The vast majority of criminal business set down in the *RCP* arose at the regular sessions of the county court. Established by statute before the Restoration and periodically given new duties by the burgesses, these courts were the backbone of the local criminal justice system. Most of the infractions brought to them were disposed of summarily. The suspect answered a grand jury presentment, a private complaint, or an information passed on to one of the justices. The justices heard the suspects and then ordered disposition of the case summarily. As magistrates, when court was not in session, they could handle breaches of the peace, but when they sat alone they were not courts of record. Our knowledge of summary jurisdiction derives largely from the sessions of the county courts.[54]

More serious crimes coming to the county court, technically termed misdemeanors, allowed suspects to ask for a trial by putting themselves upon the court or upon the country. In the latter case, the sheriff was told to bring to court a jury of twelve freeholders from the vicinity, whose property must be valued at fifty pounds sterling or more.[55] In practice, sheriffs would summon a petty jury before each session of the court, just in case it was needed for a civil or criminal trial. Refusal to serve upon a trial jury was punishable with a fine of two hundred pounds of tobacco. The judges conducted summary hearings and trials under these commissions, those portions of the common law received in the colony, and Virginia statutes.

Virginia justice of the peace commissions were granted by the crown through its agent, the governor, and were modeled upon English commissions. Despite differences in wording and a far fuller enumeration of statutory materials in the English version, the criminal jurisdiction assigned justices in Virginia and commissions in England was always similar except in two matters—game laws and slavery. Both sets of officials were enjoined to keep order, inquire into crimes, enforce statutes, arrest suspects, give bail, hold court, take recognizances, oversee lower court officers' conduct, order and collect fines, keep records, and send prisoners and evidence to the central courts for trial in felony cases. Both commissions were issued in the king's or queen's name. The English justices were also enjoined to enforce a vast array of statutes on hunting in forests and parks— preserves of privilege for the nobility. There were no comparable laws in Vir-

---

52. *Statutes at Large*, 3:86–88 (1691); 4:163–64, 168–75 (1726). On the expanding functions of the county courts, see Richard R. Beeman, "Social Change and Social Conflict in Virginia: Lunenburg County, 1746 to 1774," *William and Mary Quarterly*, 3d ser., 35 (July 1978): 458–60.

53. Benjamin W. Leigh, 1819, quoted in Charles S. Sydnor, *American Revolutionaries in the Making: Political Practices in Washington's Virginia* (New York, 1965), 80.

54. See *Statutes at Large*, 1:273 (1643), 462 (1658); 2:69–71 (1662); 3:504–16 (1710). On courts of record, see *Statutes at Large*, 3:489–90 (1710).

55. *Statutes at Large*, 3:369 (1705).

ginia. Old Dominion justices had to enforce the stipulations of "black codes"—
laws on slave conduct—which had no parallel in England.[56]

Although the Virginia justices derived their powers from the crown, the colonial government soon sought and persistently exercised a measure of autonomy
in directing criminal justice. The second charter of the colony (1609) explicitly
conferred criminal jurisdiction upon the Virginia Company governor and council, but from the first settlement at Jamestown, two years earlier, the governor
and council assumed authority to punish malingerers and thieves.[57] When the
crown reassumed direct control over the colony, the royal governor issued commissions to the local judges. The Virginia House of Burgesses enlarged and
directed the exercise of the justices' criminal jurisdiction by statute, in close but
not exact accord with changing English law and practice.[58] The burgesses jeal-
ously guarded their right to make additions to criminal law, a matter of practical
necessity as well as theoretical significance when dealing with the procedure on
crimes by slaves, discussed at length below (pp. xliv–lii).[59] The king in council
could disallow these laws but generally did not do so.

------

56. For the criminal matters in commissions for English justices see Richard Burn, *The Justice of the
Peace and Parish Officer* (London, 1755), 69–71; the powers of Virginia justices are in Webb, *Justice of
Peace*, 200–207. On the game laws of England, see P. B. Munsche, *Gentlemen and Poachers: The English
Game Laws, 1671–1831* (Cambridge, Eng., 1981), 15–27. On black codes see discussion in introduc-
tion beginning at n. 124.

57. Under the charter of 1609, the company governor and council in the colony had the right to
"correct, punish, pardon, govern, and rule" all men in Virginia; *Statutes at Large*, 1:96. In practice,
punishment was meted out soon after the first beachhead; Alden T. Vaughan, *American Genesis:
Captain John Smith and the Founding of Virginia* (Boston, 1975), 53–54. The model may have been a
military tribunal of the sort found in Northern Ireland; see David T. Konig, " 'Dales' Laws' and the
Non Common-Law Origins of Criminal Justice in Virginia," *American Journal of Legal History*, 26
(October 1982): 338–66.

58. *Statutes at Large*, 1:132–33 (1629); 2:69–71 (1662). By 1662 the county justices had obtained
jurisdiction in "all such things as by the laws of England are to be done by justices of the peace there"
(2:70). All crimes not "touching life or member" went to the county courts (2:66). On the sweeping
jurisdiction of these courts, see Webb, *Justice of Peace*, 200–207, and Warren M. Billings, "The
Growth of Political Institutions in Virginia, 1634 to 1676," *William and Mary Quarterly*, 3d ser., 31
(April 1974): 230.

In the 1710 procedure statute, a portion of the bench was regarded as members of the "Quorum,"
and they alone could direct a sheriff from a different county to take evidence from witnesses who
could not appear in civil cases. The added honor (and expertise) notwithstanding, the Quorum
concept does not appear to have been important in criminal jurisdiction of the courts under study
here. Of course, the institution itself was directly taken from English practice; *Statutes at Large*,
3:513–14 (1710); Webb, *Justice of Peace*, 200. The quorum appears in *RCP*, 245.

Despite their admission that the justices' commissions came ultimately from the crown (Webb,
Justice of Peace, 205–6), Virginia jurists viewed local criminal justice as theirs by right. See Francis S.
Philbrick, "Prefatory Note," in Susie M. Ames, ed., *County Records of Accomack-Northampton, Virginia,
1632–1640, American Legal Records—Volume 7* (Washington, D.C., 1954), xi–xii, and St. George
Tucker, *Commentaries on Blackstone* (Richmond, 1803), 1:382. The latter view was not shared in
England, but the day-to-day administration of local justice was shaped by the perceptions of Virginia
justices.

59. The treatment of slaves accused of serious crimes (which had no parallel in English criminal
law) to one side, the only major difference between Virginia and the mother country involved the
usage of the habeas corpus writ. The Habeas Corpus Act of 1679 was not reenacted in Virginia, and
Governor Alexander Spotswood, speaking for Queen Anne, was forced to introduce it by proclama-
tion in 1710. In practice, however, wrongful imprisonment does not seem to have much worried

Although the criminal jurisdiction of the English and the Virginia local judges was similar, there were differences between their roles in the larger arrangement of courts. The end of the sixteenth century saw the rise in England of a professional class of judges. These were the men who sat at the central courts and went, by twos, on circuit as courts of assize. To assize courts came all serious crimes (save piracy). The local justices were forced to surrender jurisdiction over felonies to the assize court judges (though there were exceptions to this rule early in the seventeenth century), creating a very clear hierarchy in the structure of the criminal courts.[60] Virginia had no class of professional judges to tour the provincial gaols and try offenders, no begowned high court justices to bring the formal majesty of the law into her counties. She did have a corps of local dignitaries, many of them lawyers but also planters, merchants, and doctors, who consented to devote their time to the administration of the law. To these men fell the responsibility of learning and applying the criminal law.

In the county, local judges acted as police magistrates, gathering evidence, taking testimony, and directing the actions of sheriffs and constables. The justices were the first line of social control, enforcing statutes and quelling disturbances within families, disciplining wandering servants, and humbling unruly laborers. They occupied the bench at the county court, the visible symbol of criminal law enforcement in the countryside. They dispensed with some of the formality of English justice but were no less effective enforcers of law and order for the absence of precise common-law forms and regalia.

The particular objects of the justices' criminal jurisdiction derived from English statute and case law before 1609 and Virginia statute after that time. The latter generally embodied principles of the English common law. Shortly after Jamestown was erected, crown lawyers instructed the company council and governor

> to punish the offender or offenders, either by reasonable corporal punishment and imprisonment, or else by a convenient fine, awarding damages or other satisfaction, to the party grieved . . . having regard to the quality of the offence, or state of the cause; and that aloe the said president and councel, shall have power and authority . . . to punish all manner of excesse, through drunkennesse or otherwaise, and all idle loytering and vagrant persons, which shall be found within their several limits and precincts, according to their best discretions, and with such convenient punishment, as they or the most part of them shall think fit.[61]

In addition to keeping the peace and investigating crimes brought to their attention, the English justices and their Virginia counterparts were assigned massive responsibilities for enforcing personal conduct laws. Elizabethan and early Jacobean parliaments enacted laws proscribing fornication, game-playing, sabbath-breaking, swearing, alehousekeeping, bastardy, and other forms of socially unac-

---

Virginians before the revolutionary era. See William F. Duker, *A Constitutional History of Habeas Corpus* (Westport, Conn., 1980), 100–101 and A. H. Carpenter, "Habeas Corpus in the Colonies," *American Historical Review*, 8 (October 1902): 18–27.

60. J. S. Cockburn, *A History of the English Assizes, 1558–1714* (Cambridge, Eng., 1972), 88–89.

61. "Articles, Instructions, and Orders" from James I's lawyers to the directors of the Virginia Company, 1607, *Statutes at Large*, 1:71.

ceptable behavior.[62] Some of these offenses had been the sole purview of the ecclesiastical courts but after the 1570s were thrust into the hands of the justices. Thereafter, English quarter sessions courts overflowed with bastardy, fornication, sabbath-breaking, and similar offenses. In Virginia, the justices were equally busy ordering men and women fined for swearing, fighting, barratry, drunkenness, failure to attend church services, making threats against others, disrespect to officers of the court, and sexual transgression. The profusion of laws against these offenses, including major statutory provisions in 1643, 1646, 1658, 1662, 1672, 1691, 1696, 1699, 1705, 1730, and 1744, all had the same refrain: the previous act was "insufficient to restrain and discourage wickedness and vice."[63] The penalties for these offenses ranged from incapacity to hold office, inability to sue, and three years in prison for each successive indulgence in blasphemy (though the offender could recant the words and lose nothing), to fifty pounds of tobacco for each drinking or swearing spree, one thousand pounds of tobacco for adultery, and five hundred pounds for fornication, to bonds for good behavior with security put up by others in the court to see that the recognizance was kept in cases of disturbing the peace.

In their first instructions to the colony, crown lawyers expected magistrates to carry out these duties "summarily, and verbally without writing until it come to the judgment or sentence." Though feasible, this method was not designed to gain community allegiance to the law. It did not allow, in particular, for that unique bulwark of the English system, the jury. Both the grand jury and the trial jury played a part in the county court. Virginia statutes first incorporated the English idea of a presenting jury in 1645. Twenty-four propertyholders from the county were to be assembled twice each year to present to the court their knowledge of all crimes save felonies. Grand juries at the General Court indicted free men and women for felonies. After some rearranging of procedure, the grand jury system took permanent shape in 1705. Grand juries were to be impaneled for every session of the county courts and to present, on the information of at least two of their number, all offenses not touching life or limb.[64] Seventeenth-century English and Virginia grand juries did not always follow the manualist's injunction to "diligently inquire and true presentment make"; nevertheless, in the eighteenth century, the burgesses gave to Virginia grand juries the power, hitherto reserved to the vestrymen, to present men and women for morals offenses. The grand jury was henceforth indispensable to the county court. Between 1711 and 1754, the ROB and *RCP* together recorded 282 grand jury presentments. More than two-thirds of these involved repeat offenders,

---

62. These laws include parliamentary acts on all sorts of personal conduct; see Joan R. Kent, "Attitudes of Members of the House of Commons to the Regulation of 'Personal Conduct' in Late Elizabethan and Early Stuart England," *Bulletin of the Institute of Historical Research*, 46 (May 1973): 41–71.

63. *Statutes at Large*, 1:240–43 (1643), 310 (1646), 433–34 (1658); 2:51–52 (1662), 298 (1672); 3:71–75 (1691), 137–40 (1696), 168–71 (1699), 358–62 (1705); 4:244–46 (1730); 5:225–26 (1744); R. W. Church, ed., *Laws of Virginia, Being a Supplement to Hening's the Statutes at Large, 1700–1750* (Richmond, 1971), 254–57 (1723). See also Scott, *Criminal Law*, 44.

64. *Statutes at Large*, 3:368–69 (1705); see also 4:232–33 (1727).

almost all of whom eventually came to court and paid their fines, put up bonds for good behavior, or otherwise satisfied the justices.[65]

The grand jurors' perceptions of right and wrong tended to coincide with the justices'. One example of this cooperation will illustrate its effect on the administration of justice. The *RCP* and *ROB* show a rising tide of grand jury presentments and court punishments for sex offenses in the 1720s. The number of cases peaked late in the decade, then fell sharply (Figure 1), but it is not likely that the amount of fornication and bastardy declined in the 1730s. Edward Shorter, Daniel Scott Smith and Michael S. Hindus, and Robert Wells have argued that the frequency of premarital sexual unions among Americans probably increased as the eighteenth century progressed, yet prosecution in Richmond County all but disappeared over that period.[66] An explanation lies in a shared change in perceptions among jurors and justices. At first, justices and grand jurors had responded with vigor to their recognition of heightened levels of promiscuity and incontinence. In the initial years of the 1720s, grand juries presented men and women for these offenses and the justices ordered fines and bonds for good behavior. After a century of legislating against immorality, a 1744 statute admitted that the old laws had not curbed the promiscuity of the populace.[67] The passage of additional statutes indicated that the breakdown of sexual mores continued to spread even though men and women presented for these offenses came into court and paid their fines. The decline of prosecution in Richmond after 1730 must not have been a response to a decline in offenses but a signal that the criminal justice system was shifting its attention to other problems. Presentments declined, and justices found their dockets busy with different offenses. With familiarity, sexual incontinence had become less threatening to the justices and the grand juries.

The effectiveness of the grand jury in the court system stemmed in part from its role as spokesman for the community. Its presentment of a disturber of the peace or a common drunkard expressed disapprobation shared by many. The jurors' finding might be true or false, but its force went beyond its validity. The jurors were landed freemen, who were themselves well-behaved (or they could not serve). Their eyes and ears went where the justices' did not, and they stood for the same principles of order and decorum. When Christopher Pridham made unwanted advances to his maidservant or Thomas Livack threatened to

---

65. The manualist was Sir James Astray, *A General Charge to All Grand Juries . . .* (London, 1725), 11, but the laxness of grand jurors was the subject of remedial legislation in 1677; *Statutes at Large* 2:407–8. Lambard and other English justices were sharply critical of grand jurors' negligence in England. The eighteenth-century grand juries' tasks are laid out in *Statutes at Large*, 3:367–71 (1705) and 4:232–33 (1727).

66. Edward Shorter, *The Making of the Modern Family*, 2d ed. (New York, 1977), 79–108; Daniel Scott Smith and Michael S. Hindus, "Premarital Pregnancy in America, 1640–1971: An Overview and Interpretation," *Journal of Interdisciplinary History*, 5 (Spring 1975): 553; Robert Wells, "Illegitimacy and Bridal Pregnancy in Colonial America," paper presented to the American Society for Eighteenth Century Studies, Chicago, April 1978, 11–12. The same phenomenon—a sudden, permanent decline in local prosecutions for fornication—has been traced in Massachusetts, in Hendrick Hartog, "The Public Law of a County Court: Judicial Government in Eighteenth-Century Massachusetts," *American Journal of Legal History*, 20 (1976): 300–301.

67. *Statutes at Large*, 5:225 (1744).

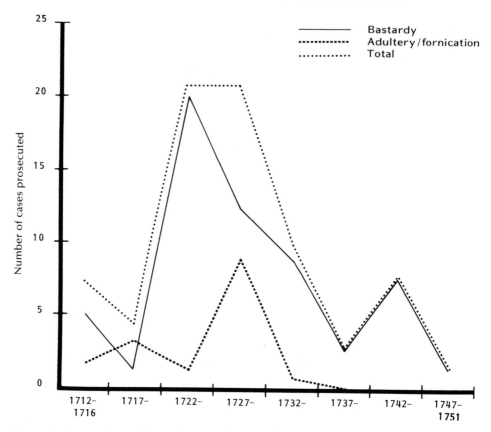

Figure 1. Prosecution of Sexual Immorality in Richmond County Courts, 1712–1751 (ROB and *RCP*)

"do some bodily hurt" to a neighbor, they knew and presented the culprits to the court.[68] Unlike modern grand jury deliberations, which are closed, these men made no secret of their findings. They could, as individuals, rise and present their own knowledge of wrongdoing—a process recalling the original presenting juries of village tithingmen in medieval England. The grand jurors might be picked by the sheriff, on some other day, to sit on a trial jury. The community was small enough that the men and women they presented for infractions of the law were their neighbors. Only a courageous or foolhardy defendant, especially one without status, would dare to challenge the presentment of the grand jury.

When could the defendant legally demand a trial in the county court, assuming he wished to challenge the "true bill" of a grand jury? Proceedings in these sessions were often informal, as they were in county courts throughout the empire,[69] and, as noted above, only the frailest evidence indicates when defen-

68. *RCP*, 70 (1724); 126 (1730). The grand jury in Richmond and elsewhere became a far more controversial institution in the 1750s and 1760s; Morgan, "Hegemony of the Laws," 232–33; Roeber, *Faithful Magistrates*, 140.

69. Julius Goebel, Jr., and T. Raymond Naughton, *Law Enforcement in Colonial New York* (1944; reprint, New York, 1970), 381.

dants may have put themselves upon the court. A technical point gives one clue: if the offense were a "misdemeanor," the accused could claim the right to a trial. At trial, he could put himself upon the country and require the court to order the sheriff to summon a jury. On the other hand, if the offense were "petty," there was no right to a trial. Even though Thomas Freshwater brought his attorney with him to answer a grand jury presentment for swearing, he was not able to contest the charge, for it was not a misdemeanor.[70] The contemporary Virginia manualist for justices did not make this distinction between petty offenses and misdemeanors into a rule—indeed, he did not regard petty offenses as an official category. He did admit that misdemeanors necessitated an "indictment" (and, therefore, a grand jury bringing in a true bill): "[Misdemeanor] is a general Word, and comprehends all Kinds of Misbehaviour; yet is not properly applicable to any one particular Crime or Offence prohibited by the Law, but to such only, which tho' not specialy provided against, are nevertheless punishable by Indictment, and the Offender may be fined and imprisoned, at the Discretion of the Court before whom he shall be convicted."[71]

Whatever their comprehension of the technical distinction between petty offenses and misdemeanors, practically speaking, the justices resorted to bonds and sureties to deal with all manner of lesser offenses: "Every Justice of Peace, by Virtue of his Office, may by his Warrant cause any Person to be brought before him, for Misdemeanors tending to the Breach of the Peace, and may require Sureties of the Offender, for his personal Appearance before the next County Court, to answer the Premises, and in the mean Time to be of Good-behavior: If the Justice see cause, he may require the Party to find Sureties to be bound in very considerable Sums, and on Refusal, commit him."[72] In certain cases, such as assaults, which might be classed as misdemeanors and not petty offenses, recognizances both ensured that suspects would appear for a hearing and underwrote their good behavior. If they comported themselves correctly, the next session of court might see them admonished and dismissed. In such cases, the distinction between a misdemeanor, requiring indictment and permitting trial, and a petty offense, handled summarily, was blurred beyond recognition.

Later generations of Virginia jurists would be more precise on this distinction. Charles Lee, defense counsel at Supreme Court Justice Samuel Chase's 1805 impeachment trial, averred that "in the practice of Virginia," misdemeanors were divided into "petty misdemeanors and those of greater malignity."[73] No doubt individual justices sitting at the sessions fifty years before had some idea of the dividing line between minor breaches of the peace and serious assaults, but these views did not reflect hard and fast rules. In the present record, one may simply assume that the judges intended to make practical, not fine, distinctions, when a defendant was entitled to a trial.

For their part, the vast majority of defendants either confessed or did not

---

70. *RCP*, 57 (1723).

71. Webb, *Justice of Peace*, 229.

72. Webb, *Justice of Peace*, 230.

73. Charles Lee to U.S. Senate, February 22, 1805, in *The Trial of Samuel Chase . . . Upon an Impeachment . . . Taken in Shorthand by Samuel H. Smith and Thomas Lloyd*, 2 vols. (Washington, D.C., 1805), 2:124.

contest the charges; between 1711 and 1754 only six put themselves upon the court. Why did only a few of those who were entitled to a trial by jury actually ask for impanelment of a petty jury? Virginians were proud that they shared with other Anglo-Americans the right to jury trial, but jury trial in criminal cases was costly and time-consuming. The county courts ordinarily met but a few days each session, seven or eight times a year, and extensive jury trials in criminal cases would extend these sessions indefinitely. The justices and potential jurors all had their own affairs to manage and could not have relished the prospect of jury trials in every eligible criminal case.[74] Some defendants did put themselves upon the court if, in the clerk's notation, the formula AB had or had not "something material to say in his own defense" meant that a bench trial took place, but this is speculation. Those defendants who pled guilty or were found guilty by the justices undoubtedly knew that it had been far cheaper to forego a jury trial, with the court costs that trial entailed, than to put themselves upon the court or even plead guilty and then produce the sureties or fines assessed against them. Even if a jury found them not guilty of the offenses charged against them, they might be ordered to bond themselves to the peace. Finally, as defendants probably knew, trial juries were likely to believe that the grand juries and the justices would not proceed to indict and try a suspect unless he or she were guilty as charged.[75]

The time and expense of trial juries did not deter a handful of defendants from seeking them. The *RCP* included all of these cases that fell under the 1710 statute. A March 1716 petty jury convicted John Henderson upon an indictment for illegally running a tipling house.[76] In September 1731, Joan Stephens was convicted by a petty jury of tending seconds of tobacco (selling inferior quality leaves—a violation of colonial statutes). The king's attorney had brought an information against her. She was ordered to pay a fine of five hundred pounds of tobacco and court costs. The same jury condemned Benjamin Hinds to pay for tending seconds.[77] In July 1733, a trial jury decided that Anthony Morgan had kept his pledge not to cohabit with a woman.[78] In July 1736, William Tillery was found guilty by a jury of wounding another man. A 1747 grand jury indicted and a petty jury convicted William Robertson for an assault. He paid a fine of two shillings.[79] The one appeal in the *RCP* from the county courts to a higher court occurred in 1719 but was not a criminal matter. Robert Beverley, acting as attorney for three planters, appealed from a judgment on a *scire facias* brought by the king's attorney. The case was a civil one, and appeals were permitted in

---

74. The criminal jury trials cited in nn. 76–80 comprise the total in the *RCP* and the ROB in which some trials were reported after 1740. Although writers such as Thomas Jefferson, *Notes on the State of Virginia* [1781], ed. William Peden (Chapel Hill, 1955), 130–31, extolled the virtues of jury trials, misdemeanor defendants in Virginia did not often demand such trials. See Warren M. Billings, "Pleading, Procedure, and Practice: The Meaning of Due Process of Law in Seventeenth-Century Virginia." *Journal of Southern History*, 47 (November 1981): 576.

75. On the presumptions of the Virginia jurors, see Billings, "Pleading, Procedure, and Practice," 580.

76. *RCP*, 24 (1716).

77. *RCP*, 136–37 (1731).

78. *RCP*, 145 (1733).

79. *RCP*, 164 (1736); 234 (1747).

cases involving any sum over £20.[80] In general, it did not improve defendants' chances very much to put themselves upon the country.

The absence of trial juries from the criminal record cannot be laid entirely to the aversion to time and expense. The ROB is filled with jury trials in civil actions. Summary criminal justice must have had a value, in addition to saving time and money, to induce defendants to forego jury trials. Without trial by jury, the disposition of criminal cases went so quickly that in many cases there could have been little attempt to establish the guilt of offenders beyond a reasonable doubt. Justices and defendants must have realized and accepted this phenomenon. The bar of the colony of Virginia was in a flourishing state but rarely involved itself in the criminal business of the county court. In the view of those present, fair trial at these sessions did not require counsel.[81]

The submissiveness of defendants in Richmond was typical of many colonies, except, perhaps, parts of New England. Viewing a similar phenomenon in New York courts, Julius Goebel, Jr., and T. Raymond Naughton proposed that "sharp distinctions" between lower-class suspects of misdemeanor and upper-class judges reinforced economic considerations in reducing the number of demands for trial.[82] Social distinctions certainly existed in the Tidewater courts of the eighteenth century and probably induced some lower-status defendants to eschew a trial when entitled to it. All requests for trial by jury came from planters, who were not always as docile before the bench as were lower-class defendants.

The conclusion suggests itself that these courts were viewed as agents of social control by those who lived in the county, criminal suspects included. In colonial Virginia, there were few institutions that could maintain order and harmony in society. The most prominent ones that could were the county courts. Defendants who made their permanent home in the county must have been wary of chal-

---

80. *RCP*, 36 (1719).

81. John H. Langbein, "The Criminal Trial before the Lawyers," *University of Chicago Law Review*, 45 (Winter 1978): 263–316. Counsel for the defense in criminal cases slowly made its way into the Old Dominion; see Alan M. Smith, "Virginia Lawyers, 1680–1776: The Birth of an American Profession" (Ph.D. dissertation, Johns Hopkins University, 1967), 280–97. Pennsylvania in 1718, Delaware in 1719, and South Carolina in 1731 provided for counsel in felonies. The last enactment was the most far-reaching, including all property offenses of a serious nature; see William S. McAnich, "Criminal Procedure and the South Carolina Jury Act of 1731," in Herbert A. Johnson, ed., *South Carolina Legal History* (Spartanburg, 1980), 190–91.

82. Goebel and Naughton, *Law Enforcement*, 78. There is some evidence that jury trial in Massachusetts county courts was demanded far more often than in similar Virginia cases. For example, David T. Konig, ed., *The Plymouth County Court Records, 1689–1859*, vol. 2: *1719–1749* (Wilmington, Del., 1978), for 1719–25, shows that three of ten cases of larceny went to trial juries. William Nelson, *Dispute and Conflict Resolution in Plymouth County, Massachusetts, 1725–1825* (Chapel Hill, 1981), 25–26; Susan C. Towne, "The Historical Origins of Bench Trial for Serious Crime," *American Journal of Legal History*, 26 (April 1982): 129; and John Murrin, "Magistrates, Sinners, and a Precarious Liberty: Trial by Jury in Seventeenth-Century New England," in David D. Hall, John M. Murrin, and Thad Tate, eds., *Saints and Revolutionaries: Essays in Early American History* (New York, 1983), agree that by the early eighteenth century, Bay Colony citizens were especially dogged in their defense of the right to jury trials. The sheer numbers of noncapital jury trials in provincial Massachusetts—an average of six per year in Middlesex County (1692–1760), twelve per year in Suffolk (1702–32, 1743–73), and five per year in Essex (1692–1740)—demonstrates that misdemeanor defendants there regularly exercised their right to trial by jury. Data courtesy of John M. Murrin, 1982.

lenging the authority of the grand juries and the justices for fear of bringing on the greater evils of social disruption, which had in the past ripped through the colony. In return for suspects' submission to the justices' decisions, the courts were often patient and lenient. As with the established church, troublemakers were disciplined but readmitted to the community when they confessed and did penance. Guilt and innocence were not the sole issues for the county courts; the willingness of the accused to submit to authority was almost as important.

The almost automatic imposition of bonds for good behavior and to keep the peace typified the social control function of the courts. Recognizances were an early and distinctive feature of the county justice system in England, preventing future misconduct by monetary penalties. Leaders of the community sometimes put up funds for the bonds and often provided the sureties, for ordinary yeomen and laborers could hardly have had the resources required. Under these conditions, the accused put themselves under a pledge not only to the crown but to the community not to threaten its members or violate its laws. More than one hundred persons are named as sureties for such recognizances in the *RCP*, a total that exceeded 10 percent of all free, propertied persons in the county. The entire community had a stake in keeping order and therefore in supporting the authority of the courts. The recognizance for "good behavior," issued at court, stated that the defendant would cease carrying on a specified unlawful activity and often required a return to the next session of court. A recognizance "to keep the peace against John Doe," which a single justice might impose, pledged the defendant not to harm a particular person. Both types were common in the *RCP*. After 1722, the justices required bonds for good behavior from men and women presented by the grand juries. This form of pledge created a network of financial obligations which supported the authority of the justices and maintained order.[83]

Defendants seemed to have respected this system; the king's attorney in Richmond had to bring suit against defendants for breach of the obligation of their bond only twice in the course of the *RCP*. Justices of the peace were also presented by the grand juries and posted bond for good behavior, found sureties, and, if required, paid fines. Justices and other court officials provided sureties for some of the defendants, tying themselves personally into the network of financial obligations. Using recognizances and other procedural instruments, the justices functioned as if they were the heads of an extended family, punishing minor offenses but permitting perpetrators to retain their identity and function within the community.

As keepers of social order as well as criminal court judges, the justices could hardly ignore breaches of the peace against themselves or their officers. When

---

83. In these proceedings, bonds tied all those concerned to the public interest, making private quarrels and misbehavior into public concerns; see Joel B. Samaha, "The Recognizance in Elizabethan Law Enforcement," *American Journal of Legal History*, 25 (July 1981): 189–204, and Bradley Chapin, *Criminal Justice in Colonial America* (Athens, Ga., 1983), 27–28. By monitoring the conduct of the parties, the justices created a warn and watch system. As the eighteenth century progressed, other colonies also stiffened economic sanctions against disturbers of the peace. Even Pennsylvania, whose first, mild criminal laws were exceptional among North American colonies, turned to stricter enforcement of bonds to keep the peace; see Paul Mermack, "Peace Bonds and Criminal Justice in Colonial Philadelphia," *Pennsylvania Magazine of History and Biography*, 100 (April 1976): 186–87.

the authority of the judge, sheriff, or underofficers was abused, the court punished not only offenders but all who failed to restrain them. In 1723, Rawleigh Chinn refused to deport himself properly in court. When he burst from the courthouse, an undersheriff was sent to summon him back. Chinn horsewhipped the officer in the courtyard and spurred away. All male bystanders who ignored the undersheriff's cry for assistance were brought before the bench and fined. Chinn himself, a perpetual disturber of the peace, was called to apologize and pay a fine.[84] Threats against justices brought bonds to keep the peace and sureties twice the amount of those required when the victim was a private citizen.[85] Persons suspected of disrespect for the justices were viewed as threats to the authority of the system and summarily punished. Even though William Goburn was acquitted of felonious taking from Justice William Jordan's stores, Goburn was still judged an "ill-behaved man" and forced to put up security for his good behavior.[86]

The paternal authority implicit in local justice extended beyond the justices' commissions and the statutory jurisdiction of these courts. Felonies were not to be dealt with in the county, but the justices, instead of convening an examining court, often reduced a charge from grand larceny or robbery to petty theft, heard the case at the county court, and gave judgment (see Table 3). Through 1729, the reduction of charges for serious offenses and imposition of punishment at the county court was as common as bringing the offense to an examining or an oyer and terminer court. In the 1730s, the latter procedures began to predominate, and by the 1740s, a few charges were reduced and handled entirely within the county court. Early in the century defendants agreed to reduction of charges, in effect renouncing their right to a trial in Williamsburg. The accused were recompensed for their relative incapacity to defend themselves in county court by the knowledge that penalties would not exceed corporal punishment or fines nor require leaving the community.[87]

This flexibility of proceeding diminished in the 1730s, and by the next decade almost all of the men and women suspected of felonious offenses against property were examined in the called courts or tried in courts of oyer and terminer. Justices at these courts could still reduce the charges and punish offenders in the county rather than sending them to Williamsburg for trial. As will shortly be apparent, the former was common in the examining court until the 1730s, when, as in the reduction of charges in the county court discussed above, suspects whose culpability was presumed were almost invariably sent to the capital for trial (see Table 4).

---

84. *RCP*, 53–55 (1723).

85. *RCP*, 183 (1738).

86. *RCP*, 184 (1738).

87. Virginia's aversion to criminal trial juries in misdemeanors may be attributable to her earliest courts' reliance on the military model; John M. Murrin and A. G. Roeber, "Trial by Jury: The Virginia Paradox," unpublished paper, courtesy of authors, here agrees with Konig (see n. 57). Another, more general explanation of why suspects bow to the "hegemony" of their social superiors, sitting as criminal judges, even to the extent of refusing to assert their rights under the law, is the subject of a growing literature on early modern social history; see Mark Tushnet, *The American Law of Slavery, 1810–1860* (Princeton, 1981), 3–25, and T. Jackson Lears, *No Place of Grace: Antimodernism and the Transformation of American Culture, 1880–1920* (1981).

**Table 3: Reduced Charges from Felony to Misdemeanor,
Richmond County Courts, 1711–1746**

Years	Felonies reduced to lesser offenses and punished in the county court (ROB and *RCP*)	Servants and slaves among the suspects (ROB and *RCP*)	Felony prosecutions in examining and oyer and terminer courts (*RCP*)
1714–16	1	0	4
1717–19	3	2	3
1720–22	12	7	6
1723–25	18	10	7
1726–28	6	6	9
1729–31	11	11	18
1732–34	4	4	10
1735–37	10	9	20
1738–40	13	11	10
1741–43	2	1	9
1744–46	1	0	10

Source: ROB and *RCP*.

Table 3 indicates that the recipients of reduced charges early in the century were almost always servants. Servants committed more than one-half of all the thefts and other property offenses recorded in the order books and the *RCP*, and reductions of charges in the 1720s mitigated their punishment. The ROB records a tidal wave of runaways, vagabonds, and mischief among servants and transported felons in these years. The growing numbers of the latter may have fueled the Richmond justices' anxiety about the misconduct of all servants, despite (or perhaps because of) the use of convict labor by the leading planters in the county.[88] In 1722, Robert Beverley warned readers of his revised history of Virginia that amassing convict servants in the colony would lead to a breakdown of local justice: "Tho' the greedy planters will always buy them yet it is to be feared they will be very injurious to the country which has already suffered murders and robberies [from them]."[89] A convict servant could corrupt other servants, as testimony in the *RCP* shows. In 1724, Virginia's Reverend Hugh Jones inveighed against transported convicts precisely because they "spoil servants that were before very good."[90] A 1748 statute mandated the recording of prior English convictions of those arrested in Virginia, for "most" capital offenses were supposedly committed by convicts.[91] Public awareness of crimes by trans-

---

88. Fears of crimes by newcomers, aliens, and lower-status minorities can become self-fulfilling prophecies as more of the outsiders are arrested and prosecuted for suspected crimes and status offenses; Sue Titus Reid, *Crime and Criminology* (Duxbury, Mass., 1977), 58–61. This theory seems to apply to Richmond. In 1730, an entire boatload of transported convicts was sold for service at Rappahannock docks. Richmond County petitioned the House of Burgesses immediately for summary jurisdiction in felony cases involving the new convicts; Morgan, "Hegemony of the Laws," 161–62, 206, 213–15.

89. Robert Beverley, *The History and Present State of Virginia* (London, 1722), 287–88. The 1722 edition expressed far more fear on this score than that of 1705.

90. Hugh Jones, *The Present State of Virginia* (London, 1724), 53.

91. Taylor's case, *RCP*, 191 (1739); Statutes at Large, 5:24–26 (1738).

ported felons in the colony stirred the *Virginia Gazette* to mourn: "When we see our papers fill'd continually with accounts of the most audacious Robberies, the most cruel Murders, and infinite other Villainies perpetrated by Convicts transported from Europe, what melancholy, what terrible Reflections must it occasion! What will become of our Posterity?"[92] Crimes by newcomers, men and women on the fringes of the community, former convicts, and servants dissolved the assumptions behind face-to-face justice. The accused did not live within the consensual network of personal and monetary ties that controlled antisocial conduct. To counter suspected crimes among runaways, transported convicts, and the slaves who shared their alienation, the justices turned increasingly toward examining and oyer and terminer courts.

Examining Courts

In the Anglo-American criminal justice system, interrogation of suspects was conducted by justices of the peace. From the time of the Marian statutes of 1554–55 (1 and 2 Philip and Mary, c.13 and 2 and 3 Philip and Mary, c.10), English justices of the peace were required to obtain written testimony in serious crimes and to bring these records to circuit courts of assize along with the suspect. English assize files invariably began with lists of the justices of peace for the county, all of whom were required to attend, but the extent of the justices' participation in actual prosecutions is uncertain.[93] Whatever the role of justices of the peace at the English assizes, the scope of their investigatory power in the county was broad. As the English manualist Michael Dalton recited: "Every [justice of peace] may and must take the examination of all such felons, or persons suspected of felony, as shall be brought before him. . . . And must take information against them (of those that bring them) . . . of the felony and fact."[94] The justices had either to bail (except in felony and treasons) or to bind over suspects to gaol. Other English treatises on evidence, including those of Dunscomb and Gilbert, as well as commentaries on crime from Hale and Hawkins to Blackstone, closely paralleled Dalton's account. By 1619, when Dalton wrote, the justices had lost jurisdiction for felony, homicide, and treason, but they still had charge of "petie larcenies, and small felonies." The latter phrase, like the "certaine felonies" Dalton later referred to, does not have a clear boundary, that is, the exact difference between a "small felony" and a serious misdemeanor was not clear-cut but a matter of categorization. If the offense was not serious enough to warrant holding the suspect in gaol until the assizes, the quarter courts might try a small felony on their own. They tried misdemeanors as well. In addition, the justices had jurisdiction over those "as convicted upon examination, and the oath of witnesses." Examinations by the justice were not trials, and Dalton's phrase "convicted upon examination" defies precise explanation.[95]

Initial examination of suspected felons under the Marian statutes was in-

---

92. *Virginia Gazette* (Williamsburg), May 24, 1751.
93. Compare John H. Langbein, *Prosecuting Crime in the Renaissance: England, Germany, France* (Cambridge, Mass., 1974), 34 ff., and Cockburn, *English Assizes*, 90ff.
94. Michael Dalton, *The Countrey Justice* (London, 1622), 42.
95. Dalton, *The Countrey Justice*, 43.

tended as a reform of arbitrary bail processes, a curb upon magisterial discretion. Suspects were set free too often with too little reason for the justices' decisions. It was, of course, a burden for the justice to commit suspects to gaol, attend to their custody, and then transport them to the county town for trial at the assizes. Yet the statutes and all of the case law that followed do not seem to have diminished the discretion of justices in matters of bail. As Blackstone wrote in 1759: "The opinion seems now to be, that the justice is to exercise a somewhat more liberal discretion, and not to commit or detain a party on bail, however positively accused, if the balance of testimony be strongly in favor of his innocence."[96]

In Virginia, as in England, justices retained final responsibility for examining suspects. The process of gathering evidence was to be guided by Dalton's *Country Justice* and other English manuals.[97] In 1705, however, the colony diverged from English procedure by introducing a new court to hear evidence of serious crime:

> When any person shall, at any time hereafter, by precept from any justice of the peace within this dominion, be committed to the goal of the county, for any such criminal offence, as shall appear to such justice to be triable in the general court only; in such case, it shall be lawful for the same justice to issue his warrant to the sheriff of the county, requiring him to summon the justices of the same county, to meet at a certain time to be appointed in the said warrant, not less than five days, nor above ten days after the date thereof, and hold a court for examining the prisoner, and all witnesses and circumstances relating to the matter whereof he or she shall be accused; and to consider whether, as the case shall appear to them, he or she may be tried in the county or must be removed from thence, to be tried at the general court. . . . And if, upon examination before the said court, they are of opinion, that the prisoner ought to be tried for the fact whereof he or she is accused, before the general court, they shall signify the same, by entring such their opinion upon record in the said court, and shall remand the said prisoner to the county goal; and thereupon, it shall be lawful for any two justices of the said court . . . to commit him or her to the said public goal, there to remain until he or she shall be thence delivered by due course of law.[98]

The examining court was not a simple enlargement of the number of examining magistrates, nor a trial court, nor a grand jury. Unlike the single magistrate, examining witnesses and suspects on his own, taking down what he wished for his own use, the "called court" was a court of record, meeting at a specified time and place, in public, under a specific instrument.[99] Though it was invariably staffed by the justices, it was separate from the regular county court. The examining court had no power to punish offenders. Failing to acquit them, it could detain suspects in gaol, but this was not itself a punishment, or it could order them to appear before the county court. The called court did not function as a

---

96. Blackstone, *Commentaries*, 4:293–297.

97. *Statutes at Large*, 2:246 (1666).

98. *Statutes at Large*, 3:390 (1705); see also 5:541–43 (1748).

99. The phrase "called court" distinguished these hearings from courts "held at. . . ." The phrase was not unique to Virginia, though the type of court was. I have found a Kent County, Delaware, "called court" convened in November 1680 to distribute land. It was not a criminal court, and the term did not appear again in the record; see Leon DeValinger, Jr., ed., *Court Records of Kent County, Delaware, 1680–1705, American Legal Records—Volume 8* (Washington, D.C., 1959), 4.

grand jury in the latter event, for though it did commit suspects for trial in other courts and certify evidence for the prosecution, its proceedings were not indictments in either the county court or the General Court. Every suspect sent to Williamsburg by the examining courts in the counties had to be indicted by a grand jury at the capital. Although not specifically provided for in the governing statute, the examining court could allow bail in "less serious felonies," a power beyond the reach of grand juries.[100] Contemporary Virginia jurists were aware that the examining court was a procedural novelty. Richard Starke's manual, published in 1775, noted:

> The Institution of a Court of Examination of criminal Offenders, previous to their Arraignment and Trial, is peculiar to this Colony, and undoubted Evidence of the Lenity of the Authors of it, who, by this Mode, have not only enlarged the Means of coming at the Truth of a supposed Fact, whereon the Life or Member of the Person charged doth depend, but also given to such Person a third Opportunity of Acquittal not to be boasted of in any other Part of the British Dominions.
>
>   The Power of Acquittal lodged with this Court is absolute and conclusive, and was calculated for the Liberty and Quiet of the Subject; but a Narrative of the Incident which gave Rise to it would not be improper in a Work of this Kind, but probably be thought impertinent.[101]

Generations of Virginians considered the examining court a safeguard of the right of accused to a public and speedy hearing in their own neighborhood, although this "right" was not specifically conferred until the 1776 Declaration of Rights.[102] Despite the patriots' boast, it is not likely that "public and speedy trial" was the intent of the 1705 Virginia act creating examining courts. They were not trial courts. What is more, except for William Penn's charters of liberties, there was little discussion of "public and speedy trial" in English or American colonial commentary.[103] Commentary that did appear was not directed to examination procedure. In England, the notion of speedy trial can be traced back to the requirement that assize justices tour the shires at least twice each year to empty the gaols. Public trials were protection against secret condemnations of Quakers and Catholics, but Virginia did not have assize circuits or secret trials of heretics. The procedural rights of the accused were not an issue mentioned in burgesses' debates on the criminal law in this era.

A better explanation of the origin of examining courts is the justices' desire to expedite the investigation of serious crimes. Virginia justices had been holding informal examining courts for all manner of crimes for at least a decade before 1705. Any justice could "call a court" to examine suspects. As in English practice, the single Virginia magistrate could order the detention of any persons sus-

---

   100. Scott, *Criminal Law*, 55–56; Webb, *Justice of Peace*, 30–38, 40; see *Statutes at Large*, 3:391 (1705), where the formula is simply "if the offence be of such a nature, as the prisoner may be admitted to bail." The *RCP* had two such cases; see pp. 30–31, 218–19.

   101. Richard Starke, *The Office and Authority of a Justice of the Peace* (Williamsburg, 1775), 115.

   102. Tucker, *Commentaries on Blackstone*, 5:300n. Section 8, Virginia Declaration of Rights, 1776, in William F. Swindler, ed., *Sources and Documents of United States Constitutions* (Dobbs Ferry, N.Y., 1979), 10:49.

   103. Bernard Schwartz, *The Great Rights of Mankind: A History of the American Bill of Rights* (New York, 1977), 73.

pected of serious crimes and take testimony from them. It was but one step further to hear this testimony, along with the evidence of other witnesses, in the courthouse "Att a court held" for that purpose.[104] The burgesses probably meant the law to be an administrative expedient. Their innovation lay not in commissioning formal hearings but in using a legislative act to formalize custom. Starke hints that a particular incident may have roused the lawmakers to codify the county justices' practice. Unfortunately, the *Journals* for the House of Burgesses are silent on this matter.[105]

Local exigency seems an even more convincing explanation for the new courts when one searches in vain for a viable precedent for them. They were not English institutions. The English Star Chamber court and certain other courts of high commission operated without impaneling juries, examining witnesses, and hearing complaints of serious crimes in an inquisitorial manner, but these were courts on whose benches sat the highest judges in the realm and whose business consisted of extraordinary cases.[106] Other colonies did not provide precedent or even move in a parallel course to that of Virginia. In Massachusetts, for example, single justices of the peace heard evidence in felony and homicide cases. The defendant did not plead, and the examination was not a public hearing.[107] The same procedures existed in the other colonies.[108] Only in Connecticut did a system of justices sitting together to hear and certify evidence in criminal cases emerge:

> Regardless of the means employed to begin process, complaint, information, or presentment, the next step in any case which ultimately arrived at the Superior Court was the preliminary hearing before one or two Justices. Arrested under a special writ and brought before "A Court of Inquiry or Examination," the accused was asked questions by means of which the examiners endeavored to establish the case of the prosecution.
>
> Every attempt was made to clinch matters at this point. If possible, a confession was secured, the first question often being such as to put to accused immediately to plead Guilty or Not Guilty. The character of the whole proceedings was that of an inquisition.[109]

---

104. Scott, *Criminal Law*, 59. For example, on September 6, 1702, Justice William Tayloe "called a court" to examine Indians suspected of murder; Richmond County "Miscellaneous Records," Book 1, p. 30. Another example appears in ROB, September 7, 1704.

105. The *Journals of the House of Burgesses* for 1702/3–1705 mention nothing of this complaint, though the criminal laws were revised extensively during these sessions, for example, *Journals*, 171.

106. John H. Langbein, *Torture and the Law of Proof: Europe and England in the Ancien Régime* (Chicago, 1977), 87–88; John Bellamy, *The Tudor Law of Treason* (London, 1979), 104–17; Plucknett, *Common Law*, 181–82, 193.

107. George L. Haskins, *Law and Authority in Early Massachusetts: A Study in Tradition and Design* (New York, 1960), 174; Joseph H. Smith, ed., *Colonial Justice in Western Massachusetts, 1639–1702: The Pynchon Court Record* (Cambridge, Mass., 1961), 144–49.

108. Goebel and Naughton, *Law Enforcement*, 630–39, notes that written evidence was taken in the locality and brought back to the principal court in revenue violations. There was no examining court in the hinterlands, however. Circuit courts were trial courts. In colonial chancery courts, commissions to persons to take depositions away from the court were common. The depositions were returned to the court under seal and read into evidence. These examinations did not deal with criminal matters.

109. John T. Farrell, ed., *The Superior Court Diary of William Samuel Johnson, 1772–1773*, American Legal Records—Volume 4, (Washington, D.C., 1942), xliii.

These examinations were not always given weight by grand juries at the Connecticut Superior Court, to which suspects were sent upon evidence of their complicity in serious crimes. Moreover, it is unlikely that the Connecticut experience motivated the Virginia burgesses to create examining courts.

The absence of external precedent leads to the conclusion that Virginians drew upon their own experience to fashion examining courts. One civil instrument used in Virginia and elsewhere might have been a model for examining courts. To aid litigants in sending evidence to the Williamsburg courts, the burgesses provided for writs of *dedimus potestatum*. Signed by the county justice, the *dedimus* included evidence taken from plantiff and defendant, as well as their witnesses, by "three or more such indifferent persons."[110] The justice sealed this examination and sent it to Williamsburg to be read at the trial. The writs permitted the hearing of cases at the General Court without great expense to witnesses and authorities. These might have suggested examining courts. In felony cases the colony had to bear the expense of sending accused and witnesses to the capital when the evidence warranted trial, so the examining court could not have been based upon the economic advantages of the *dedimus*. Common use of the *dedimus* may nonetheless have whispered to the legislators that evidence taken in the county could be certified by impartial examiners, in this case the justices sitting as a court.

Whatever part familiarity with evidentiary instruments such as the *dedimus* played in giving form to the examining court, the prime impetus for such a court grew from the exigencies of life in early eighteenth-century Virginia. As the population expanded and dispersed, the expense of bringing every accused felon to Williamsburg for trial must have increased exponentially. The General Court would not surrender jurisdiction to the local courts nor was it able (as a professional bench was) to go on circuit in the counties. The examining court provided a hybrid solution. The new institution spared the colony the cost of hearing every accusation of felony, homicide, or treason against a free person or servant at the capital. Jury trials of freemen for capital offenses remained the prerogative of the courts in Williamsburg. The expense of providing gaols for suspects in the counties and paying sheriffs and gaolers was established by statute. Sheriffs were fined for allowing escapes.[111] The cost of sending a suspect to Williamsburg remained substantial, with payments to witnesses, gaolers, and officials, not to mention the lodging of the accused, even if the grand jury there returned the bill ignoramus. Examining courts held shortly after a suspect was brought into custody prevented unnecessary trips to the capital and expedited justice for the innocent. As the century passed, counties like Richmond did send a larger and larger percentage of those its justices examined to Williamsburg, but this was not a foreseeable outcome of the introduction of examining courts.

To justices of the peace in Virginia, some of whom were also serving as its burgesses, such an innovation would have had another attraction. After the disturbances of the 1670s and 1680s these magnates steadily consolidated their

---

110. *Statutes at Large*, 2:67–69 (1662).

111. *Statutes at Large*, 2:76–77 (1662); 3:391–92 (1705). For escapes he permitted, the sheriff was fined, but only in civil cases; Webb, *Justice of Peace*, 169.

control of local affairs.[112] The statutes creating the examining courts augmented the justices' discretionary power. The crimes that most frequently came before examining courts were theft from and breaking and entering into plantation buildings. The planter who could sit in judgment on those who threatened his neighbors' property materially increased his own security as well as serving the interests of his peers.

As the Richmond criminal proceedings record indicates, examinations in court were short and succinct. Justices committed the suspect to gaol upon a warrant, then bade the sheriff call the court. The hearings were described in a number of ways in the *RCP*. The defendant "being examined," after "an examination of several evidences," and "the court having taken the said matter into examination," the justices "upon the aforesaid examination" freed the accused or bound him over for trial in Williamsburg or ordered some lesser punishment for him in the county. At the called court, suspects and witnesses confronted each other in person, but all addressed the justices. The justices did the questioning. There was no prosecutor at the examining court, for the procedure was not a trial. On occasion, one of the justices may have taken a leading role. In Livack's case (1727) justices Anthony Sydnor and William Downman left the bench to speak "on behalf of the king." The phrase "on behalf of" may have been a shortened wording of the more common "gave several evidences on behalf of the king." If so, Sydnor and Downman were merely giving firsthand evidence.[113] It is also possible that a rudimentary county prosecutorial system was emerging in Richmond alongside inquisition by the justices. These prosecutors were not the "king's attorneys" who argued cases on instructions from Williamsburg. Instead, they represented the crystallization in a separate officer of one of the multiple functions which the justices themselves performed.

Consistent with the English practice, witnesses testified on oath; the defendant did not, for defendants were not to be forced to perjure themselves on oath to defend themselves.[114] Items of physical evidence were presented and identified. Separate courts might be convened for accomplices or to take recognizances from witnesses going to Williamsburg. Accessories to the offense were heard at the same time as the principal but could be examined after the principal had fled. Every effort was made to obtain information from accessories, and perjury was severely punished. A record of the hearing was made and sent to the capital with the prisoners. If a true bill was found by the grand jury at the General Court, part of the trial jury was summoned to Williamsburg from the county of the crime (except, after 1748, in cases of transported English felons). Witnesses gave bond in the county to appear and give evidence at the capital. The examin-

---

112. Bailyn, "Politics and Social Structure," 110–15; T. H. Breen, "A Changing Labor Force and Race Relations in Virginia 1660–1710," *Journal of Social History*, 39 (Fall 1973): 3–25.

113. *RCP*, 103–4 (1727). A sample of the warrant and call for the court appears in Webb, *Justice of Peace*, 150–51, 110.

114. J. H. Baker, "Criminal Courts and Procedure at Common Law, 1550–1800," in J. S. Cockburn, ed., *Crime in England, 1550–1800* (London, 1977), 37. The justices took testimony in writing, but "this must not be upon oath"; Webb, *Justices of Peace*, 139. Anglo-American courts were moving slowly in the direction of giving privileges to the defendant. After 1702 (1 Anne, stat. 2, c. 9), defense witnesses were sworn in treason and felony cases in England. In Virginia, defense witnesses were also sworn at the General Court; *Statutes at Large*, 3:298 (1705).

ing court met while recollection was fresh, evidence at hand, and the victims' feelings still strong, reinforcing their incentive to carry on the prosecution. Once the court remanded suspects for trial, victims were bonded to go to Williamsburg and testify for the king—ensuring that their resolve did not slacken.

Bail was allowed two suspects examined for serious offenses in Richmond County called courts. Gregory Glascock put up bail in 1721 following his examination as an accessory to his father's flight from a murder scene. In May 1742, William Lee was granted bail to appear for trial in Williamsburg upon the charge of beating a slave to death. Bail might be "prayed for" and granted if the justices trusted the accused to appear at trial, except in cases of murder, treason, and petty treason. The financial guarantee that suspects provided for their compliance could be substantial; Lee put up a bond of £200 sterling and obtained a surety in the amount of £100 sterling for his appearance at the next oyer and terminer court in Williamsburg. There was no bail for murder or treason, implying that Lee was charged with manslaughter. Convicts and servants were not given the opportunity to post bail; they waited in the county gaol until the sheriff could conduct them to Williamsburg. Gentlemen and freemen could seek to remain free on bail until their trials.[115]

In the hands of the justices, examining court jurisdiction did not always conform to the statutory provisions. First, early in the 1710s, examining courts in Richmond were convened to inquire into charges of assault and wounding, offenses not included in the governing statute, for they were not to be tried in Williamsburg. The penalties imposed for these offenses were bonds for good behavior, presumably exacted under the justices' commissions of the peace, because the examining court law of 1705 did not provide for deterrent measures. As the 1720s ended, examinations came to be restricted to suspected felonies and homicides.

Second, even if the cases handled were eventually limited to those indicated in the statute of 1705, magistrates at called courts retained their discretion in dealing with suspects. Table 4 shows the percentage of felony cases heard by examining courts in Richmond County which did not, despite sufficient evidence to find the suspect culpable of an offense, result in his transportation to Williamsburg or a separate hearing at the county court. If this event occurred without a confession by the suspect, it was tantamount to reduction of the charges; if suspects admitted their guilt, it was a reduction of sentence from that which the General Court could mete out upon a guilty verdict. In effect, the examining court itself sentenced suspects. This practice was evidently common until the mid-1730s.

Discretion in charging suspects before an examining court was called could be used to cajole them to inform upon their confederates or admit their guilt. In September 1734, Anthony Dent's theft of a hat was reduced from grand larceny, a felony, to petty larceny. He had promised to give information against Charles Nicholls, suspected of stealing tobacco. Dent was given twenty-five lashes and put up a bond for good behavior in the county court—a far less severe penalty than a Williamsburg court might have inflicted had he been bound over to it. In addition, there is evidence that some defendants, rather than risk trial and

---

115. *RCP*, 218–19 (1742).

Table 4: Reduction of Charge among Suspects Found Guilty in
Felony, Homicide, and Treason Cases,
Richmond County Examining Courts, 1714–1749

Years	Number of suspects whose charges were reduced (defendant punished in the county)	Total number of suspects found culpable	Reduction of charge as percent of those found culpable
1714–16	3	3	100
1717–19	1	1	100
1720–22	4	4	100
1723–25	1	7	14.3
1726–28	4	7	57.1
1729–31	7	11	63.6
1732–34	3	7	42.9
1735–37	6	17	35.3
1738–40	2	8	25
1741–43	3	8	37.5
1744–46	2	4	50
1747–49	2	7	28.6

Source: *RCP*

conviction in the General Court, pleaded guilty and begged the examining court to order corporal punishment in the county. The arrangement, similar to modern plea bargaining, might have been made shortly after they were apprehended or could have occurred at the examining court hearing.[116]

In Richmond County the discretionary reduction of charges and/or sentences at the examining court also extended to slaves, though statute provided another form of trial for them. In September 1728, Sambo, a slave, came before an examining court on a mittimus to the gaoler for striking a man and stealing two sheep and twelve chickens. The justices did not ask the governor for a commission of oyer and terminer, as provided by a 1692 law. The matter "being proved" by the oaths of two witnesses, Sambo was given thirty-nine lashes and had both ears cropped.[117] There were few such deviations from the statutes on the trial of slaves, but those that exist show early examining courts' readiness to use discretion broadly. They did not bother to remand the cases to other courts but decided them immediately. Reduction of charges in examining courts, with corresponding changes in outcome of cases, meant that the justices preserved the independence they had in the prestatutory period, despite the limiting strictures of the 1705 act.

One may attempt to distinguish examining courts called under the statute from ad hoc examining courts held by custom by scrutinizing the headings of the sessions in the *RCP*. "Att a Called Court" was the formula applied to the examining court assembled under the 1705 law. There are very few "called courts" in the early portion of the record and many at its end, however, suggesting that the clerk may not have always used the proper "called courts" heading in the 1710s and 1720s. In Margaret Richardson's case (1715), the defendant was examined on a charge of infanticide and then sent to Williamsburg, as prescribed in the

116. *RCP*, 152–53 (1734); Scott, *Criminal Law*, 80–81.
117. *RCP*, 111 (1728).

1705 statute, but the entry was headed merely "att a court held for Richmond County."[118] In hearings labeled in both fashions the justices reduced charges and kept suspects in the county.

There is little remarkable in the justices' reduction of charges. In common law, English judges possessed this authority.[119] Nothing in Virginia statute barred her local justices from a similar claim to reduce charges. The 1705 act explicitly permitted justices at the examining court to regard a suspected felony as a misdemeanor and to hear the case in the next county court—although the justices eschewed this course in favor of the expedient of hearing and determining the matter immediately at the examining session. Discretion at the called court is important to the historian of criminal justice because its use changed over time. There was an unmistakable decline in reduced charges and sentences in the examining courts from 1711 to 1754 (R^2 = .475).[120] Each three-year period of cases, as Figure 2 indicates, resulted in a 4 percent shift away from reduction of charges and punishment in the county and toward sending the suspect to the General Court. The change raises an important historical issue: why were the justices surrendering their discretion? Comparison of the percentages of reductions over time with the conviction rate—that is, the percentage of those suspected of serious crimes who were not acquitted by the court—(see pp. lxviii) shows that they had little relationship to one another (R^2 = .153). Richmond prosecution rates for serious crimes—the number of cases divided by the adult population of the county—was declining gradually over this same period (see pp. lix–lxi); the justices cannot therefore have sent a larger percentage of suspects to Williamsburg in response to fear of a crime wave.

Two other explanations may be explored. The first lies in the characteristics of the defendants. Many were outsiders, either transients or newcomers of low status. The steepest decline in the reduction of charges begins with the period 1729–32. From these years until the end of the RCP, defendants in felony and homicide cases increasingly were slaves, whites associated with runaway slaves, and convict servants transported from England. The largest importations of slaves and convicts into the colony occurred from 1726 to 1737.[121] Criminal activity among such men and women, magnified by their growing numbers in the colony, drove colonial authorities to legislative action against slaves and convicts suspected of crimes. These defendants were not the sort of community members who would be affected by shaming in the stocks or punishment at the whipping post. The justices might have been pleased to see them leave the county.

---

118. *RCP*, 13–16 (1715).

119. Plucknett, *Common Law*, 458, citing a 1503 manual for justices.

120. R^2, called the variance, ranges between 1.0 and 0 and measures the amount of variation in the dependent variable, here reduction of charge/sentence, which the independent variable, here the passage of time, explains.

121. The number of slaves imported each year peaked in the years around 1736; see Table 2 in Herbert S. Klein, "Slaves and Shipping in Eighteenth-Century Virginia," *Journal of Interdisciplinary History*, 5 (Winter 1975): 385–86. The number of convicts coming into the colony was never as large in this century as the number of slaves, but the former also peaked in the years between 1720 and mid-century. See Abbott E. Smith, *Colonists in Bondage: White Servitude and Convict Labor in America, 1607–1776* (1947; reprint, New York, 1971), 330. See also Morgan, "Hegemony of the Laws," 186.

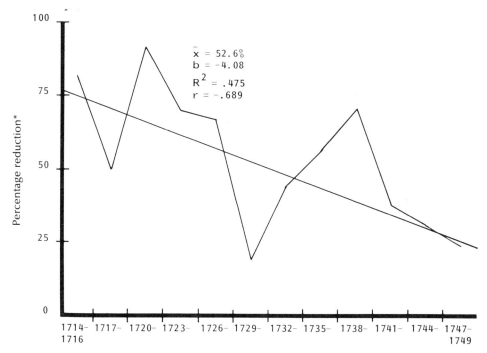

*The number of reduced sentences divided by the total number of defendants in serious property crimes.

Figure 2. Reduction of Charge and/or Sentence, Property Crimes, Examining Courts, Richmond County, 1714–1749 (*RCP*)

A second hypothesis is equally tenable but rests upon speculation. As the number of serious crimes heard in the county declined, it became financially feasible to send all those cases to the capital that under the law ought to have gone there. This explanation also fits the supposition that the justices were simply getting better acquainted with the provisions of the examining court statute, though it does not account for their abandonment of discretion. The soundest explanation is a combination of the two: worried by the criminality of certain individuals, the justices took the opportunity offered by the 1705 law to rid the county of them.

Oyer and Terminer Courts

Oyer and terminer courts for the trial of serious crimes were a fixture of Anglo-American criminal justice. The commission for judges to "hear and determine" a criminal case was commonly used in England by the end of the thirteenth century.[122] Along with the commission of general gaol delivery, bringing suspects from gaol to court, the commission of oyer and terminer gave English judges power to receive indictments and try, sentence, and punish defendants.

---

122. Plucknett, *Common Law*, 155–56; Cockburn, *English Assizes*, 21–22.

The commissions always came from the crown and by the seventeenth century went almost exclusively to assize justices on circuit and to special courts of oyer and terminer held for Middlesex and London, as well as to admiralty sessions convened to hear and determine cases of piracy and other high-seas felonies. The judges who sat in the assizes for the counties were the highest in the realm— the justices of Kings Bench and Common Pleas and the barons of the Court of Exchequer. By the late seventeenth century, English justices of the peace did not hear cases of life and limb.

Virginia's highest courts of criminal jurisdiction, sitting in the capital, were as old as the settlement of the colony and combined the English assizes and King's Bench in their power to hear and determine serious cases of crime, but trials of slaves under oyer and terminer commissions did not occur at the General Court except when the crimes were committed in or near Williamsburg.[123] By the criminal courts statute of 1692, commissions of oyer and terminer were given to past and present justices of the peace to dispose of serious crimes charged against slaves in the county where the crime occurred.[124] These were special courts, meeting by virtue of the governors' commissions. Their proceedings were distinct from those in the General Court of Virginia and other courts of oyer and terminer in North America, with the exception of the West Indian colonies, the colonial South, Pennsylvania, and Delaware.[125]

Oyer and terminer courts for slaves may appear novel and out of place in Anglo-American jurisprudence, but seen in correct perspective, they fit the development of Virginia's legal institutions. The years 1660–92 were marked by a steady deterioration in the legal status of black bondsmen and women, successive legislative acts reducing them from servants to chattel slaves.[126] The motivation for these measures has been discussed elsewhere. Suffice it to say here that the shift in the definition of slavery led to complications in the trial of slaves for serious crimes. For petty offenses, the master's discipline would be sufficient, but if the slave fled or committed a felony, or if the victim was white, the master had to turn to the regular courts. A slave did not have the same legal status as a free person in the courts, however, which made processing slaves accused of serious crimes a complicated matter. Could slaves defend themselves by examining the victim or other free persons in court? Could slaves subpoena witnesses? Could a slave have bail? The slave court act of 1692 put these questions to rest. Rather than an innovation, it was an elaboration of earlier revisions of property law.

As slavery became a fixture in all of the colonies and the number of Africans and Afro-Americans in bondage increased, interracial crimes and animosities induced colonial authorities to establish special courts for slaves. In 1661, the

---

123. Compare *Statutes at Large*, 2:63–64 (1662) with 3:102–3 (1692).

124. *Statutes at Large*, 3:102–3 (1692).

125. Why did the Privy Council allow these freeholders' courts, so contrary to English criminal law, to remain on the colonial books? The answer, in the case of similar statutes originating in the West Indian colonies, seems to be a mixture of avarice and racial bias. Richard S. Dunn, *Sugar and Slaves, Rise of the Planter Class in the English West Indies* (Chapel Hill, 1972), 245.

126. In the years before the 1692 act, the burgesses paved the way for a separate court system for slaves; see Warren M. Billings, ed., *The Old Dominion in the Seventeenth Century: A Documentary History of Virginia, 1606–1689* (Chapel Hill, 1975), 272–74, *Statutes at Large*, 2:270 (1689), 3:86–88 (1691); and Morgan, *American Slavery*, 295–337.

planters of Barbados instituted special courts for trials of slaves accused of serious crimes. These courts proceeded summarily. Their bench was composed of two justices of the peace and three freeholders. Jamaica's slaveholders created similar courts in 1664. Other English West Indian possessions soon followed suit.[127] Unlike these laws, the Virginia slave courts act of 1692 required a panel of justices, but other southern colonies followed the former, not the latter, model. In the eighteenth century, the legislatures of South and North Carolina, and later, Georgia, created "freeholders" courts, composed of two or more local justices and three to five landholders. All freeholders courts in the South tried slaves without a grand jury or a trial jury, and barring the master's appeal to the General Court, the judgment of the court was final.[128] Other colonies with large populations of slaves were moved to similar revisions of court procedure. In 1705, Pennsylvania, followed by Delaware, created special courts, composed of "two Justices of the Peace . . . who shall be particularly commissionated by the Government for that service, within the respective Counties . . . and six of the most substantial Free-holders of the Neighborhood" to "hear, examine, try and determine" slaves for capital offenses. These sessions proceeded without indictments by a grand jury or verdicts by a petty jury.[129]

Although the same fears of slaves' crimes were obviously at work in the northern and southern colonies, the former did not match the procedural inventions of the latter. Oyer and terminer courts were created on occasion to try slaves accused of felony in the northern colonies, but these courts still required grand jury indictments and petty jury verdicts.[130] Slaves in New York, Massachusetts, Connecticut, and New Hampshire were commonly brought before grand juries

---

127. Act for the Better Ordering and Governing of Negroes, 1661 (Barbados), Barbados Laws, 1645–82, CO 30/2/16–26; Jamaica Laws of 1664, CO 139/1/42, 55–58, Public Record Office, London.

128. The South Carolina Freeholders Courts Law appears in full text in Act no. 695; see John F. Grimké, ed., *The Public Laws of the State of South Carolina* (Philadelphia, 1790), 163–75, esp. 164–66. One South Carolina freeholders trial that has been preserved remains a moving account. In April 1734, a slave was tried for a burglary. He confessed to the crime and earnestly prayed for his salvation all the way to the gallows. After he was hanged, his head was severed from his body and displayed on the gallows; *South Carolina Gazette*, April 6, 1734. North Carolina created freeholders courts in 1715; see George Stevenson and Rudy D. Arnold, "North Carolina Courts of Law and Equity before 1868," *Archives Information Circular*, vol. 9 (Raleigh, 1977). The North Carolina State Archives, Raleigh, contain a more complete record of "Magistrates and Freeholders Courts" for the years 1740–89 than survive in South Carolina. Procedure in the former was swift and sanguinary. See, for example, the trial of Harry, a slave, for rape, on July 15, 1740, before a court of three justices and three "owners of slaves." The victim, Mary Busby, testified on oath to the assault on her, "against her will and consent." Harry admitted the deed. The court then pronounced a sentence of death, valued him at £240 in bills of credit, and adjourned. North Carolina State Archives, Secretary of State (SS) 311, Magistrates and Freeholders Courts Records, 1740–89. The owner's claim for the value of the slave was processed in the secretary's office on March 19, 1743. From the year 1755, freeholders courts were also convened in Georgia; see Allen D. Candler, ed., *Colonial Records of the State of Georgia* (Atlanta, 1910), 18:108–9.

129. "An Act for the Tryal of Negroes," Chapter 24 [1705], *The Laws of the Province of Pennsilvania Collected into One Volumn* (Philadelphia, 1714), 76–77; "An Act for the Tryal of Negroes" [1705], *Laws of the Government of New-Castle, Kent and Sussex upon Delaware* (Philadelphia, 1741), 65–68.

130. William M. Wiecek, "The Statutory Law of Slavery and Race in the Thirteen Mainland Colonies of British America," *William and Mary Quarterly*, 3d ser., 34 (April 1977): 276.

and, if indicted, faced trial juries at regular sessions of the superior courts. New Jersey established freeholders courts in 1713 but limited their jurisdiction to cases of murder, rape, arson, and dismemberment. Slaves' crimes against property, save arson, were left to the superior courts.[131] Rhode Island, seeking more expeditious trial of slaves accused of theft and robbery, stopped short of creating freeholders courts. Instead, her assembly created new town courts, presided over by assistants of the general court, county justices, and town wardens. Although these courts heard and determined cases without juries, their sanctions were limited to whipping and banishment.[132] Even during the 1741 crime wave in New York, slave defendants were indicted and tried in a manner similar to free defendants.[133] The Pennsylvania and Delaware freeholders courts were the exception in the North, while the Virginia oyer and terminer courts were widely, if not precisely, duplicated throughout the South.

It may be argued that another motive for Virginia oyer and terminer courts was the local demand for speedier justice. The slowness of the judicial system was one of the complaints against the English high courts that colonists had taken to heart. Other colonies did, to varying degrees, disperse justice through their counties. None of these arrangements were as thorough as Virginia's, nor as racially pointed. In the New Haven colony, a form of commission was given to certain of the the assistants to try cases away from the council, but only as an expedient.[134] Serious crimes in New York went to a circuit court presided over by a judge from the principal criminal court, at which grand juries endorsed indictments and trial juries gave verdicts. At times of emergency, or when escape seemed imminent, governors of New York created special courts of oyer and terminer to hear notorious cases, but these proceedings went forward only on grand jury indictments, and, if trial followed, petty juries were summoned to render verdicts.[135] Circuit court systems were less common throughout the colonies. In one exception, under its revised charter of 1691, Massachusetts' entire Superior Court of Judicature commenced regular circuits through the counties once or twice each year. Criminal trials in all these courts required grand jury bills and took place before trial juries, even when the suspect was a slave.[136] Overall, attempts to bring felony court justice to local populations did not discriminate against slaves accused of crimes—except in the South, Pennsylvania, and Delaware.

Although Virginia courts of oyer and terminer were not exactly the same as Carolina or Georgia freeholders courts—the Virginia commission did not specify any numerical formula for regular justices and freeholders, and all of those

---

131. "An Act for Regulating of Slaves," [1712] *The Laws, and Acts of the General Assembly of . . . New Jersey* (New York, 1717), 19–22.

132. "An Act, for the more speedy Tryal of . . . Negro and Indian Slaves," [1718] *Acts and Laws of His Majesties Colony of Rhode Island* (Boston, 1719), 101–2.

133. Daniel Horsmanden, *A Journal of the Proceedings in the Detection of the Conspiracy* (1744), ed. Thomas J. Davis (Boston, 1971), 37.

134. Charles J. Hoadley, ed., *Records of the Colony and Plantation of New Haven* (Hartford, 1857–58), 1:112–16.

135. Goebel and Naughton, *Law Enforcement,* 20, 61, 62, 80–82, 143, 147.

136. *Acts and Resolves . . . of the Province of Massachusetts Bay,* vol. 1, *1692–1717* (Boston, 1869), 72–74, 285, 371.

persons named were or had been justices for the county—all the southern colonies' handling of capital trials of slaves was clearly distinct from northern procedure. Although records of slave trials in eighteenth-century southern freeholders courts are fragmentary, the pieces appear similar to those found in the Virginia record. The far more substantial evidence on slave trials in colonial Virginia probably reflects the experience of the other southern colonies.

When a slave suspected of a serious crime had been apprehended, the sheriff informed the justices, who applied to the governor of the colony for a commission of oyer and terminer. The sheriff was responsible for assembling the court.[137] When the court met, the clerk read its commission. The governor informed the justices, the "sober men of judgment" named in the commission: "Know ye that . . . I have constituted and appointed you justices of oyer and terminer" to hold trial in "all treasons, petit treasons or misprisions thereof, felonies, murders, or other offenses or crimes" committed by the slave named.[138] A new commission was required for each case. The language of the commission varied slightly over time until printed forms were introduced in mid-century. After listing the judges, the commission recited the particulars of the offense. At the trial, the king's attorney prosecuted "on an indictment." In reality, this was an information, for there was no grand jury. Neither was there a trial jury; the bench found matters of fact. These courts had the power to take life or limb.[139] The statute of 1692 gave to the local bench greater power than was possessed by the king's criminal courts in England. In Virginia, unlike the mother country, no jury stood between the slave and the gallows. In England, there were no slaves; blacks could put themselves upon the country in trials for felony. In Virginia, slaves were arraigned to hear charges and plead to them but could not subpoena free men or women to testify or cross-examine witnesses themselves.[140] Masters alone had the statutory right to intervene on behalf of the defendants and to assist in their defense. Condemned slaves' value was ascertained, to be repaid to the master by the colony.[141]

Trial of slaves in the oyer and terminer courts was speedy and public. Local authorities feared the escape of imprisoned slaves, and nine are recorded breaking Virginia county gaols and fleeing before trial.[142] Colonial gaols were dirty, cramped, and foul smelling; a speedy trial benefited the accused as well as the

---

137. For example, Sheriff Thomas Jordan of Nansemond County to Governor Alexander Spotswood, May 4, 1718, Virginia Colonial Papers, folder 29, item 8, VSL.

138. Commission of Oyer and Terminer, recorded in York County Order book, August 15, 1748, CW. Printed forms were in use by the 1750s. The same standardization of terminology seems to have overtaken the English quarter sessions courts at this time; see, for example, Middlesex Quarter Sessions Records for 1751, Greater London Record Office.

139. Scott, *Criminal Law*, 80–81.

140. *Statutes at Large*, 4:126–34 (1723).

141. *Statutes at Large*, 4:327 (1732). *Statutes at Large*, 3:269–70 (1705), introduced the compensation principle.

142. Philip J. Schwarz, "Slave Criminality and the Slave Community: Patterns of Slave Assertiveness in 18th Century Virginia," unpublished paper, 15, reports nine escapes by slaves. One slave captured in Southhampton refused to give his name, burned down the gaol, and escaped into the countryside; see Thomas C. Parramore, *Southampton County, Virginia* (Charlottesville, 1978), 30. In Richmond, these fears were not ungrounded. In 1772, slave prisoners did burn the gaol and escape; ROB, 439 (1772).

colony, though that was not the purpose of these courts. Expedient trial in the county also saved the master the expense of transporting a slave accused of felony to Williamsburg—a necessity in the case of whites—and, equally taxing, the loss of the slave's labor while he or she waited for the General Court to convene.

The depth of detail in the *RCP* opens a window into the experience of the slave defendants. The oyer and terminer justices who found facts and ruled on law in slaves' cases were not their peers. The bench was composed of masters: white, free, propertied, and powerful. Often, justices were friend or kin to the defendant's owner. And if the slave's master or another slaveowner were the victim of slave crimes, the judges' interests were very much at stake in the trial. At the same time, slaves were valuable property, not to be regarded lightly by their masters or other slaveowners. The legislature might compensate masters for a slave hanged for a crime, but it did not compensate them for the lost time and labor of trial and punishment. Some masters were particularly fond of certain slaves and may have intervened for them even when their guilt was established. This bond was personal, not legal. Landon Carter's diary recorded his paternal kindness, exasperation, and offhanded cruelty to slaves. Once, to chastise a valuable slave, Carter vigorously prosecuted the slave for burglary, then immediately obtained a pardon for the defendant. "For a while," Carter recalled, the experience "had some good effect," improving the slave's conduct; then the man relapsed.[143]

Slaves' defenses rested upon their own and other slaves' testimony. In Dick's case, tried in 1749 by a Richmond oyer and terminer court, the defendant confessed to entering a dwelling house to steal a container of medicine. He came away with other articles as well. His intent may have been to sell his booty, to use it himself, or to give it to someone in need. He had nevertheless committed larceny (burglary if he entered at night), the penalty for which was death. A statute made the preparation or administration of poisonous medicines by slaves a felony, but Dick was not charged with this offense.[144] The record notes that after he confessed, he "put himself upon the court."[145] Technically, this plea makes no sense. He had already pleaded guilty and could no longer put himself for trial upon the justices. Indeed, he never possessed the right to ask for a jury trial, so, had he not confessed first, he would have been forced to put himself upon the court. Laying aside the possibility that the clerk had made an error, one may surmise that Dick was trying to ask for mercy from the court and, without counsel or experience to aid him, had spoken the wrong words. With this out-of-place admission of the power that the justices had over him, Dick pleaded for his life. He did not seek benefit of clergy; the *RCP* would record such a plea even when it was denied. Clergy was not allowed in a burglary, but the court could reduce the offense to a mixed larceny (if it occurred in daylight). Other slaves,

---

143. Greene, ed., *Carter, Diary,* 1:397. A few scholars have attempted to recreate the feelings of slaves on trial; see, on a much latter case, Stephen B. Oates, *The Fires of Jubilee: Nat Turner's Fierce Rebellion* (New York, 1975), 139.

144. *Statutes at Large,* 6:105 (1748). By the 1732 statute, benefit of clergy was granted slaves but did not include breaking and entering by day and taking goods worth more than 5*s.*

145. *RCP,* 240–41 (1749).

probably upon instructions from their masters or the justices (see p. lxxii), successfully pleaded benefit of clergy to felony charges. The court could have found Dick guilty of breaking and entering but not of the felony, in effect averting the death penalty, but the judges did not choose this course. Dick was hanged.

When more than one slave was accused of a felony, they invariably put up a defense. Numbers were an antidote to abject submission. Newman and Sam, for example, admitted that they had taken articles from justice of the peace Daniel Hornby's mansion house but pleaded not guilty to the felony. The court judged otherwise, and they were executed. Unlike Dick, they did not confess and then seek mercy, though their fate was the same.[146]

Behind the harsh characteristics of slave trials in the Tidewater lay the reality of increasing numbers of slave felonies, and, lurking in the shadows, the rising proportion of slaves in the population. The frequency of oyer and terminer proceedings in Richmond County increased between 1714 and 1754. There were five of these courts between 1714 and 1733 and fourteen in the next twenty-year period. The black population was increasing, but in absolute numbers it did not keep pace with the trials of blacks for serious crimes by oyer and terminer courts. What is more, early in the century justices were willing to reduce charges and penalties against some slaves accused of property offenses by trying them in the county courts, just as more planters were willing to punish slaves on the plantation rather than submit them for capital trials. For example, in 1730 the Richmond justices corporally punished a slave named Baker in the county court for felonious stealing; eighteen years later they convened an oyer and terminer court to try Harry and Aron for stealing and killing a calf.[147] It is unlikely, in the face of stern law and determined magistrates, that slave crimes were a "political" statement by the defendants, which required a sanguinary official response. Their offenses were overwhelmingly thefts of necessities, not acts of rebellion.[148] The rising numbers of slave crimes tried in the criminal courts and the increasing use of commissions of oyer and terminer to handle these cases had the same root cause: a growing subterranean unease with the visibility of black slavery in the county.

In Richmond County, as throughout the Tidewater, the number of slaves approached one-half the population by mid-century. The growing density of blacks had an effect upon their trials for crimes. As the number of slaves grew, the energy masters had to exert to control them increased, the anxiety of the surrounding white population mounted, and any incident of serious black crime, real or imagined, became a threat to social order. Even though the mass of crimes the magistrates handled remained offenses of whites against whites, each had to be investigated with care, lest a slave be implicated as an accessory, a recalcitrant witness, or a conspirator. Thus every accusation of serious crime required an immediate and unyielding response, even though masters expressed satisfaction with the extent of their control over slaves.[149]

146. *RCP*, 241–42 (1749).

147. *RCP*, 132 (1730), 239 (1748).

148. Schwarz, "Slave Criminality and the Slave Community," 15.

149. Roeber, *Faithful Magistrates*, 93. Landon Carter, from whom these assurances were most numerous, also brought more of his slaves to the oyer and terminer courts than any of his counterparts in the county.

By 1740, the number of blacks had attained a "critical mass," in which the cycle of fear, leading to harsh laws, more trials, greater visibility of black crime, and back to heightened fear could begin at any moment.[150] Serious slave offenses included leaving the plantation without a pass, "harbouring or entertaining" slaves from other plantations without permission of the master, administering to the sick without explicit consent of the master, and consorting "unlawfully" with free persons on or off the plantation.[151] Behind black codes stood a massive criminal justice system, wherein any white was absolved of killing runaway slaves, and oyer and terminer courts rendered judgment upon slaves without any of the forms of due process granted white freeholders, servants, non-English immigrants, and even, for the most part, transported English felons.

Crimes by slaves were as vexing to the highest authorities as to the local judges. The preamble to the statute of 1723 on slave gatherings grumbled that the present laws were "insufficient to restrain [the slaves'] tumultuous and unlawful meetings, or to punish the secret plots and conspiracies carried on amongst them."[152] Such apprehensions crept into the very marrow of the administration of criminal justice, inducing Governor William Gooch's appeal to the Privy Council for a pardon in a case of manslaughter:

> one Andrew Bourne [an] overseer of a Plantation who having under his Charge a Negro Slave that had frequently run away, was so transported with Anger upon his being last brought Home, that [g]ave him such imoderate Correction that the Fellow dyed under it and for which the Jury found him guilty of Murder. But the . . . Judge sett on this Tryal [is] very earnest to have his life spared not only because it did not appear that he had any Intention to Kill the Negro, but in regard as the executing of him for this offense may make the slaves very insolent and give them an occassion to condemn their Masters & Overseers, which may be of dangerous Consequence in a Country where the Negroes are so numerous and make the most valuable part of Peoples Estates. And on these considerations it is that I take the liberty to apply to your Grace on this mans behalf.[153]

Through the eighteenth century, Virginia law and procedure progressively abandoned common-law felony trial rules in order to control the slave population.[154]

Legislation creating oyer and terminer courts for slaves in the county allayed the fears of the community and transmitted a message to all slaves in the locality. A speedy trial, presided over by their masters, followed by immediate punishment, witnessed by slaves or described to them by word of mouth, offered graphic lessons in the consequences of misbehavior. Perhaps some of these slaves knew the accused, had plotted with them, or learned of their crimes through the grapevine before they were caught and tried. The solemn justice meted out by the oyer and terminer courts would have chilled these men and women to the

---

150. Jordan, *White Over Black*, 106. Peter H. Wood, *Black Majority: Negroes in Colonial South Carolina from 1670 through the Stono Rebellion* (New York, 1974), 195, uses "critical mass" in a positive sense, but the central idea remains one of population density.

151. *Statutes at Large*, 4:126–29 (1723), particularly sec. X; 6:105–9 (1748).

152. *Statutes at Large*, 4:126 (1723).

153. Gooch to the secretary of state for the Southern Department, June 29, 1752, Public Record Office CO 5/1337/M246, copy at CW.

154. Jordan, *White Over Black*, 103–4; Morgan, *American Slavery*, 295–315; A. Leon Higginbotham, Jr., *In the Matter of Color, Race and the American Legal Process: The Colonial Period* (New York, 1978), 19–60.

bone. Trial of slaves in the county transmitted a message to other slaves even when the accused was acquitted of the felony. In four Richmond County cases, slaves found not guilty of felonies were punished for offenses connected with their arrest or incarceration—an alleged escape or the destruction of prison property. It is probable that masters brought their slaves to the attention of the king's courts only when punishment on the plantation seemed too lenient, the victim was another free person, or the slaves had fled the premises. These unruly black men and women were dangerous in a slave society and received punishment whether or not the specific felony charged against them could be proven.[155]

CRIME IN THE COUNTY

Records like the *RCP* are sources on the nature and scope of crime as well as the operation of the criminal justice system. Some portion of criminal activity always escapes the attention of the authorities, but the cases that do come to court generally vary in number and character with the ebb and flow of crime in the society.[156] Because of the examining courts, the *RCP* includes a more complete record of crime than can be found in other colonies, where single magistrates must have dismissed reports of some serious crimes for lack of evidence and left no formal records. The fullness of the *RCP* allows us to analyze the distribution and rates of types of crimes, the characteristics of defendants and victims, and the disposition of cases in Richmond County and to compare these figures with other jurisdictions in Virginia, the other colonies, and the mother country.

Not all of the returns in the *RCP* may be complete. The case loads for the periods 1711–13 and 1750–54 seem too low compared with immediately adjacent years. No serious crimes are revealed in the ROB for these years; perhaps there were few. The *RCP* for the years 1740–41 has almost no entries, though again, the ROB for 1740–41 does not contain any felony investigations either. These facts cannot allay suspicion that some entries are missing from the *RCP*. Only the gaps of the years 1711–13 and 1750–54 are really nettlesome—largely because the volume of crimes in the *RCP* does not correspond to the case loads in

---

155. Unfortunately, we have no window into the minds of the justices as they deliberated the fates of accused slaves, though Thad W. Tate, *The Negro in Eighteenth-Century Williamsburg* (Charlottesville, 1965), 164–208, makes an attempt to recapture their point of view. By statute (*Statutes at Large*, 6:106 [1748]), the justices' decision to convict had to be unanimous. In this sense, they acted as a jury, finding fact as well as applying law.

156. It is impossible for the historian of crime to gauge precisely the "dark figure" of crimes. Court records, even examining court records, are one step removed from reports by victims, and not every crime is reported. The relationship between criminal court records and the actual number of crimes varies as a function of the efficiency of local magistrates and the willingness of neighbors and victims to report crimes. In general, if the relevant criminal statutes were not changed dramatically and the society remained fairly uniform in its contours, the variations in absolute numbers of cases should mirror the variations in numbers of actual crimes. See Ted Robert Gurr et al., *The Politics of Crime and Conflict: A Comparative History of Four Cities* (Beverly Hills, Calif., 1977), 21, and Beattie, "Towards a Study of Crime in Eighteenth-Century England," 314.

other Virginia counties for the same period. The years before 1714 and after 1749 therefore are omitted from the tables here. There is great variability in the number of yearly sessions for the period 1714–49, but this does not imply that sessions of the court have been lost. The average number of all criminal court sessions in that thirty-five-year span was about seven per year. The number fluctuated so much that one could just as easily expect five sessions as nine (standard deviation = 2.30). There was no significant trend in the number of sessions held as time passed (R^2 = .01 and slope = .024). There was a great deal of variation in the number of cases heard each year, but the case load did not rise or fall in relationship to the number of sessions (R^2 = .237). One may conclude that when a session was held, it went on until all crimes brought before it were disposed. The variation in number of recorded sessions thus does not imply that sessions of the various courts are missing from the record. A last confirmation of the completeness of the Richmond criminal records is physical: that the *RCP* is a bound ledger with no gaps suggests that it recorded the criminal business of every court that met. Overall, as a record of serious crimes, the *RCP* is as accurate as any historian of premodern societies could expect.

Distribution of Offenses

The Richmond County courts heard cases concerning a wide variety of crimes. Courts of oyer and terminer and of examination were reserved for serious crimes, while the county courts heard lesser offenses. Serious criminal activities included treasons and petty treasons, homicides, felonious thefts, burglaries and robberies, and arson. Misdemeanors and petty crimes included petty thefts, assaults, and violations of economic regulations. Morals offenses and failure to perform duties required by the law, such as avoidance of jury duty, were also handled in the county courts. Although the *RCP* is a less ample source on criminal law than on criminal procedure, it contains various categories of crimes.

Treasons were threats or attacks against the person of the king or his family, waging war against his government, or aiding enemies of the realm. In England, treason included a category of "constructive" acts, permitting the courts and the House of Lords to pursue those whose plots, words, or actions may have endangered the king, his advisers, or his policies. Colonial courts never went this far,[157] but in Virginia, under this "constructive" doctrine, slave conspiracies against their masters and farmers' conspiracies to destroy tobacco plants were regarded as treason. Petty treason, the murder of husband by wife or master by servant, was a heinous offense, for which both English and Virginia law prescribed capital punishment.[158] Homicides included murder (killing with premeditation, from ambush, or by stealth), as well as manslaughter (killing in the sudden heat of passion), justifiable homicide (for example, self-defense), and accidental homicide. In a first offense of manslaughter, as well as most larcenies and breaking and entering, the defendant could plead benefit of clergy. In 1732,

---

157. Clayton Roberts, "The Law of Impeachment in Stuart England: A Reply to Raoul Berger," *Yale Law Journal*, 84 (June 1975): 1419–39. Slave meetings in excess of five persons were construed to be conspiracies to "advise . . . rebellion"; see Webb, *Justice of Peace*, 32.

158. Hawkins, *Treatise of Pleas of the Crown*, 1:87; Webb, *Justice of Peace*, 343.

a Virginia statute extended this medieval English ecclesiastical formula to all men and women, whether or not they proved able to read the appropriate verses from the Bible.[159] Defendants were not culpable for justifiable and accidental homicides. If the suspect had taken all reasonable steps to avoid killing an attacker (the example often given was that the defendant had reached the end of an alley and had to turn upon his assailant), killing in self-defense was not a felony. This rule applied to the capture of criminals and the apprehension of runaway slaves.[160] If a defendant was carrying on a lawful activity (practicing musketry with the militia, for example) and the victim was shot and died without any intent by the defendant, there was no felony. Grand larcenies, involving goods valued at more than one shilling, were felonies, but clergyable. Breaking and entering a dwelling by night to steal was burglary and punishable by death. No clergy was allowed. A burglary might or might not include felonious taking, which by itself had lesser penalties and permitted benefit of clergy. A burglary could be reduced to a felonious theft in Virginia if the justice or the jury wished to avert the defendant's execution.[161] A jury finding or judicial ruling that the stolen goods were less than one shilling in value reduced the charge to a misdemeanor. In England as well one finds verdicts from juries of "guilty of the larceny, but not of the felony." In addition, juries reduced the value of goods stolen to make offenses clergyable.[162] Robberies were thefts from a person put "in fear for his life," a capital offense, without benefit of clergy. Knowingly receiving stolen goods was a felony and was heard at examining courts or, in the special case of stolen hogs, at the regular sessions of the county court.[163] House burning was a felony, bringing death without benefit of clergy; it was the common-law crime of arson, a felony in both England and Virginia because it endangered life and property.[164]

Common lesser offenses included assaults, batteries, and woundings, violations of the mass of antiswearing and sexual laws passed in the Virginia House of Burgesses, disobedience by servants, illegal selling of spirits and alehousekeeping, and disturbances of public order. These offenses can be found in all of the surviving Virginia county court order books. The most frequent, assault, was a common-law offense.[165] Battery meant unlawful touching. The eighteenth-century Vir-

---

159. *Statutes at Large*, 4:325–27 (1732); George W. Dalzell, *Benefit of Clergy in America and Related Matters* (Winston-Salem, N.C., 1955), 100–104.

160. Homicide (including manslaughter, fatal accident, justifiable and excusable homicide) and murder (killing with premeditated malice) were different crimes. See Webb, *Justice of Peace*, 175–78, 231–38.

161. Larceny was felonious taking (Hawkins, *Treatise of Pleas of the Crown*, 1:89, 91), and simple larceny was felonious taking of another's goods without entering his house or taking from his person. If the goods exceeded twelve pence in value, the larceny was grand and punishable by death. For a first offense, the accused could plead his clergy. Petty larceny brought corporal punishment and loss of chattels; Webb, *Justice of Peace*, 208–11. Robbery was a capital offense, in which the owner of the goods was put in fear of his life or the goods were taken from his person or house.

162. Cockburn, *English Assizes*, 128; John H. Langbein, "*Albion's* Fatal Flaws," paper presented at the American Society for Legal History Conference, October 1981, revised January 1982, 12–13, quoted by permission of the author.

163. Webb, *Justice of Peace*, 63, 146; *Statutes at Large*, 3:278 (1705).

164. Hawkins, *Treatise of Pleas of the Crown*, 1:105; Webb, *Justice of Peace*, 67–69.

165. Plucknett, *Common Law*, 457–58.

ginia county courts heard civil cases termed "trespass with assault and battery."
These differed from criminal charges of assault in that damages were sought by
the injured party, the plaintiff, from the defendant instead of or in addition to
the infliction of punishment and the assurance of good behavior.[166] Legislation
in England and Virginia assigned regulation of domestic life to justices of the
peace. Control of the behavior of servants and landless laborers was a major part
of this jurisdiction. In England and Virginia, a series of increasingly severe laws
directed magistrates to punish runaways and send vagabonds back to the parish
of their origin.[167] Aiding a runaway, providing a servant with a false pass, and
kidnapping a servant or slave were serious offenses and heard in the examining
courts. Disturbances of public order among servants and others were also matters of public concern. Virginia justices could summarily proceed against these
individuals as trespassers. Serious riots were common in England, and some
were tried in the assize courts as felonies. No "riots" are mentioned in the *RCP*,
but Webb devoted a great deal of space to the investigation of unlawful assembly,
affray (accidental mob combats), and deliberate mob violence (riots).[168]

The variety of offenses handled in the *RCP* is displayed in Table 5. Failure to
perform public duties, morals offenses, violations of economic regulations, non-
fatal assaults, serious thefts and felonious breaking and entering, and homicides
are grouped as categories. Only in the last periods of years, when the clerk
limited himself to serious crimes and used the ROB for minor offenses, did
felony and homicide combined approach half the total number of cases noted in
the *RCP*. Over the entire record, serious crimes accounted for about one-fourth
of the cases in the *RCP*, that is, about one-fourth of all the offenses requiring
fines, bonds, or more serious action by all the county courts.

Distribution of the types of offenses recorded in the *RCP* remained more or
less stable until the 1730s, but there was an important shift over time in the
manner of bringing cases into the courts before that period (see Table 6). A
shifting, or tightening, of definitions of serious crimes by the justices led to an
increase in the percentage of cases—from an average of 19 percent between
1714 and 1728 to an average of 35 percent between 1729 and 1749—heard in
oyer and terminer and examining courts. The shift first appeared in the years
1726–29 and coincides with a large increase in the total number of criminal
cases recorded in the *RCP*. The growing recourse to the special courts is thus not
an artifact of a change in recordkeeping (the later transformation of the *RCP* to
a record of felony and homicide trials exclusively). Instead, the leap in total
volume of criminal cases is the key to the shift in manner of prosecution. An

---

166. The civil action for damages in trespass with assault (and battery, with touching) left the size
of the award to the jury, though the amount of damages was alleged in the action. The plaintiff's
claim of assault in these cases, especially if no blood was shed, might not have convinced a grand jury
to present the defendant, whereas a jury in a civil action, regarding the preponderance of evidence,
might award damages.

167. Paul A. Slack, "Vagrants and Vagrancy in England, 1598–1664," *Economic History Review*, 2d
ser., 27 (August 1974): 360; Carl Bridenbaugh, *Vexed and Troubled Englishmen, 1590–1642*, rev. ed.
(New York, 1976), 375. The immense increase in vagrancy in London in this period is discussed in
A. L. Beier, "Social Problems in Elizabethan London," *Journal of Interdisciplinary History*, 9 (Autumn
1978): 203–21.

168. Webb, *Justice of Peace*, 281–87, 272–78.

Table 5: Distribution of Offenses, by Cases, Richmond County, 1714–1749 (percent of total)

Years	Regulatory* and Moral	Peace, Assault	Crimes† against Property	Homicide	Total
1714–16	25 (61.5%)	8 (20.5%)	4 (10.3%)	3 (7.69%)	40 (100%)
1717–19	9 (42.9)	9 (42.9)	3 (14.3)	0 (0.0)	21
1720–22	12 (44.4)	8 (29.6)	6 (22.2)	1 (3.7)	27
1723–25	50 (65.8)	18 (23.7)	6 (7.89)	2 (2.6)	76
1726–28	27 (52.9)	8 (15.7)	10 (19.6)	6 (11.8)	51
1729–31	27 (54.0)	8 (16.0)	14 (28.0)	1 (2.0)	50
1732–34	13 (59.1)	3 (13.6)	5 (22.7)	1 (4.5)	22
1735–37	8 (20.0)	21 (52.5)	11 (27.5)	0 (0.0)	40
1738–40	11 (29.7)	15 (40.5)	9 (24.3)	2 (5.4)	37
1741–43	3 (15.8)	8 (42.1)	7 (36.8)	1 (5.3)	19
1744–46	1 (4.54)	13 (59.1)	8 (36.4)	0 (0.0)	22
1747–49	2 (11.1)	9 (50.0)	6 (33.3)	1 (5.6)	18
Totals	188 (44.3%)	128 (30.3%)	89 (21.1%)	18 (4.3%)	423 (100%)

Source: *RCP.*

* Includes violation of economic and licensing laws.

† Includes robbery, burglary, larceny, and theft.

increase in the number of actual crimes may have induced the justices to turn to special courts. The latter explanation fits the growing unwillingness of examining court justices to reduce charges and/or sentences and punish offenders in the county after 1730 (see pp. xli–xlii).

The relationship between crimes against the person and crimes against property presents no clear pattern. In other societies, depressed economic conditions have stimulated property offenses while dampening violent crimes. Conversely, flush times induced more crimes against persons and held down thefts, burglaries, and similar offenses. Figure 3 shows that the relationship between the number of crimes against persons and the number of crimes against property in Richmond County was not reciprocal: the rise and fall of the former was unrelated to the rise and fall of the latter. The one exception to this overall pattern occurred in the period 1726–31. Tobacco prices declined in these years, and property crimes increased.[169] A detailed comparison of property crime rates and price levels (see pp. lxi–lxii) traces this phenomenon.

The rates of all types of crimes in Richmond declined over time (pp. lix–lxi). This apparent common trend may be merely a function of a hidden prior cause that affected all types of criminal behavior, rather than the result of a relationship among the types of crimes themselves. When violent crimes and property crimes are "detrended"[170] one finds no relationship over time between their rises and falls (R^2 = .014).

---

169. Earle, *Tidewater Settlement System,* 228–29, gives prices for tobacco exports for the 1730s. These, of course, apply to Maryland, not Richmond County.

170. "Trended" data is a sequence of data points which shows a clear upward or downward motion caused by some common, underlying factor. For example, most price series have a trend—they go up. Comparison of two sets of such data will invariably show some degree of correlation, measuring the effect of the common, underlying factor (in this case, inflation), when perhaps there is no real relationship between the variables. They must be "detrended" to be truly compared. The

Table 6: Manner of Prosecution, by Cases, Richmond County, 1714–1749 (percent of total)

Years	Oyer and Terminer/ Examining Court	Justice's Order	Complaint	Grand Jury Presents	Other
1714–16	7 (17.5%)	17	0	16	0
1717–19	3 (14.3)	15	0	2	1
1720–22	6 (22.2)	14	3	2	2
1723–25	11 (14.5)	17	0	43	5
1726–28	13 (25.5)	5	2	29	2
1729–31	18 (36.0)	1	6	20	5
1732–34	7 (31.8)	6	0	4	5
1735–37	13 (32.5)	7	1	13	6
1738–40	11 (29.7)	15	1	8	2
1741–43	8 (42.1)	8	0	3	0
1744–46	8 (36.4)	9	3	2	0
1747–49	7 (38.9)	7	0	3	1
Totals	112	121	16	145	29

Source: *RCP*.

* Includes prosecutions brought by the king upon writs of *scire facias*

The distribution of serious personal and property crime in Richmond County is similar to that in other Virginia counties. For the years 1742–56, the balance between serious offenses against the person (homicide) and serious crimes against property (arson, robbery, grand larceny, and burglary) in Surry County, on the south side of the James River, was six cases (24 percent) of the former against nineteen cases (76 percent) of the latter.[171] In Louisa County, to the west of Richmond, between 1743 and 1748, five examining and oyer and terminer courts met. Three cases involved felonious taking and two, murder.[172] In Augusta County, on the western mountain frontier, six serious crimes were investigated in 1746 and 1747; four were felonies against property and two were homicides.[173] From 1748 to 1753, York County magistrates heard twenty-three cases of serious crimes, eighteen of which concerned breaking and entering, felonious taking, or robbery.[174] King George's County clerk kept a full record of serious crimes from 1722 to 1737, in which he entered thirty-seven felonies and ten fatal attacks upon persons.[175] In all of these county records, the ratio of felonious property crimes to homicides was between 2.5 and 3 to 1, roughly equivalent to that in Richmond.

The Richmond County pattern of serious offenses is essentially that of a rural area. More densely populated areas in the eighteenth century had higher pro-

"first differences" method removes long-term up and down trends by calculating the amount of difference, up or down, between each data point and the one preceding it. These new measures of change from period to period can then be compared with other detrended variables or variables without trends to find real relationships.

171. Surry County, "Criminal Proceedings vs. Free Persons, Slaves, etc., from 1742 to 1822," Surry County, Virginia, Courthouse Archives; copy courtesy of Kevin Kelly, CW.

172. Louisa County Order Book, 1742–48, reel 29, VSL.

173. Augusta County Order Books, Nos. 1–3, 1745–53, reel 62, VSL.

174. York County Order Books, Judgments and Orders, 1746–54, reel 29, CW.

175. King George County Order Books, 1721–34, reels 22 and 23, VSL.

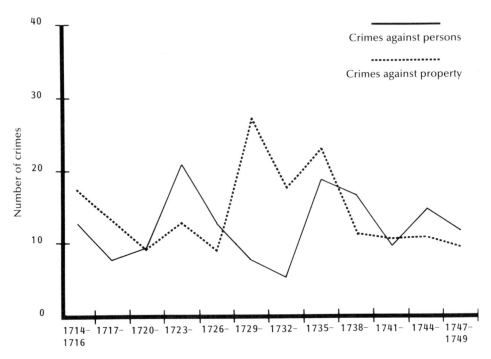

Figure 3. Distribution of Crimes against Property and Crimes against Persons, Plotted by the Total Numbers of These Crimes, Richmond County, 1714–1749 (RCP)

portions of crimes against persons. In Charleston, South Carolina, from 1769 to 1776, crimes against persons were 53.6 percent of the total offenses and crimes against property but 37.8 percent.[176] In New York City during much of the eighteenth century, crimes against persons and against property were each 20.9 percent of the total. These figures, provided by Douglas Greenberg, do not include homicides, which would have increased the total and percentage of crimes against persons.[177] The Massachusetts Superior Court of Judicature in the years 1711–54 heard 207 felonies against property and eighty homicides, respectively 72.1 percent and 27.9 percent of the total of serious crimes. This ratio was roughly equivalent to that in Richmond, but when only those cases coming from large towns in Massachusetts are counted, the ratio of violent crimes to property crimes approached one to one.[178] In less dense populations there may be less chance for interpersonal violence. Conversely, the teeming eighteenth-century city was a hotbed of duels, street fights, gang wars, and accidental

176. Michael Stephen Hindus, *Prison and Plantation: Crime, Justice, and Authority in Massachusetts and South Carolina, 1767–1878* (Chapel Hill, 1980), 64.

177. Douglas Greenberg, *Crime and Law Enforcement in the Colony of New York, 1691–1776* (Ithaca, N.Y., 1976), 54.

178. Records of the Superior Court of Judicature, Massachusetts, New Suffolk County Court House, Boston, volumes for 1711–1714 through 1749–1750; data courtesy of N. E. H. Hull.

violence.[179] Sociologists have linked "subcultures of violence" with the density and alienation of urban life.[180]

Rates of Prosecution of Crimes

Without reports of crimes by police, the closest the scholar can come to measuring the rate of criminal activity is to count presentments, indictments, and orders in the courts. This rate measures community and court attitudes toward certain types of reported offenses as much as it measures real crimes—and perhaps the former more than the latter. The rate of recorded offenses for any period of time is the number of suspects named in the court over that period of time divided by the population at risk to commit those crimes over the same period of time. This population includes adult men and women. The number of people in Richmond County fitting this description can be approximated. Lists of tithables for Virginia counties included all free males over sixteen years and all servants and slaves over sixteen. Free adult females were not counted among the tithables. To include these women in the rates of recorded crimes I assumed that free adult women were roughly equal in number to free white adult men, as was true in eighteenth-century Maryland and Massachusetts. "Infants" under the law could not be found guilty of committing a felony or homicide and are not included in the at risk population calculations.

Three-year average rates of serious criminal prosecutions for Richmond County are plotted in Table 7.[181] The reader should note that the unit of analysis shifts from the case—the crime incident—to the defendant, because the rate of prosecution should measure the extent of personal misbehavior rather than the volume of courtroom business. Recidivists—repeat offenders—were counted each time they committed an offense. Table 7 presents the rates of crimes first by major types: crimes against property and crimes against persons, and then by the more restrictive categories of felonies and homicides. Crime rates in the county show both a cyclical and a linear trend. The bulge in all types of crime in the years 1729–39, visible in Figure 4, followed hard upon the period of the largest percentage increase in importation of convicts and slaves—the defendants who swelled the dockets in these years. Whether they committed more crimes than free laborers or were more carefully monitored and more often arrested for crimes in which the perpetrator was unknown, the justices in the county certainly found more and more servants standing before them in the dock as the century passed.

Nevertheless, the overall trend in serious crimes was a slight decrease. Crimes

---

179. On crime in the city of London, see John Jacob Tobias, *Crime and Industrial Society in the Nineteenth Century* (New York, 1967), 22–27.

180. See, for example, Marvin E. Wolfgang and Franco Ferrecuti, *The Subculture of Violence: Towards an Integrated Theory in Criminology* (London, 1967), passim.

181. The rates of crime for Richmond County have been standardized in these calculations for a population of ten thousand. Thus every rate entry indicates the number of crimes one would find each year of the three-year period if the population of the county were ten thousand. To do this, one need only multiply the actual rate by ten thousand. Standardization permits the scholar to compare criminal indictments in Richmond with those elsewhere despite the difference in population between Richmond and other jurisdictions.

Table 7: Criminal Prosecution Rates, Serious Property and Violent Crimes per 10,000 Adults per Year, by Defendants, Richmond County, 1714–1749
(number of defendants in parentheses)

Years	Crimes against Property	Crimes of Violence	Property Felony	Homicide	Total
1714–16	21.5/10,000 adults/year (16)	16.1 (12)	5.38 (4)	5.38 (4)	48.4
1717–19	17.0 (13)	11.8 (9)	3.90 (3)	0	28.7
1720–22	14.3 (9)	14.3 (9)	9.53 (6)	1.59 (1)	28.7
1723–25	20.7 (13)	33.3 (21)	11.2 (7)	3.49 (2)	54.1
1726–28	13.8 (9)	21.3 (14)	13.8 (9)	9.19 (6)	35.3
1729–31	37.3 (26)	12.9 (9)	25.9 (18)	1.43 (1)	50.4
1732–34	26.2 (18)	10.2 (7)	14.6 (10)	5.83 (4)	36.3
1735–37	31.1 (22)	25.4 (18)	28.4 (20)	0	56.6
1738–39*	23.4 (11)	36.2 (17)	21.3 (10)	4.28 (2)	59.6
1742–43†	19.8 (10)	17.8 (9)	17.8 (9)	1.98 (1)	37.5
1744–46	13.0 (10)	16.8 (13)	13.0 (10)	0	29.9
1747–49	11.2 (9)	12.5 (10)	11.2 (9)	1.25 (1)	23.7

Source: *RCP*.

*Omitting the year 1740; therefore the rate is for two years: 1738–39.

† Omitting the year 1741; the rate is for the years 1742–43.

against property declined slowly as the century passed (b = −.198, r = −.090).[182] The felonies among these offenses, crimes whose punishment could be capital, actually increased during these years at the rate of one offense each three-year period. The correlation between property felony charges and the passage of time (r = .480) was stronger than the comparable statistic for other types of crimes.[183] The change over time explained 23 percent of the variation in the indictment rates (R^2 = .230), reflecting, perhaps, the collective shift in justices' charging of offenders with a felony instead of a misdemeanor. Rates of prosecution for crimes against the person fluctuated greatly from year to year but remained more or less stable throughout the period 1714–49 (b = .188, r = .080, R^2 = .006). Violence against persons, a characteristic of southern counties long after the colonial era ended, did not decrease as the community became more settled and the institutions of local justice more firmly established in

---

182. The "b" statistic is the slope of the least squares regression line approximating the trend of the curve for these criminal indictments.

183. The "r" statistic—Pearson's correlation coefficient—is a measure of association between one variable and another. It ranges from −1.0 to +1.0, showing the direction of the association as well as strength. Unlike its square (R^2), it is not a measure of causality.

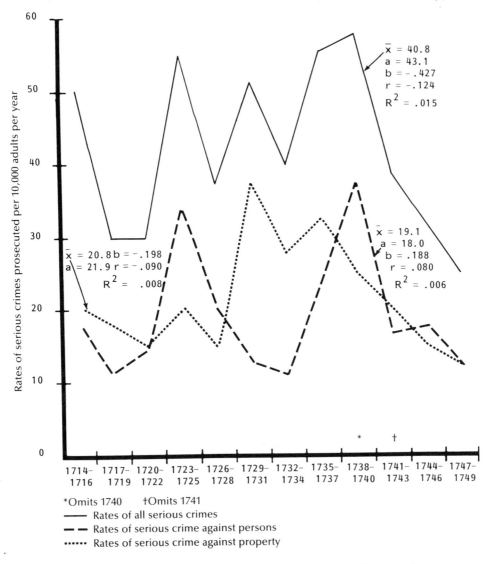

Figure 4. Prosecution Rates for Serious Crimes, by Defendants, Richmond County, 1714–1749 (*RCP*)

Richmond.[184] As a whole, serious crime did decline, but very slowly ($b = -.427$, $r = -.124$, $R^2 = .015$).

The relationship between rates of prosecution for serious crime against prop-

---

184. On violence and violent crime in the South, see Raymond D. Gastil, "Homicide and a Regional Culture of Violence," *American Sociological Review*, 36 (June 1971): 412–27; Sheldon Hackney, "Southern Violence," in Hugh D. Graham and Ted Robert Gurr, eds., *The History of Violence in America: Historical and Comparative Perspectives* (New York, 1969), 505–12; Austin L. Porterfield, "Indices of Suicide and Homicide by States and Cities: Some Southern–Non-Southern Contrasts with Implications for Research," *American Sociological Review*, 14 (August 1949): 481–90.

erty and economic conditions can be explored somewhat more concretely using economic data from the first section of this introduction. In general, one can say that as the productivity of the county—measured by tobacco exports—rose, the property crime rate declined. For the brief period 1737 through 1750 for which export figures are available, the comparison of property crimes and economic prosperity shows the expected inverse relationship: as exports rose, property crime rates fell ($r = -.389$, $R^2 = .152$). The correlation is not large, but it fits the hypothesis.

The criminal records of the Massachusetts Superior Court of Judicature and the general gaol delivery courts of London and Middlesex County in England permit a broader comparative view of Richmond County prosecution rates. Comparison of a single county with an entire New England colony and the most populous of England's shires can produce only tentative conclusions. Nevertheless, a comparison of Richmond's figure with those for Massachusetts, displayed in Table 8, does suggest changing directions in overall rates of criminal prosecutions.[185] The same overall downward movement and the same ratio of felony rate to homicide rate mark the Massachusetts data as those for Richmond. The absolute rate of criminal prosecutions was far lower in the New England colony than in any of the Virginia counties. On the evidence of rates of recorded serious crime, the former were indeed "peaceable kingdoms." The relative absence of convict and slave labor might explain part of this difference. The intrusiveness of neighbors, magistrates, and ministers in the Bay Colony, not so visible in Virginia, might have also dampened the crime rate.[186]

Evidence from the records of criminal courts in London and Middlesex County can also be compared with the *RCP*. "The Old Bailey Sessions Papers" from 1726 to 1756 accurately reported all serious crimes that came before the general gaol delivery and oyer and terminer courts of the city of London and Middlesex County.[187] The rates of indictments for serious crimes varied during these years between 13.1 and 8.9 per ten thousand adults. The figures obtained

185. The adult population of Massachusetts was not racially comparable to the adult population of Richmond County because of the large numbers of slaves in the latter. Blacks never amounted to more than 3–4 percent of the inhabitants of the Bay Colony. In addition, few servants were imported into the New England colonies, and fewer convicts were sent there than to Virginia. Massachusetts population estimates are from U.S. Bureau of the Census, *A Century of Population Growth* (Washington, D.C., 1909), 9.

186. A more speculative assessment of these comparative rates is Peter Charles Hoffer, "Deference and Disorder: Paradoxes of Criminal Justice in the Colonial Tidewater," in David J. Bodenhamer and James T. Ely, eds., *Ambivalent Tradition, Legal History of the South* (Oxford, Miss., 1984).

187. The childbearing rate was lower in London than in the colonies, and the flood of immigrants to the city tended to be adults, necessitating a different multiplier to equate greater London population to Richmond population. If 70 percent of the population of London and its environs was adult, then .70 × gross population gives an estimate equivalent to adult population in Virginia. English population and birth statistics are in Phyllis Deane and W. A. Cole, *British Economic Growth, 1688–1959: Trends and Structure*, 2d ed. (Cambridge, Eng., 1967), 103, 115. Criminal data are from the "Old Bailey Sessions Papers," *Proceedings on the Commissions of Oyer and Terminer and General Gaol Delivery of London and Middlesex*, held at the Old Bailey. These are printed shorthand accounts of trials of serious crimes, available at the Guildhall Library Collection, London, the Library of Congress Law Library, Library of Congress, Washington, D.C., and the Langdell Library, Harvard University School of Law, Cambridge, Massachusetts. They are quite accurate; see Langbein, "Albion's Fatal Flaw," 4–5.

**Table 8: Indictment Rates per 10,000 Adults per Year for Property
Felony and Homicide, by Defendants, Massachusetts, 1711–1750**

Years	Rate of Prosecution of Suspects for Felonies against Property	Homicide Prosecution Rate
1711–20	1.14	0.32
1721–30	0.83	0.36
1731–40	0.46	0.23
1741–50	0.40	0.16

Source: N. E. H. Hull, "Female Felons, Women and Serious Crime in Colonial
Massachusetts, 1674–1776" (Ph.D. dissertation, Columbia University, 1981).

for Middlesex, including the metropolis, lie between the low rates of New England and the higher rates of Virginia, suggesting that black-white or other
social tensions in the latter colony led to more crime than did the class conflict
assigned by some historians as a cause of crime in the greater London area.[188]
This extreme conclusion must be tempered by realization that densely populated, unpoliced eighteenth-century London probably had a much higher rate of
unreported crime than did Richmond or any other Tidewater county. In addition, one must bear in mind that Virginia examining courts recorded cases which
individual New England and English justices of the peace heard and dismissed
for lack of evidence without keeping any record. Perhaps the soundest conclusion is one based upon a common phenomenon: the decline of the criminal
prosecution rates in all these jurisdictions as the eighteenth century passed im-
plies that serious crimes in all of them were declining.[189]

Defendants and Victims

The defendants in Richmond's serious crimes were male and female, black
and white, free, slave, and servant (see Table 9). Only 14 free females were
accused of serious crimes; three female slaves were charged with major offenses.
Female servants were named in eight cases. Among the 120 men suspected of

---

188. The class consciousness in eighteenth-century English criminal justice is discussed in Doug-
las Hay, "Property, Authority, and the Criminal Law," in Hay et al., *Albion's Fatal Tree: Crime and
Society in Eighteenth-Century England* (London, 1975), 17–39, and Robert W. Malcolmson, " 'A set of
ungovernable people': The Kingswood colliers in the eighteenth century," in John Brewer and John
Styles, eds., *An Ungovernable People: The English and Their Law in the Seventeenth and Eighteenth Centuries*
(New Brunswick, N.J., 1980), 85–127.

189. Generalizations about crime rates over a long span of time are invariably speculative. Nevertheless, eighteenth-century data lend themselves to the conclusion that crimes against property
and persons were moving downward. See Gurr et al., *Politics of Crime and Conflict*, chap. 1. The gross
comparison of thirteenth- and sixteenth-century English assize court records with eighteenth-
century English and American records indicates that the downward movement of crime goes back at
least to the late medieval period. For example, from data in James B. Given, *Society and Homicide in
Thirteenth Century England* (Stanford, 1977), one can estimate an indictment rate for homicide in
selected English counties of between 18.9 cases and 6.8 cases per hundred thousand people per year.
These rates had declined by the reign of Elizabeth I to 3.3 cases per hundred thousand people per
year (Essex); Joel Samaha, *Law and Order in Historical Perspective; The Case of Elizabethan Essex* (New
York, 1974), 125–27.

Table 9: Suspects of Serious Crimes by Race and Sex, Richmond County, 1714–1749

Years	Felonious Property Offenses				Homicide			
	Male/Female		White/Black		Male/Female		White/Black	
1714–16	4	0	3	1	3	1	4	0
1717–19	3	0	2	1	0	0	0	0
1720–22	5	1	5	1	1	0	1	0
1723–25	7	0	6	1	1	1	2	0
1726–28	9	0	8	1	6	0	5	1
1729–31	18	8	21	5	1	0	0	1
1732–34	8	2	10	0	4	0	2	2
1735–37	14	6	18	2	0	0	0	0
1738–40	9	1	10	0	2	0	2	0
1741–43	8	1	8	1	1	0	1	0
1744–46	7	3	7	3	0	0	0	0
1747–49	9	0	1	8	0	1	1	0
	—	—	—	—	—	—	—	—
Totals	101	22	99	24	19	3	18	4
	(82.1%)	(17.9)	(80.5)	(19.5)	(86.4)	(13.6)	(81.8)	(18.2)

Source: *RCP.*

serious crimes, thirteen were servants and twenty-three were slaves. Suspects' characteristics in the Richmond criminal record remained fairly uniform over time, with two exceptions: a brief surge in the number of women accused in the 1730s and a jump in the number of slaves tried at the end of the 1740s. Overall, 101 (82.1 percent) of the property felony defendants were male, and twenty-two (17.9 percent) were female. When the number of felonies rose sharply in the period 1729–37, the number of females peaked more rapidly; as the crime rate declined, the number of females went down even more steeply. Examination of the record shows that there were a series of thefts carried out by gangs of thieves, for which women worked as informants, lookouts, and receivers of stolen goods. The eight slaves suspected of felony at the end of the record reflected the growing black presence in the county and, perhaps more to the point, their growing visibility among the population.[190]

Neither women nor black slaves were prosecuted for serious crimes in proportion to their numbers in the population. The commission of serious crimes depends upon opportunity and prior criminal training. Women had far less opportunity to take and conceal others' goods than did men. They found themselves far less often in violent confrontations than did men. They were not

190. The percentage of women prosecuted for murder in North Carolina from 1663 to 1740 was but 13 percent of the total; only one-fifth of the defendants for theft were women; Donna J. Spindel and Stuart W. Thomas, Jr., "Crime and Society in North Carolina, 1663–1740," *Journal of Southern History,* 49 (May 1983): 238. A similar pattern appears in Massachusetts and New York City. On the question of slave crime, Gerald W. Mullin, *Flight and Rebellion: Slave Resistance in Eighteenth-Century Virginia* (New York, 1972), 61–62, finds comparatively few slaves tried for crimes compared to the mass of trials, hearings, and orders in criminal cases in the Richmond County courts. One must note, however, that slaves' offenses were not ordinarily heard in the king's courts but punished on the plantation. Slave trials in the county courts—invariably for very serious crimes—should be compared only to white felony and homicide hearings.

trained in crime or violence, as men were. Slaves were given even less opportunity to move about than women, restricting their capacity to steal, except on the plantation, in which case the planter often acted as constable, prosecutor, and judge. They had less chance to commit sophisticated crimes against property—to forge notes, counterfeit currency, or defraud others. There was violence among them, but they were not permitted weapons and thus found homicide far more difficult than did free white males.

Homicide was overwhelmingly a white person's crime. The racial balance of suspects for homicide did not change as the century continued. In other words, blacks were not increasingly suspected of homicide as they were of property felonies. Homicide was always a matter of intense local concern, and the culprit was pursued whatever his color.

The division between the sexes and races of suspects in Richmond's serious crimes was similar to that occurring elsewhere in the colony. In King George County, Virginia, in the years 1721–38, suspects of serious offenses showed exactly the same proportion of male to female, 82.1 percent to 17.9 percent, as in Richmond. The racial division was 78.6 percent white and 21.4 percent black, slightly more evenly balanced than Richmond. Only one female and no blacks were charged with the thirteen homicides heard in the county during those years.

To the North, the pattern was slightly different. In the Superior Court of Judicature of Massachusetts, during the years 1711–50, there were 230 felony suspects. Of these seventeen (7.4 percent) were female and twenty (8.9 percent) were black, fewer than in Virginia. The Superior Court heard eighty-one defendants plead to homicide indictments; twenty-eight defendants were women (34.8 percent) and three (3.8 percent) were black. The greater freedom some New England women exhibited outside the home compared to Virginia women might offer an explanation for the higher percentage of female homicide suspects in New England were it not that twenty-two of the Massachusetts women's homicides were murders of their own newborn children, committed in or near their homes. There were two cases of suspected infanticide in the Richmond County record as well, two of the three women's homicide cases there. This similarity in typology of female crimes cannot be ignored. A glance at the much higher rate of prosecution of male homicide in Virginia than in Massachusetts suggests that the comparatively smaller percentage of women among Virginia homicide suspects is the result not of the different roles assigned to women in these two colonies but of the greater propensity of Virginia men to kill each other. Were the male homicide rate in Virginia scaled down to the rate found in Massachusetts, the proportion of women accused of homicide in the two colonies would be similar.

In Richmond, homicides and assaults tended to be crimes with single suspects. In only three cases can one find an accessory to the fact. Felonious thefts presented a different picture. In eighteen of eighty-nine cases (20.2 percent) there was more than one accomplice to the crime. In all, fifty-three defendants (49.5 percent) acted in concert to steal. The composition of these gangs was racially homogenous. All ten black defendants worked only with other blacks, all of whom were male. Among the white defendants, males and females worked with one another.

Recidivism did appear in the Richmond County records but was almost entirely limited to petty offenses. A handful of notorious characters periodically were brought to court to give bond for good behavior or to pay fines for offenses against morality or the peace. Members of the Pridham clan, in particular Christopher Pridham, were paraded before the county courts for ill behavior, swearing, lewd living, drunkenness, and wife beating at one time or another. Overall, slightly less than 19 percent of all defendants mentioned in the *RCP* appeared on more than one occasion. Recidivism was much more pronounced in the ROB (approaching two-thirds of all persons charged), for obvious reasons. Very rarely was one of these returnees to court accused of a serious crime. Only three of eighty-three recidivists in the *RCP* were accused of a serious offense. Unlike modern courts, whose criminal business overwhelmingly concerns individuals with prior arrests and convictions, courts of justice in colonial Virginia had a recidivism rate of but 5 percent for serious crimes.[191] This low rate stemmed in part from the severity of punishments for property crimes and in part from the ease with which a suspect could flee a place in which he or she had committed a serious crime.

The victims of serious crimes are rarely as well studied as the perpetrators. Today, victims of violent offenses often know the attacker and may precipitate the crime.[192] This seems to be true of an earlier era as well. In eighteenth-century Richmond, eighteen of forty-three serious assaults and homicides were committed upon individuals well known to the attacker, and in ten of these cases the victim was the spouse or child of the defendant. In serious offenses against property, the victim lived outside the family circle. The dwellings and warehouses of the wealthy were the most prominent targets. Blacks were not among the recorded victims of property offenses, for they held little personal property and thefts among them were evidently not brought to the attention of the civil authorities. Two cases of slaves assaulting other slaves were brought to court by masters. Given the number of cases of whites assaulting whites in the record, forty-three, and the proportion of blacks to whites in the total population, one must assume that blacks' quarrels among themselves were not taken to the criminal courts. Slaves settled their own differences on the plantation.[193] There were only five black victims of white defendants in assault cases, but this figure seriously underestimates the extent of interracial violence. Corporal punishment was integral to the slave system, and if planters' diaries are any indication, corporal punishment was common and severe on the plantation.[194] When interracial

---

191. Modern recidivism rates vary according to the manner in which they are calculated, but the range is 30 to 70 percent for serious crimes. See Marvin E. Wolfgang et al., *Delinquency in a Birth Cohort* (Chicago, 1972), 254, and Sue Titus Reid, *Crime and Criminology*, 2d ed. (New York, 1979), 755–60.

192. On victim-induced violent crimes, see Marvin E. Wolfgang, "A Sociological Analysis of Criminal Homicide," in Wolfgang, ed., *Studies in Homicide* (New York, 1967), 27.

193. On conflicts among slaves on the plantation, see Allan Kulikoff, "The Origins of Afro-American Society in Tidewater Maryland and Virginia, 1700 to 1790," *William and Mary Quarterly*, 3d ser., 35 (April 1978): 254–55.

194. Mullin, *Flight and Rebellion*, 24–25 ff. Even mild masters could condone savage beatings of slaves on the plantation; see *Journal and Letters of Philip Vickers Fithian, 1773–1774*, ed. Hunter D. Farish (Charlottesville, 1957), 38–39, and Greene, ed., *Carter, Diary*, 2:845. Richmond County planters were no exception to this rule; Morgan, "Hegemony of the Laws," 118–19, 147.

violence did come to court, the victims were invariably black. The recorded incidence of such violence was not significant.[195]

Convictions

The fate of suspects depended upon the proceeding in which they found themselves. If they confessed or put themselves upon the country or oyer and terminer court (the latter a forced option for slaves), or were judged summarily, the justices decided if they were innocent or guilty. If they obtained a jury trial in the county court, twelve of their peers rendered a verdict on the case. If they were brought before an examining court, the justices could acquit, bind over for indictment and trial in Williamsburg, or reduce the charge and dispose of the case in the county. Those defendants sent to Williamsburg for trial from the county of Richmond during our period have disappeared from the record, for the General Court dockets for these years were destroyed in the Civil War. The *Virginia Gazette,* which kept informal watch on trials in the capital in the mid-eighteenth century, does not mention the names of suspected felons sent from the Richmond examining courts.

To understand Richmond conviction rates in their historical context one must trace them over time and compare them with other jurisdictions. For the county courts this exercise is no problem because all persons presented by the grand jury or ordered to court by the justices were found guilty and bound in some way to reform their conduct or were punished for it. As has been suggested, most of these men and women admitted their guilt. Others, putting themselves on the court, were found guilty by the justices. With one exception, those who put themselves upon the country were also convicted. This pattern of conviction in the county courts was common throughout the empire.

Far more important and difficult to study is the disposition of serious crimes. To compare conviction rates for felony and homicide in Richmond County with those elsewhere in the colony and the empire, I have combined two categories of results of hearings. The first is a finding of guilt by the justices by examining and oyer and terminer courts. Although judges at the former could not technically find guilt (though they could acquit), they did reduce charges and punish suspects at the examining courts. This action I regard as a conviction. To this category I have added the number of suspects sent on for indictment and trial in Williamsburg. These men and women were not yet convicted of crime; in fact, the General Court dismissed charges against one-fourth of all suspects sent there for capital offenses. Nevertheless, the Richmond judges did not acquit these suspects. A better name for this measure of outcomes of cases may be "nonacquittal rate." Over the span of years covered by the *RCP,* 70.4 percent of all suspects brought to examining or oyer and terminer courts were not acquitted. As Figure 5 indicates,

---

195. Contemporary violent crimes are overwhelmingly intraracial. Despite the high visibility of interracial crimes today, segregated residential patterns are responsible for the preponderance of intraracial offenses. See President's Commission on Law Enforcement and Administration of Justice, *Task Force Report: Crime and Its Impact, An Assessment* (Washington, D.C., 1967). Cross-tabulation of Richmond victims and defendants by race shows that intraracial violence was the rule, phi = .51, significant at the 10 percent level, by chi square test.

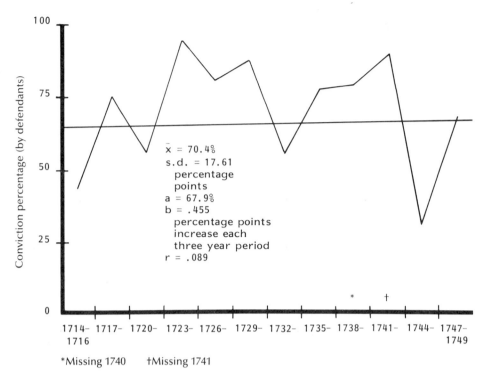

Figure 5. Percentage Conviction and/or Transportation to Williamsburg, Serious Crimes, Richmond County, 1714–1749

the nonacquittal rate rose slightly but not significantly over time. During the eighteenth century, Anglo-American jurists generally took a harsh view of crime, and Richmond County judges were no exception.[196] Even dropping the cases sent to Williamsburg for trial from the nonacquittal rate leaves it four times higher than that found in modern American county courts.[197]

Several variables demonstrably influenced the justices' findings. Race, a major contributor to the justices' fears of crime, had an important effect on the outcomes of cases. Analysis of judges' findings in the county by race of suspect shows that blacks were three times as likely to be convicted as acquitted for serious crimes (74.2 percent of the cases ended in nonacquittal) and penalties for their crimes were not often reduced. Whites were twice as likely as blacks to be found not guilty of the original charges in serious crimes, that is, to be acquitted or have their charges reduced from felony to misdemeanor. The association

196. Samuel Sewall, chief justice of the Massachusetts Superior Court of Judicature, wrote in his diary concerning one case that "GOD furnish'd the Court with such a series and Frame of evidence that [the verdict] was brought in Guilty"; see M. Halsey Thomas, ed., *The Diary of Samuel Sewall* (New York, 1973), 2:677. See also Douglas Hay, "Property, Authority and the Criminal Law," 17, and Graeme Newman, *The Punishment Response* (Philadelphia, 1978), 125–30.

197. During the period from 1969 to 1971 Ohio and California state courts convicted about 13 percent of the men and women indicted for serious crimes; see Rita James Simon, *Women and Crime* (Lexington, Mass., 1975), 63.

between race and the end result of prosecution in the county is moderately strong (phi = 35, p <. 10). The Richmond County racial differential in judgments was typical of the colony. The conviction of whites in the principal courts at Williamsburg for the years 1732 through 1756 ran at about 74 percent—151 out of the 205 defendants known to have been brought there for indictment and trial.[198] If one assumes that examining courts in the various counties dismissed 30 to 35 percent of the white suspects who came before them, the overall nonacquittal rate of whites for felonies cannot be much above or below 50 percent.[199] In contrast to this figure, slaves were not acquitted at Virginia oyer and terminer proceedings 71.2 percent of the time for crimes against property; 70.3 percent of the time for crimes against persons; and 89.3 percent of the time for conspiracies, though not all of those found guilty were capitally punished.[200]

The outcome of cases in the county also varied according to the type of crime and the gender of the suspect. In property felony cases, eighty-three of 114 Richmond County defendants (72.8 percent) were either found guilty of an offense and punished on the spot or sent to the General Court. Only nine of twenty-two suspects of homicide (40.8 percent) were in any way judged culpable and either punished or held for trial. In part, this wide difference in judgments was created by reduction of charges of property offenses by the discretion of the justices at examining courts, occurring in forty of the eighty-three cases in which guilt was established. Benefit of clergy was also granted to four slaves at oyer and terminer courts for their first felony offenses. Examining courts could not allow this plea for white felons, though General Court judges could.

Gender was a last variable that appears to have affected findings in the courts. Women suspected of serious crime were judged guilty and punished in the county or sent to the General Court in fourteen of twenty-two cases (63.6 percent), slightly lower than the average for both sexes and eleven percentage points below the nonacquittal percentage of male defendants in the county. Only one of the three women charged with homicide was not acquitted, as opposed to eight of the eighteen men brought to the dock for the same offense. The comparative leniency of the justices toward women may be attributed to cultural presumptions about the weakness of women or the fact that these women seemed less threatening to social order than men, although the percentages of nonacquittal in Richmond for the different sexes are close enough to have resulted from incidental factors.

Overall nonacquittal percentages for the Richmond County courts corre-

---

198. According to the surviving issues of the *Virginia Gazette*, 151 of 205 tried at the General Court and oyer and terminer courts in Williamsburg were convicted and (presumably) executed. Forty-eight were acquitted outright; the remainder were pardoned or had their charges reduced to misdemeanor.

199. This overall nonacquittal rate for whites is the result of adding to the nonacquittal rate in the county—60 percent of all accused—another figure representing the fate of those sent to Williamsburg for indictment and trial. These men and women, 40 percent of the total processed in the county, were acquitted 25 percent of the time. Thus one should subtract .25 × .40 or 10 percent from the nonacquittal rate of 60 percent for the county courts (which, the reader will recall, counted all cases sent to Williamsburg as nonacquittals), giving an overall nonacquittal rate for serious crimes of 50 percent.

200. Schwarz, "Slave Criminality," 15.

spond to results elsewhere in the colony. In Surry County, 61.3 percent of the defendants in serious crimes were not acquitted of the charges. In Orange County examining courts eighty-two defendants faced the justices between 1735 and 1775; only twenty-three were discharged without any penalty. In York County, thirty-six cases were heard in examining courts during the period 1702–75 (there are gaps of thirty-two years), in which twenty-four individuals were sent to Williamsburg and three were punished in the examining court. In Henrico County, during the years 1752–69, twenty-three examinations for serious crime led to four discharges, seven punishments in the county, eleven defendants sent to Williamsburg, and one case held over to the county court. In Elizabeth City County, records for the period 1731–69 show twenty-eight defendants coming before the examining court, ten of whom were discharged without any penalty.[201] In these counties the percentage of nonacquittals varied somewhat, but always exceeded 60 percent when the imposition of some form of punishment in the county is added to transportation to the capital. In later years, the percentage of nonacquittal in Virginia may have declined. At the city of Richmond hustings court, percentages for convictions for serious crimes in the years 1784–1820 went from the high of 52 percent for free black males, to 43 percent for white males and 44 percent for male slaves, down to 32 percent for female slaves, 29 percent for white women, and 10 percent for free black women.[202]

Conviction rates in Massachusetts and New York were slightly but consistently lower than average nonacquittal rates in Virginia. One must bear in mind that the examining court was the Virginia equivalent of examination by single magistrates elsewhere, and, even if suspects were sent to Williamsburg for indictment and trial, the principal courts there could still acquit them. If acquittals at Williamsburg are added to the totals of dismissed and unproven cases in the counties, one would find a rough average of 60 percent nonacquittal rate for serious crime in Virginia. Bear in mind that this figure includes conviction on reduced charges at the county level, which is slightly higher than nonacquittal rate for serious crime of 55.6 percent in the Massachusetts Superior Court of Judicature between 1711 and 1750. That figure can be broken down into 64.7 percent guilty of property felony and 32.1 percent guilty of homicide—numbers close to but lower than those for Richmond. In the New York Supreme Court between 1691 and 1704 (omitting confessions and quashed indictments), crown prosecutions for serious offenses resulted in fourteen convictions and nineteen acquittals.[203] Over the entire span of time from 1691 to 1776, courts in the New York colony found 53.5 percent of defendants accused of theft and 47.9 percent of those charged with violent crimes to be guilty. The latter figure, drawn from Greenberg, does not include homicides, which probably would have lowered the overall conviction rate further.[204]

---

201. Data from Scott, *Criminal Law*, 60–61. This includes slaves, of course.

202. Robert M. Saunders, "Crime and Punishment in Early National America: Richmond, Virginia, 1784–1820," *Virginia Magazine of History and Biography*, 86 (January 1978): 33–44.

203. Paul M. Hamlin and Charles E. Baker, eds., *Supreme Court of Judicature of the Province of New York, 1691–1704, New York Historical Society Collections*, 78 (New York, 1952), 1:233–34.

204. Greenberg, *Crime and Law Enforcement*, 84, 87–91.

Verdicts in Massachusetts and New York rendered by trial juries parallel at a lower figure the proportions of conviction for different types of crime handed down by Virginia judges and juries when one takes two particulars into account. First, findings of criminal culpability in the Virginia examining courts were a bit more frequent than in other colonial courts, but one must remember that these were only preliminary findings upon which the suspect was sent to Williamsburg. A second, and far more important source of difference, was the treatment of blacks. The higher percentage of convictions of blacks in Virginia is not found in Massachusetts and New York, a fact which, by itself, could explain the differences in overall conviction rates. In Massachusetts, only eight of nineteen blacks were found guilty of property felony, though all three blacks tried for homicide were convicted. Overall, the percentage of conviction for blacks was 52.4 percent, essentially the same as for whites. In New York, blacks were found guilty of 55.1 percent of the thefts for which they stood accused, slightly but not significantly higher than the percentage for whites charged with theft. Blacks were not acquitted in 81.3 percent of cases of nonfelonious violent crime, but many of the crimes in New York were assaults, and had they come to court in Virginia, they would have raised the blacks' conviction rates there. As it was, in the Old Dominion such crimes were handled by the master or overseer. In serious offenses, Virginia courts convicted blacks more frequently than Massachusetts and New York courts, raising the conviction rates of the former's courts three to four percentage points.

Sentence and Punishment

Courts in the Virginia counties meted out punishments for an array of offenses. The penalties did not always involve afflictive sanctions; economic deterrents were also assessed. Fines were regularly imposed upon morals offenders to curb disorderliness, drunkenness, swearing, and fornication. Bonds for good behavior were so routinely assessed that little guilt or shame could have been attached to this form of deterrence. The two sureties required from neighbors, friends, or superiors to pressure the defendant to keep his pledge show that in deterrence, as in arrest and trial, the criminal justice system of the county depended upon the active assistance of the community. Passive consent was not enough to control deviance.

Punishment for serious offenses was more severe, in part to deter repetition, but also to incapacitate the wrongdoer. Lashes might supplement other corporal punishments, gaol terms, and fines in cases of petty theft, wounding, stealing livestock, and breaking gaol. The most severe and painful punishments performed in the county were ordered in courts of oyer and terminer. Slave perjurers in these courts lost their ears; suspected thieves were given the maximum thirty-nine lashes, and some defendants were executed. Richmond County justices at these sessions imposed the death penalty for nine of the twenty-three slaves who came before them. One of the nine was recommended to the governor for mercy as an insane person who did not understand his crime. Even when oyer and terminer courts imposed a lesser penalty for defendants, it tended to be more severe than that ordered by examining court justices for equivalent offenses by free men. Unruly and rebellious slaves had to be made to "stand in fear" lest others join them or copy their example.[205] In November 1730, James, a slave, was arrested for the murder of Mary Petty, the daughter of his master. Though he died in gaol before his trial, the court nevertheless ordered his corpse quartered and the head placed upon a pole. The display was a gory message to other slaves in the county.[206] The sentences for some slaves accused of felony were reduced in the Richmond courts. After 1732, benefit of clergy was extended to slaves, and four Richmond slaves avoided the death penalty when their pleas of benefit of clergy were accepted by the justices. Elsewhere in the colony, benefit of clergy saved at least thirty convicted slaves' lives between 1733 and 1749. Benefit of clergy was not a punishment, though it did involve a branding of the thumb or head to ensure that it was not pled twice by the same person. Helpful masters or the justices themselves may have guided the slaves to this plea.[207] A 1705 statute formally condoned such assistance by masters in the courts. Other slaves, although cleared of felony accusations, were corporally punished for attempted gaolbreaks, insolence to sheriffs, and other breaches of the peace while they were in custody. Some of these slaves were known to the justices to be rebellious or destructive. The troublesome slave, proven innocent of the particular charge of felony, could still be humbled before his potential followers by a public whipping for resisting authority. Nonslave suspects were bound by bonds and sureties to their good behavior after serious charges against them were dismissed. Slaves could not produce such a bond to ensure their future obedience.

As the century passed, the courts of Richmond County imposed more and more severe sentences and punishments. In the years 1714–33, only fifteen of forty-four cases of serious crimes went to Williamsburg or ended in death. Simple whipping was by far the largest of all categories of punishment (twenty cases). By the next decade, this pattern had changed. The courts ordered thirty-three of fifty-four defendants to be sent to the capital for indictment and trial or to be hanged in the county. The cropping of ears and other disfigurement now comprised one-third of all corporal punishments. By the period 1744 to 1753, ten of sixteen serious cases ended in the loss of life or limb. Only three resulted in mere whipping. The shift in severity of punishment matched the trend toward higher percentages of nonacquittals. The statutory provisions for punishments had changed little in these years; the administration of existing law had become more severe.

---

205. Kenneth M. Stampp, *The Peculiar Institution* (New York, 1956), 145.

206. *RCP*, 133 (1730).

207. The availability of benefit of clergy reduced the percentage of convicted slave felons actually executed from almost two-thirds to under one-half. Figures for Virginia oyer and terminer courts, 1706–39, courtesy of Philip Schwarz.

APPENDIX
THE JUSTICES OF THE RICHMOND
COUNTY COURTS

The justices of Richmond County named in commissions of the peace were by and large men of substance and status. Although this office was only the first step toward power in colonial affairs, and was consequently attained by many in their twenties, few justices relinquished their powers and authority. The following table lists the justices holding commissions between 1711 and 1754 in the order that they appear in the *RCP*. The table also provides information on the approximate ages at which they first sat with the court and their tenure on it through 1754.

It is clear from the table that the judicial offices of the county passed down, in many cases, through a family. This was particularly true among the Peacheys, Tarpleys, Barbers, Woodbridges, Tayloes, Griffins, and Fauntleroys, all of whose representatives tended to be conscientious attenders of the sessions. Families with status and wealth wishing to take a major role in the local judiciary found access to office easy.

Justice	Personal data	Appears in RCP
Samuel Peachey I	fl. 1710–1715	1711–1715
Samuel Peachey II	1699–1750	1723–1749
John Tarpley	fl. 1699–1723	1711–1723
Charles Barber	1676–1727	1703–1726
William Woodbridge	1668–1726	????–1715
John Tayloe, Jr.	1688–1747	1710–1732
John Tavener	1683–1711	1710–1711
Alexander Doniphan	1653–1717	1692–1716
William Thornton	d. 1727	1710–1726
Thomas Griffin	16??–1745	1710–1730
Edward Barrow	16??–1721	1705–1721
Joseph Deeke	16??–1718	1712–1715
George Hale	——	—1712
*Thomas Fitzhugh	d. 1719	1712–1719
Nicholas Smith	1666–1734	1713–1721
Richard Taliferro	16??–1715	1712–1715
Jonathan Gibson	16??–1729	1712–1719
Moore Fauntleroy	1680–1739	1714–1738
Moore Fauntleroy, Jr.	1716–1791	1739–1754
J. Griffin	——	—1715
Austin Brockenborough	d. 1717	1712–1717
Charles Brockenborough	fl. 1715	—1715
William Robinson	168?–1737	1708–1721
William Downman	——	1718–1730
James Ingo	1680–1725	1718–1724

The Justices of the Richmond County Courts (continued)

Justice	Personal data	Appears in RCP
James Strother	fl. 1720	1718–1720
Joseph Belfield	16??–1738	1721–1734
Robert Tomlin	fl. 168?–1734	1721–1734
Charles Colston	1691–1724	1721–1724
John Metcalfe	d. 1728	1721–1728
Charles Grymes	fl. 1721–1738	1721–1738
Newman Brockenborough	d. 1740	1723–1740
Samuel Barber	17??–1735	—1726
Thomas Wright Belfield	fl. 1705–1743	1728–1740
Willoughby Newton	fl. 1710–1752	1728–1731
John Woodbridge	1706–1769	1728–1754
Thomas Barber	fl. 1730–1753	1730–1753
William Glasscock	1704–177?	1730–1753
*George Glasscock	——	—1732
Samuel Glasscock	fl. 1730–1734	1730–1734
Thomas Beale	d. 1729	—1729
Richard Barnes	16??–1760	1732–1734
William Jordan	d. 1757	1732–1754
Anthony Sydnor	1683–1759	1732–1754
Leroy Griffin	1711–1750	1733–1749
Daniel Hornby	d. 1750	1733–1749
Landon Carter	1710–1778	1735–1754
Gilbert Hamilton	fl. 17??–1749	1735–1749
William Fauntleroy, Jr.	1713–1793	1736–1754
William Brockenborough	d. 1778	1739–1754
John Smith	fl. 1734–1754	1740–1754
John Plumer	——	—1742
Travers Tarpley	17??–1768	1743–1754
Alvin Mountjoy	1700–1760	1743–1754
John Tarpley Jr.	fl. 1743–1754	1743–1754
Thomas Plumer	fl. 1735–1749	1743–1749
Thomas Peachey	——	—1744
John Tayloe, Jr.	1721–1779	1744–1754
Nicholas Flood	1715–1768	1744–1754
Nicholas Plumer	fl. 1746–1750	—1747
John Peachey	——	—1748
*William Glasscock, Jr.	——	—1752

Key: d. = died   fl. = flourished

*Does not appear in *RCP;* commission taken from ROB.

EDITORIAL NOTE

The manuscript *RCP* was written in three distinct clerks' hands in a bound ledger. There are very few corrections in it, no additions or deletions longer than a single word, and no inserted pages. Twice recognizances were entered out of their chronological order, but with the relevant case, suggesting that the *RCP* was a compilation of rough minutes and file papers produced after the courts met. Therefore, although a mirror image copy of the original would not pose difficulties to modern scholars, we have nevertheless made a number of changes and additions. The object of the American Legal Records Series has been to make valuable documents of general interest available to a large readership. Even the cleanest of eighteenth-century American legal documents has peculiarities of spelling, abbreviation, organization, and presentation, which, left in their original state, would puzzle the layman. No material has been deleted. The changes and additions have the sole purpose of making the *RCP* more accessible. All of them fall under the specific rules given below.

Guided by the American Historical Association Committee on Legal History's "Rules for Style, American Legal Records Series," we have made certain alterations consistently through the text of the document. All antiquated abbreviations are expanded into their modern equivalent. Some would have been obvious from the text, for example, "s^d" for said, "&" for and, "Hon." for Honorable, and so forth. Others would have been cryptic except for a glossary, for example "als" for "also known as," "Ma^s" for Majesties, "P^{sh}" for parish, and "p^{ds}" for pounds, currency. Readers can often guess at these terms from the context in which they appear, but there is no need to force a reader to make an incorrect stab at the meaning of a word. All superscripts are lowered and then, if they fall under the previous rule, expanded. All obsolete letters are replaced with their modern equivalents. For example, the "y" in Y^t—that—was spoken as "th" and is so rendered. If the spelling is unintelligible in the text, a modern version appears after it in brackets. New style years follow old style dates when necessary for accuracy. For example, January 10, 1720, old style, appears as January 10, 1720 [1721]. Each case and entry begins a new paragraph and is indented. Each case or entry ends with a period. The archaic "stroke" is printed as a period. Otherwise, punctuation is left untouched. Marginal case references are brought into the text, in italics. Columns of names of justices present at a called court are presented as lists of names, separated by commas.

The wealth of verbatim testimony that the clerk entered into the *RCP* is one of its unique features but poses problems not precisely covered in the series' style guide. Victims, witnesses, and defendants came to these courts to tell their stories, which the clerk set down with little punctuation. Although study of these firsthand accounts gives the scholar an idea of the justices' experience and affords a vivid picture of the way the common people expressed themselves, many passages would be baffling to the reader without editorial additions. We therefore have taken the liberty of supplying punctuation in brackets to clarify the speakers' tale when absolutely necessary. Nothing in the original text has been removed or altered, save for these essential emendations and those suggested in the series' manual of style.

CRIMINAL PROCEEDINGS IN COLONIAL VIRGINIA

[Records of] Fines, Examination of Criminals, Trials
of Slaves, etc., from March 1710 [1711] to [1754]

[Richmond County, Virginia]

[1] At a Court held for Richmond County the Seventh Day of March One thousand Seven hundred and Tenn [1711].

Present: Samuel Peachey, John Tarpley, Charles Barber, William Woodbridge, John Tayloe Sr., John Taverner, Gentlemen Justices.

Erwin fined

George Erwin Being Summoned to show Cause why he did not appear as a Juryman on the Land in difference between William Fantleroy Plaintiff and Mathew Thornton Defendant, he this Day appearing, but showing noe sufficient Cause why he did not appear, It is therefore Ordered that he be fined Two hundred and Fifty Pounds of Tobacco to her Majesty, which the Sheriff of this County is hereby Ordered to Collect of him, upon refusall of payment by Distress and that the said Sheriff Account for it with William Byrd Esq. her Majestys Receiver General in this Country.[1]

Bowen fined

John Bowen being Summoned to show Cause why he did not appear as a Juryman on the Land in difference between William Fantleroy plaintiff and Mathew Thornton Defendant, but not appearing; It is therefore Ordered that he be fined Two hundred and Fifty pounds of Tobacco to her Majesty, which the Sheriff of this County is hereby Ordered to Collect of him, upon refusall of payment by Distress, and that the said Sheriff Account for it with William Byrd Esq. her Majestys Receiver Generall in this Country.

Fennell fined

John Fennell being summoned to show Cause why he did not appear as a Juryman on the Land in difference between William Fantleroy plaintiff and Mathew Thornton Defendant, but not appearing; It is therefore Ordered that he be fined Two hundred and Fifty pounds of Tobacco to her Majesty, which the Sheriff of this County is hereby Ordered to Collect of him, upon refusall of payment by Distress, And that the said Sheriff Account for it with William Byrd Esq. her Majestys Receiver Generall in this Country.

---

1. Grand juries and trial juries, panels of twenty-four and twelve respectively, were summoned by the sheriff for the county court session. The statutory penalty for nonappearance was two hundred pounds of tobacco for grand jurors and four hundred pounds for trial jurors, if the latter, by their refusal, prevented a jury from sitting. Only freemen with property in excess of £100 sterling were eligible for jury duty; *Statutes at Large*, 3:367–71 (1705).

Smith fined

[2] William Smith being Summoned to show Cause why he did not appear as a Juryman on the Land in Difference between William Fantleroy plaintiff and Mathew Thornton Defendant but not appearing; It is therefore Ordered that he be fined Two hundred and Fifty pounds of Tobacco to her Majesty, which the Sheriff of this County is hereby ordered to Collect of him, upon refusal of payment by Distress; And that the said Sheriff Account for it with William Byrd Esq. her Majesty's Receiver General in this Country.

Lockhart fined

James Lockhart being Summoned to Show Cause why he did not appear as a Juryman on the Land in difference between William Fantleroy plaintiff and Mathew Thornton Defendant, but not appearing; It is therefore Ordered that he be fined Two hundred and Fifty pounds of Tobacco to her Majesty, which the Sheriff of this County is hereby Ordered to Collect of him, upon refusall of payment by Distress, And that the said Sheriff Account for it with William Byrd Esq. her Majesties Receiver General in this Country.

At a Court held for Richmond County the Second Day of May One thousand Seven hundred and Eleven.
Present: Samuell Peachey, Alexander Doniphan, John Tarpley, Charles Barber, William Woodbridge, William Thornton, and Thomas Griffin, Gentlemen Justices.

Fantleroy fined

Griffin Fantleroy being returned upon the Pannell of the Grand Jury to attend this Court this Day, and not appearing when called is hereby fined two hundred pounds of Tobacco to Our Sovereign Lady the Queen according to Law.

Ingo fined

[3] James Ingo being returned upon the Pannell of the Grand Jury to attend this Court this Day, and not appearing when called, is hereby fined Two hundred pounds of Tobacco to Our Sovereign Lady the Queen according to Law.

At a Court Continued and held for Richmond County the Third Day of May One thousand Seven hundred and Eleven.
Present: Samuel Peachey, Alexander Donaphon, John Tarpley, Charles Barber, William Woodbridge, William Thornton, Gentlemen Justices.

Downing and others fined

George Downing, William Seale and William Sims being by Order brought before this Court to Answer to what should be objected against them Relating to the breaking open the Prison of this County and Rich Clathierbucks makeing his Escape from thence,[2] On hearing the Evidence of James Ingo, James Wilson, Samuell Short, Elizabeth Smith and Martha Hayton in this behalfe, and the said George Downing, William Seale and William Sims being separately Examined and offering nothing materiall in barr of what was laid to their charge in this matter, and of Opinion that they are guilty of the Fact aforesaid; It is thereupon Ordered that they be each of them fined One thousand pounds of Tobacco to Our Sovereign Lady the Queen, and that each of them give good and sufficient Security for their good Behaviour One Year.

Downing bound to the Peace

George Downing and Henry Berry Came into Court and acknowledged themselves Indebted to Our Sovereign Lady the Queen her heirs and Successors in the Sum of Tenn pounds Sterling to be levyed on their Lands and Tenements Goods and Chattles; Upon Condition that if the said George Downing shall well and truely keep the Peace as well towards our said Sovereign Lady the Queen, as to all her Leige People dureing the term of One whole Year, then the Recognizance to be void, otherwise to remain in force.

Seale bound the Peace

[4] William Seale and William Berry Came into Court and Acknowledged themselves Indebted to Our Sovereign Lady the Queen her heirs and Successors in the Sum of Tenn pounds Sterling and One thousand pounds of Tobacco to be levyed on their Lands and Tenements Goods and Chattles; Upon Condition that if the said William Seale shall well and truely keep the Peace as well toward our said Sovereign Lady the Queen, as to all her Leige people During the terme of One whole Year and also pay One thousand pounds of Tobacco (it being the Fine laid on him by this Court) then this Recognizance to be void, otherwise remain in force.

Sims bound to the Peace

William Sims and Thomas Dickenson came into Court and Acknowledged themselves Indebted to Our Sovereign Lady the Queen her heirs and Successors in the Sum of Tenn pounds Sterling to be Levyed on their lands and Tenements

---

2. "Rescue" was a felony (Webb, *Justice of Peace*, 169), but the Downing case does not seem to have been a rescue. The prison was allegedly broken open, but the perpetrator was not named. The penalty, a fine and surety for good behaviour, did not fit a felony charge. It may be that Downing and his co-defendants were bystanders who aided or concealed Clathierbuck's flight. In colonial Virginia, as in England, the entire community was obliged to pursue escaped felons. See Webb, *Justice of Peace*, 15.

Goods and Chattles, Upon Condition that if the said William Sims shall well and truely keep the Peace as well towards our said Sovereign Lady the Queen, as to all her Leige People, dureing the Terme of one whole Year, then this Recognizance to be void, otherwise to remain in force.

Att a Court Continued and held for Richmond County August the 7th 1712.
Present: Alexander Doniphan, John Tarpley, Charles Barber, Edward Barrow, Joseph Deeke, George Heale and Thomas Griffin, Gentlemen Justices.

Hill fined

Upon the Grand Jurys Presentment of Richard Hill for keeping an Ordinary without Lycence the said Hill being called and offering nothing Material in Barr, It is hereby Ordered that he be fined Two Thousand pounds of Tobacco to our Sovereign Lady the Queen According to Law.

[5] Att a Court Continued and held for Richmond County the 6th Day of August 1713.
Present: Alexander Doniphan, John Tarpley, Charles Barber, Joseph Deeks, William Woodbridge, Thomas Griffin, Gentlemen Justices.

Champ fined

John Champ being Summoned as a Juryman to Survey and layout the land in dispute between John Lomax Plaintiff and Henry Butler Defendant and appearing accordingly upon the said Land, but Refusing to be Sworne It is Ordered that he be fined the Sume of Two hundred pounds of Tobacco to her Majestie[3] which the Sheriff of this County is hereby Impowered to Collect of him and in Case of Refusall by Distress. And it is further Ordered that he Account for and pay the same to her Majesties Receiver Generall of this Country.

Minton fined

Joseph Minton the same.

Edmund fined

Cornelius Edmund the same.

Carter fined

William Carter the same.

---

3. The offense was contempt of court, not failure to appear for jury duty.

White fined

Daniell White the same.

Brown fined

Maxfield Brown the same.

Burrows fined

Mathew Burrows the same.

Att a Court held for Richmond County the Second Day of September 1713.
Present: Alexander Doniphan, John Tarpley, Charles Barber, Edward Barrow, Nicholas Smith and Richard Taliferro, Gentlemen Justices.

Thornton fined

[6] Thomas Thornton being Summoned to Show Cause why he did not appear according to Summons as a Juryman to Survey and layout the Land in Dispute between John Lomax Plaintiff and Henry Butler Defendant the said Thomas Thornton this day appeared in Court but the reasons he gave for his not appearing as a Juryman on the Land aforesaid not being allowed, It is therefore Ordered that he be fined the Sume of Two hundred pounds of Tobacco to her Majestie which the Sheriff of this County is hereby Impowered to Collect of him, and in Case of Refusall by Distress; And it is further Ordered that he Account for and pay the same to her Majesties Receiver Generall of this Country.

Dozier fined

Leonard Dozier being Summoned to show Cause why he did not appear according to Summons as a Juryman to Survey and layout the Land in dispute between John Lomax Plaintiff and Henry Butler Defendant the said Leonard Dozier failing to appear to show any Cause to the Contrary; It is therefore Ordered that he be fined the Sume of Two hundred pounds of Tobacco to her Majestie, which the Sheriff of this County is hereby Impowered to Collect of him, and in Case of Refusall by Distress; And it is further Ordered that he Account for and pay the same to her Majesties Receiver Generall of this Country.[4]

Att a Court held for Richmond County the Sixth Day of January 1713/4.
Present: John Tarpley, Charles Barber, Nicholas Smith, William Thornton, Jonathan Gibson, Richard Taliafero and Thomas Griffin, Gentlemen Justices.

4. Misconduct by jurors and officers of the court was entered in the *RCP* because of the fines involved. In later years, these proceedings were entered in the ROB.

Welsh fined

James Welsh of the Parish of North Farnham in the County of Richmond, being presented by the Grand Jury for Publick Selling of Brandy by Retail in the Race Ground of Thomas Dews in the said Parish and County on the 23d and 24th Days of October last Contrary to Law, was returned by the Sheriff not to be found in his Bayliwick and now failing to appear. It is therefore Ordered that he be fined the Sume of Two thousand pounds Tobacco to her Majestie, which the Sheriff of this County is thereby [7] Impowered to Collect of him, and in Case of Refusall by Distress, And it is further Ordered that he Account for and pay the same to her Majesties Receiver Generall of this County.[5]

Dew fined

Andrew Dew of the Parish of North Farnham in the County of Richmond being Summoned to Answer the Presentment of the Grand Jury against him for Publick Selling of Cyder by Retaile, in the said County and Parish the 23d Day of October last past, Appeared in Court and Refusing to undergo the punishment the Law directs; It is therefore Ordered that he be fined the Sume of Two Thousand pounds of Tobacco to her Majestie,[6] which the Sheriff of this County is hereby Impowered to Collect of him, and in Case of Refusall by Distress, And it is further Ordered that he Account for and pay the same to her Majesties Receiver Generall of this County.

Caine fined

John Caine of the Parish of North Farnham in the County of Richmond being Summoned to Answer the Presentment of the Grand Jury against him for the publick Selling of Cyder by Retaile in his house in the Parish and County afore-said the 5th Day of September last past, Appeared in Court, and Refusing to undergo the Punishment the Law directs; It is therefore Ordered that he be fined the Sume of Two Thousand pounds of Tobacco to her Majestie which the Sheriff of this County is hereby Impowered to Collect of him, and in Case of Refusall by Distress, And it is further Ordered that he Account for and pay the same to her Majesties Receiver Generall of this Country.

Boyles fined

Thomas Boyles of the Parish of St. Maryes[7] in the County of Richmond being Summoned to Answer the Presentment of the Grand Jury against him for pub-lick Selling of Cyder by Retail in a Race Ground and att his own house in the said Parish and County about the last of August last past Appeared in Court, and

---

5. English quarter sessions records in this era were filled with sheriffs' reports that suspects were no longer to be found in the vicinity. This was not as common in the *RCP*, but criminal suspects certainly fled from justice in Richmond County. See, for example, pp. 59–60 below.

6. Dew was ordered to pay the statutory fine of two-thousand pounds of tobacco; *Statutes at Large,* 3:396 (1705).

7. After 1720, St. Mary's became a part of King George County.

Refusing to undergo the Punishment the Law directs, It is therefore Ordered that he be fined the Sume of Two Thousand pounds of Tobacco to her Majestie which the Sheriff of this County is hereby Impowered to Collect of him, and in Case of Refusall by Distress, And it is further Ordered that he Account for and pay the same to her Majesties Receiver Generall of this Country.

Dalton fined

[8] William Dalton of the Parish of Sittenburn[8] in the County of Richmond appeared in Court to Answer the Presentment of the Grand Jury against him for the Public Selling of Cyder by Retaile, on a Race Ground in the said Parish and County the last day of August last past, and Refusing to undergo the Punishment the Law directs, It is therefore Ordered that he be fined the Sume of Two Thousand pounds of Tobacco to her Majestie which the Sheriff of this County is hereby Impowered to Collect of him, and in Case of Refusall by Distress; And it is further Ordered that he Account for and pay the same to her Majesties Receiver Generall of this Country.

Strother fined

James Strother of the Parish of St. Maryes in the County of Richmond being Summoned to Answer the Presentment of the Grand Jury Against him for the publick Selling by Retaile of Cyder in his house in the said Parish and County the 28th Day of October last past, Appeared in Court and refuseing to undergo the Punishment as the Law directs, It is therefore Ordered that he be fined the Sume of Two Thousand pounds of Tobacco to her Majestie which the Sheriff of this County is hereby Impowered to Collect of him, and in case of Refusall by Distress; And it is further Ordered that he Account for and pay the same to her Majesties Receiver Generall of this Country.

Robinson fined

Major William Robinson came into Court and acknowledged himself Indebted to Our Sovereign Lady the Queene her heirs and Successors in the full and just Sume of Two Thousand pounds of Tobacco, to be paid to our said Sovereign Lady the Queene her heirs and Successors in Case James Strother of the Parish of St. Maryes in the County of Richmond do not pay, att the Cropp, his Fine according to Law, upon the Presentment of the Grand Jury against him for publick Selling and Retailing Cyder in his house in the said Parish and County the 28th Day of October last past.

Att a Court Continued and held for Richmond County the Eighth Day of April 1714.

---

8. Part of this parish lay south of the Rappahannock.

Present: John Tarpley, Charles Barber, Edward Barrow, William Woodbridge, Jonathan Gibson, Thomas Griffin, Gentlemen Justices.

Taylor Sheriff fined

[**9**] In an Action of Trespass between John Lomax Plaintiff and Henry Butler Defendant the Order for Survey with a Jury by this Court not being Complyed with at the Motion of Daniell McCarty Attorney for the Plaintiff, It is Ordered that the Sheriff of this County for his default therein be fined the Sume of One Thousand pounds of Tobacco.[9]

Att a Court held for Richmond County the Fifth Day of May 1714.
Present: Alexander Doniphan, Charles Barber, Edward Barrow, William Thornton, Moore Fantleroy, Jonathan Gibson, Richard Taliaferro, Gentlemen Justices.

Dye fined

Arthur Dye being returned upon the Pannell of the Grand Jury to attend this Court this Day, and not appearing when called, Is hereby fined Two hundred pounds of Tobacco to Our Sovereign Lady the Queen according to Law.

Littman fined

William Littman being brought before this Court the Seventh Day of April last for raising malitious and scandalous Reports of Elizabeth and Frances the Wife and Daughter of Charles Kipp, did then Contemptuously goe away from the said Court after his Appearance, Whereupon it was then Ordered that the Sheriff of this County should apprehend the said Littman, and him safely keep till he should give Security for his Appearance at the next Court to Answer for his said Contempt;[10] And the said Littman now appearing pursuant to the said Order, but offering nothing materiall to Excuse himself for his said Contempt It is therefore Ordered that the said William Littman be fined the Sume of Five hundred pounds of Tobacco to Our Sovereign Lady the Queen for his said Contempt to this Court; and that he give Security for the payment [**10**] of the said fine, Whereupon John Doyle Came into Court and Obliged himself his

---

9. The sheriff failed to carry out an order of the court and was fined. Sheriffs (who were by law also justices of the peace) had other, full-time occupations in addition to their duty as officers of the court, and fines kept these men's minds on their official responsibilities. *Statutes at Large*, 3:248 (1705), specifies the one-thousand-pound fine.

10. Littman was in court to answer a charge of libel against the Kipps. His unauthorized departure was a contempt, for which offense he was fined. Cases of scandal mongering and libel were recorded in the ROB, while contempts of the court, involving fines, were placed in the *RCP* until the 1740s. Littman's libel, for which he received thirty lashes, can be found in the ROB, No. 6, 203 (1714).

heirs etc. pay the said Five hundred pounds of Tobacco, in Case the said William Littman did not pay the same according to the aforesaid Order against him.

Att a Court Continued and held for Richmond County the Second Day of December 1714.

Present: William Woodbridge, John Tayloe, Jonathan Gibson, Richard Taliaferro, Gentlemen Justices.

Hooper fined

Thomas Hooper being returned upon the Pannell of the Grand Jury to attend this Court this Day and not appearing when called, is hereby fined Two hundred pounds of Tobacco to Our Sovereign Lord the King according to Law.

Heaford bound to his good behaviour

John Heaford being bound over to this Court by John Tayloe Gentleman one of his Majesties Justices of the Peace for this County on Suspition of Hogg Stealing,[11] and he now appearing, It is Ordered that he give Security for his good Behaviour for One Year; Whereupon George Gaydon together with the said Heaford Acknowledged themselves Indebted to Our Sovereign Lord the King his heirs and Successors in the Sume of Tenn pounds Sterling, to be Levyed on their Lands and Tenements Goods and Chattles, with Condition that if the said John Heaford shall keep the Peace of Our Sovereign Lord the King as well as towards his Majestie, as all his Leige People, that then this Recognizance to be void and of noe Effect, or else to remain in full force.

Hinds bound to good behaviour

Benjamin Hinds being bound over to the Court by John Tayloe Gentleman one of his Majesties Justices of the Peace for this County on Suspition of Hogg Stealing and he now appearing, It is Ordered that he give Security for his good Behaviour for One Year; Whereupon Thomas Thorne together with the said [11] Hinds Acknowledged themselves Indebted to Our Sovereign Lord the King his heirs and Successors in the Sume of Tenn pounds Sterling to be Levyed on their Lands and Tenements Goods and Chattles, with Condition that if the said Benjamin Hinds shall keep the Peace of Our Sovereign Lord the King, as well as towards his Majestie as all his Leige People, that then this Recognizance to be void and of none Effect, or else to remain in full force.

---

11. Although stealing hogs was a statutory offence (*Statutes at Large*, 3:276–79 [1705]), suspicion of hog stealing was not mentioned in the statute. Under their commissions of the peace, justices could detain and require bond for good behavior from suspects of criminal offenses; Webb, *Justice of Peace*, 325.

[*Phillips bound to good behavior*]

William Phillips Jr. being bound over to the Court by John Tayloe Gentleman one of his Majesties Justices of the Peace for this County on Suspition of Hogg Stealing, and he now appearing; It is Ordered that he give Security for his good Behaviour for One Year; Whereupon George Gaydon together with the said Phillips Acknowledged themselves Indebted to Our Sovereign Lord the King his heirs and Successors in the Sume of Tenn pounds Sterling, to be Levyed on their Lands and Tenements, Goods and Chattles, With Condition that if the said William Phillips Jr. shall keep the Peace of Our Sovereign Lord the King, as well as towards his Majestie as all his Leige People, that then this Recognizance to be void and of none Effect, or else to remain in full force.

At a Call'd Court[12] held at the Court house of Richmond County on Fryday the Seventh Day of January 1714/5.
Present: Alexander Doniphan, Edward Barrow, Nicholas Smith, John Tayloe, and Moore Fantleroy, Gentlemen Justices.

Jones Acquitted

John Jones been Committed Prisoner to the Goal of this County by the vertue of a Warrant[13] of John Tarpley Gentleman one of his Majesties Justices of the Peace for this County on Suspition of killing one Richard Garrett, this Day the Court haveing taken the said matter into Examination haveing heard the Evidence of Griffin Humphreys on behalf of the King against the Prisoner, no sufficient Cause appearing to them upon the Evidence to remove him to the Public Goal, He is therefore Ordered to be Acquitted.

[12] Att a Court held for Richmond County the Fourth Day of May 1715.
Present: Alexander Doniphan, John Tarpley, Edward Barrow, Nicholas Smith, Gentlemen Justices.

Bayley fined

Ordered that William Bayley Constable for not duely Executing a Warrant Granted by John Tayloe Gentleman one of his Majesties Justices of the Peace for this County against William Smith Cordwainer to Answer the Complaint of Austin Brockenbrough be fined the Sume of One hundred pounds of Tobacco to Our sovereign Lord the King.

---

12. This formula introduced the examining court. When the phrases "upon examination" or "taken under examination" appeared in the record, the justices also were sitting as an examining court.

13. The justice issued the warrant to the sheriff or a constable, who executed it.

Smith Fined

Ordered that William Smith Cordwainer for Contemning a Warrant Granted by John Tayloe Gentleman against him to Answer the Complaint of Austin Brockenbrough be fined the Sume of five hundred pounds of Tobacco to Our Sovereign Lord the King.[14]

Att a Court held for Richmond County the First Day of June 1715.
Present: John Tarpley, Edward Barrow, William Thornton, John Tayloe, and Richard Taliferro, Gentlemen Justices.

Richardson's Examination

Whereas Margaret Richardson was by Warrant of John Tarpley Gentleman one of the Justices of this Court Committed to the County Goal on Suspition of Murdering her Bastard Child which by her own Confession she privately buryed and being now brought before his Majesties Justices here present was Examined by the Court as followeth.[15]

Court. Margaret Richardson was it your Child that was found buryed in Mrs. Dew's Tobacco Grounds?
Answer. Yes.
Court. Whether was it a Boy or a Girl?
Answer. A Girl.
[13] Court. Was it you that buryed it there?
Answer. Yes.
Court. Was any Body with you when you were delivered?
Answer. No.
Court. Was the Child born alive or dead?
Answer. Dead.
Court. Who was the Father of this Child?
Answer. One John Stanley.
Court. Was you ever marryed to the said Stanley[?]
Answer. No.
Court. How farr do you think you were from Mrs. Dew's house when you were delivered?
Answer. Within Sight of the house.
Court. Why did you not discover it to Mrs. Dew as soon as you went to her house[?]

---

14. The constable had not brought the cordwainer to court; the cordwainer resisted legal authority. Warrants were commands to appear binding on all; *Statutes at Large*, 3:510 (1710).

15. In 1710, the Virginia House of Burgesses had received 21 James I, c.27 (1624), making concealment of the death of a newborn bastard by its mother presumptive evidence that she murdered it, unless someone could testify to its stillbirth; *Statutes at Large*, 3:516–17 (1710). Note that Richardson, the defendant, did not testify on oath. Defendants in England and her colonies were not sworn to their testimony in criminal trials.

Answer. I was a fool and knew no better.

Court. How long had you been delivered of the Child before you were apprehended[?]

Answer. Almost a Week.

Mary Bluford Aged 38 yeares or thereabouts being
Sworn was Examined by the court as followeth.

Court. Mary Bluford doe you know Margaret Richardson the Prisoner at the Bar?

Answer. Yes.

Court. What day was it that the Prisoner at the Bar came to your house?

Answer. The Fryday after she was delivered of her Child as since appears.

Court. What Discourse had you with her when she came to your house?

Answer. I said, soe Margaret which way now, she answered she was come to pay the rest of her time, and I asked her what became of her great Belly? She answered she thanked God Almighty that he had eased her of what she had been long time troubled with, ever since last May, and that they broke upon her upon a Tobacco hill in Mrs. Dew's Tobacco ground, and that they might have tracked her all the way she came, but that the Rain washed it out.

Court. What did you apprehend she meant by her Saying they had broke upon her?

Answer. I understood by it she meant that it then was with her after the manner of other Women.[16]

Court. How Came you to ask those Questions[?]

Answer. She seemed to be gaunter then what I saw her before. [14] and I had formerly thought her to be with Child and charged her with it, but she always denyed it.

Court. Had you any further Discourse with her at that time?

Answer. Yes. She told me that the first place they broke out upon her was upon a Tobacco hill in Mrs. Dew's tobacco ground and that they came from her to the Quantity of a Porringer full, and that she threw some dirt upon them.

Court. How long did she stay at your house?

Answer. From Fryday Night, till Monday Morning.

Court. What were her reasons doe you think that caused her to goe away soe soon?

Answer. I told her I heard the people talk abroad that she had had a little one, and had made away with it, She told me she had not had a Child, for she had often told me the reasons that caus'd her Belly to swell, and that she had never gott anything in the County, therefore would not stay in it; Whereupon I told her if she knew she had not had a great Belly she need not fear but stay, nevertheless she went away the next Morning.

Mary Brady Aged 25 Yeares or thereabout being
Sworn was Examined by the Court as followeth.

---

16. Her menstrual period.

Court. Mary Brady Doe you know Margaret Richardson the Prisoner at the Bar[?]

Answer. I do know her by Sight, and that's all.

Court. When was the first time you saw her?

Answer. On a Sunday, she was going to Mr. Thorn's towards the last of Aprill.

Court. Doe you believe she was with Child that time you saw her?

Answer. I don't know, I took no Notice of her, she just Came within the Ground-sell of the Door, and went away again.

Court. When was the Second time you saw her[?]

Answer. The Fryday following after the Sunday.

Court. What Discourse did you have with her[?]

Answer. I asked her where she lay last Night? She Answered at Mrs. Dew's and sometime after she began the Discourse and told me people said she was with Child, but she thanked God she had seen more Yesterday between Betty Morris's and Mrs. Dew's than she had seen a Twelve Month Whereupon I asked what that was? She told me them broke upon her, and she hoped in a little time her great Belly would fall.

[15] Court. What did you understand she meant when she told you them broke upon her?

Answer. I understood she meant it was the Flowers of women.

George Bluford Aged 47 Yeares or Thereabouts being
Sworn, was Examined by the Court as followeth.

Court. George Bluford do you know Margaret Richardson the Prisoner at the Barr?

Answer. Yes I know her.

Court. What doe you know concerning her having a Child?

Answer. I know nothing, only the Fryday after she was delivered of a Child as she has since Confest she Came to my house I not being at home, but when I came home which was on Saturday my Wife told me that Margaret was come again to serve the rest of her time; on Sunday after John Flemings Wife came to my house, and my little Boys went home with her, and when they came back at Night I heard them tell the Prisoner at the Barr that John Fleming's Wife said that she doubted the Prisoner at the Barr had done something she ought not to have done, and that she had a good Mind to come down on Monday Morning and search her to see whether she had any Milk in her Breasts; Whereupon the Prisoner at the Barr Swore by her Maker's Blood that if she or any body else came to search her she would Stave their Brains out with the first thing she could gett in her hands, and the next Morning before I gott up she was gone away.

Court. Doe you know anything further?

Answer. I was one of the Jury on the Body of the Child,[17] and the Prisoner at the Barr showed us where the Child was buryed goeing before us to the place she pointed with her hand, and said there is my poor Babe.

---

17. The coroner's jury. Verdicts of these juries were not recorded in the *RCP*, except when the jury suspected foul play and the justices began an examination.

Court. What Posture did the Jury find the Child in?

Answer. When we came to the place where the Child was, one of Mrs. Dew's Negroes put a hoe under it, and lifted the Child up dirt and all, and the Armes were extended up over it's head.

Court. Did the Child seem to be bruis'd?

Answer. On the back part of the head seemed to be a blow.

[**16**] It appearing to the Court upon the aforesaid Examinations that there is just Cause for trying the said Prisoner at the next Court of Oyer and Terminer to be held at his Majesties Royall Capitoll for the Crime aforesaid whereof she is Accused; It is therefore Ordered that the said Margaret Richardson be remanded to the Prison of this County under the Custody of the Sheriff and from thence to be Conveyed to the Publick Goal of Williamsburgh as the Law in such Cases directs.

[*Bluford's recognizance*]

George Bluford and Mary his Wife in open Court before his Majesties Justices acknowledged themselves indebted to Our Sovereign Lord the King his heirs and Successors in the Sum of Twenty pounds Sterling to be levyed of their Lands and Tenements Goods and Chattles with Condition if they the said George and Mary shall appear before the Honorable Court of Oyer and Terminer to be held at his Majesties Royall Capitoll on the Second Tuesday in this instant June and so attend from time to time as the said Court shall direct, then and there to give Evidence for Our said Lord the King against Margaret Richardson who stands Committed to the Goal of this County on Suspition of Murdering her Bastard Child. Then this Recognizance to be void, or else to be and remain in full force and vertue. Mary Brady in Open Court before his Majesties Justices acknowledged her self indebted to Our Sovereign Lord the King his heirs and Successors in the Sum of Twenty Pounds Sterling to be levyed of her Lands and Tenements Goods and Chattles with Condition if she the said Mary Brady shall appear before the Honorable Court of Oyer and Terminer to be held in his Majesties Royall Capitoll on the Second Tuesday in this instant June and so attend from time to time as the said Court shall direct, then and there to give Evidence for Our said Lord the King against Margaret Richardson who stands Committed to the Goal of this County on Suspition of Murdering her Bastard Child then this Recognizance to be void or else to remain in full force and vertue.

Negro Will his Tryall

[**17**] Att a Session of Oyer and Terminer held at Richmond Court house on Monday the Thirteenth Day of June 1715 in the First Year of the Reign of Our Sovereign Lord George by the Grace of God King of Great Brittain France and Ireland Defender of the Faith etc. by Virtue of a Speciall Commission for the Tryall of all Treasons, Petty Treasons or Misprisions thereof Felonies, Murthers

or other Offences or Crimes whatsoever Committed within the County of Richmond by a Negro Slave called Will directed to Alexander Donophan, John Tarpley, Edward Barrow, Nicholas Smith, Joseph Deeke, William Woodbridge, William Thornton, Thomas Griffin, John Tayloe, Moore Fanteroy, Jonathan Gibson, Richard Talliaferro, and Austin Brockenbrough Gentlemen.

Present: Edward Barrow, Nicholas Smith, John Tayloe, Moore Fantleroy, Gentlemen Justices.

Memorandum. That on this Day being the Thirteenth Day of June 1715 an Indictment[18] was preferred against a Negro Man Slave called Will in these Words . . . Richmond Ss/[19] May in the First Year of the Reigne of Our Sovereign Lord George by the Grace of God of Great Brittain France and Ireland King Defender of the Faith etc. Anno/Dom: 1715.

To his Majesties Justices of Oyer and Terminer for the said County Daniell McCarty Attorney of Our said Lord the King Presents and gives the said Justices to understand and be informed That one Will a Negro Man Slave belonging to William Robinson of the County afore said Gentleman on the Second Day of February in the Year aforesaid of the Reign aforesaid and in the Year of Our Lord Christ 1714 [1715] at the Parish of Sittenburn in the County of Richmond aforesaid By force and Armes an Assault upon the Body of one Richard Copley at the Parish and County aforesaid in the Peace of God and Our aforesaid Lord the King being feloniously did make and him the said Richard Copely feloniously did Steal and Carry away sundry peices of Silver Money to the value of five Pounds Sterling, Contrary to the Peace of our said Lord the King his Crown and Dignity.

DANIELL MCCARTY/Dom Rex[20]

[18] Whereupon the said Will was brought to the Barr and Arraigned for the said Felony and there pleaded, Not Guilty, and no Evidence appearing to prove the aforesaid Fact against him It is therefore Ordered that he be Acquitted.[21]

Also another Indictment was this Day preferred against the said Will breaking Goal in these Words . . . Richmond Ss/ May in the First Year of Reigne of Our Sovereigne Lord George by the Grace of God of Great Brittain France and Ireland King Defender of the Faith etc. Anno Dom. 1715.

To his Majesties Justices of Oyer and Terminer for the said County Daniell

---

18. This memorandum was not properly an indictment, for there was no grand jury to find it. Instead, it was an information, giving the justices "to understand and be informed" of the facts in the case according to the crown. The slave was then permitted to plead, that is, he was brought to the bar to answer the charge; *Statutes at Large*, 3:269–70 (1705).

19. "Ss" may have been an abbreviation for "special sessions" but more commonly denoted "the venue of. . . ." Oyer and terminer courts to try slaves accused of felonies were held in the county from 1692, under commissions from the governor; *Statutes at Large*, 3:102–3 (1692).

20. McCarty, prosecutor "Pro Dominus Rex" for the king, merely filled in the blanks in the memorandum: the dates and details of the crime and the names and identities of the defendants and victims. The formula included the allegation that from malicious intent ("feloniously"), that is, with *mens rea*, Will committed a criminal act. As in England, the "indictment" was read to the defendant, at which time he could object to any errors in it. There were no traverses of oyer and terminer memorandums in the Richmond records.

21. Will heard the memorandum and then made his plea at the opening of proceedings. There is no evidence that slaves were informed of the precise charges or the evidence against them before they stood at the bar. In this case, the victim did not come to give evidence.

McCarty Attorney of Our said Lord the King Presents and gives the said Justices to understand and be Inform'd That Negroe Will a Man Slave belonging to William Robinson of the County aforesaid Gentleman being on the Fifth day of March now Last past Duely committed to the Publick Goal of the County aforesaid for haveing feloniosly Rob'd and from the Body of one Richard Copley Stole sundry peices of Money to the vallue of Five Pounds Sterling the said Negroe Will Indeavoring and Designing to fly from Justice on the 8th Day of March in the Year aforesaid of the Reigne aforesaid by force and Armes the said Goal and Prison did feloniously break and therefrom did fly and make his Escape Contrary to the Peace of Our said Lord the King his Crown and Dignity and his Laws and Statutes in that behalf made and provided.

DAN. McCARTY Dom. Rex

Whereupon the said Will was brought to the Barr and Arraigned for the said Felony and there pleaded Not Guilty and thereupon the Court proceeding in his Tryall (After the hearing the Evidence of John Doyle against him, and which he had to say in his Defence)[22] Are of Opinion that he is not Guilty of the Felony for which he stands Indicted. It is therefore Ordered that he be Acquitted.

John Doyle being Sworne as an Evidence on the behalf of the King Deposed that the Prisoner at the Barr Will was by Vertue of a Mittimus[23] for Felony put into the Goal of this County, and that the Goal was broke and the said Will absent severall Days.

[19] Att a Court Continued and held for Richmond County the Seventh Day of July 1715.

Present: Alexander Doniphan, Edward Barrow, Nicholas Smith, William Thornton, and John Tayloe, Gentlemen Justices.

Davis fined

John Davis Jr. of Sittenbourn Parish haveing been presented by the Grand Jury for being a Common Disturber of the Peace this Day appeared in Court to Answer the said Presentment, but offering nothing materiall to discharge himself from the same; It is therefore Ordered that the said John Davis be fined the Sume of Five Pounds Sterling to Our Sovereign Lord the King and that he remain in the Sheriffs Custody till he gives good and sufficient Security for his good behavior and keeping the Peace in the Sume of One hundred pounds Sterling. Whereupon Mathew Davis and Edmond McLinchy together with the said John Davis Acknowledged themselves Indebted to Our Sovereign Lord the King his heirs and Successors in the Sume of One hundred pounds Sterling, to

---

22. The jailor, Doyle, gave evidence under oath, but Will was not sworn. A 1705 law prevented blacks, slave and free, from giving evidence of any kind under oath; *Statutes at Large*, 3:298 (1705). In 1723, slaves were permitted to testify under oath against other slaves in capital offenses; *Statutes at Large*, 4:127–28. In 1744, free Christian blacks and mulattoes could testify under oath against other blacks and mulattoes in all cases; *Statutes at Large*, 5:245 (1744).

23. The writ from a justice commanding commitment of a suspect.

be Levyed on their Lands and Tenements Goods and Chattles with Condition that if the said John Davis shall be of good Behaviour and also shall keep the Peace of Our Sovereign Lord the King and as well towards his Majestie as all his Leige People for the term of One Year and One Day, That then his Recognizance to be void and of none Effect, or else to remain in full force.

Griffin fined

William Griffin of Sittnbourn Parish having been presented by the Grand Jury for not keeping lawfull Measures in his Mill, this Day appeared in Court to Answer the said Presentment but offering nothing materiall in Barr thereof; It is therefore Ordered that he be Fined Fifteen Shillings to Our Sovereign Lord the King.

Pavey bond etc.

Webley Pavey being presented by the Grand Jury for being generally Suspected to live in Adultery with Sarah Yeats, It is therefore Ordered that the said Webly Pavey enter into Bond with good and sufficient [20] Security in the Sum of Fifty pounds Sterling for his dismissing the said Sarah Yeats from her dwelling and Cohabitation with him in his house, as also for his refraining himself from resorting to or frequenting her Company, and that the Sheriff take him into Custody and him safely keep untill he shall give such Bond with Security as aforesaid;[24] Whereupon the said Webly Pavey appeared in Court and together with David Berrick his Security Acknowledged themselves Indebted to Our Sovereign Lord the King his heirs and Successors in the Sume of Fifty pounds Sterling to be Levyed of their Land and Tenements, Goods and Chattles if the said Webly Pavey did not Comply with and fulfill the purport and Contents of the above order.

Williams bond etc.

Francis Williams being presented by the Grand Jury for being generally Suspected to live in Adultory with a Mulatto Woman. It is therefore Ordered that the said Francis Williams enter into Bond with good and sufficient Security in the Sume of One hundred pounds Sterling for his dismissing the said Mulatto Woman from her dwelling and Cohabitation with him in his house as also for his refraining himself from resorting to or frequenting her Company, and that the Sheriff take him into Custody with Security as aforesaid; Whereupon the said Francis Williams appeared in Court and together with John Bowen and Francis Williams Jr. his Security Acknowledged themselves Indebted to Our Sovereign

---

24. Either Pavey or Yeats was married. Punishment for this offense was mild compared with Massachusetts, whose courts still considered adultery a serious (if no longer capital) crime. A Virginia statute (*Statutes at Large*, 3:361 [1705]) provided for a fine of one thousand pounds of tobacco upon conviction or confession. Pavey neither confessed nor was convicted. The £50 was a pledge for good behavior only. The actual presentments of the grand jury were entered in the ROB, in the form of a list of names and offenses, ordinarily twice each year.

Lord the King his heirs and Successors in the Sume of One hundred pounds
Sterling to be Levyed of their Lands and Tenements Goods, and Chattles if the
said Francis Williams did not Comply with and fulfill the Purport and Contents
of the above Order.

Champ bound

John Champ being presented by the Grand Jury for being generally Suspected
to live in Adultry with Mary Carter, It is therefore Ordered that the said John
Champ enter into Bond with good and sufficient Security in the Sume of One
hundred pounds Sterling for his dismissing the said Mary Carter from her
dwelling and Cohabitation with him in his house, as also for his refraining
himself from resorting to or frequenting her [21] Company and that the Sheriff
take him into Custody and him safely keep untill he shall give such Bond with
Security as aforesaid.

Copley fined etc.

Richard Copley haveing been Commanded by James Philips one of the Under
Sheriffs of this County to assist him in the apprehending of One James Ellkins
who for Contempt of Authority was by this Court Ordered to be taken into
Custody, the said James Philips this Day made complaint to this Court that the
said Richard Copley not only denyed giveing his Assistance, but alsoe used
severall threatening Speeches to him, and likewise Assaulted and beat him, the
said Richard Copley appearing but offering nothing materiall to Excuse himself,
It is therefore Ordered that the said Richard Copley be Fined the Sume of Ten
pounds Sterling to Our Sovereign Lord the King and that he be Imprisoned One
Month, and also that he give good and sufficient Security for his good Behaviour
in the Sume of One hundred Pounds Sterling.[25]

Champ fined

John Champ Surveyor of the Highwayes between the Court house and
Charles Beaver Dam being Summoned to Answer the Presentment of the Grand
Jury against him for not clearing the Road according to Law, he this Day appear-
ing, but offering nothing materiall in Barr; It is therefore Ordered that he be
Fined Fifteen Shillings to Our Sovereign Lord the King.[26]

Carter fined

William Carter Surveyer of the Highwayes between Charles Beaver Dam and
the Gravelie Run being Summoned to Answer the Presentment of the Grand

25. Copley's imprisonment was a rare instance of confinement used as a punishment in itself.
Most often a defendant was put in jail until he could settle his fines and court costs and give security
for payment should he violate the conditions of his bond.

26. The offense was treated in *Statutes at Large*, 3:392–95 (1705). The 15*s.* was to go to an
informer, making this a *qui tam* proceeding (*Statutes at Large*, 3:393). The *RCP* did not mention the
informer, in which case one assumes the fine went to the crown.

Jury against him, he this Day appearing, but offering nothing materiall in Barr; It is therefore Ordered that he be Fined Fifteen Shillings to Our Sovereign Lord the King.

Wilson fined

James Wilson Surveyer of the Highwayes between the Court house and Rappahanock Run being Summoned to Answer the Presentment of the Grand Jury against [22] him, he this Day appearing, but offering nothing material in Barr; It is therefore Ordered that he be Fined Fifteen Shillings to Our Sovereign Lord the King.

Copley Discharged from imprisonment

The Court takeing into Consideration the Order passed this Day against Richard Copley for his Fine and Imprisonment upon the said Copley's appearing in Court and with humble Submission acknowledging his Offence, have Ordered that he be discharged from the said Imprisonment.[27]

Att a Court held for Richmond County the Seventh Day of September 1715. Present: John Tarpley, Nicholas Smith, William Thornton, John Tayloe, Moore Fantleroy, Jonathan Gibson and Richard Taliaferro, Gentlemen Justices.

Pratt bound to Peace

John Pratt being by Vertue of a Warrant of Nicholas Smith Gentlemen one of his Majesties Justices of the Peace for this County bound over to appear at this Court to Answer the Complaint of William Whitesides of Whitehaven Mariner for Assaulting beating and bruising him the said John Pratt accordingly appeared this Day in Court and severall Evidences being Examined who fully proved the Fact; It is therefore Ordered that he give good and sufficient Security in the Sum of One hundred pounds Sterling for his keeping the Peace.[28]

Whereupon the said John Pratt together with Thomas Paise and Cornelius Edmonds Acknowledged themselves Indebted to Our Sovereign Lord the King his heirs and Successors in the Sume of One hundred pounds Sterling to be Levyed on their Lands and Tenements, Goods [23] and Chattles, with Condition that if the said John Pratt shall keep the Peace of Our Sovereign Lord the King towards his said Majestie and all his Leige People and Especially towards William Whitesides Mariner of Whitehaven; That then this Recognizance to be void and of none Effect, or else to remain in full force.

---

27. Copley had now bowed to the authority of the court, the jail sentence evidently acting as a spur (which may have been the original intent of the court).

28. The justices sat as an examining court, but assault was not a crime that went to the General Court. This hearing was thus covened under the pre-1705 custom rather than the letter of the 1705 act. *Statutes at Large*, 3:389–92 (1705).

Carwick to give security for Behavior

David Carwick being by vertue of a Warrant of John Tarpley Gentlemen one of his Majesties Justices of the Peace for this County brought before this Court to Answer the complaint of John Naylor against him upon Oath that he was in fear of receiving some bodily hurt from the said Daniel Carwick, the said Carwick appearing and offering nothing materiall to Excuse himself; It is Therefore Ordered that the said Daniel Carwick be Committed to the Sheriffs Custody there to remaine till he give good and sufficient Security in the Sume of Fifty pounds Sterling for his keeping the Peace.[29]

Henley fined

William Henley being by Vertue of a Warrant from John Tarpley Gentlemen one of his Majesties Justices of the Peace for this County bound over to appear at this Court to Answer the Complaint of John Doyle one of the Under Sheriffs of this County against him for refusing to aid and assist the said John Doyle to Carry one Margaret Richardson a Criminal then in his Custody to the Publick Goal at Williamsburgh which matter being fully proved by the Oath of the said John Doyle, and the said William Henley appearing but offering nothing materiall to Excuse himself; It is Ordered that the said William Henley be Fined the Sume of Five hundred pounds of Tobacco to Our Sovereign Lord the King, and that he give Security for the payment thereof.

[Mills fined]

John Mills came into Court and Acknowledged himself Indebted to Our Sovereign Lord the King his heirs and Successors in the full and just sume of Five hundred pounds of Tobacco, to be paid to Our said Sovereign Lord the King his heirs and Successors, in Case William Henley do not pay, att the Cropp,[30] the Sume of five hundred pounds of Tobacco, being the Fine laid on him by this Court for refusing to aid and Assist John Doyle to Carry Margaret Richardson a Criminal in his Custody [24] to the Publick Goal at Williamsburgh.

Reeves fined

Thomas Reeves Constable being bound over to appear at this Court by vertue of a Warrant from John Tarpley Gentleman one of his Majesties Justices of the Peace for this County for refusing to execute severall Warrants directed to him by the said John Tarpley, the said Thomas Reeves appearing but offering nothing materiall to excuse himself; It is therefore Ordered that the said Thomas Reeves be Fined the Sume of Five hundred pounds of Tobacco to Our Sovereign

---

29. An example of a bond to keep the peace; see Webb, *Justice of Peace*, 54–55. A single justice could swear a person to the peace and take security for performance, although, from the evidence of the *RCP*, it was common for recognizances for the peace to find their way onto the county court docket.

30. At harvest time.

Lord the King, as also that he give good and sufficient Security for his good Behaviour in the Sume of Fifty pounds Sterling.

Whereupon the said Thomas Reeves together with John Mills acknowledged themselves Indebted to Our Sovereign Lord the King his heirs and Successors in the Sume of Fifty pounds Sterling to be Levyed on their Lands and Tenements Goods and Chattles with Condition that if the said Thomas Reeves shall be of good Behaviour as well towards his said Majesties as all his Liege People, That then this Recognizance to be void and of none Effect, or else to remaine in full force.

Att a Court Continued and held for Richmond County the Eighth Day of September 1715.

Present: John Tarpley, Nicholas Smith, William Thornton, John Tayloe, Jonathan Gibson, Richard Taliafero, Gentlemen Justices.

Carwick bound to the Peace

Pursuant to an Order of Court past Yesterday Daniel Carwick together with Thomas Thorne acknowledged themselves Indebted to Our Sovereign Lord the King his heirs and Successors in the Sume of Fifty pounds Sterling to be Levyed on their Lands and Tenements Goods and Chattles with Condition that if the said Daniel Carwick [25] shall keep the Peace of Our Sovereign Lord the King toward his said Majestie and all his Liege People and Especially towards John Naylor; That then this Recognizance to be void and none Effect, or else to remain in full force.

Att a Court held for Richmond County the Seventh Day of March 1715/6.

Present: Alexander Doniphan, William Robinson, Nicholas Smith, William Thornton, John Tayloe, William Fantleroy, Gentlemen Justices.

Johnson bound to the Peace

Robert Johnson being by Vertue of a Warrant of William Robinson Gentleman one of his Majesties Justices of the Peace for this County bound over to appear at this Court to Answer the Complaint of William Tippet beating, wounding and maiming him, the said Robert Johnson accordingly appeared this Day in Court, and it appearing that he is a person of an ill behaviour: It is therefore Ordered that he give good and sufficient Security in the Sume of Ten Pounds Sterling for his keeping the Peace.

Whereupon the said Robert Johnson together with Henry Long acknowledged themselves Indebted to Our Sovereign Lord the King his Heirs and Successors in the Sume of Ten Pounds Sterling to be Levyed on their Land and Tenements, Goods and Chattles, with Condition that if the said Robert Johnson shall keep the Peace of Our Sovereign Lord the King towards his said Majestie and all his Liege [people] and especially towards William Tippet, That then this Recognizance to be void and of none Effect, or else to remain in full force.

Att a Court Continued and held for Richmond County the Eighth Day of March 1715/6.

Present: John Tarpley, William Robinson, Edward Barrow, William Fantleroy, Gentlemen Justices.

Leach fined

[26] William Williams being by Order of this Court putt in the Stocks for appearing drunk before the Court the said Williams being lett out of the Stocks by a Woman by the Advise of William Leach. It is therefore Ordered that he be fined the Sume of Fifty Shillings Currant Money to Our Sovereign Lord the King, also that he be putt in the Stocks there to remain the space of four hours, And it appearing to the Court that Sarah Kemp lett the said William Williams out of the Stocks; It is thereupon Ordered that she ask the Courts pardon for her said offense, and give good and sufficient Security for her good Behaviour.

[Kemp bound to her behavior]

Whereupon Martin Kemp the said Sarah Kemp's husband Acknowledged himself Indebted to Our Sovereign Lord the King his heirs and Successors in the Sume of Ten Pounds Sterling to be Levyed on his Lands and Tenements Goods and Chattles, with Condition that if the said Sarah Kemp shall be of good Behaviour as well towards his said Majestie as all his Leige People That then this Recognizance to be void and of none Effect or else to remain in full force.

Present:[31] Nicholas Smith, William Thornton and John Tayloe, Gentlemen [Justices].

Henderson fined

Att a Court held for this county the First Day of June 1715 John Henderson was presented by the Grand Jury upon the Information of John Doyle for keeping a Tipling house and retailing Drinks in Sittenbourn Parish the 15th of January last, to which the said John Henderson at a Court held for the said County the Seventh day of July last pleaded Not Guilty and thereupon put himself upon the Countrey,[32] and the same being Continued to this Court for

---

31. The clerk recorded the arrival of three more justices.
32. See ROB, No. 6, 284 (1715).

Tryall the Jury for Tryall of the matter in Issue were this Day Sworne by Name Thomas Taylor, Gabriell Alloway, George Paine, Robert Harrison, Robert Reynolds, Henry Wood, Thomas Petty John Naylor, Arthur Dye, Samuell Bayly, Hugh Harris and Thomas Paise who having heard the [27] Evidence and received their Charge were sent out, and soon after returning into Court gave in their Verdict in these words Wee of the Jury do find the Defendant Guilty of the Fact for which he is presented by the Grand Jury Thomas Paise Foreman, which Verdict at the Motion of Daniell McCarty the Kings Attorney is Ordered to be Recorded, whereupon it is Considered by the Court and the Court doth hereby Order that the said John Henderson doe give Security to pay at the Cropp unto Our Sovereign Lord the King One thousand pounds of Tobacco, as also to the said John Doyle the Informer One thousand Pounds of Tobacco (pursuant to the Law in that Case made and provided) together with Costs, Also Execution[;] Whereupon Francis Williams, James Henderson and Samuell Bayly came into Court and obliged themselves their Heirs etc. for the said John Hendersons payment of the said Two thousand Pounds of Tobacco and Cost as before Ordered at the Ensueing Cropp.[33]

Att a Court continued and held for Richmond County the Ninth day of March 1715 [1716].
Present: John Tarpley, William Robinson, Edward Barrow, William Fantleroy, Gentlemen Justices.

Leach's fine remitted

The Court taking into Consideration the Order passed on Wednesday last against William Leach upon the said William Leach's appearing in Court and with humble Submission on his Knees acknowledging his Offence and begging the Courts pardon, have Ordered that the Fine of Fifty Shilling Currant Money imposed on him by the said Order be remitted.

Att a Court Continued and held for Richmond County the Fifth Day of Aprill 1716.
Present: William Robinson, Edward Barrow, William Thornton, William Fantleroy, Gentlemen Justices.

Tippett bound to his Behaviour

[28] William Tippett according to Order this Day appeared and it appearing to the Court that he is a person of an ill behaviour, It is therefore Ordered that he give good and sufficient Security for his good Behaviour.

---

33. Another *qui tam*, with the informant given his share of the two-thousand-pound fine; *Statutes at Large*, 3:534–35 (1710).

Whereupon the said William Tippett together with Isaac Arnold and William Pitman acknowledged themselves Indebted to Our Sovereign Lord the King his heirs and Successors in the Sume of Forty Pounds Sterling to be Levyed on their Lands and Tenements Goods and Chattles with Condition that if the said William Tippett shall be of good Behaviour as well towards his said Majestie as all his Liege People, That then this Recognizance to be void and of none Effect, or else to remaine in full force.[34]

Att a Court Continued and held for Richmond County the Third Day of May 1716.

Present: John Tarpley, William Robinson, William Thornton, John Tayloe and William Fantleroy, Gentlemen Justices.

Arnold fined

Isaac Arnold being Summoned as a Jury Man to attend the Court this Day and not appearing when called Is hereby fined Two hundred pounds of Tobacco to Our Sovereign Lord the King according to Law.

Arnold's fine remitted

On the Motion of Isaac Arnold the fine of two hundred pounds of Tobacco laid on him by this Court this Day for his not appearing as a Jury Man is hereby remitted and it is Ordered that the same be not Levyed.

Rogers Bound to his Behavior

It appearing to this Court that Nicholas Rogers is a person of an ill Behaviour, It is therefore Ordered that he give good and sufficient Security for his good Behaviour.

[**29**] Whereupon the said Nicholas Rogers together with John Doyle acknowledged themselves Indebted to Our Sovereign Lord the King his heirs and Successors in the Sume of Ten Pounds Sterling to be Levyed on their Lands and Tenements Goods and Chattles, with Condition that if the said Nicholas Rogers Shall be of good Behaviour as well towards his said Majestie as all his Liege People, That then this Recognizance to be void and of none Effect, or else to remain in full force.

Att a Court held for Richmond County the First Day of August 1716.

Present: William Robinson, Nicholas Smith, John Tayloe, William Fantleroy, Gentlemen Justices.

---

34. Webb, *Justice of Peace*, 49–50, noted that, unlike swearing the peace, recognizances for good behavior were commonly ordered by two or more justices at the county court.

Davis fined

Complaint haveing been made the last Court by Edward Barrow Gentleman one of the Magistrates[35] of this County that Walter Davis was a Common Disturber of the Peace It was thereupon Ordered that the said Davis should be taken into Custody, who this Day appearing but offering nothing materiall to Excuse himself, It is therefore Ordered that the said Walter Davis be fined the Sume of Twenty Shillings to Our Sovereign Lord the King, and that he remain in the Sheriffs Custody untill he gives good and sufficient Security for his good Behaviour.

Att a Court Continued and held for Richmond County the Second Day of August 1716.
Present: Edward Barrow, Nicholas Smith, John Tayloe, William Fantleroy, Gentlemen Justices.

Davis's Fine remitted

The Court takeing into Consideration the Order passed Yesterday against Walter Davis, upon the said Davis's appearing in Court and with humble Submission acknowledging his Offence have ordered that the Fine of Twenty Shillings laid on him by the said Order be remitted.

[30] Att a Court held for Richmond County the fifth Day of December 1716.[36]
Present: John Tarpley, William Robinson, Charles Barber, Edward Barrow, Nicholas Smith, William Thornton, John Tayloe, William Fantleroy, Gentlemen Justices.

Arnold bound to his Behaviour

Isaac Arnold[37] together with Thomas James being by Vertue of a Warrant from William Robinson and Nicholas Smith gentlemen two of his Majesties Justices of the Peace for this County bound over to Appear at this Court on Suspition of Murthering one William Willis the said Isaac Arnold is a person of an ill behaviour, It is therefore Ordered that he give good and sufficient Security for his good Behaviour.[38] Whereupon the said Isaac Arnold together with Henry

---

35. Synonym for justices of the peace.

36. This hearing was obviously an examining court, though the clerk did not use the heading "At a Called Court." The latter phrase was not consistently used to introduce examining courts until 1727.

37. Arnold was late for jury duty on May 3, 1716 (see above), but his fine was remitted upon his petition.

38. Arnold bound himself to come to the court when it met the following day. In effect, this allowed him bail, though technically the bond was for good behavior.

Wood and John Breen acknowledged themselves Indebted to Our Sovereign Lord the King his heirs and Successors in the Sume of One hundred Pounds Sterling to be Levyed on their Lands and Tenements Goods and Chattles with Condition that if the said Isaac Arnold shall be of good Behaviour as well toward his said Majestie as all his Liege People, That then this Recognizance to be Void and of none Effect, or else to remaine in full force.

Att a Court Continued and held for Richmond County the Sixth Day of December 1716.

Present: John Tarpley, Edward Barrow, Nicholas Smith, William Fantleroy, Gentlemen Justices.

James bound to his Behaviour

Isaac Arnold and Thomas James being by Vertue of a Warrant from William Robinson and Nicholas Smith Gentlemen two of his Majesties Justices of the Peace for this County bound over to Appear at this Court on Suspition of murthering one William Willis, the said Thomas [31] James accordingly appeared and severall Evidences being produced and Examined but not proving the Fact,[39] Yet it appearing to the Court that the said Thomas James is a person of an ill behaviour, It is therefore Ordered that he give good and sufficient Security for his good Behaviour.

Whereupon the said Thomas James together with William James Acknowledged themselves Indebted to Our Sovereign Lord the King his heirs and Successors in the Sume of One hundred Pounds Sterling to be Levyed on their Lands and Tenements Goods and Chattles with Condition that if the said Thomas James shall be of good Behaviour as well towards his said Majestie as all his Liege People That then this Recognizance to be Void and none Effect or else to remain in full force.

Att a Court held for Richmond County the Third Day of April 1717.

Present: William Robinson, Charles Barber, Edward Barrow, Nicholas Smith, John Tayloe, William Fantleroy, Gentlemen Justices.

Dowling Whipt

It appearing to this Court that Nicholas Dowling feloniously[40] stole Tobacco from Joseph Belfield: It is therefore Ordered that the Sheriff give the said

---

39. The examining court had the power to dismiss charges. Arnold presumably appeared, for no order was issued upon his bond. Charges against him were evidently dropped, since he was not bound over to the county court or the General Court or punished by order of the justices at this hearing.

40. If the theft was grand larceny, that is, if the tobacco was valued at more than 12*d.*, the case should have gone to the General Court. If the court valued the tobacco at less than 12*d.*, the offense

Dowling One and Thirty Lashes on his bare Back well laid on, and that he give good and sufficient Security for his good Behaviour at the next Court.

Att a Court Continued and held for Richmond County the Second Day of May 1717.

Present: John Tarpley, William Robinson, Charles Barber, Nicholas Smith, John Tayloe, William Fantleroy, Gentlemen Justices.

Nugent for his Behaviour

It appearing to this Court that Dominick Nugent is a person of very ill behaviour, It is therefore Ordered that he give good and sufficient Security in the Sume of One hundred Pounds Sterling for his good Behaviour [32] and that he remain in the Common Goal untill he gives such Security before a Magistrate of this County.

Att a Court held for Richmond County the Fourth Day of September 1717.

Present: John Tarpley, William Robinson, Charles Barber, Nicholas Smith, John Tayloe, William Fantleroy, Gentlemen Justices.

Washington Judgement against him

William Deacon of this County having Sworn the Peace before William Robinson Gentleman one of his Majesties Justices of the Peace for this County against Lansdown Washington of Westmoreland County Carpenter thereupon the said William Robinson Issued out his Warrant for the apprehending the said Lansdown Washington, who being taken by Vertue thereof was Carryed before the said William Robinson and entered into a Recognizance in the Sume of Twenty Pounds to Our Sovereign Lord the King as also Charles Snead his Security in the Sume of Ten Pounds for his appearance at this Court, which he failing to doe Judgement is therefore Granted Our Sovereign Lord the King against the said Lansdown Washington for the said Twenty Pounds which is Ordered to be paid with Costs also Execution. And upon Consideration the Court are of Opinion and do accordingly Order that the said Charles Snead be discharged from his aforesaid Suretyship.[41]

---

was petty larceny, and Dowling should have had his day at the county court. In point of fact, the justices heard and determined the case in the examining court, ordering Dowling's punishment before they closed the session. The adjective "feloniously" connoted malicious intention rather than denoting the severity of the crime.

41. Washington swore the peace before a single justice, but when he failed to keep the peace against Deacon, the court ordered him to pay the bond and costs. Washington's surety, Snead, was discharged from his financial responsibility.

Davis, Junior bound to his Behaviour

John Davis Jr. this Day appeared according to Order of last Court to give Security for his good Behaviour etc., Whereupon the said John Davis Jr. together with James Wilson and Mathew Davis acknowledged themselves Indebted to Our Sovereign Lord the King his heirs and Successors in the Sume of Forty Pounds Sterling to be Levyed on their Lands and Tenements Goods and Chattles with Condition that if the said John Davis Jr. shall be of good Behaviour and keep the Peace as well towards [33] his said Majestie as all his Liege People for one Year and a Day That then this Recognizance to be void and of none Effect otherwise to remain in full force.

Att a Court Continued and held for Richmond County the Fifth Day of September 1717.

Present: John Tarpley, William Robinson, Charles Barber, Edward Barrow, Nicholas Smith, John Tayloe, and William Fantleroy, Gentlemen Justices.

Davis bound to his Behaviour

Mathew Davis appearing this Day drunk before the Court and being a person of an ill behaviour it is therefore Ordered that he give good and sufficient Security for his good Behaviour.

Whereupon the said Mathew Davis together with Thomas Mountjoy acknowledged themselves Indebted to Our Sovereign Lord the King his heirs and Successors in the Sume of Forty Pounds Sterling to be Levyed on their Lands and Tenements Goods and Chattles, With Condition that if the said Mathew Davis shall be of good Behaviour as well towards his said Majestie as all his Liege People for One Year and a Day that then this Recognizance to be Void and of none Effect, or else to remain in full force.

Att a Court Continued and held for Richmond County the Sixth Day of September 1717.

Present: William Robinson, Charles Barber, Nicholas Smith, John Tayloe and William Fantleroy, Gentlemen Justices.

Davis Junior Judgement against him

John Davis Jr. being on Wednesday last by Recognizance in the Sume of Forty Pounds Sterling bound to the Peace and his good Behaviour and he haveing Yesterday in the presence of these Magistrates broke the same [34] therefore on the Motion of the King's Attorney, Judgment is Granted Our Sovereign Lord the King against the said John Davis Jr. and James Wilson and Mathew Davis his Securityes for the said Sume of Forty Pounds Sterling which is Ordered to be paid with Costs also Execution.

Davis bound to his Behaviour

It appearing to this Court that Walter Davis is a refractory person and of an ill behaviour, It is therefore Ordered that he give good and sufficient Security for his good Behaviour and keeping the Peace. Whereupon the said Walter Davis together with Thomas Harper acknowledged themselves Indebted to Our Sovereign Lord the King his heirs and Successors in the Sume of Forty Pounds Sterling to be Levyed on their Lands and Tenements Goods and Chattles with Condition that if the said Walter Davis shall be of good Behaviour and keep the Peace as well towards his said Majestie as all his Liege People for One Year and a Day; That then this Recognizance to be void and of none Effect, or else remain in full force.

Davis Junior bound to his Behaviour

It appearing to this Court that John Davis Jr. is a person of very ill Behaviour, it is therefore Ordered that he give good and sufficient Security for his good Behaviour and keeping the Peace. Whereupon the said John Davis Jr. together with Thomas Harper Acknowledged themselves Indebted to Our Sovereign Lord the King his heirs and Successors in the Sume of Eighty Pounds Sterling to be levyed on their Lands and Tenements Goods and Chattles with Condition that if the said John Davis Jr. shall be of good Behaviour and keep the Peace as well towards his said Majestie as all his liege People for One Year and a Day; That then this Recognizance to be Void and of none Effect or else to remain in full force.

Mulatto Sawny his Tryall

[35] Att a Session of Oyer and Terminer held at Richmond Court house on Thursday the Third Day of Aprill 1718 in the Fourth Year of the Reign of Our Sovereign Lord George by the Grace of God King of Great Brittain France and Ireland Defender of the Faith and by Virtue of a Speciall Commission for the Tryall of all Treasons, petty Treasons or Misprisons thereof, Felonies Murthers or other Offenses or Crimes whatsoever Committed within the County of Richmond by a Mulatto Slave called Sawney belonging to Robert Carter Esq. directed to John Tarpley, William Robinson, Charles Barber Edward Barrow, Nicholas Smith, Thomas Griffin, John Tayloe Moor Fantleroy, Samuel Mathews and William Fantleroy Gentlemen.

Present: John Tarpley, Charles Barber, Edward Barrow, Nicholas Smith, John Tayloe and William Fantleroy, Gentlemen Justices.

Memorandum That on this Day being the Third Day of Aprill 1718 an Indictment was preferred against Sawney a Mulatto Slave belonging to Robert Carter Esq. in these words Richmond Ss April in the 4th Year of his Majesties Reign Anno. Do 1718.[42]

The Worshipfull his Majesties Justices of Oyer & Terminer for this County

---

42. *Anno Dominus*, in the year of our Lord.

aforesaid Daniel McCarty Attorney of Our said Lord the King for the County
afforesaid Came into Court and Gives the said Justices to understand and be
informed that Whereas Sawney a Mulato Slave belonging to Robert Carter Esq.
was lately Arrested and taken in the Parrish of North Pharnham in the County
afforesaid for Suspition of Felony in the same County by him Committed, that
is to say, for breaking a Mill house[43] there belonging to the said Robert Carter
Esq. and from thense stealing severall baggs of Meal to persons unknown
belonging and one of the Mill Measures with sundry other things and for
which he was duly Committed to the Sheriff of the County aforesaid to be by
him kept till he should thense be duly Delivered according to Law[;] who there
upon Committed the said Sawney to the Common Goal of the County afforesaid and the said Sawney in the said Goal of the said County in the Custody of
said Sheriff being the 10th Day of January in the Year of Our Lord afforsaid
[did] with Force and Arms the said Goal and Feloniously break, and out of the
said Goal and the Custodie of the said Sheriff did then and there Feloniously
goe at large whether he would, and against the will of the said Sheriff, and
against the Peace etc.

Da. McCarty Dom. Rex

[36] Whereupon the said Sawney was brought to the Barr and Arraigned for
the said Felony and then pleaded not Guilty and thereupon the Court proceeding on his Tryall and on hearing the Evidence, the Court are of Opinion that the
Fact is sufficiently proved, but that he ought not to dye for the same.[44] It is
therefore Ordered that he be Acquitted.

Also another Indictment was this Day preferred against the said Sawney for
breaking open the Mill house of the said Robert Carter and stealing Goods there
out in these Words.

Richmond Ss. April in the 4th Year of his Majesties Reign Anno Domini 1718.
The Worshipfull his Majesties Justices of Oyer and Terminer for the County
aforesaid Daniel McCarty Attorney of Our said Lord the King for the County
afforsaid Came into Court and Gives the said Justices to understand and be
informed, That whereas Sawney a Mulato Slave belonging to Robert Carter Esq.
on the last Day of August in the Year of Our Lord 1717 in the Afternoon of the
same Day in the Parrish of North Pharnham in the County afforsaid the Millhouse of the afforsaid Robert Carter with Force and Armes Feloniously and
Burglary did break and Enter[,] no person in the said Millhouse then being, and
from thense did and and carry away two Mill Peaks of the value of 2 Shillings
and one hatchett to the ax value of three Shillings of the Goods and Chattles of
the said Robert Carters did Feloniously take and Carry away. And also the said

43. That is, for breaking into the mill.
44. The justices found Sawney guilty of the felony of breaking jail but did not order his death for
that offense. They may have reasoned that Sawney did not understand he was committing a crime in
breaking jail when he was innocent of the original charge. Carter probably interceded for his slave,
for if he was guilty of the fact, and his conduct was criminal, there should have been some punishment. Perhaps Carter punished Sawney on the plantation, though this had nothing to do with the
oyer and terminer proceeding. Even if Sawney knew he was not guilty, "any suspected person, 'tho
upon common fame only, may be taken" when a felony has been discovered. In felony cases the
justices were supposed to order the confinement of a suspect already taken or give warrant for the
capture of one on the loose; Webb, *Justice of Peace*, 15.

Sawney on the 8th Day of December in the Year afforsaid in the Night of the same Day into the afforsaid Mill did again Feloniously break and Enter, and from thense did take and Carry away sundry Peices of the Cart Gear or hors harness of the Value of five Shillings to the said Robert Carter belonging and one bagg of Wheat Flour of the Value of Foure Shilling to a Certain Edward Bucklin belonging, no person [in] the said Mill then being[,] did Feloniously Steal and Carry away Contrary to the Peace.

Da. McCarty Dom. Rex.

Whereupon the said Sawney was brought to the Barr and Arraigned for the said Felony and there pleaded Not guilty and thereupon the Court proceeded on his Tryall and on hearing the Evidence the Court is of Opinion that he is not Guilty of the Felony for which he stands Indicted, It is therefore Ordered that he be Acquitted.

[37] Att a Court Continued and held for Richmond County the Fourth Day of September 1718.

Present: William Robinson, William Fantleroy, William Downman, and James Ingo, Gentlemen Justices.

Griffin whipt

It appearing to this Court that Richard Gifffin hath been Guilty of Forgery It is therefore Ordered that the Sheriff give the said Griffin One and Twenty Lashes on his bare Back well laid on and that he give good and sufficient Security for his good behaviour.

Att a Court held for Richmond County the First Day of October 1718.

Present: William Robinson, Nicholas Smith, John Tayloe, William Fantleroy, and Joseph Strother, Gentlemen Justices.

Taylor Committed to his Behaviour

It appearing to this Court that Humphrey Taylor is a person of an ill Behaviour; It is therefore Ordered that he give good and sufficient Security for his good Behaviour.

Lewis whipt

John Lewis Convicted at this Court for assisting Negro Will in Stealing of Hoggs; It is therefore Ordered that the Sheriff give the said Lewis Thirty Lashes on his bare Back well laid on, and that he give good and sufficient Security for his good Behaviour, as also for his refraining keeping Company with Mary Taylor.[45]

[38] Att a Court Continued and held for Richmond County the Fifth Day of March 1718 [1719].

Present: John Tarpley, Charles Barber, William Thornton, James Ingo and Joseph Strother, Gentlemen Justices.

Worsdell fined etc.

Richard Worsdell being bound over by John Tayloe Gentleman one of his Majesties Justices of the Peace for this County to appear at this Court to Answer the Complaint of Garratt Brickey for stollen Goods belonging to the said Brickey found in the said Worsdells Tobacco house among his Corn, the said Richard Worsdell accordingly appeared and Confessed the Fact; It is therefore Ordered that the said Richard Worsdell be fined the Sume of Five hundred pounds of Tobacco to Our Sovereign Lord the King, as also that he give good and sufficient Security for his good Behaviour. Whereupon the said Richard Worsdell together with Patrick Short and Owen Jones Acknowledged themselves Indebted to Our Sovereign Lord the King, the said Richard Worsdell in the Sume of Forty Pounds Sterling and the said Patrick Short and Owen Jones each in the Sume of Twenty Pounds Sterling to be Levyed on their Lands and Tenements, Goods and Chattles, with Condition that if the said Richard Worsdell shall be of good Behaviour as well towards his said Majestie as all his Liege People, That then this Recognizance to be Void and of none Effect, or else to remain in full force.

Dixon bound to his behaviour

It appearing to this Court that Luke Dixon is a person of an ill Behaviour; It is therefore Ordered that he give good and sufficient Security for his good Behaviour. Whereupon the said Luke Dixon together with William Grant Acknowledged themselves Indebted to Our Sovereign Lord the King in the Sume of Twenty Pounds Sterling to be Levyed on their Lands and Tenements Goods and Chattles with Condition that if the said Luke Dixon shall be of good Behaviour as well towards his said Majestie as all his Liege People That then this Recognizance to be Void and of none Effect or else to remain in full force.

Deekins bound to his behaviour

It appearing to this Court that William Deekins is a person of an ill Behaviour; It is therefore Ordered that he give good and sufficient Security for his good Behaviour.

[39] Present: Nicholas Smith, John Tayloe, Gentlemen Justices.

45. The statutory penalty for a freeman's first offense of stealing hogs was twenty-five lashes; *Statutes at Large*, 3:276 (1705). Assuming that "assisting" the theft was regarded as theft (the statute did not mention assistance), Lewis's five additional stripes probably resulted from the legal status of the man he helped. Assisting a slave commit a crime was more serious than committing the crime oneself, at least on this occasion. The justices appear to have regarded statutory rules for corporal punishment as coming within their discretion.

Davis fined

It appearing to this Court that Mathew Davis one of the Under-Sheriffs of this County received a Bribe of Five Shillings from one Thomas Phillips to put him on the Pannell of the Grand Jury for this County and to strike out of the said Pannell one Christopher Pridham, who he had before Summoned to be on the said Grand Jury; It is therefore Ordered that the said Mathew Davis be Fined the Sume of Five Pounds Sterling to Our Sovereign Lord the King.

Att a Court Continued and held for Richmond County the Seventh Day of May 1719.
Present: William Robinson, Charles Barber, Nicholas Smith, William Fantleroy, James Ingo, and Joseph Strother, Gentlemen Justices.

Ward fined

Henry Ward one of the Under Sheriffs of this County not haveing Summoned a sufficient number of able Grand Jury Men pursuant to an Order of this Court made the Second Day of Aprill last It is therefore Ordered that the said Henry Ward be Fined the Sume of Twenty Shillings Sterling to Our Sovereign Lord the King.

Att a Court Continued and held for Richmond County the Second Day of Aprill 1719.
Present: Charles Barber, William Thornton, William Fantleroy, James Ingo, and Joseph Strother Gentlemen Justices.

[Smith fined]

Robert Smith of the Parish of North Farnham haveing been presented by the Grand Jury for Tending of Seconds,[46] this Day appeared in Court to Answer the said Presentment, but offering nothing materiall in Barr there of, It is therefore Ordered that he be Fined Five hundred Pounds of Tobacco to Our Sovereign Lord the King for One Tythable person.

George Fined

[40] Richard George of the Parish of North Farnham haveing been presented by the Grand Jury for Tending of Seconds, being called this Day to Answer the said Presentment but not appearing, It is therefore Ordered that he be fined Six

---

46. Second quality tobacco; see *Statutes at Large*, 3:435–36 (1705). The fine was proportionate to the number of tithables who worked in the defendant's fields that year, five hundred pounds per tithable.

hundred Pounds of Tobacco to Our Sovereign Lord the King for Six Tythable persons.

Att a Court held for Richmond County the First Day of July 1719.
Present: Charles Barber, Nicholas Smith, John Tayloe, William Fantleroy, James Ingo and Joseph Strother, Gentlemen Justices.

The King v. Pratt and others

On the Seize [scire] facias at the Suit of Our Sovereign Lord the King against John Pratt, Cornelius Edmonds and Thomas Paise upon a Recognizance entered into by them to Our said Lord the King for One hundred Pounds Sterling at a Court held for this County the Seventh Day of September 1715[47] the Defendants haveing pleaded to the same Daniell McCarty Esq. the Kings Attorney on the behalf of his Majestie demurred to the said Pleas, which being now argued the said Pleas are over ruled and the Defendants being at the Barr and refusing to say anything further in stay of Judgment, therefore on the Motion of the said Daniell McCarty the Kings Attorney Judgment is Granted to Our Sovereign Lord the King against the said John Pratt, Cornelius Edmonds and Thomas Paise for the aforesaid Sume of One hundred Pounds Sterling, which is Ordered to be paid also Execution from which Judgment the Defendants by Robert Beverley their Attorney prayed an Appeal to the next Generall Court, which is Granted giveing Security Whereupon the said John Pratt together with John Morton Jr. in open Court Acknowledged themselves bound to Our Sovereign Lord the King in the Sume of Two hundred Pounds Sterling For Prosecuting the said appeal and paying all Damages according to Law.

[**41**] Att a Court held for Richmond County the Second Day of September 1719.
Present: William Robinson, Charles Barber, Nicholas Smith, William Thornton, John Tayloe, Jonathan Gibson, William Fantleroy, and James Ingo, Gentlemen Justices.

Battaly bound to his Behaviour

It appearing to this Court that Moseley Battaly is a person of an ill Behaviour, It is therefore Ordered that he give good and sufficient Security for his good Behaviour. Whereupon the said Moseley Battaly together with William Skrine

---

47. See p. xxx above. The case appears in the *RCP* because a judgment for the crown has been given. See *Statutes at Large*, 3:511–12 (1710) on "matters relating to her majesty's revenues."

Acknowledged themselves Indebted to Our Sovereign Lord the King the said Mosely Battaly in the Sume of Forty Pounds Sterling and the said William Skrine in the Sume of Twenty Pounds Sterling to be Levyed on their Lands and Tenements, Goods and Chattles, with Condition that if the said Mosely Battaly shall be of good Behaviour as well towards his said Majestie as all his Liege People that then this Recognizance to be Void and of none Effect, or else to remain in full force.

Att a Court held for Richmond County the Fourth Day of November 1719.
Present: William Robinson, Charles Barber, Nicholas Smith, William Thornton, William Fantleroy, James Ingo and Joseph Strother, Gentlemen Justices.

Reily Whipt etc.

Enoch Flower, Joseph Walker and John Reily haveing been committed to the common Goal of this County by Vertue of a Warrant from two of his Majesties Justices of the Peace for this County and they being now brought to the Barr of this Court and it being proved by the Oaths of the said Enoch Flower and Joseph Walker that the said John Reily had forged passes for them to travel from Pensilvania to North Carolina,[48] it is therefore Ordered that the Sheriff give the said John Reily Thirty Lashes on his bare back well laid on and it is further Ordered that the said John Reily remain in the said common Goal of this County untill the next Court without Bail or Mainprize. [42] And it is also Ordered that the said Enoch Flower and Joseph Walker be discharged upon paying fees etc.

Att a Court Continued and held for Richmond County the Third Day of March 1719/20.
Present: Charles Barber, Nicholas Smith, William Thornton, Joseph Strother, Gentlemen Justices.

Brenaugh Discharg'd

Samuell Brenaugh being this Day brought before this Court for the killing of Margaret Fossakey, It appearing to the Court by the Verdict of the Coroners Judgment that the Misfortune happen'd by the accidental firing of a Gun Charg'd with Powder and Lead that was in the hand of the said Samuell Bre-

---

48. Debtors, servants, and slaves needed passes to travel out of the colony. The colonial secretary appointed someone in each district to issue passes; *Statutes at Large*, 3:270–75 (1705). Using a forged pass was a misdemeanor, punishable by standing two hours in the pillory and making reparation for lost working time. Forging the pass was more serious, punishable with a £10 fine or thirty-nine lashes; *Statutes at Large*, 3:455 (1705). This was still a less severe penalty than for the common-law felony of forgery.

naugh a lad of about Ten Years of Age, It is therefore Ordered that the said Samuell Brenaugh be Discharged.[49]

Att a Court held for Richmond County the Fourth Day of May 1720.
Present: John Tarpley, Charles Barber, John Tayloe, William Fantleroy, William Downman, James Ingo, Gentlemen Justices.

Hornby fined

Daniell Hornby[50] being Summoned as a Jury to attend the Court this Day and not appearing when called Is hereby Fined Two hundred pounds of Tobacco to Our Sovereign Lord the King according to Law.

Barrow fined

Edward Barrow[51] Gentleman Sheriff of this County not haveing Summoned a competent number of Men duely Qualified for a Grand Jury to appear at this Court pursuant to an Order of last March fined Five Pounds Sterling to Our Sovereign Lord the King.

Roberts bound to his Behaviour

[43] It appearing to this Court that Robert Roberts is a person of an ill Behaviour, It is therefore Ordered that he give good and sufficient Security for his good Behaviour. Whereupon the said Robert Roberts together with John Spicer Gentleman Acknowledged themselves Indebted to Our Sovereign Lord the King in the Sume of Twenty Pounds Sterling to be Levyed on their Lands and Tenements Goods and Chattles with Condition that if the said Robert Roberts shall be of good Behaviour as well towards his said Majestie as all his Liege People for the term of Twelve Months next Ensueing, That then this Recognizance to be void and of none Effect, or else to remain in full force.

Att a Court held for Richmond County the Seventh Day of December 1720.
Present: Nicholas Smith, William Thornton, John Tayloe, William Downman and Joseph Strother, Gentlemen Justices.

---

49. Accidental death was excusable homicide if the defendant was not breaking the law when the incident occurred and had no intention of harming or threatening the victim. Killing a bystander by discharging a weapon accidentally was not a crime; Webb, *Justice of Peace*, 175. The coroner's jury (whose report was read at court) did not find that Brenaugh had any malice in discharging the weapon. Brenaugh's case is special. The suspect was a boy of ten, and under English statute (3 Henry VII, c.1) "infants," minors under fourteen years, were not to be presumed to have "felonious" intent. Without malice and premeditation, it was impossible for a minor to be charged with felonious homicide. If the infant had knowledge of "good and evil" and planned the murder, he could be tried and convicted for it, however; Webb, *Justice of Peace*, 176.

50. Hornby would join the county bench in 1733.

51. Barrow was a justice; he stepped down in 1721.

Nelson fined etc.

James Nelson Constable in Sittenbourn Parish by Virtue of a Warrant Granted by Nicholas Smith and James Ingo Gentlemen two of his Majesties Justices of the Peace for this County this Day appeared to Answer the Complaint of William Thornton Gentleman one of his Majesties Justices of the Peace for this County against him for refusing to obey the Order of the said William Thornton on the Fifth Day of October last past at the Court house of this County to take into his Custody two Runaway Servant Men, but haveing nothing materiall to offer to Excuse himself; It is therefore Ordered that the said James Nelson be fined the Sume of Five hundred Pounds of Tobacco to Our Sovereign Lord the King, as also that he give good and sufficient security for his good Behaviour, and that he remain in the Sheriffs Custody untill he gives such Security.

Yeats fined

Elias Yeats this Day appearing before this Court by Virtue of a Warrant issued out against him by John Tayloe Gentleman one of his Majesties Justices of the Peace for this County for Contemning a Warrant Granted by the said John Tayloe against him to Answer the Complaint of Samuell Godwin [**44**] but haveing nothing materiall to say for himself It is therefore Ordered that the said Elias Yeats be fined the Sume of Five hundred Pounds of Tobacco to Our Sovereign Lord the King as also that he give good and sufficient Security for his good Behaviour.

Whereupon the said Elias Yeats together with John Brown Acknowledged themselves Indebted to Our Sovereign Lord the King in the Sume of Twenty Pounds Sterling to be Levyed on their Land and Tenements Goods and Chattles with Condition that if the said Elias Yeats shall be of good behaviour as well towards his Majesty as all his Liege People That then this Recognizance be Void and of none Effect or else to remain in full force.

Wood bound to his Behaviour

It appearing to this Court that Henry Wood is a person of an ill Behaviour, It is therefore Ordered that he give good and sufficient Security for his good Behaviour, and that he remain in the Sheriffs Custody untill he gives such Security.

Rymer and all bound to their Behaviour

It appearing to this Court that Mark Rymer and Grace his Wife are persons of an ill Behaviour, It is therefore Ordered that they give good and sufficient Security for their good Behaviour, and that they remain in the Sheriff's Custody untill they give such Security.

At a Court held for Richmond County the First Day of March 1720/1.
Present: William Robinson, Nicholas Smith, John Tayloe, and James Ingo,
Gentlemen Justices.

Sawyer bound to his Behaviour

It appearing to this Court that Humphrey Sawyer is a person of an ill Behaviour, It is therefore Ordered that he give good and Sufficient Security for his good Behaviour and that he Remaine in the Sheriffs Custody untill he gives such Security.

[**45**] At a Court held for Richmond County the Seventh Day of June 1721.
Present: Charles Barber, Edward Barrow, John Tayloe, William Fantleroy,
William Downman and James Ingo, Gentlemen Justices.

Connell whipt etc.

Whereas Edmond Connell by Virtue of a Warrant from William Downman Gentleman One of the Magistrates of this County was brought before this court on Suspicion of Stealing of Sundry goods out of the Store house of Mr. Charles Brown and on Examination of Severall Evidences Touching the same It is the Opinion of this Court that the said Edmund Connell is guilty of the Crimes laid to his Charge It is therefore Ordered that the Sherrif take him and Carry him to the Common whiping post and give him Twenty Lashes on his bare Back well laid on, and then to keep him in his safe Custody till Saturday next at which Time the said Sherrif is Ordered to give him Nineteen Lashes more at the Store house Door where the Fact was Committed Then to keep him in his safe Custody till he Enters into bond with good and Sufficient Security or his good Behaviour.[52]

At a Court held for Richmond County the Fifth Day of July 1721.
Present: Charles Barber, Edward Barrow, John Tayloe, William Fantleroy,
James Ingo, Joseph Belfeild and Robert Tomlin, Gentlemen Justices.

Burroes bound to his Behaviour

It appearing to this Court that Mathew Burroes is a person of an ill Behaviour, It is therefore Ordered that he give good and Sufficient Security for his good Behaviour. Whereupon the said Matthew Burroes Together with Marmaduke Beckwith[53] and Michael Burroes Acknowledged themselves Indebted to Our Sovereign Lord the King the said Mathew Burroes in the Sume of Forty Pounds

---

52. The crime was evidently a pretty larceny. The court (not a trial jury because none was impaneled to hear this case) decided the goods were less than 1s. (12d.) in value.

53. The clerk of the county court.

Sterling and the said Marmaduke Beckwith and Michael Burroes in the Sume of Twenty pounds Sterling Each of them, to be Levyed on their Lands and Tenements goods and Chattles with [46] Condition that if the said Mathew Burroes shall be of good Behaviour as well Towards the said Majestie as all his Liege People That then this Recognizance be Void and of none Effect or Else to Remaine in full force.

At a Court Continued and held for Richmond County the Sixth Day of July 1721.

Present: Charles Barber, John Tayloe, William Fantleroy, James Ingo, Charles Colston, and Robert Tomlin, Gentlemen Justices.

Davis's fine Renew

On a Seize [Scire] Facias at the Suit of Our Sovereign Lord the King[54] against Mathew Davis on a fine Laid upon him for Five pounds Sterling to our said Sovereign Lord the King by Order of the Court Dated the 5th Day of March 1710 [1711] the said Mathew Davis being Duely Summoned to Show why the said Order should not be Renewed and being now Called but not Appearing the said Order is hereby Renewed for the said Sume of Five pounds sterling and it is Ordered that the said Mathew Davis pay the same to Our said Lord the King also Execution.

Negro Frank his Tryall

At a Session of Oyer and Terminer held at Richmond Court house on Wednesday the Second Day of August 1721 By Vertue of a Special Commission for the Tryall of all Treasons Petty Treasons or Misprisons thereof Fellonys Murthers or other Offences or Crimes whatsoever Committed within the County of Richmond by a Negro Slave Called Frank Directed to Charles Barber Edward Barrow John Taylor William Fantleroy William Downman James Ingo Charles Grymes Joseph Belfeild Charles Colston Robert Tomlin and John Metcalfe Gentlemen.

Present: Charles Barber [47], John Tayloe, William Fantleroy, James Ingo, Charles Grymes, Charles Colston, Robert Tomlin and John Metcalfe, Gentlemen Justices.

Memorandum That on this Day being the Second Day of August 1721 an Indictment was preferred against a Negroe Slave Called Frank in these words [Richmonds Ss] George Eskridge for and behalfe of Our Sovereign Lord the King Doth present that Frank a Negro man belonging to Henry Long of the

---

54. The crown sought to make Davis pay his fine. The ROB entry has not been found. The *scire facias* was a common-law writ used, in this case, to seek renewal of the original judgment or order, which expired a year and a day after it was originally issued.

parish of Hanover Late the County of Richmond now King Georges County for that he the said Negro Frank on the ninth Day of February In the year of Our Lord One Thousand Seven hundred and Twenty [1721] in the Night of the Same Day at the parish and County aforesaid into a Certaine Store house belonging to One Jonathan Gibson gentleman did with force and Arms etc. Feloniously and Burglariously Break and Enter and Ten gallons of Rum of the Vallue of Forty Shillings Sterling and Ten pounds of Sugar of the Value of Five Shillings Sterling[,] being the proper goods of the said Jonathan Gibson[,] Did then and there in a Felonious and Burglarious maner Steal and Carry away Contrary to the peace of our Lord Lord the King his Crown and Dignity.

G. ESKRIDGE

Whereupon the said Frank was brought to the Barr and Arraigned for the said Fellony and there pleaded not Guilty and noe Prosecutor,[55] nor Evidence appearing to prove that aforesaid Fact against him It is Therefore Ordered that he be Acquitted.

At a Court held for Richmond County the Second Day of August 1721.

Present: Charles Barber, William Fantleroy, James Ingo, Charles Grymes, Joseph Belfeild, Robert Tomlin and John Metcalfe, Gentlemen Justices.

Winn Acquitted

Thomas Winn this Day Appearing According to his Recognizance to Answer the Complaint of John Gower Concerning a Certain Quantity of wheat taken out of his house and on Examination of Several Evidences Touching the Same It is the Opinion of this Court that the aforesaid Crime Laid to [48] his Charge is not Sufficiently proved; It is therefore Ordered that he be Acquitted giveing Security for his good Behaviour. Whereupon the said Thomas Winn Together with Edward Bryan and Roger Thornton Acknowledged themselves as Indebted to Our Sovereign Lord the King the said Thomas Winn in the Sume of Forty Pounds Sterling and the said Edward Bryan and Roger Thornton in the Sume of Twenty pounds Sterling Each of them to be Levyed on their Lands and Tenements goods and Chattles with Condition that if the said Thomas Winn shall be of good Behaviour as well Towards his said Majestie as all his Liege people That then this Recognizance to be Void and of none effect or Else to Remaine in full Force.

McCarty Judgement against Robinson

Daniell McCarty brought his Action of Debt in this Court against William Robinson and Declared against him the said William Robinson for the Sume of Five hundred Pounds of Tobacco Due to Our Sovereigne Lord the King and the

---

55. Either Eskridge, prosecutor for the crown, or Gibson, the victim, who was the prosecutor in the older English sense of the party injured, failed to appear. The latter was far more likely because no oyer and terminer court ever convened in Richmond without the presence of the king's attorney.

said Daniel [McCarty] for that the said William Robinson Altho he had noe free hold in the County of Westmoreland on the 16th Day of September In the year of our Lord 1720 Did on the same Day at the County of Westmoreland Afore-said at an Election of Burgesses for the said County Presume to give his Vote for and to Elect a Burgess for the said County Contrary to the Force form and Effect of the Act of Assembly[56] in that Case made and provided etc. as in the Declaration is more at large Set forth the said Defendant being now Called to Come Forth to Answer the Same but not Appearing the Judgment of Last July Court is therefore Confirmed against the said Defendant and John Tarpley Gentlemen Sheriff of this County and Ordered that the said Defendant and the said Sherrif pay to Our Sovereign Lord the King and the said Daniel McCarty the Aforesaid Sume of Five hundred pounds of Tobacco also Execution.

At a Court held for Richmond County the Third Day of January 1721/2.
Present: Charles Barber, John Tayloe, William Fantleroy, William Downman, Joseph Belfeild, and Robert Tomlin, Gentlemen Justices.

Phillips whipt

Whereas Thomas Phillips by Vertue of a Warrant from Charles Barber gentleman One of the Magistrates of this County was brought before this Court on Suspicion of Picking open the Lock of George Sissons Chamber and taking out the Keg of his Syder house and Disposing of his Syder and on Examination of Severall Evidences Touching the Same, It is the Opinion of this Court that the said Thomas Phillips is Guilty of the Crime Laid to his Charge. It is therefore Ordered [49] that the Sherrif take him and Carry him to the Common whiping post and give him Tenn Lashes on his bare back well laid on.

Lewis fined

Whereas Charles Lewis One of the under Sherrifs of this County being Ordered by this court to take into his Custody Thomas Phillips and give him Ten Lashes on his bare back at the Common whiping post of his County, the said Thomas Phillips haveing made his Escape, It is therefore Ordered that the said Charles Lewis be fined for the Same Two hundred and Fifty pounds of Tobacco to Our Sovereign Lord the King.

At a Court held for Richmond County the Seventh Day of March 1721/2.
Present: Charles Barber, John Tayloe, William Downman, Charles Grymes, Joseph Belfeild, Charles Colston and Robert Tomlin, Gentlemen Justices.

---

56. The penalty for conviction for unlawfully voting in an election for the House of Burgesses was recoverable by an action of debt against the voter for the statutory amount; *Statutes at Large,* 3:172 (1699).

Squib whipt etc.

Whereas William Squib by Vertue of a Warrant from John Metcalfe Gentleman one of the Magistrates of this County was brought before this Court on Suspition of Stealing a parcell of Stem'd Straight Laid Tobacco and on Examination of Severall Evidences touching the Same, It is the Opinion of this Court that the said William Squib is guilty of the Crime Laid to his Charge, It is therefore Ordered that the Sherrif take him and Carry him to the Common Whiping post and give him Twenty Lashes on his bare back well Laid on and then to keep him in his safe Custody till the next Sitting of the Court, at which Time the said Sherrif is Ordered to give him Nineteen Lashes more on his bare back as aforesaid and then to keep him in his Safe Custody till he Enters into Bond with good and Sufficient Security for his good Behaviour.

Dawlton whipt etc.

Whereas Frances Dawlton by Vertue of a Mittimus from Charles Grimes gentleman One of the Magistrates of this County was Committed to the County Goal on Suspicion of Stealing of Sundry goods from the house of Mr. Samuell Bonum, and being [50] now brought before this Court and on Examination of Severall Evidences Touching the same, It is the Opinion of this Court that the said Frances Dawlton is guilty of the Crime laid to her Charge. It is Therefore Ordered that the Sherrif take her and Carry her to the Common whiping post and give her Twenty Lashes on her bare Back well Laid on, and then to keep her in his safe Custody till the next Sitting of the Court At which Time the said Sherrif is Ordered to give her Nineteen Lashes more on her bare back as aforesaid.

At a Court held for Richmond County the Fourth Day of Aprill 1722.
Present: Charles Barber, John Tayloe, William Fantleroy, William Downman, Joseph Belfeild, Robert Tomlin, Gentlemen Justices.

Martins Recognizance

Nicholas Martin in Open Court before his Majesties Justices Acknowledged himself Indebted to Our Sovereign Lord the King his heirs and Successors In the Sume of Tenn pounds Sterling To be Levyed of his Lands and Tenements goods and Chattles with Condition if he the said Nicholas Martin shall appear before this Court to give Evidence for Our said Lord the King against Frances Dawlton on Suspicion of Fellony, then this Recognizance to be Void or else to Remaine in Full Force.

At a Court held for Richmond County the Second Day of May 1722.
Present: Charles Barber, John Tayloe, William Faunteroy, William Downman, Charles Grymes, Joseph Belfeild, Robert Tomlin and John Metcalfe, Gentlemen Justices.

Lee's Recognizance

John Lee in Open Court before his Majesties Justices Acknowledged himself Indebted to Our Sovereign Lord the King his heirs and successors In the Sume of Tenn pounds Sterling to be Levyed of his Lands and Tenements goods and Chattles with Condition if he the said John Lee shall Appear [**51**] before this Court to give Evidence for Our said Lord the King against Thomas Swinley Then this Recognizance to be Void or Else to Remaine in full force.

At a Court held for Richmond County the Fourth Day of July 1722.

Present: John Tarpley, Charles Barber, John Tayloe, William Fantleroy, Charles Grymes, Joseph Belfeild, Robert Tomlin and John Metcalfe, Gentlemen Justices.

McClinchey fined

Jane McClinchey of Sittinbourne Parish haveing been Summoned to answer the Presentment of the Grandjury against her for Stoping and turning the Rolling Road to Churchills Quarter. And being now Called and not Appearing, It is Ordered that she be Fined for the same Tenn Shillings Currant money to Our Sovereign Lord the King.[57]

Davis Fined

Walter Davis of Sittenborne parish this Day Appearing to answer the present-ment of the grandjury against him for Concealing his Tythable, but Offering nothing Materiall in his Defence, It is Ordered that he be Fined for the same One Thousand pounds of Tobacco to Our Sovereigne Lord the King.[58]

At a Court Continued and held for Richmond County the Fifth Day of July 1722.

Present: John Tarpley, Charles Barber, John Tayloe, Charles Colston, Joseph Belfeild, and Robert Tomlin, Gentlemen Justices.

[*Swinley bound to his behavior*]

It Appearing to this Court that Thomas Swinley is a person of an ill Behav-iour; It is therefore Ordered that he give good and Sufficient Security for his good Behaviour Whereupon the said Thomas Swinley Together with John

---

57. This was the same 10*s*. fines he would pay to the informer under the statute on obstructing public roads; *Statutes at Large*, 3:392–93 (1705). No informer appeared, and the fine presumably went to the crown. The justices were flexible in such cases.

58. *Statutes at Large*, 3:258–61 (1705).

Gower and Edward Bryan Acknowledged themselves Indebted to Our Sovereigne Lord the King the said Thomas Swinley in the Sume of Tenn pounds Sterling and the said [52] John Gower and Edward Bryan in the Sume of Five pounds Sterling Each of them To be Levyed on their Lands and Tenements goods and Chattles with Condition that if the said Thomas Swinley shall be of good Behaviour as well Towards his said Majestie as all his Leige people Then this Recognizance to be Void and of none Effect or Else to Remaine in full Force.

At a Court held for Richmond County the First Day of August 1722.
Present: John Tarpley, Charles Barber, John Tayloe, James Ingo, Charles Grymes, Joseph Belfeild, Charles Colston and Robert Tomlin, Gentlemen Justices.

Chinn Fined

Whereas Mr. Rawleigh Chin haveing on the Second Day of May Last at the Court house of this County made Severall Breaches of the Peace before Two of the Magestrates of this County, It is therefore Ordered that he be Fined for same Twenty pounds Sterling to Our Sovereign Lord the King.

At a Court held for Richmond County the Fifth Day of September 1722.
Present: John Tarpley, Charles Barber, John Tayloe, William Fantleroy, Joseph Belfield, Robert Tomlin, Gentlemen Justices.

Wells Fined

The Information brought by George Eskridge who Sues as well for Our Sovereign Lord the King as himself against Stephen Wells for keeping Ordinary without Lycence the said Stephen Wells this Day Appeared and Produced Two Receipts for Twelve Shillings from the Clerk of this Court for keeping Ordinary Foure months which this Court Adjudged Insufficient And the said Stephen Wells Saying Nothing Further It is Considered by this Court and the [53] Court Doth hereby Order that the said Stephen Wells Doe pay at the Crop unto Our Sovereigne Lord the King One Thousand pounds of Tobacco As alsoe to the said George Eskridge the Informer One Thousand pounds of Tobacco Pursuant to the Law in that Case made and Provided Together with Costs also Execution.[59]

---

59. *Statutes at Large*, 3:395–96 (1705). This evidently was a *qui tam* proceeding, in which the informant received a part of the judgment, one thousand pounds of tobacco, though the statute does not mention informants. An earlier statute (*Statutes at Large*, 2:189 [1663]), did specify that the informer was to receive one-half of the fine collected from a violation of the penal laws.

Sherman Fined

Martin Sherman being Summoned as a Jury Man to attend the Court this Day and not appearing when called is hereby Fined Two hundred pounds of Tobacco to Our Sovereigne Lord the King according to Law.

At a Court held for Richmond County the Third Day of October 1722.

Present: Charles Barber, John Tayloe, William Fantleroy, James Ingo, Charles Grymes, Joseph Belfield, Robert Tomlin, John Metcalfe, Gentlemen Justices.

[Tune bound to his behaviour]

It appearing to this Court that William Tune is a person of an ill Behaviour, It is therefore Ordered that he give good and Sufficient security for his good Behvaviour.

Whereupon the said William Tune Together with Hugh Harriss Acknowledged themselves Indebted to Our Sovereigne Lord the King in the Sume of Twenty pounds Sterling to be Levyed on their Lands and Tenements goods and Chattles with Condition that if the said William Tune shall be of good behaviour as well Towards his said Majestie as all his Leige people for the Terme of Twelve months next Ensuing that then this Recognizance to be void and of none Effect or Else to Remaine in Full Force.

At a Court Continued and held for Richmond County the 7th Day of February 1722/3.

Present: John Tarpley, Charles Barber, John Tayloe, William Fantleroy, James Ingo, Charles Grymes, Joseph Belfeild, Charles Colston, Robert Tomlin and John Metcalfe, Gentlemen Justices.

Hinch bound to his Behaviour

It appearing to this Court that Gregory Hinch is a person of an ill Behaviour It is therefore Ordered that he give good and [54] Sufficient security for his good Behaviour.

Whereupon the said Gregory Hinch Together with John Tarpley Gentleman Acknowledged themselves Indebted to our Sovereigne Lord the King in the Sume of Twenty pounds Sterling to be Levyed on their Lands and Tenements goods and Chattles with Condition that if the said Gregory Hinch shall be of good behaviour as well Towards his said Majestie as all his Leige people for the Terms of Twelve months next Ensueing that then this Recognizance to be void and of none Effect or Else to Remaine in full Force.

Absent John Tarpley Gentleman.[60]

---

60. Tarpley stepped down from the bench as he was to be presented. His sureties were also justices of the peace, a show of solidarity and friendship within the country elite.

Tarpley bound to his Behaviour

Colonel John Tarpley of North Farnham parish haveing been Summoned to answer the presentment of the grand Jury against him for being a Common and Notorious Swearer to the Dishonour of Almighty God Contrary to Law and the evill Example of others and this Day appearing but Offering Nothing Materiall to Excuse himself it is the Opinion of this Court and accordingly Ordered that for the said Offence he give good and sufficient security for his good Behaviour Dureing the Terme of one year.[61] Whereupon the said John Tarpley Together with Charles Barber and Robert Tomlin in open Court acknowledged themselves Indebted to our Sovereigne Lord the King his heirs and Successors In the sume of Twenty pounds Sterling to be Levyed on their Lands and Tenements goods and Chattles with Condition that if the said John Tarpley shall be of good behaviour as well Towards his said Majestie as all his Leige people That then this Recognizance to be void and of none Effect or Else to Remaine in full Force.

Smith bound to his Behaviour

William Smith of the ponds of North Farnham parish haveing been Summoned to answer the presentment of the Grandjury against him for being a Common and Notorious Swearer to the Dishonour of Allmighty God Contrary to Law and the Evill Example of others and this Day appearing but offering Nothing materiall to Excuse himself it is the Opinion of the Court and Accordingly Ordered that for the said Offence he give good and sufficient security for his good behaviour Dureing the Terme of one year.

Whereupon the said William Smith Together with John Pursell in open Court Acknowledged themselves Indebted to our Sovereigne Lord the King his heirs and Successors In the Sume of Twenty pounds Sterling to be Levyed on their [55] Lands and Tenements, goods and Chattles with Condition that If the said William Smith shall be of good behaviour as well Towards his said Majestie as all his Leige people That then this Recognizance to be void and of none Effect or Else to Remaine in full Force.

Taylor bound to his Behavior

Docter Robert Taylor of North Farnham parish haveing been Summoned to answer the presentment of the Grandjury against him for being a Common and Notorious Swearer to the Dishonour of Allmighty God Contrary to Law and the Evill Example of others and this Day appearing but Offering Nothing Materiall to Excuse himself it is the Opinion of this Court and Accordingly Ordered that for the said Offence he give good and sufficient security for his good behaviour Dureing the Terme of one year.

Whereupon the said Robert Taylor together with George Thomson in open Court Acknowledged themselves Indebted to our Sovereigne Lord the King his heirs and Successors In the Sume of Twenty pounds Sterling to be Levyed on

---

61. A statutory fine of 5s. or fifty pounds of tobacco for each count of swearing could have been levied, but was not; *Statutes at Large*, 3:359–60 (1705).

their Lands and Tenements goods and Chattles with Condition that if the said Robert Taylor shall be of good Behaviour as well Towards his said Majestie as all his Leige people That then this Recognizance to be void and of none Effect or Else to Remaine in full force.

[Pridhams bound to their behavior]

Christopher Pridham of North Farnham parish having been Summoned to answer the presentment of the Grand jury against him for being a Common and Notorious Swearer to the Dishonour of Allmighty God Contrary to Law and the evill Example of others and this Day appearing but Offering Nothing Materiall to Excuse himself it is the opinion of this Court and accordingly Ordered that for the said Offence he give good and sufficient security for his good behaviour Dureing the Terme of one year.

Whereupon the said Christopher Pridham Together with John Yeatman and William Landman in open Court Acknowledged themselves Indebted to our Sovereign Lord the King his heirs and Successors In the Sume of Twenty Pounds Sterling To be levyed on their Lands and Tenements goods and Chattles with Condition that if the said Christopher Pridham shall be of good behaviour as well towards his said Majestie as all his Leige people That then this Recognizance to be void and of none Effect or Else to Remaine in full Force.

[56] John Pridham of North Farnham parish haveing been Summoned to answer the presentment of the grandjury against him for being a Common and Notorious Swearer to the Dishonour of Allmighty God Contrary to Law and the Evill Example of others and himselfe It is the Opinion of this Court and Accord-Accordingly Ordered that for the said Offence he give good and sufficient security for his good behaviour Dureing the Terme of one year. Whereupon he said John Pridham together with John Kinchelow in open Court Acknowledged themselves Indebted to our Sovereign Lord the King his heirs and Successors in the Sume of Twenty pounds Sterling to be Leveyed on their Lands and Tenements goods and Chattles with Condition that if the said John Pridham shall be of good behaviour as well towards his said Majestie as all his Leige people That then this Recognizance to be void and of noe Effect or Else to Remaine in full force.

Absent John Metcalfe gentleman.

Metcalfe Fined

John Metcalfe Surveyer of the Road from Champs Rolling house to a bridge known by the name of Barrows Bridge being Summoned to [answer] the presentment of the grandjury against him for not Clearing the said Road or Repairing his part of the said Bridge According to Law he this Day Appearing But offering Nothing Materiall in Barr It is therefore Ordered that he be Fined Fifteen Shillings to Our Sovereign Lord the King.

Absent Joseph Belfeild gentleman.

Belfield Fined

Joseph Belfeild Surveyer of the Road from Naylors hole to Barrows Bridge being Summoned to answer the presentment of the Grandjury against him for not Clearing the said Road or Repairing his part of the said Bridge According to Law he this Day appearing but offering nothing materiall in barr It is therefore Ordered that he be Fined Fifteen shillings to Our Sovereign Lord the King.

G. Webb Fined

Giles Webb Surveyor of the Road that Leads from Bolers Ferry to the County Road being Summoned to answer the presentent of the Grandjury against him for not Clearing the said Road According to Law he this Day Appearing but Offering Nothing materiall in Barr It is therefore Ordered that he be Fined Fifteen Shillings to our Sovereign Lord the King.

Clark Fined

William Clark Surveyer of the road that Leads from Mr. Glascocks Mill to Collonell Carters Coach Road being Summoned to answer the presentment of the grandjury against him for not Clearing the said Road According to Law he this Day appearing but Offering Nothing materiall in [57] Barr It is therefore Ordered that he be fined Fifteen Shillings to Our Sovereign Lord the King.

At a Court held for Richmond County the Sixth Day of March 1722/3.
Present: John Tarpley, Charles Barber, William Fantleroy, James Ingo, Charles Grymes, Robert Tomlin and John Metcalfe, Gentlemen Justices.

Yeat's Judgment Against him Renewed

On the Seize [scire] Facias at the Suit of Our Sovereign Lord the King against Elias Yeates and John Brown upon a Recognizance Entered into by them to our said Lord the King for Twenty pounds Sterling at a Court held for this County the Seventh Day of December 1720[62] the said Elias Yeats and John Brown being now Called and not appearing on the motion of Daniell McCarty the Kings Attorney Judgment is granted to our Sovereeigne Lord the King against the said Elias Yeats and John Brown for the aforesaid Sume of Twenty pounds Sterling which is Ordered to be paid also Execution.

Murrah bound to his Behaviour

It appearing to this Court that Gilbert Murrah is a person of an Ill Behaviour It is therefore Ordered that he give good and Sufficient security for his good

---

62. See p. 39 above. Yates had given bond for good behavior, and when he did not appear at the "next session," part of the condition of his pledge, the court ordered him and his surety, Brown, to pay the £20 to the crown.

behaviour. Whereupon the said Gilbert Murrah Together with Newman Brock-enbrough gentleman Acknowledged themselves Indebted to our Sovereigne Lord the King in the Sume of Twenty pounds Sterling to be Levyed on their Lands and Tenements goods and Chattles with Condition that if the said Gilbert Murrah shall be of good behaviour as well towards his said Majestie as all his Leige people for the Terme of Twelve months next Ensueing That then this Recognizance to be Void and of none Effect or Else to Remaine in full force.[63]

Draper bound to his Behaviour

Thomas Draper of North Farnham parish haveing been Summoned to answer the presentment of the Grandjury against him for being a Common and Notorious Swearer to the Dishonour of Allmighty God contrary to Law and the evill Example of others and this Day Appearing but Offering nothing Materiall to Excuse himself it is the Opinion of this Court and accordingly Ordered that for the said Offence he give good and Sufficient Security for his good behaviour Dureing the Terme of one year.

[58] Whereupon the said Thomas Draper Together with William Brocken-brough In open Court Acknowledged themselves Indebted to our Sovereign Lord the King his heirs and Successors in the Sume of Twenty pounds Sterling to be Levyed on their Lands and Tenements goods and Chattles with Condition that if the said Thomas Draper shall be of good behaviour as well towards his said Majestie as all his Leige people That then this Recognizance to be void and of none Effect or Else to Remaine in full force.

Smoot bound to her Behaviour

Jane Smoot of North Farnham parish haveing been Summoned to answer the presentment of the Grandjury against her for being a Common and Notorious Swearer to the Dishonour of Allmighty God Contrary to Law and the evill Example of others and this Day appearing but Offering Nothing Materiall to Excuse herselfe It is the Opinion of this Court and Accordingly Ordered that for the said Offence she give good and sufficient securty for her good behaviour Dureing the Terme of one year.

Whereupon the said Jane Smoot Together with Thomas Durham in open Court acknowledged themselves Indebted to Our Sovereigne Lord the King his heirs and Successors In the Sume of Twenty pounds Sterling to be Levyed on their Lands and Tenements goods and Chattles with Condition that if the said Jane Smoot shall be of good behaviour as well towards his said Majestie as all his Leige People That then this Recognizance to be void and of none Effect or Else to Remaine in Full Force.

Stone bound to his good Behaviour

William Stone of North Farnham parish haveing been Summoned to answer the presentment of the Grandjury against him for being a Common and Notori-

---

63. These and other recognizances to keep the peace were entered in the *RCP* because the bond might be paid to the crown if the offender did not keep his pledge.

ous Swearer to the Dishonour of Allmighty God Contrary to Law and the Evill Example of others and this day appearing but Offering Nothing materiall to Excuse himself It is the Opinion of this Court and Accordingly Ordered that for the said Offence he give good and Suffcent Security for his good behaviour Dureing the Terme of one year. Whereupon the said William Stone Together with Newman Brockenbrough gentleman in open Court Acknoweledged themselves Indebted to our Sovereign Lord the King his heirs and Successors In the Sume of Twenty pounds Sterling to be Levyed on their Lands and Tenements goods and Chattles with Condition that if the said William [59] Stone shall be of good behaviour as well Towards his said Majestie as all his Leige people That then this Recognizance to be void and of none Effect or Else to Remaine in full force.

Thornton bound to his Behaviour

Thomas Thornton of Sittenbourn parish having been Summoned to answer the presentment of the Grandjury against him for being a Common Drunkard and Common Disturber of the Peace to the Dishonour of God Contrary to Law and the Evill Example of others and this Day appearing but Offering nothing materiall to Excuse himselfe it is the Opinion of this Court and Accordingly Ordered that for the said Offence he give good and sufficient Security for his good behaviour Dureing the Terme of one year.

Whereupon the said Thomas Thornton Together with Stephen Wells in open Court Acknowledged themselves Indebted to our Sovereign Lord the King his heirs and Successors In the Sume of Twenty pounds Sterling to be Levyed on their Lands and Tenements goods and Chattles with Condition that if the said Thomas Thornton shall be of good behaviour as well towards his said Majestie as all his Leige people That then this Recognizance to be Void and of none Effect or Else to Remaine in full force.

At a Court held for Richmond County the Third Day of July 1723.

Present: Charles Barber, John Tayloe, William Fantleroy, James Ingo, Charles Grymes, Joseph Belfeild, Robert Tomlin, John Metcalfe, Samuell Peachey and Newman Brockenbrough, Gentlemen Justices.

Doniphan Fined

Daniel Doniphan by Vertue of a Warrant Granted by John Tayloe gentleman One of his Majesties Justices of the Peace for this County this Day Appeared to answer the Complaint of John Molloney for breaking open his house threatening to beat wound and [60] Evill intreat [evilly treat] him and haveing Nothing Materiall to Offer to Excuse himselfe It is therefore Ordered that the said

Daniel Doniphan be fined the Sume of Ten pounds Currant money to our Sovereign Lord the King and that he Remaine in Prison till he give good Security for his payment of it And also for his keeping the Peace and for his good behaviour.

At a Court Continued and held for Richmond County the Fourth Day of July 1723.

Present: Charles Barber, Thomas Griffin, John Tayloe, Joseph Belfeild, John Metcalfe and Samuell Peachey, Gentlemen Justices.

Chinn Fined

Whereas Mr. Rawleigh Chinn by Vertue of a Mittimus from Charles Barber Gentleman one of the Magestrates of this County was bound over to this Court for breaking the peace of our Sovereigne Lord the King by abusive words used to Colonel John Tarpley and this Day appearing but Offering Nothing materiall to Excuse himself It is therefore Ordered that he be fined for the same Five Shillings to our Sovereign Lord the King.

Present: James Ingo and Robert Tomlin gentlemen.

Dale Fined

Thomas Dale According to his Summons this Day appearing to Show Cause why he Refused to Assist the Sheriff in Conveying Mr. Rawleigh Chinn to the Goal of this County but Offering Nothing Material to Excuse himselfe It is therefore Ordered that he be fined for the same Five Shillings or Fifty Pounds of Tobacco to Our Sovereign Lord the King.

Dew Fined

[61] Ishmaell Dew According to his Summons this Day Appearing to Show Cause why he Refused to Assist the Sherrif in Conveying Mr. Rawleigh Chinn to the Goal of this County but Offering Nothing materiall to Excuse himself It is therefore Ordered that he be fined for the Same Ten Shillings or One hundred Pounds of Tobacco to our Sovereigne Lord the King.

Tune Fined

John Tune According to his Summons this Day appearing to Show cause why he Refused to Assist the Sherrif in Conveying Mr. Rawleigh Chinn to the Goal of this County but Offering Nothing materiall to Excuse himself It is therefore Ordered that he be fined for the same Five Shillings or Fifty Pounds of Tobacco To our Sovereigne Lord the King.

Bryan Fined

Wilfree Bryan according to his Summons this Day appearing to Show Cause why he Refused to Assist the Sherrif in Conveying Mr. Rawleigh Chinn to the Goal of this County but offering Nothing materiall to Excuse himself It is therefore Ordered that he be fined for the same Five Shillings or Fifty pounds of Tobacco to our Sovereigne Lord the King.

Hightower Fined

John Hightower According to his Summons this Day appearing to Show Cause why he Refused to Assist the Sherrif in Conveying Mr. Rawleigh Chinn to the Goal of this County but Offering Nothing Materiall to Excuse himself It is Therefore Ordered that he be Fined for the Same Five Shillings or Fifty pounds of Tobacco to our Sovereign Lord the King.

[Hightowre fined]

Charnell Hightowre According to his Summons this Day Appearing to Show Cause why he Refused to Assist the Sherrif in conveying Mr. Rawleigh Chinn to the Goal of this County but Offering Nothing materiall to Excuse himself It is therefore Ordered that he be fined for the Same five Shillings or fifty pounds of Tobacco to Our Sovereigne Lord the King.

Chapman Fined

[62] John Chapman being Summoned to Show Cause why he Refused to Assist the Sherrif in Conveying Mr. Rawleigh Chinn to the Goal of this County and being now Called and not appearing It is therefore Ordered that he be fined for the same Five Shillings or Fifty pounds of Tobacco to our Sovereign Lord the King.

Morris Fined

Edward Morris According to his Summons this Day Appearing to Show Cause why he Refused to Assist the Sherrif in Conveying Mr. Rawleigh Chinn to the Goal of this County but Offering Nothing materiall to Excuse himself It is Therefore Ordered that he be fined for the Same Five Shillings or Fifty pounds of Tobacco to Our Sovereign Lord the King.

Harris Fined

Hugh Harris According to his Summons this Day Appearing to Show Cause why he Refused to Assist the Sherrif in Conveying Mr. Rawleigh Chinn to the Goal of this County but Offering Nothing materiall to Excuse himself It is therefore Ordered that he be Fined for the same Five Shillings or Fifty pounds of Tobacco to Our Sovereign Lord the King.

Walker Fined

William Walker According to his Summons this Day appearing to Show Cause why he Refused to Assist the Sherrif in Conveying Mr. Rawleigh Chinn to the Goal of this County but Offering Nothing materiall to Excuse himself It is therefore Ordered that he be Fined for the same Five Shillings or Fifty pounds to Our Sovereign Lord the King.

Chinn Fined and Bound to Peace

Mr. Rawleigh Chinn being by Vertue of a Warrant from John Tarpley gentleman One of his Majesties Justices of the peace for this County bound over to Appeare at this Court to answer the Complaint of Alexander Clarke one of the under Sherrifs of this County against him for Laying Violent hands on him and Whiping him with his horse whip without any Provocation which matter being fully proved by the said Allexander Clarke [63] And the said Rawleigh Chinn Offering Nothing materiall to excuse himself It is therefore Ordered that the said Rawleigh Chinn be Fined the Sume of Twenty Shillings to our Sovereign Lord the King. And also that he give good and sufficient Security for his keeping the peace in the sume of Forty pounds Sterling.

Whereupon the said Rawleigh Chinn Together with Tobias Phillips in open Court Acknowledged themselves Indebted to Our Sovereign Lord the King his heirs and Successors In the Sume of Forty Pounds Sterling to be Levyed on their Lands and Tenements goods and Chattles[64] with Condition that if the said Rawleigh Chinn Shall keep the peace of our Lord the Sovereign King Towards his said Majestie and all his Leige People and especially towards Allexander Clarke That then this Recognizance to be Void and of none Effect or Else to Remaine in full force.

Taylor Bound to his Behaviour

Thomas Taylor of North Farnham parish haveing been summoned to answer the presentment of the grandjury against him for being a Wicked and Common profaine Swearer and this Day Appearing but offering nothing materiall to excuse himselfe It is the Opinion of this Court and accordingly Ordered that for the said Offence he give good and Sufficient Security for his good Behaviour Dureing the Terme of one yeare.

Whereupon the said Thomas Taylor together with Robert Tomlin in open Court Acknowledge Themselves Indebted to Our Sovereign Lord the King his heirs and Successors in the Sume of Twenty Pounds Sterling to be Levyed on their Lands and Tenements goods and Chattles with Condition that if the said Thomas Taylor shall be of good Behaviour as well towards his said Majestie as all his Liege people, that then this Recognizance to be Void and of none Effect, or Else to Remaine in full force.

---

64. The court fined male bystanders in the courtyard for failing to assist the court's officers in detaining Chinn and Chinn himself for violently mishandling the officer. Using financial penalties, the court reimposed its authority on Chinn and the men who let him flee the scene. A disruptive incident was thus contained.

Sconce bound to his Behaviour

John Sconce of North Farnham parish haveing been Summoned to answer the presentment of the Grandjury against him for being a Wicked and Common Profaine Swearer and this Day appearing but offering nothing materiall to excuse himselfe It is the Opinion of this Court and Accordingly Ordered that for the said Offence he give good and Sufficient Security for his good Behaviour Dureing the Terme of One yeare.

Whereupon the said John Sconce together with John Benjer [64] in Open Court Acknowledged themselves Indebted to our Sovereign Lord the King his heirs and Successors In the Sume of Twenty pounds Sterling to be Levyed on their Lands and Tenements goods and Chattles with Condition that if the said John Sconce shall be of good Behaviour as well Towards his said Majestie as all his Leige People, That then this Recognizance to be Void and of none Effect or Else to Remaine in full force.

Webster bound to his Behaviour

Moses Webster of North Farnham parish having been Summoned to answer the presentment of the grandjury against him for being a Wicked and Common profaine Swearer and this Day appearing but offering nothing materiall to Excuse himselfe It is the Opinion of this Court and Accordingly Ordered that for the said Offence he give good and Sufficient Security for his good Behaviour Dureing the Terme of one yeare.

Whereupon the said Moses Webster Together with Robert Davis in open Court Acknowledged themselves Indebted to Our Sovereign Lord the King his heirs and Successors In the Sume of Twenty Pounds Sterling to be Levyed on their Lands and Tenements goods and Chattles with Condition that if the said Moses Webster shall be of good Behaviour as well towards his said Majestie as all his Leige people that then this Recognizance to be Void and of none Effect or Else to Remaine in full force.

At a Court held for Richmond County the Seventh Day of August 1723.
Present: Charles Barber, William Fantleroy, James Ingo, Charles Grymes, Joseph Belfeild, Robert Tomlin, Samuell Peachey and Newman Brockenbrough, Gentlemen Justices.

Jones Bound to his Behaviour

John Jones of North Farnham parish haveing been Summoned to Answer the Presentment of the Grandjury [65] against him for being a Wicked and Common profaine Swearer and this Day appearing but Offering nothing materiall to Excuse himselfe It is the Opinion of this Court and accordingly Ordered that for the said Offence he give good and Sufficient security for his good Behaviour Dureing the Terme of one yeare.

Whereupon the said John Jones Together with John Branham in open Court Acknowledged themselves Indebted to our Sovereign Lord the King his heirs and Successors in the Sume of Twenty pounds Sterling to be Levyed on their Lands and Tenements goods and Chattles with Condition that if the said John Jones shall be of good Behaviour as well towards his said Majestie as all his Leige People that then this Recognizance to be Void and of none Effect or Else to Remaine in full force.

Freshwater bound to his Behaviour

Thomas Freshwater of North Farnham parish having been Summoned to answer the presentment of the Grandjury against him for being a Wicked and Common Profaine Swearer and this Day by his Attorney appearing but Nothing materiall being Offering to Excuse him It is the Opinion of this Court and accordingly Ordered that for the said Offence he give good and Sufficient Security for his good Behaviour dureing the Terme of one yeare.

Whereupon George Eskriege and John Tarpley Jr. gentlemen In Open Court acknowledged themselves Indebted to our Sovereign Lord the King his heirs and Successors In the Sume of Twenty Pounds Sterling To be Levyed on their Lands and Tenements goods and Chattles with Condition that if the said Thomas Freshwater shall be of good Behaviour as well towards his said Majestie as all his Leige People That then this Recognizance to be void and of none Effect or Else to Remain in full force.

[66] At a Court held for Richmond County the Fourth Day of September 1723.

Present: Charles Barber, Thomas Griffin, John Tayloe, James Ingo, Charles Grymes, Joseph Belfield, Robert Tomlin and Samuell Peachey, Gentlemen Justices.

Renolds's Examination

Whereas Elizabeth Renolds was by warrant of Charles Barber gentleman One of the Justices of this Court Committed to the County Goal on Suspition of privately burying of a Child born of her body which by Law was a bastard and being now brought before his Majesties Justices here present being Examined saith that she had a Child Lately borne of her body but that the same was born Dead and that Burgess Longworth was a Witness to the same whereupon the said Burgess Longworth was Called and being Sworn saith that he was with the said Elizabeth Renolds when she was Delivered of a Child but that the same was borne Dead.[65] It is therefore Ordered that she be Discharged out of Custody Paying Fees.

At a Court Continued and held for Richmond County the Fifth Day of December 1723.

Present: Charles Barber, John Tayloe, William Fantleroy, Joseph Belfield, Robert Tomlin and John Metcalfe, Gentlemen Justices.

Davis Fined

George Davis of Sittenboure Parish having been summoned to answer the Presentment of the Grandjury against him for breaking the Peace of our Sovereign Lord the King and being this Day Called and not appearing It is Ordered that for his said Offence he be Fined Five [67] pounds Currant money to our said Sovereigne Lord the King.

Jones bound to his Behaviour

Jonathan Jones of North Farnham Parish haveing been Summoned to answer the Presentment of the Grandjury against him for being a Wicked and Common Profaine Swearer and this Day appearing but Offering Nothing materiall to excuse himself It is the Opinion of this Court and Accordingly Ordered that for the said Offence he give good and sufficient Security for his good Behaviour Dureing the terme of one yeare.

Whereupon the said Jonathan Jones together with Benjamin Rust in Open Court Acknowledged themselves Indebted to our Sovereign Lord the King his heirs and Successors in the sume of Twenty pounds Sterling to be Levied on their Lands and Tenements goods and Chattles with Condition that if the said Jonathan Jones shall be of good behaviour as well Towards his said Majestie as all his Leige People that then this Recognizance to be void and of none Effect or Else to Remaine in full Force.

At a Call'd Court held at the Court house of Richmond County the Eleventh Day of January 1723/4.

Present: Charles Barber, Thomas Griffin, John Tayloe, James Ingoe, Joseph Belfield, John Metcalfe, Samuell Peachey and Newman Brockenbrough, Gentlemen Justices.

---

65 English and Virginia law after 1710 provided that testimony of a witness to the stillbirth of a bastard child absolved the mother of the charge of murdering the infant. See n. 15 above.

Glascock's Examination

Whereas Gregory Glascock was by Warrant of Charles Barber gentleman One of the Justices of this Court Committed to the County Goal on Suspicion of Conveying away in a Small boat Thomas Glascock who made an Assault on the Body of William Forrester by Stabbing him [68] with a knife by means whereof the said Forrester Instantly Dyed and the said Gregory Glascock being now brought before his Majestie Justices here present the Depositions of the Evidences, and the Examination of the said Gregory Glascock are as followeth.

Glascock's Deposition

John Glascock aged Twenty Four years or thereabouts being Sworn saith that on the Fifth of November last about midnight he see Thomas Glascock and Gregory Glascock set of in a boat from Thomas Glascocks Landing on Farnham Creek and that the said Gregory Glascock assisted in Carrying Down from the house to the said boat Provisions and other goods and that he alsoe see the said Gregory Glascock Set the said Boat of[f] from the Landing with an Oar about the Distance of Forty yards and further saith not.

T. Glascocks Deposition

Thomas Glascock aged Eighteen years or thereabouts being Sworn Saith that on the Fifth of November Last about midnight he see Thomas Glascock and Gregory Glascock set of in a boat from Thomas Glascocks Landing on Farnham Creek and that the said Gregory Glascock Assisted in Carrying Down from the house to the said boat Provisions and other goods and that he alsoe see the said Gregory Glascock set the said Boat of from the Landing with an oar about the Distance of Forty yards and further saith not.

Gregory Glascock being Examined saith that on the Fifth of November Last about midnight he set of in a boat with his father Thomas Glascock from their Landing, and the next morning his Father put him on Shoar the other side of the River about five miles below Moratticoe Creek, and then he Travelled to [69] Glocester Town and went over the Ferrey to York Town and from thence went to Hampton Town and soe went over James River and Landed at one Willsons. And from thence Traveled through Norfolk Town and went to a Place Called the Northwest Landing, and then came back about Two Days before Christmass to the house of one Nehimiah Jones, and from thence made the best of his way home.

On hearing of the Evidences and Confession of the party the Court are of Opinion that the said Gregory Glascock is an Accessary after the murther Committed by his father Thomas Glascock on William Forrester but the principall not being Attaineed,[66] that noe Indictment will lye against the Accessary, therefore the said Gregroy Glascock is Admitted to Baile.

---

66. Possibly "attainted," meaning convicted or outlawed for a felony. Attainder was a parliamentary act condemning an offender; no trial was involved. The defendant forfeited his goods and chattels. The world also may have meant "attained," as in captured. In any case, the younger Glascock was accused of being an accessory to a felony but was bailed. See "Introduction," p. xxi.

Glascock's Recognizance

Whereupon the said Gregory Glascock together with George Devonport and Hugh Harris Acknowledged themselves Indebted to our Sovereigne Lord the King the said Gregroy Glascock in the sume of Forty Pounds Sterling and the said George Devonport and Hugh Harris Each in the sume of Twenty Pounds Sterling to be Levyed on their Lands and Tenements goods and Chattles with Condition that if the said Gregory Glascock shall make his Personall appearance before the Court of this County at any time when thereunto Called within a Twelve month and Day, Then this Recognizance to be void and of None Effect or Else to Remaine in full Force.

At a Court held for Richmond County the Fifth Day of February 1723/4.
Present: Charles Barber, William Fantleroy, James Ingo, Joseph Belfield and Robert Tomlin Gentlemen Justices.

[Douglas's Examination]

[**70**] Whereas Randolph Douglas was by Vertue of a Mittimus from John Tayloe gentleman One of the Justices of this Court Committed to the County Goal for Felioniously Robbing the house of George Walton on monday the Thirtieth Day of December 1723 and being now brought before his Majesties Justices here present was Examined by the Court as Followeth.

Court: You hear what is Laid to your Charge, was it you that Robbed the house of George Walton[?]
Answer: Yes, I went into the house of George Walton Between the houres of Twelve and One a Clocke in the Day Time, the Doores being Open, and I took Two pair of Breeches, two Jackets, two Pair of Stokins and One hatt.

It appearing to the Court upon the aforesaid Examination that there is Just Cause for Trying the said Prisoner at the Generall Court for the Crime of Fellony whereof he is Accused, It is therefore Ordered that the said Randolph Douglas be Remanded to the Prison of this County under the Custody of the Sheriff and from thence to be Conveyed to the Publick Goal of Williamsburgh as the Law in such Cases Direct.

Walton's Recognizance

George Walton in Open Court before his Majesties Justices Acknowledged himself Indebted to Our Sovereigne Lord the King his Heirs and Successors in the sume of Ten Pounds Sterling to be Levyed of his Lands and Tenements goods and Chattles with Condition that if the said George Walton shall personally appeare at the next Generall Court on the Fourth Day thereof and then and there give such Evidence as he knows against Randolph Douglas Concearning

his Feloniously [71] Stealing of two pair of Breeches, two Jackets, two pair of Stokins, and One hatt, the goods of the said George Waltons, and Doe not Depart
thence without Leave of that Court That then this Recognizance to be void Or
Else to Remain in full Force.

At a Court held for Richmond County the Fourth Day of March 1723/4.

Present: Charles Barber, John Tayloe, William Fantleroy, James Ingo, Charles
Grymes, Joseph Belfeild, Charles Colston, Robert Tomlin, John Metcalfe, Samuell Peachey and Newman Brockenbrough, Gentlemen Justices.

Dodson and Draper Fined and bound to their Behaviour

Whereas Batholomew Richard Dodson and Thomas Draper being by Vertue
of A Warrant from John Tayloe Gentleman One of the Magestrates of this
County bound over to appear at this Court to answer the Complaint of Christopher Pridham for that they the said Dodson and Draper came to his Ordinary
at the Court house of this County on Thursday the 13th Day of February Last
and then and there without any Provokation Did Assault the body of the said
Pridham Robert Mathews and William Rust and then did beat wound and Pursue with Staves, Clubbs, Stones, and Chaires; that the said Pridham and his
Family being in Danger of their Lives barred themselves up in his house which
the said Draper and Dodson with Force and Armes Attempted Diverse Times to
Break open Contrary to the Kings Peace etc., The said Bartholomew Richard
Dodson and Thomas Draper Accordingly appeared this Day in Court and Severall Evidences being Examined who fully Proved the Facts laid to their Charge, It
is therefore Ordered that they Each of them be Fined Tenn [72] Pounds Current
Money to Our Sovereign Lord the King, and that they give good and Sufficient
security for the Payment of it, and alsoe that they Each of them give good and
sufficient Security in the sume of Forty Pounds Sterling and their Securitys Each
of them in the sume of Twenty Pounds Sterling for keeping the Peace, and that
they Remaine in the Sherrifs Custody untill they give such Security.

Draper's Recognizance

Thomas Draper Hugh Harris and Henry Fann Came into Court and Acknowledged themselves Indebted to our Sovereign Lord the King his heirs and
Successors the said Thomas Draper in the sume of Forty Pounds Sterling and
the said Hugh Harris and Henry Fann Each of them in the sume of Twenty
Pounds Sterling to be Levied on their Lands and Tenements Goods and Chattles
upon Condition that if the said Thomas Draper shall pay Ten pounds Current
money when Ordered it being a Fine Laid upon him by this Court and shall keep
the Peace of Our Sovereign Lord the King Towards his said Majestie and all his
Leige People and Especially towards the said Christopher Pridham Robert Mathews and William Rust That then this Recognizance to be Void and of None
Effect or Else to Remaine in full Force and Vertue.

Molloney bound to his Behaviour

It appearing to this Court that John Molloney is a person of an ill Behaviour It is therefore Ordered that he give good and sufficient Security for his good behaviour.

Whereupon the said John Molloney Together with William Nash Acknowledged themselves Indebted to Our Sovereign Lord the King the said John Molloney in the sume of Forty Pounds sterling and the said William Nash in the sume of Twenty Pounds Sterling To be Levied on their Land and Tenements Goods and Chattles with Condition that if the said John Molloney shall be of Good Behaviour as well Towards his said Majestie as all his Leige People That then this [73] Recognizance to be Void and of None Effect or Else to remaine in full Force.

Velden's Recognizance

Francis Velden in Open Court before his Majesties Justices Acknowledged himself Indebted to Our Sovereign Lord the King his heirs and Successors in the sume of Tenn Pounds Sterling to be Levied of his Lands and Tenements Goods and Chattles with Condition if he the said Francis Velden shall Appeare before the Honorable The Generall Court next Comeing on the Fourth Day thereof and soe Attend from time to time as the said Court shall Direct then and there to give Evidence for Our said Lord the King against Randolph Douglas Concearning his Feloniously Stealing of Two pairs of Breeches Two Jackets Two Paire of Stokins and one hatt, the goods of George Waltons[,] and Doe not Depart thence without Leave of that Court That then this Recognizance to be void or Else to Remaine in full Force.

At a Court held for Richmond County the First Day of Aprill 1724.
Present: Charles Barber, John Tayloe, William Fantleroy, James Ingo, Robert Tomlin and Samuell Peachey, Gentlemen Justices.

Dodson's Recognizance

Bartholomew Richard Dodson William Stone and Lambert Dodson Came into Court and Acknowledged themselves Indebted to Our Sovereign Lord the King his heirs and Successors the said Bartholomew Richard Dodson in the Sume of Forty pounds Sterling and the said William Stone and Lambert Dodson Each of them in the sume of Twenty Pounds Sterling to be Levied on their Lands and Tenements Goods and Chattles upon Condition that if the said Bartholomew Richard [74] Dodson shall pay Tenn Pounds Current money when Ordered[,] It being a fine Laid upon him by this Court, and shall keep the Peace of Our Sovereign Lord the King Towards his said Majestie and all his Liege People and Especially Towards Christopher Pridham Robert Mathews and William Rust

That then this Recognizance to be void and of None Effect or Else to Remaine in full Force and Vertue.

At a Court held for Richmond County the First Day of Aprill 1724.

Present: Charles Barber, Thomas Griffin, John Tayloe, William Fantleroy, James Ingo, Charles Colston, Robert Tomlin and Samuell Peachey, Gentlemen Justices.

[*Geithings's Examination*]

Whereas Andrew Geithings being by Vertue of a Warrant from John Tayloe Gentlemen One of the Magestrates of this County Bound over to appeare at this Court to answer the Complaint of James Hill for that the said Andrew Geithings without any Provokation gave the said James Hill a very Large and Dangerous wound in his Back with an Ax being at the same Time in the Peace of Our Sovereign Lord the King etc. The said Andrew Geithings accordingly appeared this Day in Court and the said James Hill and Francis Suttle being Examined upon Oath who Fully proved the Fact Laid to his Charge, It is the Opinion of this Court that he has Forfeited his Former Recognizance Entered into in February Court last, It is Therefore Ordered that he give good and Sufficient Security In the sume of Forty Pounds Sterling, and his Two Securitys Each of them in the sume of Twenty Pounds Sterling for keeping the Peace, and that he remaine in the Sherrifs Custody untill he give such Security.

[**75**] At a Court held for Richmond County the Sixth Day of May 1724.

Present: Charles Barber, John Tayloe, Thomas Griffin, William Fantleroy, James Ingo, Joseph Belfield, Robert Tomlin and John Metcalfe, Gentlemen Justices.

Tomlinson Fined

Edward Tomlinson being Summoned as a Jury Man to Attend the Court this Day and not appearing when Called Is hereby Fined Four hundred Pounds of Tobacco to Our Sovereign Lord the King according to Law.

Present Charles Colston Gentleman.

Fann bound to the Peace

Whereas Mary Clarke Haveing Sworn the Peace against Winifred Fann before Charles Barber gentleman One of the Magistrates of this County, It is therefore Ordered that she give Security for Keeping the same. Whereupon William Stone and Leonard Hart Acknowledged themselves Indebted to Our Sovereigne Lord the King his heirs and Successors Each of them in the sume of Twenty pounds Sterling to be Levied on their Lands and Tenements goods and Chattles with Condition that if the said Winifred Fann shall keep the Peace of our Sovereign Lord the King as well Towards his said Majestie as all his Liege People but more Especially Towards the said Mary Clarke, That then this Recognizance to be Void and of none Effect or Else to Remaine in full Force.[67]

[76] At a Court Continued and held for Richmond County the Seventh Day of May 1724.

Present: Charles Barber, John Tayloe, William Fantleroy, James Ingo, Joseph Belfield, Charles Colston, Robert Tomlin, John Metcalfe and Newman Brockenbrough, Gentlemen Justices.

Russell bound to his Behaviour

Whereas William Russell was bound over to appear at this Court by Vertue of a Warrant from John Tayloe gentleman one of Magistrates of this County for Assaulting beating and bruising of John Kinchiloe It is therefore Ordered that the said William Russell give good and sufficient Security for his good behaviour.

Whereupon the said William Russell Together with Joseph Russell Acknowledged themselves Indebted to Our Sovereign Lord the King the said William Russell in the sume of Twenty Pounds Sterling and the said Joseph Russell Jr. in the sume of Tenn Pounds sterling to be Levied on their Lands and Tenements goods and Chattles with Condition that if the said William Russell shall be of good Behaviour as well Towards his said Majestie as all his Liege people That then this Recognizance to be void and of none Effect or Else to Remaine in Full Force.

At a Court held for Richmond County the Third Day of June 1724.

Present: Charles Barber, Thomas Griffin, William Fantleroy, Charles Colston, Robert Tomlin, John Metcalfe, Samuell Peachey, Newman Brockenbrough, Gentlemen Justices.

Dew bound to his Behaviour

[77] Thomas Dew of North Farnham parish haveing been Summoned to answer the presentment of the Grandjury against him for being a Common Swearer and this Day appearing but Offering Nothing material to Excuse him-

---

67. Clark swore an oath before a single justice that Fann had done or threatened to do some specific violent act against her. In open court, the justices bound Fann to the peace with Stone and Hart as her sureties. The single justice to whom Clark brought the problem could have made this decision, but the entire court could do it as well. Convenience played a part in these proceedings; Webb, *Justice of Peace*, 49–55.

self, It is the Opinion of the Court and accordingly Ordered that for the said Offence he give good and sufficient security for his good behaviour Dureing the Terme of one Yeare.

Whereupon the said Thomas Dew Together with William Hill Acknowledged themselves Indebted to Our Sovereigne Lord the King his heirs and Successors In the Sume of Twenty Pounds Sterling To be Levied on their Lands and Tenements goods and Chattles with Condition that if the said Thomas Dew shall be of good behaviour as well Towards his said Majestie as all his Liege people That then this Recognizance to be void and of None Effect or Else to Remaine in full Force.

McMahone bound to his Behaviour

Arthur Mcmahone of North Farnham parish haveing been Summoned to answer the presentment of the Grandjury against him for being a Profaine and Common Swearer and this Day appearing but Offering Nothing material to Excuse himselfe, It is the Opinion of this Court and accordingly Ordered that for the said Offence he give good and Sufficient Security for his good behaviour Dureing the Terme of One yeare.

Whereupon the said Arthur Mcmahone Together with Robert Baylis Acknowledged themselves Indebted to Our Sovereigne Lord the King his heirs and Successors In the sume of Twenty pounds Sterling to be Levied on their Lands and Tenements goods and Chattles with Condition that if the said Arthur Mcmahone shall be of good Behaviour as well Towards his said Majestie as all his Liege People That then this Recognizance to be void and of None Effect of Else to Remain in full Force.

Anderson bound to his Behaviour

[78] George Anderson of North Farnham haveing been Summoned to answer the presentment of the Grandjury against him for being a Common Swearer and this Day appearing but Offering Nothing materiall to Excuse himselfe it is the Opinion of this Court and accordingly Ordered that for the said offence he give good and sufficient security for his good behaviour Dureing the Terme of one yeare.

Whereupon the said George Anderson Together with Thomas Nash Acknowledged themselves Indebted to Our Sovereigne Lord the King his heirs and Successors in the Sume of Twenty Pounds Sterling To be Levied on their Lands and Tenements goods and Chattles with Condition that if the said George Anderson shall be of good behaviour as well Towards his said Majestie as all his Leige people That then this Recognizance to be void and of None Effect or Else to Remaine in full Force.

Grymes's Recognizance

Charles Grymes John Tayloe and William Downman Gentlemen in open Court Acknowledged themselves Indebted unto Our Sovereign Lord the King his heirs and Successors in the Sume of One Thousand pounds Sterling etc. upon Condition that if the said Charles Grymes (who by vertue of a Commission from the Honourable Lt. Governour is appointed high Sherriff of this County)[68] Doe and shall from Time to Time and at all Times Dureing the Time of his Sherrivalty well and Truly Collect gather up and Secure all his Majesties Revenues and Dues which shall become Due in the said County also Render an Account of all Fines Estreates and amerciaments whatsoever to the Auditor for the Time being or such other person as shall be appointed to Receive the same and Doe and shall Dureing the Time of his Sherrivalty Act performe and Doe in all things Relateing to the said Office as is usuall in the like Cases and by the Laws of this Colony appointed and Required to be Done then this Recognizance to be void Otherwise to Remaine in full Force.

[79] At a Court held for Richmond County the First Day of July 1724.
    Present: Charles Barber, William Fantleroy, Joseph Belfield, Robert Tomlin and Samuell Peachey, Gentlemen Justices.

Taylor bound to the Peace

Whereas Thomas Taylor a Sailor was bound over to appeare at this Court by Vertue of a Warrant from Charles Barber Gentleman One of the Magestrates of this County To answer the Complaint of Samuel Baley for Threatning to Beat Wound maime or kill him, It is therefore Ordered that the said Thomas Taylor give good and Sufficient Security for his Keeping the peace of Our Sovereign Lord the King.
    Whereupon the said Thomas Taylor Together with Thomas Nash Acknowledged themselves Indebted to our Sovereign Lord the King his heirs and Successors Each of them in the Sume of Twenty pounds Sterling to be Levied on their Lands and Tenements goods and Chattles with Condition that if the said Thomas Taylor shall keep the peace of our Sovereign Lord the King as well Towards his said Majestie as all his Leige people, but more especially Towards the said Samuel Baley, That then this Recognizance to be void and of none Effect or Else to Remaine in full Force.

[80] At a Court held for Richmond County the Fifth Day of August 1724.
    Present: Charles Barber, John Tayloe, William Fantleroy, Joseph Belfield, Charles Colston, Robert Tomlin, John Metcalfe, Samuell Peachey and Newman Brockenbrough, Gentlemen Justices.

------

68. The sheriff held office upon a commission from the governor. He had to be a justice and was nominated for the additonal office by the county bench. He served a term of two years and had to put up a bond for the performance of his duties; *Statutes at Large*, 3:246–50 (1705).

Geithings Examination

Whereas Andrew Geithings A Servant to John Byard was by vertue of a mitti-mus from John Tayloe Gentleman One of the Justices of this Court Committed to the County Goal for Robbing a Flatt[69] in Mr. Peter Murrahs Employ at Ann Reanolds's Landing, and being now brought before his Majesties Justices here present was Examined by the Court as Followeth:

Court: Andrew Geithings You hear what you are Charged with, what have you to say in your Defence.
Answer: About the 6th Day of July last I run away from my Master John Byard and Carryed away with me One Duroy Coat, One Hatt, One Shirt, One pair of Shoos, One pair of Stokins, One pair of Garters, One pair of Leather Breeches, and One Pistoll, which goods belonged to my said Master alsoe about the 15th Day of July Last I being along with Edward Lambert, alias John Hearles, alias Morris Jones, near the house of Ann Reanolds, the said Edward Lambert left me and after some small Time Returned againe with a wallet of dry Goods and gave me part of them which goods are part of them Claim'd by James McClunpitt, I also wrote one pass for to Travel by.

William Russell Aged 22 years or thereabouts being Sworn Saith about the 25th Day of July Last he took out of Andrew Geithings's Pocket three knives, One Razor, One [81] Silk Handerchief, Two Black Neck Cloths, One Ink horn, Six passes, Two Needles, and a small parcell of thread, and by Direction of the said Andrew Geithings he found Two wallets with Diverse goods in them.

James McClumpitt a Sailor aged 21 years or thereabouts being sworn saith that about the 15th Day of July last he lost out of a Flatt at the Widow Reanolds's Landing One Silk Handerchief three pair of Buckles, three packs of Cards, about 3/4 of a Pound of Thread and One Remnant of Fustaine, part of which goods William Russell took out of Andrew Geithings's pocket.

John Byard aged 30 years or thereabouts being Sworn saith that about the 7th Day of July last in the Night he Lost the Following Goods out of his house (vizt.) about One yard of Red Check Linning, One pair of wooden heeled Shoes, One New Shirt, One pair of yarn Stokins, One pair of Garters, One Duroy Frock, One Pistoll, One Fine Hatt and one pair of Leather Breeches, part of which said goods he since took from the said Andrew Geithings when he was in Prison (that is to say) One Hatt, One pair of Shoes, One Shirt, One pair of Garters, One pair of Stokins, and one pair of Breeches.

Jane Geithings aged 16 years or thereabouts being Sworn saith that about Three weeks agoe Andrew Geithings the prisoner at the Barr gave her One yard of Red Check Linning.

It Appearing to the Court upon the aforesaid Examination that there is Just Cause for Trying the said Prisoner at the General Court for the Crime aforesaid whereof he is accused It is therefore Ordered that the said Andrew Geithings be Remanded to the prison of this County under the Custody of the Sherriff and

---

69. A flatboat or barge. Geithings had already run afoul of the court; see p. 63 above.

from thence to be Conveyed to the publick Goal of Williamsburgh as the Law in such Cases Directs.

Russell's Recognizance

[82] William Russell in open Court before his Majesties Justices Acknowledged himself Indebted to Our Sovereign Lord the King his heirs and Successors In the sume of Ten pounds Sterling to be Levyed of his Lands and Tenements goods and Chattles with Condition that if the said William Russell shall personally appear at the next General Court on the Fourth Day thereof and then and there give such Evidence as he knows against Andrew Geithings on Suspicion of Robbing a Flatt in the Employ of Mr. Peter Murrah lying at Ann Reanolds's landing and Doe not Depart thence without Leave of that Court that Then this Recognizance to be void Or Else to Remaine in full Force.

Byard's Recognizance

John Byard in open Court before his Majesties Justices Acknowledged himselfe Indebted to our sovereign Lord the King his heirs and Successors in the sume of Ten pounds Sterling to be Levied of his Lands and Tenements goods and Chattles with Condition that if the said John Byard shall personally appeare at the next General Court on the Fourth Day thereof and then and there give such Evidence as he knows against Andrew Geithings on Suspicion of Robbing a Flatt in the Employ of Mr. Peter Murrah lying at Ann Reandolds's Landing and do not Depart thence without leave of that Court That then his Recognizance to be void Or Else to Remaine in full Force.

Lambert's Examination

Whereas Edward Lambert, alias John Hearles, alias Morris Jones, a Servant to William Griffin who Confesseth that he was Convicted in England for Stealing a Silver Ring for which Fact he was Transported into this County; being brought before this Court on Suspicion of Fellony and being Examined saith that about Five weeks agoe he Run away from his said Master William Griffin and went to One John Byards about a week afterwards and mett with Andrew Geithings who was this Day Examined at [83] the Barr and being in Discourse with the said Geithings the said Geithings told him that he would take his masters Cloaths and goe along with him to North Carolina and about Two Nights afterward the said Geithings did take part of his Masters goods and they went down to the Plantation of Ann Reanolds and Two or Three Days after seeing off Two Flatts Comeing up [to] the said Reanolds's Landing they hid themselves and seeing the Sailors goe onshore they went and took a Bag of goods out of one of the said Flatts[,] some of which goods are now produced[,] and soone after went back into the Woods and Devided the goods between them and then went to the house of one James Coward with an Intent to goe Clear away.

Court: Where did you Gett that Ticken Jackett which now lies before you[?]
Answer: Why some small Time before the Boat was Robb'd I went into a house
  Near Totoskey Ferry the Doors being open and I took it Out.

Henry Killbourn aged 31 years or thereabouts being Sworn saith that about a
month agoe he lost a Ticken Jackett out of his house which is now produced in
Court and was taken from Edward Lambert etc. the prisoner at the Barr.

It Appearing to the Court upon the aforesaid Examination that there is Just
Cause for Trying the said prisoner at the General Court for the Crime aforesaid
whereof he is Accused It is therefore Ordered that the said Edward Lambert etc.
be Remanded to the Prison of this County under the Custody of the Sherrif and
from thence to be Conveyed to the publick Goal of Williamsburgh as the Law in
such Cases Directs.

Killbourn's Recognizance

[84] Henry Killbourn in Open Court before his Majesties Justices Acknowledged himselfe Indebted to Our Sovereign Lord the King his heirs and
Successors In the sume of Ten Pounds Sterling to be Levyed of his Lands and
Tenements goods and Chattles with Condition that if the said Henry Killbourn
shall personally appeare at the Next General Court on the Fourth Day thereof
and then and there give such Evidence as he knows against Edward Lambert etc.
on Suspicion of Robbing a Flatt in the Employ of Mr. Peter Murrah lying at Ann
Reanolds's Landing and taking out Diverse Goods as alsoe for Stealing a Ticken
Jacket from him And do not Depart thence without Leave of that Court That
then this Recognizance to be void or Else to Remaine in full Force.

At a Court Continued and held for Richmond County the Sixth Day of August
1724.

Present: Charles Barber, John Tayloe, Robert Tomlin and John Metcalfe,
Gentlemen Justices.

McClinchey bound to her behavior

Jane McClinchey of Sittenbourn Parish haveing been Summoned to answer
the Presentment of the Grand Jury Against her for being a Common Swearer,
but offering Nothing Material to Excuse herselfe, It is the Opinion of this Court
and Accordingly Ordered that for the said Offence she give good and Sufficient
security for her good Behaviour Dureing the Terme of one year.

Whereupon the said Jane McClinchey Together with John Jenings in open
Court Acknowledged themselves Indebted to our Sovereign Lord the King his
Heirs and Successors in the Sume of Twenty Pounds Sterling To be Levyed on
their Lands and Tenements Goods and Chattles with Condition that if the said
Jane McClinchey shall be of good Behaviour as well Towards his said Majestie as

all his Leige People That then this Recognizance to be Void and of None Effect, or Else to Remaine in full Force.

[85] Present Joseph Belfield Gentleman.

Newgent Bound to the Peace

Whereas Mary Clarke haveing Sworn the Peace against Ann Newgent before Charles Barber gentleman One of the Magistrates of this County, It is therefore Ordered that she Give Security for keeping the same and that she Remaine in the Sherriffs Custody untill she gives such Security.

At a Court held for Richmond County the Second Day of September 1724.

Present: Charles Barber, Thomas Griffin, William Fantleroy, William Dowman, Joseph Belfeild and Robert Tomlin, Gentlemen Justices.

Pridham Bound to his Behaviour

Whereas Christopher Pridham by vertue of a Warrant from Charles Barber Gentleman One of the Magestrates of this County was Bound over to appeare at this Court to answer the Complaint of his Servant woman Named Margret Conner for that the said Christopher Pridham doth Continually Importune the said Margret Conner by all ways and means to prostitute her body to him which he Dayly Practices to the other Servant Woman belonging to him and because she Refuses to Gratify his Vitious Inclinations he abuses her in a very Grose manner both by words and Actions etc. The said Christopher Pridham accordingly appeared this Day in Court and Severall Evidences being Examined who fully Proved the Facts laid to his Charge It is therefore Ordered that he give good and sufficient Security for his good Behaviour.

Whereupon the said Christopher Pridham Together with Richard Worsdell Acknowledged themselves Indebted to our Sovereign Lord King his Leige and Successors the said Christopher Pridham in the Sume of Forty Pounds Sterling and the said Richard Worsdell in [86] In the Sume of Twenty Pounds Sterling To be levyed on their Lands and Tenements Goods and Chattles with Condition that if the said Christopher Pridham shall be of good behaviour as well Towards his said Majestie as all his Leige people That then this Recognizance to be void and of None Effect Or Else to Remaine in full Force.

Present Samuell Peachey gentleman.

Griffin's Recognizance

Thomas Griffin gentleman in open Court Acknowledged himselfe Indebted to our Sovereigne Lord the King in the sume of Forty Pounds Sterling to be Levied on his Lands and Tenements Goods and Chattles with Condition that if Ann Newgent (who was Last Court Committed into the Sherriffs Custody for her ill Behaviour untill she gave Security) shall be of good Behaviour as well

Towards his said Majestie as all his Leige People Dureing the Terme of one year That then this Recognizance to be void and of none Effect or Else to Remaine in full Force.

Davis Bound to his Behaviour

It appearing to this Court that George Davis is a person of an ill Behaviour it is therefore Ordered that he give good and Sufficient Security for his good Behaviour, and that he Remaine in the Sherriffs Custody untill he gives such Security.

At a Court held for Richmond County the Third Day of February 1724/5.

Present: Charles Barber, William Fantleroy, Joseph Belfeild, Robert Tomlin, John Metcalfe, Samuell Peachey and Newman Brockenbrough, Gentlemen Justices.

Hughs bound to his Behaviour

[87] William Hughs of North Farnham parish haveing been Summoned to answer the presentment of the Grandjury against him for being a Common and Notorious Swearer and this day appearing but offering Nothing material to Excuse himselfe. It is the Opinion of this Court and accordingly Ordered that for the said Offence he give good and sufficient security for his good behaviour Dureing the Terme of one Year.

Whereupon the said William Hughs Together with Thomas Durham and John Hightower in open Court acknowledged themselves Indebted to our Sovereign Lord the King his heirs and Successors in the Sume of Twenty pounds Sterling to be Levyed on their Lands and Tenements goods and Chattles with Condition that if the said William Hughs shall be of good behaviour as well towards his said Majestie as all his Leige people That then this Recognizance to be void and of None Effect or Else to Remaine in full Force.

Cornelius bound to his Behaviour

Richard Cornelius of North Farnham parish haveing been Summoned to answer the presentment of the Grandjury against him for Profainly Spending the Day being the 25th of October Last in Drinking and Danceing at Mrs. Rebecca Colstons Quarter[70] and this Day appearing but Offering Nothing material to Excuse himselfe It is the Opinion of this Court and accordingly Ordered that for the said Offence he give good and sufficient security for his good Behaviour Dureing the Terme of one Yeare.

Whereupon the said Richard Cornelius Together with Lambert Dodson in

---

70. Cornelius violated the laws on keeping the sabbath by not going to church; *Statutes at Large*, 3:360–61 (1705), an offense which by this time was relegated to the ROB. The riotous behaviour of the defendant resulted in the order for him to give bond for good behavior and led to the recording of his offense in the *RCP*.

open Court Acknowledged themselves indebted to our Sovereign Lord the King his heirs and Successors In the Sume of Twenty pounds sterling to be Levyed on their Lands and Tenements goods and Chattles with Condition that if the said Richard Cornelius shall be of good behaviour as well Towards his said Majestie as all his Leige People That then this Recognizance to be Void and of None Effect or Else to Remaine in full Force.

Pridham bound to his behaviour

Christopher Pridham of North Farnham Parish [88] haveing been Summoned to answer the presentment of the Grandjury against him for being a Common and Notorious swearer and this Day appearing but Offering Nothing material to excuse himselfe It is the Opinion of this Court and accordingly Ordered that for his said Offence he give good and sufficient security for his good behaviour Dureing the Terme of one Yeare.

Whereupon the said Christopher Pridham Together with Tobias Pursell in open Court acknowledged themselves Indebted to our Sovereign Lord the King his heirs and Successors in the sume of Twenty pounds sterling each of them to be Levyed on their Lands and Tenements Goods and Chattles with Condition that if the said Christopher Pridham shall be of good behaviour as well Towards his said Majestie as all his Leige people That then this Recognizance to be void and of None Effect or Else to Remain in full Force.

Osgriffin bound to Behaviour

Jane Osgriffin of North Farnham parish haveing been summoned to answer the presentment of the Grandjury against her for a Common and Notorious Swearer and being now Called and not appearing It is the Opinion of this Court and accordingly Ordered that for the said Offence she give good and sufficient security for her good behaviour Dureing the Terme of one Yeare.

Whereupon William Osgriffin and Thomas Jeffreys in open Court Acknowledged themselves Indebted to our Sovereign Lord the King his heirs and successors in the sume of Twenty pounds Sterling to be Levyed on their Lands and Tenements Goods and Chattles with Condition that if the said Jane Osgriffin Shall be of good behaviour as well towards his said Majestie as all his Leige people That then this Recognizance to be Void and of None Effect or Else to Remaine in full Force.

Grimston bound to behaviour

Thomas Grimston of Sittenbourn Parish haveing been Summoned to answer the presentment of the Grandjury against him for his Rude and Disorderly behaviour at his parish Church[71] and this Day appearing but Offering Nothing material to excuse himself It is the opinion of this Court and accordingly

---

71. Grimston, as Cornelius before him, added disorderly conduct at the church to violation of the sabbath laws.

Ordered that for the said Offence he give good and Sufficient security for his good behaviour Dureing the Terme of one Yeare.

[89] Whereupon the said Thomas Grimston Together with Edmond Collinsworth in open Court acknowledged themselves Indebted to our sovereign Lord the King his heirs and Successors in the sume of Twenty Pounds Sterling to be Levyed on their Lands and Tenements goods and Chattles with Condition that if the said Thomas Grimston shall be of good behaviour as well Towards his said Majestie as all his Leige people That then this Recognizance to be void and of None Effect or Else to Remaine in full Force.

Burroes bound to behaviour

Michael Burroes of Sittenbourn parish haveing been Summoned to answer the presentment of the Grandjury against him for a Common Swearer and this Day appearing but offering Nothing Material to Excuse himselfe It is the Opinion of this Court and accordingly Ordered that for the said Offence he give good and suffcent security for his good behaviour Dureing the Terme of One Yeare.

Whereupon the said Michael Burroes Together with Edward Tomlinson in open Court acknowledged themselves Indebted to Our Sovereign Lord the King his heirs and successors in the sume of Twenty pounds Sterling To be Levyed on their Lands and Tenements goods and Chattles with Condition that if the said Michael Burroes shall be of good behaviour as well towards his said Majestie as all his Leige people That then this Recognizance to be void and of None Effect or Else to Remaine in full Force.

Packet bound to behaviour

Gabriel Packet Jr. of North Farnham parish haveing been Summoned to answer the Presentment of the Grand jury against him for a Common swearer and this Day appearing but Offering Nothing material to excuse himselfe It is the opinion of this Court and accordinly Ordered that for the said Offence he give good and sufficient security for his good behaviour Dureing the Terme of one Yeare.

Whereupon the said Gabriel Packet Jr. Together with Solomon Redman in open Court acknowledged themselves Indebted to Our Sovereign Lord the King his heirs and Successors in the Sume of Twenty pounds sterling To be Levyed on their Lands and Tenements goods and Chattles with Condition that if the said Gabriel Packet Jr. shall be of good behaviour as well Towards his said Majestie as all his Leige People That then this Recognizance [90] to be void and of None Effect or Else to Remaine in full Force.

Packet bound to his behaviour

Gabriel Packet of North Farnham Parish haveing been Summoned to answer the presentment of the Grandjury against him for a Common swearer and this Day appearing but offering Nothing material to Excuse himself, It is the Opinion of this Court and accordingly Ordered that for the said Offence he give good and sufficient security for his good behaviour Dureing the Terme of one Yeare.

Whereupon the said Gabriel Packet Together with Gabriel Packet Jr. in open Court acknowledged themselves Indebted to our Sovereign Lord the King his heirs and Successors in the Sume of Twenty pounds Sterling to be Levyed on their Lands and Tenements goods and Chattles with Condition that if the said Gabriel Packet shall be of good behavior as well Towards his said Majestie as all his Leige people That then this Recognizance to be Void and of None Effect or Else to Remaine in full Force.

Nicholls bound to his Behaviour

Charles Nicholls of North Farnham parish haveing been Summoned to answer the presentment of the Grandjury against him for a Common and Notorious Swearer and this Day appearing but Offering Nothing material to excuse himselfe It is the opinion of this Court and accordingly Ordered that for the said Offence he give good and sufficient security for his good behaviour Dureing the Terme of one Yeare.

Whereupon the said Charles Nicholls Together with Thomas Smith in open Court acknowledged themselves Indebted to our sovereign Lord the King his heirs and Successors In the sume of Twenty pounds sterling to be Levyed on their Lands and Tenements goods and Chattles with Condition that if the said Charles Nicholls shall be of good behaviour as well Towards his said Majestie as all his Leige people That then this Recognizance to be Void and of None Effect or Else to Remaine in full Force.

[91] At a Court Continued and held for Richmond County the Fourth Day of February 1724/5.

Present: Charles Barber, John Tayloe, William Fantleroy, Joseph Belfeild, Robert Tomlin, John Metcalfe, Samuell Peachey and Newman Brockenbrough, Gentlemen Justices.

Durham Fined

Thomas Durham Constable according to Order this day appearing to answer for his Contempt in not Returning a Mittimus about Col. Tarpleys Negro, but offering Nothing Material to excuse himselfe, It is therefore Ordered that he be Fined Fifty shillings Current money to our sovereign Lord the King.

Plumer's Tryall

At a Session of Oyer and Terminer held at Richmond Court house on Wednesday the Third Day of March 1724/5 In the Eleaventh yeare of the Reign of our Sovereign Lord George by the Grace of God King of great Brittaine

France and Ireland Defender of the Faith etc. and by Vertue of a Special Commission for the Tryall of all Treasons Petty Treasons or misprisions thereof Felonys murthers or other Offences or Crimes whatsoever Committed within the County of Richmond by a mulattoe Slave Called William Plummer Directed to Charles Barber Thomas Griffin John Tayloe William Fantleroy William Downman Joseph Belfeild Robert Tomlin John Metcalfe Samuel Peachey and Newman Brockenbrough Gentlemen.

Present: Charles Barber, Thomas Griffin, John Tayloe, William Fantleroy, William Downman, Joseph Belfield and Robert Tomlin, Gentlemen Justices.

Memorandum that on this Day being the Third day [**92**] of March 1724/5 an Indictment was preferred against a Mulatto Man Slave Called William Plummer in these words Richmond Ss. Our Sovereign Lord the King George of Great Brittaine etc. Doth hereby Arrain and indict William Plumer otherwise Called Plumer a Mulatto Slave belonging to John Tarpley gentleman of the parish of North Farnham and County aforesaid for that the aforesaid Plumer not having the Fear of God before his Eyes but Instigated by the Devill did on the Tenth the Seventeenth the Twenty Fourth and the Thirty First Day of January Last past break open the Dwelling house of a Certaine John Bruce one of his Majesties Leige Subjects and then and there did in the parish and County aforesaid break and Enter the said house and Did Commit Burglary and Felony by stealing takeing and Carrying away One great Coate of grey broad Cloath one Jacket of the same Cloath a pair of broad Cloath Breeches one Fire Lock and a Lathing hammer of the vallue of Forty shillings being the goods and Chattles of the aforesaid Bruce[,] being then in the said house[,] there found and Carried away by the said Plumer and that the aforesaid Plumer the Eighth Day of December Last past did Commit Burglary and Felony[72] by stealing takeing and Carrying away one Fine Castor or Carolina hat and one pair Shoes of the vallue of Ten shillings being in the Kitchin of the said house, all against the peace of our Sovereign Lord King George etc. and against Several Acts of Parliament and of our General Assembly for such Cases made and Provided.

JOHN TARPLEY JR. Dom Rex[73]

Whereupon the said William Plummer was brought to the barr and arained for the said Felony and there Pleaded not Guilty, and thereupon the Court proceeding on his Tryal, after the hearing the Evidence of John Bruce against him and what he had to say in his Defence are of the Opinion that he is Guilty of the Felony for which he stands Indicted.[74] [**93**] It is therefore Ordered that the said William Plummer Return to the Place from whence he Came from thence to the place of Excecution, and there to be hanged by the Neck till he be Dead.

Pursuant to an Act of Assembly made in the yeare 1723 Concerning the Tryall of Slaves Committing Capitoll Crimes this Court in pursuance thereof Doe vallue William Plummer a Mulatto Slave belonging to John Tarpley gentleman (who was this Day Condemned to Dye for Felony) to Fifty shillings Current

---

72. If burglary was charged, the breaking and entering must have occurred at night.

73. The king's attorney was the son of the victim. With so few crown officials, all of whom were drawn from the propertied classes, such conflicts of interest were not unusual.

74. Breaking and entering a dwelling to commit a felony, whether or not anything was taken, was a felony; Webb, *Justice of Peace*, 63.

money and Ordered that the Clerk of this Court Certifye the same to the next Assembly.[75]

At a Court held for Richmond County the Third Day of March 1724/5.
Present: Charles Barber, Thomas Griffin, William Fantleroy, Robert Tomlin and Samuell Peachey, Gentleman Justices.

Jackson bound to his Behaviour

It appearing to this Court that John Jackson is a person of an ill Behaviour, It is therefore Ordered that he give good and sufficient security for his good Behaviour Whereupon the said John Jackson Together with Richard Brown and Thomas Smith acknowledged themselves Indebted to our Sovereign Lord the King In the sume of Twenty pounds sterling to be Levyed on their Lands and Tenements goods and Chattles with Condition that if the said John Jackson shall be of good Behaviour as well Towards his said Majestie as all his Liege people for the Terme of Twelve months next Ensueing That then this Recognizance to be void and of none Effect or Else to Remaine in full Force.

[94] At a Court held for Richmond County the Seventh Day of Aprill of 1725.
Present: Charles Barber, John Tayloe, William Downman, Joseph Belfield, Robert Tomlin, John Metcalfe, Samuell Peachey, Gentlemen Justices.

Hill bound to his Behaviour

James Hill of North Farnham parish haveing been taken into Custody to answer the Presentment of the Grandjury against him for being a Common and Notorious swearer and Drunkard and this Day appearing but offering Nothing material to excuse himselfe It is the opinion of this Court and accordingly Ordered that for the said Offence he give good and sufficient security for his good behaviour Dureing the Terme of one yeare.

Whereupon the said James Hill Together with Edward Jones and John Foushee in open Court acknowledged themselves Indebted to our sovereign Lord the King his heirs and Successors the said James Hill in the Sume of Forty pounds Sterling and the said Edward Jones and John Foushee in the Sume of Twenty pounds Sterling Each of them To be Levyed on their Lands and Tenements goods and Chattles with Condition that if the said James Hill shall be of good behaviour as well Towards his said Majestie as all his Liege people That then this Recognizance to be void and of none effect or else to Remaine in full Force.

75. Under *Statutes at Large,* 4:128 (1723), the court valued the slave so that the next session of the House of Burgesses might adequately recompense the owner. Public compensation was required by law; *Statutes at Large,* 3:461 (1705).

At a Court Continued and held for Richmond County the Eighth Day of Aprill 1725.

Present: Charles Barber, John Tayloe, William Fantleroy, Joseph Belfield, Robert Tomlin, John Metcalfe and Samuell Peachey, Gentlemen Justices.

Pridham bound to his Behaviour

Whereas Christopher Pridham by vertue of a Warrant from Robert Tomlin gentleman one of the Magistrates [95] of this County was bound over to appear at this Court to answer the Complaint of Thomas Freshwater Jr. for being a person of lude Life and Conversation and Common Disturber of the peace by Drinking Quareling Swearing threatning and all manner of Impiousness and impurity etc. the said Christopher Pridham this Day appearing in Court and acknowledging his Offence. It is therefore Ordered that he give good and Sufficient security for his good Behaviour.

Whereupon the said Christopher Pridham Together with Thomas Walker and William Nash in open Court acknowledged themselves Indebted to our soveriegn Lord the King his heirs and Successors the said Christopher Pridham in the sume of Forty pounds Sterling and the said Thomas Walker and William Nash in the sume of Twenty pounds sterling each of them To be Levied on their Lands and Tenements goods and Chattles with Condition that if the said Christopher Pridham shall be of good behaviour as well towards his said Majestie as all his Leige people That then this Recognizance to be void and of none Effect or else to remaine in full Force.

Morgan bound to his Behaviour

William Morgan Jr. of North Farnham Parish having been taken into Custody to answer the presentment of the Grand Jury against him for being a Common Drunkard and this Day appearing but offering Nothing material to excuse himselfe It is the opinion of this Court and accordingly Ordered that for the said Offence he give good and sufficient security for his good behaviour Dureing the Terme of one Yeare.

Whereupon the said William Morgan Jr. Together with Hugh Lambert in open Court acknowledged themselves Indebted to our sovereign Lord the King his heirs and Successors in the sume of Twenty pounds sterling To be Levyed on their Lands and Tenements goods and Chattles with Condition that if the said William Morgan Jr. shall [96] Be of good behaviour as well Towards his said Majestie as all his Leige People That then this Recognizance to be void and of None Effect or Else to Remain in full Force.

At a Court held for Richmond County the Fifth Day of May 1725.

Present: Charles Barber, John Tayloe, William Fantleroy, Joseph Belfield, Robert Tomlin, John Metcalfe and Newman Brockenbrough, Gentlemen Justices.

Deane bound to his Behaviour

It appearing to this Court that Charles Deane is a Person of an ill Behaviour. It is therefore Ordered that he give good and Sufficient security for his good Behaviour.

Whereupon the said Charles Dean Together with John Jenings in open Court acknowledged themselves Indebted to our Sovereign Lord the King his heirs and Successors the said Charles Deane in the sume of Twenty pounds sterling and the said John Jenings in the sume of Ten pounds sterling To be Levied on their Lands and Tenements goods and Chattles with Condition that if the said Charles Deane shall be of good behaviour as well Towards his said Majestie as all his Liege people That then this Recognizance to be void and of none Effect or else to Remaine in full Force.

Casey bound to his Behaviour

Mr. Peter Casey being brought before this Court for his Rude behaviour this Day before Two of the Majestrates of this County. It is therefore Ordered that he give good and Sufficient Security for his good Behaviour Dureing the Terme of one year Whereupon the said Peter Casey Together with Marmaduke Beckwith and William Walker in open Court acknowledged themselves Indebted to our Sovereign Lord the King his heirs and Successors the said [97] Peter Casey in the Sume of Twenty pounds sterling and the said Marmaduke Beckwith and William Walker In the sume of Ten pounds sterling Each of them To be Levied on their Lands and Tenements Goods and Chattles with Condition that if the said Peter Casey Shall be of good behaviour as well Towards his said Majestie as all Liege people That then this Recognizance to be void and of none Effect or Else to Remaine in full Force.

Whereas Mr. Peter Casey haveing this Day Uttered abusive Languidge to two of the Majestrates of this County. It is therefore Ordered that he be Fined for the same Fifty shillings Current money to our Sovereign Lord the King, and that he give security for the payment of it Whereupon Marmaduke Beckwith in open Court Obliged himselfe his heirs etc. to pay the said Fine as before Ordered.

At a Court held for Richmond County the Second Day of June 1725.
Present: Charles Barber, Thomas Griffin, John Tayloe, William Fantleroy, William Downman, Joseph Belfield, Robert Tomlin, John Metcalfe and Samuell Peachey, Gentlemen Justices.

Pridham bound to his Behaviour

It appearing to this Court that John Pridham is a person of an ill behaviour It is therefore Ordered that he give good and sufficient security for his good behaviour Dureing the terme of one yeare.

Whereupon the said John Pridham Together with John Bramham and John

Hefford in open Court acknowledged themselves Indebted to our Sovereign Lord the King his heirs and successors the said John Pridham in the Sume of Forty pounds sterling and the said John Bramham and John Hefford in the sume of Twenty pounds sterling Each of them To be Levied on their Lands and Tenements [98] Goods and Chattles with Conditions that if the said John Pridham shall be of good Behaviour as well Towards his said Majestie as all his Leige people That then this Recognizance to be void and of None Effect or Else to Remaine in full Force.

Molony bound to his Behaviour

John Molloney of North Farnham parish haveing been Summoned to answer the presentment of the Grandjury against him for being a Common swearer and this Day appearing but Offering Nothing materiall to Excuse himself It is the Opinion of this Court and accordingly Ordered that for the said Offence he give good and sufficient security for his good Behaviour Dureing the Terme of one yeare.

Whereupon the said John Molloney Together with Sollomon and David Caverner in open Court acknowledged themselves Indebted to our sovereign Lord the King his heirs and Successors In the sume of Forty pounds sterling To be Levied on their Lands and Tenements goods and Chattles with Condition that if the said John Molloney shall be of good behaviour as well Towards his said Majestie as all his Liege people That then this Recognizance to be void and of none Effect Or else to Remain in full Force.

Osborne bound to his Behaviour

Thomas Osborne of North Farnham parish haveing been Summoned to answer the presentment of the Grand Jury against him for being a Common swearer and this Day appearing but offering Nothing materiall to Excuse himself It is the opinion of this Court and accordingly Ordered that for the said Offence he give good and sufficient security for his good behaviour dureing the Terme of one Yeare.

Whereupon the said Thomas Osborne Together with David Caverner in open Court acknowledged themselves Indebted to our Sovereign Lord the King his heirs and Successors In the sume of Twenty pounds sterling To be Levied on their Lands and Tenements goods and Chattles with Condition that if the said Thomas Osborne shall be of good behaviour as well Towards his said Majestie as all his [99] Liege people That then this Recognizance to be Void and of None Effect or Else to Remaine in full Force.

Kelly bound to his behaviour

James Kelly of North Farnham parish haveing been summoned to answer the presentment of the Grandjury against him for being a Common swearer and this Day appearing but Offering Nothing material to Excuse himselfe it is the Opinion of this Court and accordingly ordered that for the said Offence he give good and sufficient security for his good behaviour Dureing the Terme of one yeare.

Whereupon the said James Kelly Together with Hugh Lambert in open Court acknowledged themselves Indebted to our sovereign Lord the King his heirs and Successors in the sume of Twenty pounds sterling To be Levied on their Lands and Tenements goods and Chattles with Condition that if the said James Kelly shall be of good behaviour as well Towards his said Majestie and all his Liege people That then this Recognizance to be void of None Effect or Else to Remaine in full Force.

Oneale Bound to his behaviour

James Oneale of North Farnham parish haveing been Summoned to answer the presentment of the Grandjury against him for being a common swearer and Drunkard and this Day appearing but offering nothing Material to Excuse himself. It is the opinion of this Court and Accordingly Ordered that for the said offence he give good and sufficient security for his good behaviour Dureing the Terme of one Yeare.

Whereupon the said James Oneale Together with Thomas Dale and Caron Brannon in open Court acknowledged themselves Indebted to our sovereign Lord the King his heirs and successors in the sume of Twenty pounds Sterling To be Levied on their Lands and Tenements goods and Chattles with Conditions that if the said James Oneale shall be of good behaviour as well Towards his said Majestie as all his Liege people That then this Recognizance to be void and of none Effect or Else to Remaine in full Force.

Hanks bound to his behaviour

William Hanks of North Farnham parish haveing been Summoned to answer the presentment of the Grandjury against [**100**] him for being a Common Swearer and Drunkard and this Day appearing but Offering Nothing material to excuse himself It is the opinion of this Court and accordingly Ordered that for the said offence he give good and sufficient Security for his good behaviour Dureing the Terme of one Yeare.

Whereupon the said William Hanks Together with William Walker his Security in open Court acknowledged themselves Indebted to our sovereign Lord the King his heirs and Successors In the sume of Twenty pounds Sterling To be Levyed on their Lands and Tenements goods and Chattles with Condition that if the said William Hanks shall be of good behaviour as well Towards his said Majestie as all his Liege people That then this Recognizance to be void and of none Effect or Else to remaine in full Force.

Mullis bound to his behaviour

Richard Mullis of North Farnham parish haveing been Summoned to answer the presentment of the Grandjury against him for being a Common swearer and this Day appearing but offering Nothing material to Excuse himself it is the opinion of this Court and accordingly Ordered that for the said Offence he give good and sufficient security for his good behaviour Dureing the terme of one yeare.

Whereupon the said Richard Mullis Together with David Williams and Humphery Thomas in open Court acknowledged themselves Indebted to our Sovereign Lord the King his heirs and Successors In the sume of Twenty pounds sterling To be Levied on their Lands and Tenements goods and Chattles with Condition that if the said Richard Mullis shall be of good behaviour as well Towards his said Majestie as all his Liege people That then this Recognizance to be void and of none Effect or Else to Remaine in full Force.

Barnes bound to his behavior

Whereas Mr. Richard Barnes of North Farnham Parish was presented by the Grandjury for being a common swearer It is therefore Ordered that he give Security for his good behaviour Dureing the Terme of One Yeare.

Whereupon George Eskriege gentleman in open Court acknowledged himselfe Indebted to our Sovereign Lord the King [101] his heirs and successors in the sume of Twenty pounds sterling To be Levied on his Lands and Tenements goods and Chattles with Condition that if the said Richard Barnes shall be of good behaviour as well towards his said Majestie as all his Liege People That then this Recognizance to be void and of none Effect or Else to Remaine in full Force.

Thornton bound to his Behaviour

Thomas Thornton of Sittenbourn Parish haveing been summoned to answer the presentment of the Grandjury against him for being a common swearer and Drunkard and this Day appearing but offering Nothing materiall to excuse himselfe It is the opinion of this Court and accordingly Ordered that for the said offence he give good and sufficient security for his good behaviour Dureing the Terme of one yeare.

Whereupon the said Thomas Thornton Together with Avery Dye and Robert Welch in open Court acknowledged themselves Indebted to our sovereign Lord the King his heirs and Successors In the sume of Twenty pounds sterling To be Levied on their Lands and Tenements goods and Chattles with Condition that if the said Thomas Thornton shall be of good behaviour as well towards his said Majestie as all his Liege people that then this Recognizance to be void and of None effect or else to Remaine in full Force.

Kelly bound to his Behaviour

John Kelly of Sittenbourn parish haveing been summoned to answer the presentment of the Grandjury against him for being a Common swearer and this Day appearing but offering Nothing material to excuse himself it is the opinion of this Court and accordingly Ordered that for the said Offence he give good and sufficient security for his good behaviour Dureing the Terme of one yeare.

Whereupon the said John Kelly Together with John Morton in open Court acknowledged themselves Indebted to our Sovereign Lord the King his heirs and successors In the sume of Twenty pounds sterling To be levied on their Lands and Tenements goods and Chattles with Condition that if the said John Kelly shall be of good behaviour as well Towards his said Majestie as all his Liege people That then this Recognizance to be void and of none effect or Else to Remaine in full Force.

[102] At a Court held for Richmond County the Seventh Day of July 1725.
Present: Charles Barber, William Fantleroy, Joseph Belfield, Robert Tomlin, John Metcalfe and Samuell Peachey, Gentlemen Justices.

Bruss's Examination

Whereas Thomas Bruss a Servant to William Walker (who confesseth that he was Convicted in England for stealing a Mare for which fact he was Transported into this County)[76] was by Vertue of a Mittimus from William Downman gentleman one of the Justices of this Court Committed to the County Goal for Feloniously takeing of Goods out of the house of Richard Mills on the 25th of June Last at Night (vizt.) one suit of Duroys Cloaths, a Fine hatt, two pair shoos, a pair shoo buckles, 3 pair stokins a fine Shirt, Neck Bands, some fine thred and a Raiser [razor] and being now Brought before his Majesties Justices here present was Examined by the Court as Followeth.

Court: Thomas Bruss you hear what you are Charged with Concearning your stealing of goods out of the house of Richard Mills[?]
Answer: About the 25th Day of June I unlockt the Door of Richard Mills's house and I took out of the said house One suit of Duroys Cloaths, a fine hat, 2 pair shoos, a pair Shoo Buckles, 3 pair Stokins, a fineshirt, 3 Neckbands Some fine thred, a Raiser, 1 Stript holland Jacket and 1 pair Garters.

Richard Mills aged 30 years or thereabouts being sworn saith that about the 21st Day of June he Lost out of his house one suit of Duroys Cloaths, a fine hatt, 2 pair Shoes, a pair Shoo Buckles, 3 pair Stokins, a fine Shirt 3 Neck bands, some fine Thred, a Raiser, 1 Stript holland Jacket, and 1 pair Garters some of which goods he took from the Prisoner at the Barr.
[103] William Walker aged 30 years or thereabouts being sworn saith that the coat and Jacket which was taken from his Servant man Thomas Bruss the prisoner at the Barr belongs to Richard Mills.
It Appearing to the court upon the aforesaid Examination that there is just Cause for trying the said Prisoner at the Generall Court for the Crime aforesaid where of he is accused, It is therefore Ordered that the said Thomas Bruss be Remanded to the Prison of the County under the Custody of the Sherriff and

76. A 1748 statute ordered the justices to note this fact upon the papers they sent to the General Court; *Statutes at Large,* 5:545 (1748). Long before this time, however, justices were aware of the importance of previous convictions in weighing the likelihood of guilt.

from thence to be Conveyed to the publick Goal of Williamsburgh as the Law in such Cases Direct.

Mills's Recognizance

Richard Mills in open Court before his Majesties Justices Acknowledged himselfe Indebted to our sovereign Lord the King his heirs and successors in the sume of Ten pounds sterling to be Levyed of his Lands and Tenements goods and Chattles with Condition that if the said Richard Mills shall personally appeare at the Next General Court on the fourth Day thereof and then and there give such Evidence as he knows against Thomas Bruss Concerning his stealing divers goods out of the said Mills's house and Doe not Depart thence without Leave of that Court That then this Recognizance to be void or else to Remaine in full Force.

Walker's Recognizance

William Walker in open Court before his Majesties Justices acknowledged himselfe Indebted to Our Sovereign Lord the King his heirs and successors In the sume of Ten pounds sterling To be Levyed of his Lands and Tenements goods and Chattles with Condition that if the said William Walker shall personally appeare at the next General Court on the fourth Day thereof and then and there give such Evidence as he knows against Thomas Bruss for Feloniously takeing of Diverse goods out of the house of Richard Mills and Doe not Depart thence without Leave of [104] that Court That then this Recognizance to be void or Else to Remaine in full Force.

At a Court held for Richmond County the First Day of September 1725.

Present: Charles Barber, John Tayloe, William Fantleroy, Robert Tomlin, John Metcalfe and Newman Brockenbrough, Gentleman Justices.

Taylor bound to his behaviour

Robert Taylor of North Farnham parish haveing been taken into Custody to answer the presentment of the Grandjury against him for being a Common and Notorious swearer and this Day appearing but offering Nothing materiall to Excuse himselfe, It is the opinion of this Court and accordingly Ordered that for the said Offence he give good and Sufficient security for his good Behaviour Dureing the Terme of One Year.

Whereupon the said Robert Taylor Together with Edward Jones in open Court Acknowledged themselves Indebted to our Sovereign Lord the King his heirs and Successors In the Sume of Twenty pounds sterling To be Levyed on their Lands and Tenements goods and Chattles with Condition that if the said Robert Taylor shall be of good behaviour as well Towards his said Majestie as all his Leige people That then this Recognizance to be void and of none Effect or Else to Remaine in full Force.

At a Court held for Richmond County the Third Day of November 1725.

Present: Charles Barber, John Tayloe, William Downman, Joseph Belfeild, Robert Tomlin, John Metcalfe and Newman Brockenbrough, Gentlemen Justices.

[*Mulenton examined*]

[**105**] Whereas Joseph Mulenton was by vertue of a mittimus from John Tayloe gentleman one of the Justices of this Court committed to the County Goal on Suspicion of Feloniously breaking open a house belonging to Christopher Pridham and takeing Rum and Suggar and being now brought before his Majesties Justices here Present and Together with severall Witnesses being Diligently Examined touching the said Fact. It appearing to the Court that there is Just Cause for Trying the said Prisoner at the Next Court of Oyer and Terminer to be held at his Majesties Royall Capitol for the Crime aforesaid Whereof he is Accused It is therefore Ordered that the said Joseph Mulenton be Remanded to the prison of this County under the Custody of the Sherriff and from thence to be Conveyed to the Publick Goal of Williamsburgh as the Law in such Cases Directs.

Nash's Recognizance

William Nash in open Court before his Majesties Justices acknowledged himselfe Indebted to our Sovereign Lord the King his heirs and Successors In the sume of Ten pounds sterling to be Levyed of his Lands and Tenements goods and Chattles with Condition if he the said William Nash shall appeare before the Honorable Court of Oyer and Terminer to be held at his Majesties Royall Capitol on the second Tuesday in December Next And so Attend from Time to Time as the Said Court shall Direct Then and there to give Evidence for our said Lord the King against Joseph Mulenten who stands Committed to the Goal of this County on Suspicion of Feloniously breaking open a house belonging to Christopher Pridham and takeing Rum and Suggar, Then this Recognizance to be Void, or Else to be and Remaine in full Force and Vertue.

Barnes's Recognizance

Mary Barnes in open Court before his Majesties Justices Acknowledged herselfe Indebted to Our Sovereign Lord the King his heirs and Successors In the sume of Ten pounds sterling To be Levyed of her Lands and Tenements goods and Chattles with Condition if she the said Mary Barnes shall appeare before the Honorable Court of Oyer and Terminer to be held at his Majesties Royall Capitol on the second Tuesday [**106**] In December Next and so attend from Time to Time as the said Court shall Direct Then and there to give Evidence for our said

Lord the King against Joseph Mulenton who stands Committed to the Goal of this County on Suspicion of Feloniously breaking open a house belonging to Christopher Pridham and Takeing Rum and Suggar, Then this Recognizance to be void or else to Remaine in full force and Vertue.

[*Anderson's recognizance*]

Edward Anderson in open Court before his Majesties Justices Acknowledged himselfe Indebted to our Sovereign Lord the King his heirs and successors in the sume of Ten pounds sterling to be Levyed of his Lands and Tenements goods and Chattles with Condition if he the said Edward Anderson shall appear before the Honorable Court of Oyer and Terminer to be held at his Majesties Royal Capitoll on the second Tuesday in December Next and so attend from Time to Time as the said Court shall Direct. Then and there to give Evidence for our said Lord the King against Joseph Mulenton who stands Committed to the Goal of this County on Suspicion of Feloniously breaking open a house belonging to Christopher Pridham and takeing Rum and suggar, Then this Recognizance to be void, or Else to be and Remaine in full Force and Vertue.

Bartlet's Recognizance

John Bartlet in open Court before his Majesties Justices Acknowledged himselfe Indebted to our sovereign Lord the King his heirs and successors In the sume of Ten pounds sterling To be Levyed of his Lands and Tenements goods and Chattles with Condition of the said John Bartlets servant man named Richard Hancock shall appeare before the Honorable Court of Oyer and Terminer to be held at his Majesties Royall Capitoll on the second Tuesday in December Next And so attend from Time to Time as the said Court shall Direct Then and there to give Evidence for our said Lord the King against Joseph Mulenton who stands Committed to the Goal of this County on Suspicion of Feloniously breaking open a house belonging to Christopher Pridham and takeing Rum and Suggar Then this Recognizance to be void or Else to [**107**] be and Remaine in full Force and Vertue.

At a Court held for Richmond County the third Day of March 1725/6.
Present: John Tayloe, William Fantleroy, Joseph Belfield, Robert Tomlin and Samuell Peachey, Gentlemen Justices.

Tayler bound to his behaviour

Thomas Tayler of Northfarnham parish haveing been Summoned to answer the presentment of the Grandjury Against him for Common Swearing and this Day Appearing but Offering Nothing Materiall to Excuse himselfe it is the Opinion of this Court and accordingly Ordered that for the said Offence he give good and Sufficient Security for his good behaviour dureing the Terme of one year.

Whereupon the said Thomas Tayler together with Stanley Gower his Security in Open Court Acknowledged themselves Indebted to our Sovereign Lord the King his heirs and Successors in the sume of Twenty pounds sterling to be Levied on their Lands and Tenements goods And Chattles with Condition of the said Thomas Taylor shall be of good behaviour as well towards his said Majestie as all his Leige people That then his Recognizance to be Void and of None Effect or else to remaine in full Force.

Smith Bound to his behaviour

William Smith of Northfarnham parish haveing been Summoned to Answer the presentment of the Grandjury Against him for Common Swearing and this Day Appearing but Offering Nothing Materiall to Excuse himselfe it is the Opinion of this Court and Accordingly Ordered that for the said Offence he give good and Sufficient Security for his good behaviour dureing the Terme of one year.

[108] Whereupon the said William Smith together with Owen Jones his Security in Open Court Acknowledged themselves indebted to Our Sovereign Lord the King his heirs and Successors in the Sume of Twenty pounds Sterling to be Levyed on their Lands and Tenements goods and Chattles with Condition of the said William Smith shall be of good behaviour as well Towards his Majestie as All his Leige people That then his Recognizance to be Void and of None Effect or else to Remaine in full Force.

Anderson bound to his behaviour

Edward Anderson of Northfarnham Parish haveing been Summoned to Answer the presentment of the Grandjury Against him for Common Swearing and this Day Appearing but Offering Nothing Materiall to Excuse himselfe it is the Opinion of this Court and Accordingly Ordered that for the said Offense he give good and Sufficient Security for his good behaviour dureing the Terme of one year.

Whereupon the said Edward Anderson together with John Pyeraat his Security in Open Court Acknowledged themselves Indebted to Our Sovereign Lord the King his heirs And Successors in the Sume of Twenty pounds Sterling to be Levyed on their Lands and Tenements goods and Chattles with Condition if the said Edward Anderson shall be of good behaviour as well towards his said Majestie as all his Leige people That then his Recognizance to be void and of None Effect or else to remaine in full Force.

At a Court held for Richmond County the Sixth day of Aprill 1726.
Present: John Tayloe, William Fantleroy, Joseph Belfield, Robert Tomlin and John Metcalfe, Gentlemen Justices.

Vernon bound to the Peace

Whereas Thomas Nash Jr. haveing Sworn the peace Against Ephraim Vernon before Charles Barber Gentleman one of the Magistrates of this County it is therefore Ordered that he give Security for keeping the same.

[**109**] Whereupon the said Ephraim Vernon together with Martin Sherman his Security Acknowledged themselves Indebted to Our Sovereign Lord the King his heirs and Successors both of them in the Sume of Twenty pounds Sterling to be Levyed on their Lands and Tenements goods and Chattles with Condition that if the said Ephraim Vernon shall keep the peace of our Sovereign Lord the King as well towards his Majestie as all his Leige people but more Especially towards the said Thomas Nash Jr. That then this Recognizance to be Void and of None Effect or else to remaine in full Force.

Present: Charles Barber and Samuell Peachey, Gentlemen

Deboard bound to his Peace

Whereas John Deboard was bound Over to Appear at this Court by Virtue of a Warrant from John Tayloe Gentlemen one of the Magestrates of this County to Answer the Complaint of Thomas Williams for that the said John Deboard on the Twenty First day of October last past did Violently Assault him on the road and in a Most barbarous Maner beat kick and Bruise him it is therefore Ordered that the said John Deboard give good And Sufficient Security for his Keeping the peace of our Sovereign Lord the King.

Whereupon the said John Deboard together with Patrick Short And David Phillips his Securitys Acknowledge themselves Indebted to Our Sovereign Lord the King his heirs and Successors each of them in the Sume of Twenty pounds Sterling to be Levyed on their Lands and Tenements goods and Chattles with Condition that if the said John Deboard shall keep the peace of our Sovereign Lord the King as well towards his Majestie as all his Leige people but More Especially the said Thomas Williams. That then this Recognizance to be Void And of None Effect or else to remaine in full Force.

Mahon bound to his behaviour

Whereas Mathew Mahon Collier of Northfarnham Parrish this day Appearing to Answer the presentment of the Grandjury Against him for Common Swearing but Offering Nothing Materiall to Excuse himselfe. It is the Opinion of this Court And Accordingly Ordered that for the said Offence he give good and Sufficient Security for his good behaviour dureing the Terme of one year.

Whereupon the said Mathew Mahon together with Aurthur McMahon his Security in Open Court Acknowledge themselves Indebted to Our Sovereign Lord the King his heirs and Successors in the sume of Twenty pounds Sterling to be Levyed on their Lands and Tenements goods and Chattles wtih Condition of the said Mathew Mahon shall be of good behaviour as well towards his Majestie as all his Leige people That then his Recognizance to be Void and of None Effect or else to remaine in full Force.

[**110**] Present Newman Brockenbrough Gentleman

[*Taylor bound to his behaviour*]

Whereas John Taylor Wiggmaker of Northfarnham Parrish this day Appearing to Answer the presentment of the Grandjury against him for Common Swearing But Offering Nothing Materiall to Excuse himselfe It is the Opinion of this Court and Accordingly Ordered that for the said Offence he give good and Sufficient Security for his good behaviour dureing the Terme of one Year.

Whereupon the said John Taylor together with George Eskridge his Security in Open Court Acknowledged themselves Indebted to our Sovereign Lord the King his heirs and Successors in the Sume of Twenty pounds with Condition of the said John Taylor shall be of good behaviour As well towards his Majestie as all his Liege people, That then his Recognizance to be Void and of None effect or else to remaine in full Force.

At a Court held for Richmond County the Third Day of August 1726.

Present: Charles Barber, John Tayloe, William Fantleroy, Robert Tomlin, John Metcalf, Samuell Peachey, Gentlemen Justices.

Haley bound to his behaviour

It Appearing to this Court that Andrew Haley is a person of An ill behaviour It is therefore Ordered that he give good and Sufficient Security for his good behaviour.

Whereupon the said Andrew Haley together with Owin Jones his Security Acknowledged themselves Indebted to our Sovereign Lord the King the said Andrew Haley in the Sume of twenty Pounds Sterling and the said Owen Jones in the Sume of Tenn Pounds Sterling to be Levyed on their Lands and Tenements goods and Chattells with Condition that if the said Andrew Haley shall be of good behaviour as well towards his said Majestie as all his Leige People that then this Recognizance to be void and of none Effect or Else to Remaine in full Force.

Negro Ben's Tryal

[**111**] At a Session of Oyer and Terminer held at Richmond Court house on tuesday the Sixteenth of August 1726 In the Thirteenth Year of the reign of Our Sovereign Lord George By the grace of God King of Great Brittain France and Ireland Defender of the Faith etc. By Virtue of a Speciall Commission for the Tryall of All Treasons petty Treasons or Misprisions Thereof Felonys Murders or other Offences or Crimes Whatsoever Committed Within this County of Richmond by a Negro Man Slave Named Ben belonging to Thomas Griffin

Gentleman and Directed to Charles Barber John Tayloe William Fantleroy William Downmen Charles Grymes Robert Tomlin John Metcalfe Samuell Peachey and Newman Brockenbrough Gentlemen.

Present: Charles Barber, William Fantleroy, William Downman, Robert Tomlin and John Metcalfe, Gentlemen Justices.

Memorandom that on this day being the Sixteenth Day of August 1726 an Indictment was preferred against a Negro Man Slave Called Ben in these words Richmond Ss Negro Ben a Slave to Mr. Thomas Griffin of the Parrish of Northfarnham in the County of Richmond are in his Majesties Name appealed[77] and hereby arrained for the felonious Murdering and Killing of a Certain Negro Woman slave late belonging to the aforesaid Thomas Griffin And in the parrish and County aforesaid named Winney by Cutting of her throat and Mortally wounding her with a knife on the twenty seventh of June 1726 as Appears by an Inquest taken on the view of the body of the said Winney by Charles Barber Gentleman one of his Majesties Coroners for the County aforesaid dated the twenty eigth of June 1726 for which willfull felonious Murder you Must Now Answer before his Majesties Commissioners of Oyer and Terminer Now Present.

Whereupon the said Ben was brought to the Barr and Arraigned for the said Felony and there pleaded Not Guilty and thereupon the Court proceeding on his Tryall (After haveing heard the Evidence Against him and that he had to say in his Defence) are of Oppinion that he is guilty of Feloniously Murdering the said Negro Winney for which he stands Indicted.

It is therefore Ordered that the said Negro Ben return to the place from which he Came from thence to the place of Execution and there to be hanged by the Neck till he be dead.

[112] Pursuant to an Act of Assembly made in the Year 1723 Concerning the Tryall of Slaves Comitting Capital Crimes this Court in pursuance thereof do Value Ben a Negro Man Slave belonging to Thomas Griffin Gentleman (Whereas this day Condemned to dye for Feloniously Murdering a Negro Woeman Named Winney belonging to the said Thomas Griffin) to Twenty pounds Currant Money and Ordered that the Clerk of this Court Certifye the same to the next assembly.

At a Court held for Richmond County the 7th day of September 1726.

Present: Charles Barber, John Tayloe, William Downman, Robert Tomlin and Samuel Peachey, Gentlemen Justices.

Allgood bound to his Behaviour

It appearing to this Court that Edward Allgood Is a person of an ill behaviour It is therefore ordered that he give good and sufficient Security for his good Behaviour.

Where upon the said Edward Allgood together with Ishmaell Dew and An-

---

77. Meaning "accused" of the crime. In medieval English criminal law, private individuals could "appeal" a person for a crime when the king's courts had not indicted the person for it; Plucknett, *Common Law*, 117ff. This use of the term was long out of date by the eighteenth century.

drew Dew his Securitys Acknowledged themselves Indebted to Our Sovereign Lord the King the said Edward Allgood in the Sume of forty pounds sterling and the said Ishmaell Dew and Andrew Dew in the sume of twenty pounds each sterling to be Levyed on their lands and Tenements goods and Chattels with Condition that if the said Edward Allgood shall be of good behaviour as well towards his said Majestie As All his Leige people that then this Recognizance to be Void And of None Effect or else to remaine in full Force.

[**113**] At a Court held for Richmond County the Fifth Day of October 1726.
Present: Charles Barber, Thomas Griffin, John Tayloe, William Fantleroy, Robert Tomlin and Samuell Peachey, Gentlemen Justices.

Smith bound to his Behaviour

It appearing to this Court That Thomas Smith is a person of an ill behaviour it is therefore ordered that he give good and Sufficient Security for his good behaviour.

Whereupon the said Thomas Smith together with Thomas Osborne his Security Acknowledged themselves Indebted to our Sovereign Lord the King The said Thomas Smith in the Sume of twenty pounds sterling and the said Thomas Osborne in the Sum of Tenn Pounds Sterling to be levyed on their lands and Tenements goods and Chattels with Condition that if the said Thomas Smith shall be of Good Behaviour as well towards his said Majesty as all his Leige people That then this Recognizance to be Void and of None Effect or else to remaine in Full Force.

At a Court Continued and held for Richmond County the Sixth Day of October 1726.
Present: Charles Barber, John Tayloe, William Fantleroy and Robert Tomlin, Gentlemen Justices.

Pridham bound to his behaviour

Christopher Pridham being brought before this Court for beating and Abuseing his Wife, It is Therefore ordered That he give good and Sufficient Security for this good behaviour the said Pridham in the Sum of forty pounds and two Securitys Each in twenty pounds And ordered that he remain in the Sherriffs Custody untill he Give Such Security.

At a Court held for Richmond County the second day of November 1726.
Present: Charles Barber, William Fantleroy, Robert Tomlin and Samuel Barber, Gentlemen Justices.

Charlton whipt and give Security for his Behaviour

Whereas John Charlton was by Virtue of a Mittimus from John Metcalfe Gentleman one of the Justices of this Court Committed to the County Goal on Suspicion of felloniously Killing of a Beef belonging to [114] Col. Robert Carter and being now brought before his Majesties Justices here present and Together with Severall Evidences being Diligently Examined touching the said Fact it is the Opinion of this Court that the said John Carlton is Guilty of the Crime Laid to his Charge it is therefore Ordered that for the said Offence, the sherriff take him and Carry him to the Common Whipping post and give him thirty nine Lashes on his bare back well laid on, As also that he give good and Sufficient Security for his good behaviour the said Charlton in the Sum of forty Pounds Sterling and two Securities Each in twenty pounds Sterling and that he Remain in the Sherriffs Custody until he gives Such Security.[78]

At a Call'd Court held at the Court house of Richmond County the 17th day of January 1726/7.

Present: Thomas Griffin, John Tayloe, William Fantleroy, William Downman, Robert Tomlin, John Metcalfe and Samuell Peachey, Gentlemen Justices.

Parson's Examination

Whereas Jesper Parsons second mate of the ship Call'd the Tayloe was by Vertue of a Mittimus from John Tayloe Gentleman one of the Justices of this Court Committed to the County Goal on Suspicion of Murdering Cap. John Heard, late Master of the said shipp and others And also for plundering the said shipp and being Now brought before his Majesties Justices hereto Gentleman was Examined by the Court as Followeth.

COURT:	ANSWER:
What day did the shipp call'd the Tayloe run ashore[?]	The Eighteenth Day of December last[.]
What sort of Weather had you[?]	Thick Hazy Weather[.]
What wind put you on shore[?]	South S: Easter thereabouts.
What time of the Day was it[?]	About Ten a Clock at Night.
Did not the Master and you think by your Reckening that you were upon the Coast[?]	Yes about 12 a Clock in the day wee had thirty five fathom water[.]

78. The offense was the common-law one of malicious mischief. The law required that the offender have animus against the victim and destroy his property out of cruelty or revenge; Blackstone, *Commentaries*, 4:243–44. By 23 and 24 Charles II, c.7 (1667), it was a felony maliciously to kill another man's cattle, the penalty for which was usually reduced to transportation for seven years. Evidently Virginia did not regard this statute as holding in the colony, perhaps because it was passed after 1607.

What part of the Coast Did you think you were upon[?]	Just upon the Cape.
Did you not heave the lead and line of ten[?]	Every halfe hour[.]
[115] What water had you at Eight a Clock at Night[?]	About Twelve Fatham.
What Course did you steer[?]	West S: West halfe South.
What time after the Shipp Run a ground did the Master and the Rest that went with him leave the Ship and take to the Yawle[?]	Soon After.
Did he take Anything along with him[?]	I was told that the Captain went into his Cabbin and took a bag but do not know whether it was Gold or Silver.
How many of the Crew went with him[?]	Four.
Did the storm Continue long after[?]	Sometimes Moderate Breezes and Storms after[.]
How long did you stay on board after the Master Went off[?]	I went ashore Betimes in Each Morning.
How Farr Might it be to the Shore[?]	The first stroak she gave was about two hundred yards from the Shore and wee Left her within ten or fourteen yards of the Shore.
What things had you from the shipp[?]	Nothing but what I have upon my back.
Did the Shipp split in pieces[?]	Not all only the Rudder.
Why did you not stay on board and Secure the goods[,] sales and rigging[?]	I thought it not proper to meddle with anything because I thought it might bring us into a prison[.]
Did you know when the Long boat over sett[?]	Yes about 11 a Clock at Night there was 3 hands in her[.]
Why did not they secure the papers[?]	They were burning them before I Came down Staires at Timothy Eves's.
What Water was there about the shipp when you left her[?]	About three Fatham a stern and Ten foot a head.
Did not you go on board afterward[?]	No, only that Morning I left her[.]

What became of the Yawle and long boat[?] Did not they drive a shore and were they Dry or full of Water[?]

They Drove ashore, there was No Water in the Long boat and Little or None in the Yawle. They Satt up upon their bottoms.

Was any of the Men that came ashore present on Board the Man of Warr[?]

Yes I saw the Boatswain present.

What became of the Captains Escrtore[?][79]

I saw it stave upon the Beach.

Doe you know of any Quarrelling or Blood shed on board the Shipp[?]

None at all only one Man Cutt his hand.

Had the Captain and you any Quarell on board[?]

Only once for Swearing.

What Chests did you Carry on shore[?]

We did not Carry one on shore[.]

Where was the Grind stones stowed[?]

Abaft Under the baild goods[;] they Could not be Came at[.]

[**116**] What liquor did you Carry on Shore[?]

A dozen and halfe or 2 Dozen pint bottles of White wine[,] bottles brandy and 3 or 4 Caces Sugar[.]

How many perriwigs did you see on shore[?]

With two or three[.]

[*Court*]

What goods, Money or Merchanizes, Did you See or hear of being gott a shore by any body from first to Last[?]

[*Answer*]

There was the Captains box of books, bed, quilt, table Linen, Morning Gown and his Wearing Apparell, There was about Eight or Tenn Course hatts, Four or Five Dozen of Shoo's, Six Musketts, Two pistolls, one or two pieces of Garlick Holland, three or four papers of Book Cambrick, about a dozen and halfe of Handkercheifs, one Brass Compass, one Book Call'd the English Laws, some Letters, one Speaking Trumpett, three iron potts, two basketts of Close, three Cask of Chese, Nineteen Chears, the Ships Jack Ensigne and penant, the Fore-saile Foretopsailes and flying Gibb, and Cask of Flower, one Cooking Glass, Some Chests, Three parts of a Cask of Butter, some Silver plate, Two watches, twelve Coines, one spie glass, and Two small Cooking Glasses.

---

79. A writing table or desk.

It appearing to the Court upon the Aforesaid Examination that there is Just Cause for trying the said prisoner at the Generall Court for the Crime aforesaid where of he is Accused, It is therefore ordered that the said Jesper Parsons, be remanded to the Prison of this County Under the Custody of the Sherriff, And from thence to be Conveyed to the publique Goal of Williamsburgh as the Law in such Cases Directs.

At a Call'd Court held at the Court house of Richmond County the 24th day of January 1726/7.

Present: Thomas Griffin, John Tayloe, William Fantleroy, William Downman, Robert Tomlin and John Metcalfe, Gentlemen Justices.

Hescocks Examination

Whereas John Hescock a Servant to Edward Hinkley late of North Farnham parrish in this County (who confesseth that he was Convicted in England for Stealing a Mare for which fact he was Transported into this Country) was by Vertue of an Order of this Court dated this 17th Instant, Committed to the County Goal on Suspition of Murdering his said Master, and being now brought before his Majesties Justices here present, Was Examined by the Court as Followeth.

[117] Court: John Hescock did you kill your Master Edward Hinkley[?]
Answer: Yes Kill'd him with an Ax.
Court: What reason had you to doe it[?]
Answer: None att all that I knew of.
Court: Did you strike your Mistress with the same ax[?]
Answer: Yes one blow, And then threw her down into the potatoe hole and threw the same Ax along with her[.]
Court: Did you robb the house[?]
Answer: Yes I took a parsell of Dowlass and some white Tape out of a chest that was not Lockt[.] I took out of a box that was lockt one pair worsted Stockings one Ivory knife and Fork. one Jacklegg knife, some Pinns one bagg of Flints, buttons, and one Leather purse with Four Fifteen pound peices in it; one Razour, two powder goards with powder in them. I took out of My Mistresses pockett one Gold Ring and one Ink Case. I took out of the house one brass pockett Compass, one horse Whipp, And one pair of pistolls, and then I went away and Design'd to make my Escape on board some Shipp.

It appearing to the Court upon the aforesaid Examination that there is Just Cause for trying the said prisoner at the Generall Court for the Crime aforesaid whereof he is Accused, It is therefore ordered that the said John Hescock be Remanded to the prison of this County Under the Custody of the Sherriff and from thence to be Conveyed to the publique Goal of Williamsburgh as the Law in Such Cases Directs.

Thornton Recognizance

Thomas Thornton of Sittenburn parrish in Richmond County, in open Court before his Majesties Justices Acknowledged himself Indebted to our Sovereign Lord the King his heirs and Successors in the Sum of Tenn pounds Sterling to be levyed of his Lands and Tenements goods and Chattles with Condition that if the said Thomas Thornton shall personally Appear at the Next General Court on the Fourth day thereof and then and there give Such Evidence as he knows against John Hescock, who stands Committed for petty Treason in Murdering his Master Edward Hinkley late of the said County and do not Depart thence without Leave of that Court, That then this Recognizance to be Void, or else to Remain in Full Force.

Bruce [and Ford] Recognizance[s]

Andrew Bruce of Sittenburn parrish in Richmond County in Open Court before his Majesties Justices Acknowledged himself Indebted to our Sovereign Lord the King his heirs and Successors in the sum of Tenn pounds Sterling to be Levyed of his Lands and Tenements goods and Chattles with Condition that if the said Andrew Bruce shall personally appear at the Next General Court on the Fourth day thereof, And then and there give such Evidence as he knows Against John Hescock, who stands Committed for petty Treason in Murdering his Master Edward Hinkley Late of the said County, And do not Depart thence without Leave of that Court, That then this Recognizance to be Void, or else to Remain in full Force.

[**118**] John Ford of Sittenburn parrish in Richmond County in Open Court before his Majesties Justices Acknowledged himself Indebted to our Sovereign Lord the King his heirs and Successors in the sum of Tenn pounds Sterling to be Leveyed on his Lands and Tenements goods and Chattles with Condition that if the said John Ford shall personally appear at the Next General Court on the Fourth day thereof, And then and there give Such Evidence as he knows Against John Hescock, who stands Committed for petty Treason in Murdering his Master Edward Hinkley late of the said County and do not Depart thence without Leave of that Court, That Then this Recognizance to be Void, or else to Remaine in Full Force.

At a Court held for Richmond County the Seventh Day of June 1727.
Present: John Tayloe, William Fantleroy, William Downman, Charles Grymes, John Metcalfe and Samuell Peachey, Gentlemen Justices.

Booth bound to his Behaviour

Whereas James Booth of Northfarnham parrish this day Appearing to Answer the presentment of the Grandjury Against him for being a Common Swearer but offering Nothing Matteriall to Excuse himselfe It is the Opinion of this Court, and Accordingly Ordered that for the said Offence he give Good and Sufficient Security for his Good Behaviour During the Term of one Year.

Whereupon the said James Booth Together with Tobias Phillips and William Walker his Security in open Court Acknowledged themselves Indebted unto our Sovereign Lord the King his heirs and Successors in the sum of twenty pounds Sterling to be Levyed on their Lands and Tenements Goods and Chattles with Condition that if the said James Booth shall be of Good Behaviour as well towards his Majestie as all his Leige people, That then his Recognizance to be void and of None Effect or else to Remain in full Force.

Nicholls bound to his Behaviour

Whereas Charles Nicholls of North Farnham parrish this day appearing to answer the presentment of the Grandjury Against him for being a Common Swearer but Offering Nothing Matteriall to Excuse himself It is the opinion of this Court, And Accordingly Ordered that for the said Offence he give Good and Sufficient Security for his Good behaviour During the Terme of one Year.

Whereupon the said Charles Nicholls Together with Thomas Nash his Security, in Open Court Acknowledged themselves Indebted unto our Sovereign Lord the King his heirs and Successors in the Sum of twenty pounds Sterling to be Levyed on his Lands and Tenements Goods and Chattles with Condition that of the said Charles Nicholls shall be of Good [119] behaviour as well towards his Majestie as all his Leige people, That then this Recognizance to be Void and of None Effect or else to remain in full Force.

At a Court held for Richmond County the Seventh Day of June 1727.
Present: John Tayloe, William Fantleroy, William Downman, Charles Grymes, John Metcalfe and Samuell Peachey, Gentlemen Justices.

Grandjury Walker and Others

At a Court held for this County the Fifth day of May 1725 William Walker, Edmund Northen, William Smith and John Brown, was presented by the Grandjury for not going to their parrish Church for a month, to which the said William Walker, Edmond Northen, William Smith and John Brown at a Court held for the said County the third day of March following putt in their plea to which John Tarpley Jr. Gentlemen the Kings Attorney Demur'd there to, Upon arguing the same, the said Demurrer is Overruled.[80]

At a Court held for Richmond County the Fifth Day of July 1727.
Present: Thomas Griffin, John Tayloe, William Fantleroy, Robert Tomlin, Samuell Peachey and Newman Brockenbrough, Gentlemen Justices.

---

80. A demurrer is an objection to the sufficiency of the facts alleged to constitute the offense under the law.

Taylor Bound to his Behaviour

John Taylor planter of Northfarnham parish this day Appearing to Answer the presentment of the Grandjury against him for being a Common Disturber of the peace but Offering Nothing Matteriall to Excuse himself it is the Opinion of this Court and accordingly Ordered that for the said Offence he give good and Sufficient Security for his good behaviour During the Terme of one year.

Whereupon the said John Taylor Together with Thomas Jesper his Security in open Court Acknowledged themselves Indebted unto our Sovereign Lord the King his heirs and Successors in the sum of Twenty pounds Sterling to be Levyed on their Lands and Tenements goods and Chattles with Condition that if the said John Taylor shall be of Good Behaviour as well towards his Majestie as all his leige people, That then his Recognizance to be Void and of None Effect or Else to Remain in full Force.

Jones bound to his behaviour

[120] Richard Jones of Northfarnham Parish haveing been Summoned to Answer the presentment of the Grandjury against him for being a Common Swearer and this day Appearing but Offering Nothing Matteriall to Excuse himself It is the Opinion of this Court and accordingly ordered that for the said Offence he Give Good and Sufficient Security for his Good Behaviour Dureing the Terme of one Year and that he Remain in the Sherriffs Custody untill he Gives Such Security.

Molony bound to his behaviour

John Molony of Sittenburn Parish haveing been Summoned to Answer the Presentment of the Grand Jury Against him for being a Common Swearer and this Day Appearing but Offering Nothing Matteriall to Excuse himself It is the Opinion of this Court, and Accordingly Ordered that for the said Offence he Give good and Sufficient Security for his Good Behaviour During the Terme of one year.

Whereupon the said John Molony Together with Thomas Osborne And Humphry Thomas his Security's in Open Court Acknowledged themselves Indebted unto our Sovereign Lord the King his heirs and Successors in the Sum of Twenty pounds Sterling to be Levyed on their Lands and Tenements goods and Chattles with Condition that if the said John Moloney shall be of Good Behaviour as Well toward his majestie as all his Leige People, That then this Recognizance to be Void and of None effect or Else to Remain in full Force.

[Rooker's Examination]

Roger Rooker being by Vertue of a Warrant of Newman Brockenbrough Gentleman one of his Majesties Justices of the Peace for this County, brought before this Court to Answer the Complaint of John Dunlop Merchant on Suspicion of the said Rookers taking one hundred twenty Seven pounds of Tobacco out of a hogshead of Tobacco belonging to the said Dunlop of Captain Crawleys Quarters, And Several Evidences being Examined Concerning the same, This Court are of Opinion that the said Rooker is Guilty of the Crime laid to his Charge, It is Therefore Ordered that the Sherriff take him and Carry him to the Common Whipping post and Give him Twenty Lashes on his bare back Well laid on, and then to Remain [Remand] him to the Goal of this County untill he Gives Good and Sufficient Security for his Good Behaviour During the Terme of one year.

[**121**] At a Court held for Richmond County the Second day of August 1727. Present: John Tayloe, William Fantleroy, William Downman, Charles Grymes, Robert Tomlin, John Metcalfe and Samuell Peachey, Gentlemen Justices.

Toole Whipt

Christian Toole a Servant Woeman belonging to James Wilson this day Acknowledging in Court that she stole out of her said Masters house about Twenty Eight pounds Current Money It is Therefore ordered that for the said Offence the Sherriff take her and Carry her to the Common Whipping post and give her Thirty nine Lashes on her bare back Well laid on.

Molony Whipt

John Molony being by Vertue of a Warrant of William Fantleroy Gentleman one of his Majesties Justices of the peace for this County brought before this Court for Concealing Stolen Goods brought to his house by Captain Thomas Marshalls Saylors [sailors] and several Evidences being Examined concerning the same, this Court are of Opinion that the said Molony is Guilty of the Crime laid to his charge.[81] It is therefore ordered that the Sherriff take him and Carry him to the Common Whipping post and Give him thirty nine Lashes on his Bare back Well laid on and that he Remain in the Sherriffs Custody untill he gives Good and Sufficient Security for his good Behaviour During the Terme of one Year.

Thornton bound to his Behaviour

Thomas Thornton of Sittenburn Parish this day Appearing to Answer the Presentment of the Grandjury against him for being a Common Swearer and a Common Drunkard But offering Nothing Materiall to Excuse himself, It is the

---

81. In common law, accessories to a felony, including knowing receivers of stolen goods, could not be convicted unless and until the principal was taken and found guilty; Blackstone, *Commentaries*, 4:318–19. The sailors were not in custody, but the magistrates punished Molony for concealing allegedly stolen goods anyway. He was not punished as severely as he might have been if tried and convicted of being an accessory to a felony at the General Court. A statute of 1730 (*Statutes at Large*, 4:271–73) closed this loophole by permitting fine and imprisonment of knowing receivers or sellers of stolen goods when the principal was not yet taken.

Opinion of this Court And accordingly ordered that for the said Offence he Give good and Sufficient Security for his good Behaviour During the Terme of one Year.

Whereupon the said Thomas Thornton Together with Avery Dye his Security in Open Court Acknowledged themselves [122] Indebted unto our Sovereign Lord the King his heirs and Successors in the Sum of Twenty pounds Sterling to be Levyed on their Lands and Tenements Goods and Chattles, with Condition that if the said Thomas Thornton shall be of good Behaviour as Well Towards his Majestie as all his Leige people That then this Recognizance to be void and of None Effect or else to Remain in full Force.

At a Call'd Court held at the Court house of Richmond County the 19th day of August 1727.

Present: John Tayloe, William Fantleroy, William Downman, John Metcalfe, Samuel Peachey and Newman Brockenbrough, Gentlemen Justices.

Gourly Whipt

Whereas James Gourly by Vertue of a Mittimus from Samuell Peachey gentleman one of the Justices of this Court was Committed to the County Goale on Suspicion of Stealing from David Copley of Westmoreland County one Large Black horse and some other things and being now brought before his Majesties Justices here present on Examination of Severall Evidences touching the same, It is the Opinion of this Court, That the said James Gourly is Guilty of the Crime laid to his Charge, It is therefore Ordered that the Sherriff take him and Carry him to the Common Whipping post and Give him Twenty Lashes on his bare back well laid on and Then to keep him in his Safe Custody till the Next Sitting of the Court, at which time the said Sherriff is Ordered to Give him Nineteen Lashes More on his bare back as aforesaid and then to keep him in his Safe Custody till he enters into bond with good and Sufficient Security for his Good Behaviour During the Terme of one Year.

At a Call'd Court held at the Court house of Richmond County the twenty Seventh day of October 1727.

Present: Charles Grymes, Robert Tomlin, Samuel Peachey and Newman Brockenbrough, Gentlemen Justices.

Gormorly's Examination

Whereas Patrick Gormorly was by Vertue of a Mittimus from Charles Grymes gentleman one of the Justices of this Court Committed to [123] the County Goal for Felonious Stealing Sundry Goods found in his Custody and for Inticeing two Servants belonging to Christopher Petty and a Servant belonging to Robert

Mathews to Run away,[82] and being Now brought before his Majesties Justices here present was Examined by the Court as followeth.

Court—Patrick Gormorly[,] how came you by that bay horse that was found in your possession[?]

Answer—I had him from one Phillip Harris that lives in Charles County in Maryland and Gave him a Mare in Exchange he was going into King and Queen County.

Court—Who was by when you made the Exchange[?]

Answer—Two men that came out of Maryland along with him.

William Bird Servant to Robert Mathews of this County aged Twenty one years or thereabouts being sworn saith that Some time Ago he had Discourse with Patrick Gormorly the prisoner at the barr who told him that if he would goe along with him he would Carry him where his Master should not find him againe and that he would provide a horse for him, upon which this Despondent told the said Gormorly that he was willing one John Williams servant to Christopher Petty should goe along with him, and then they would appoint a place to Meet in the woods and goe of[f] and Accordingly they Did afterwards Meet, and Appointed Tuesday the 17th Instant to Meet Two hours within Night at a Certain place in the woods, whereupon this Depondent and John Williams went and found the prisoner at the barr Sitting by a fire and he had along with him a bay horse two Saddles and Some shirts and other things, and this Depondent and John Williams Imediately took him and Tyed his hands, and the Next day Carryed him before Col. Grymes.

John Williams Servant to Christopher Petty aged 27 years or thereabouts being Sworn saith that on Tuesday the 17th Instant within Night he went along with William Bird into the woods [124] and there found Patrick Gormorly the prisoner at the Barr Sitting by a fire, and he had along with him a bay horse two saddles some shirts and other things, and they Imediately took and tyed his hands and the next day Carryed him Before Col. Grymes.

John Webb of Northumberland County aged thirty years of thereabouts being Sworn saith, that on Monday the Sixteenth Instant towards the Evening he and one John Wheeler rode to Madam Balls Mills in Lancaster County, and tyed their horses near the Mill Door, and soon after the bay horse which belonged to John Wheeler was gone away, and this Depondent further saith that the bay horse which was Taken from Patrick Gormerly the Prisoner at the Barr by John Williams and William Bird and Now in the Sherriffs possession is the same horse that was rode to Madam Balls Mill that Evening, and that the horse belongs to John Wheeler.

Robert Duack of Northumberland County Aged Forty years or thereabouts Being Sworn Saith, that the bay horse which was taken from Patrick Gormerly by John Williams and William Bird and now in the Sherriffs possession belongs to John Wheeler.

---

82. No statute explicitly governed enticing servants to run away from their masters, though the case might conceivably be covered by the prohibition upon harboring and entertaining runaways; *Statutes at Large*, 3:454–55 (1705).

William Ross of Stafford County aged forty five years or thereabouts being Sworn saith, that some time agoe he lost out of his house a Coat and about three Yards of Course Linnen and that the Linnen Now produced which was taken in Patrick Gormerlys Custody he beleives to be the same which he lost out of his house.

George James of Stafford County aged Twenty two Years or thereabout being Sworn Saith, that about five weeks agoe he lost out of his Father's house where he lives one paire of Leather Breeches, and that the Leather Breeches which Patrick Gormerly the prisoner at the Barr has now on, is the same Breeches which he lost out of his Fathers house, and this Depondent further saith, that his Father lost a Saddle and Bridle out of his house Much about the same time, and that [125] the Saddle and Bridle now produced, and was taken from the prisoner is the same Saddle and Bridle which his Father lost.

It appearing to the Court upon the aforesaid Examination that there is Just Cause for trying the said prisoner at the Next Court of Oyer and Terminer to be held at his majesties Royall Capitol for the Crime aforesaid where of he is Accused, It is therefore Ordered that the said Patrick Gormerly be Remanded to the prison of this County Under the Custody of the Sherriff, And from thence to be Conveyed to the publique Goale of Williamsburgh as the Law in such Cases Directs.

Mathew's Recognizance

Robert Mathews in open Court before his Majesties Justices Acknowledged himselfe Indebted to our sovereign Lord the King his heirs and Successors in the sum of Tenn pounds Sterling to be Levyed of his Lands and Tenements, Goods and Chattles, with Condition if the said Robert Mathews Servant Man Named William Bird shall appear before the Honorable Court of Oyer and Terminer to be held at his Majesties Royal Capitol on the Second Tuesday in December Next and soe attend from time to time as the said Court shall Direct, Then and there to Give Evidence for our said Lord the King against Patrick Gormerly who stands Committed to the Goal of this County for Stolen Goods, Then this Recognizance to be Void, or Else to be and remaine in full Force and vertue.

[Webb's Recognizance]

John Webb of Northumberland County in Open Court before his Majesties Justices Acknowledged himselfe Indebted to our Sovereign Lord the King his heirs and Successors in the sum of Tenn pounds sterling to be Levyed of his Lands and Tenements Goods and Chattles with Condition if he the said John Webb shall appear before the Honorable Court of Oyer and Terminer to be held at his Majesties Royall Capitol on the second Tuesday in December next, and soe attend from time to time as the said Court shall Direct, Then and there to Give Evidence for our said Lord the King against Patrick Gormerly who stands Committed to the Goal of this County for stolen Goods, Then this Recognizance to be Void, or Else to be and remain in full Force and Vertue.

Duack's Recognizance

[**126**] Robert Duack of Northumberland County in Open Court before his Majesties Justices acknowledged himselfe Indebted to our Sovereign Lord the King his heirs and Successors in the sum of Tenn pounds Sterling to be Levyed of his Lands and Tenements Goods and Chattles with Condition if he the said Robert Duack shall Appear before the Honorable Court of Oyer and Terminor to be held at his Majesties Royall Capitol on the Second Tuesday in December Next and soe attend from time to time as the said Court shall Direct, Then and there to Give Evidence for our said Lord the King against Patrick Gormerly, who stands Committed to the Goal of this County for Stolen Goods, Then this Recognizance to be Void, or Else to be and remain in full Force and Vertue.

Ross' Recognizance

William Ross of Stafford County in Open Court before his Majesties Justices Acknowledged himself Indebted to our Sovereign Lord the King his heirs and Successors in the sum of Tenn pounds Sterling to be Levyed of his Lands and Tenements Goods and Chattles with Condition if the said William Ross shall appear before the Honorable Court of Oyer and Terminer to be held at his Majesties Royall Capitol the second Tuesday in December next and soe attend from time to time as the said Court shall Direct, Then and there to Give Evidence for our said Lord the King against Patrick Gormerly who stands Committed to the Goal of this County for stolen Goods, Then this Recognizance to be Void, or Else to be and remain in full Force and Vertue.

James's Recognizance

George James of Stafford County in Open Court before his Majesties Justices Acknowledged himself Indebted to our Sovereign Lord the King his heirs and Successors in the sum of Tenn pounds Sterling to be Levyed of his Lands and Tenements Goods and Chattles with Condition if he the said George James shall Appear before the Honorable Court of Oyer and Terminer to be held at his Majesties Royall Capitoll on the second Tuesday in December Next and soe Attend from time to time as the said Court shall Direct Then and there to give Evidence for our said Lord the King against Patrick Gormerly who stands Committed to the Goal of this County for Stolen Goods, Then this Recognizance to be Void, or Else to be and remain in full Force and Vertue.

[**127**] At a Court held for Richmond County the First Day of November 1727. Present: Thomas Griffin, John Tayloe, William Fantleroy, Charles Grymes, Samuell Peachey and Newman Brockenbrough, Gentlemen Justices.

[Petty's recognizance]

Christopher Petty in Open Court before his Majesties Justices Acknowledged himselfe Indebted to our Sovereign Lord the King his heirs and Successors in the sum of Tenn pounds Sterling to be Levyed of his Lands and Tenements Goods and Chattles with Condition if the said Christopher Petty's Servant Man named John Williams shall Appear before the Honorable Court of Oyer and Terminor to be held at his Majesties Royall Capitoll on the Second Tuesday in December Next and Soe Attend from time to time as the said Court shall Direct, Then and there to Give Evidence for our said Lord the King against Patrick Gormerly Who Stands Committed to the Goal of this County for Stolen Goods, Then this Recognizance to be Void, or Else to be and remain in full Force and Vertue.

At a Court held for Richmond County the sixth day of September 1727.

Present: John Tayloe, William Fantleroy, William Downman and Robert Tomlin, Gentlemen Justices.

Gourly bound to his behaviour

Whereas James Gourly (at a Call'd Court held at the Courthouse of this County the Nineteenth day of August Last) was Committed to the Sherriffs Custody untill he should Give Good and Sufficient Security for his good behaviour dureing the Terme of one Year.

Whereupon the said James Gourly together with Marmaduke Beckwith his Security Acknowledged themselves Indebted to our Sovereign Lord the King, the said James Gourly in the sum of Twenty pounds sterling and the said Marmaduke Beckwith in the sum of Tenn pounds sterling to be Levyed on their Lands and Tenements goods and Chattles with Condition that if the said James Gourly shall be of good behaviour as well towards his said Majestie as all his Leige [128] people, that then this Recognizance to be Void and of None Effect, or Else to remain in full Force.

At a Call'd Court held at the Court house of Richmond County the 20th Day of October 1727.

Present: John Tayloe, William Fantleroy, Charles Grymes, Robert Tomlin, Samuell Peachey, Newman Brockenbrough, Gentlemen Justices.

Livack bound to his Behaviour

Thomas Livack being committed prisoner to the Goal of this County by Vertue of a Mittimus from Charles Grymes Gentleman one of his Majesties Justices of the peace for this County on Suspicion of Counterfeiting and Disperseing false

Coin Contrary to Law,[83] This day the Court having taken the said Matter into Examination and having heard the Evidence of Mr. William Downman and Mr. Anthony Sidnor on behalf of the King against the Prisoner, Noe Sufficient Cause appearing to them upon the said Evidence to Remove him to the publick Goal at Williamsburgh he is therefore ordered to be Acquitted Giveing Security for his good behaviour during the Terme of one Year.

Whereupon the said Thomas Livack together with William Downman and Marmaduke Beckwith his Securitys acknowledged themselves Indebted to our sovereign Lord the King the said Thomas Livack in the sum of Twenty pounds Sterling and the said William Downman and Marmaduke Beckwith Each in the sum of Tenn pounds Sterling to be Levyed on their Lands and Tenements goods and Chattles with Condition that if the said Thomas Livack shall be of good behaviour as well towards his said Majestie as all his Leige people, That then this Recognizance to be Void and of None Effect, or Else to remain in full Force.

[**129**] At a Court Continued and held for Richmond County the Second Day of November 1727.

Present: Thomas Griffin, John Tayloe, William Fantleroy, William Downman, Charles Grymes, Robert Tomlin and Samuell Peachey, Gentlemen Justices.

Smith bound to his Behaviour

William Smith of the ponds of Northfarnham parrish having been Summoned to Answer the presentment of the Grandjury against him for being a Common Drunkard and a Common Swearer and this Day appearing but offering Nothing Materiall to Excuse himselfe, It is the Oppinion of this Court and Accordingly Ordered that for the said Offence he give good and Sufficient Security for his good behaviour During the Terme of one Year.

Whereupon the said William Smith together with Daniell Hornby his Security, Acknowledged themselves Indebted to our sovereign Lord the King the said William Smith in the sum of Twenty pounds Sterling and the said Daniell Hornby in the sum of Tenn pounds Sterling to be Levyed on their Lands and Tenements goods and Chattles with Condition that if the said William Smith shall be of good behaviour as well towards his said Majestie as all his Leige People, That then this Recognizance to be Void and of None Effect or Else to Remain in full Force.

At a Call'd Court held at the Courthouse of Richmond County the 21st day of November 1727.

Present: John Tayloe, William Fantleroy, Charles Grymes, Robert Tomlin, John Metcalfe, Newman Brockenbrough, Gentlemen Justices.

83. In Virginia, as in England, counterfeiting coins was treason; *Statutes at Large*, 4:219–20 (1727). Protection of the specie supply in the colony was an economic as well as a criminal matter, and the provision against counterfeiting appeared in a specie valuation law rather than a statute on crime per se.

Minors Examination

Mr. Nicholas Minor of Westmoreland County being brought before this Court on Suspicion of Murdering [130] one Richard Clifton This day the Court haveing taken the said Matter into Examenation and haveing heard Severall Evidences on behalf of the King against the said Nicholas Minor, Noe Sufficient reason appearing to them upon the said Evidence to remove him to the publick Goal at Williamsburgh, It is therefore ordered that the said Nicholas Minor be Discharged.

At a Call'd Court held at the Court house of Richmond County the 3d Day of January 1727/8.
Present: Thomas Griffin, John Tayloe, William Fantleroy, William Downman, Charles Grymes, Robert Tomlin, John Metcalfe, Samuell Peachey, Gentlemen Justices.

[Booth's Examination]

James Booth of Northfarnham parish in this County being this day brought before this Court for the Killing of John Lee, It appearing to the Court by the Verdict of the Coroners Inquest that the Misfortune hapend by the said James Booths fireing of a Gunn Charged with powder and wadd Not knowing that the said John Lee was near him, It is therefore Ordered the the said James Boooth be Discharged.

At a Court held for Richmond County the sixth day of March 1727/8.
Present: Thomas Griffin, William Fantleroy, Robert Tomlin, John Metcalfe, Samuell Peachey and Newman Brockenbrough, Gentlemen Justices.

Underwood Acquitted giving bond for his behaviour

Whereas Muta Underwood by Virtue of a Mittimus from John Tayloe Gentleman one of the Magistrates of this County was Committed to the County Goale on Suspicion of having stolen a quantity of Tobacco from Joseph Russell Jr. and being now brought before this Court and Severall Evidences being produced and Examined, but Not [131] proving the fact, Yet it Appearing to the Court that the said Muta Underwood is a person of an Ill behaviour. It is therefore Ordered that he Give good and sufficient Security for his good behaviour. And that he remain in the Sheriffs Custody Until he Gives such Security.

At a Court held for Richmond County the First day of May 1728.
Present: John Tayloe, William Fantleroy, William Downman, Robert Tomlin, Samuell Peachey, Newman Brockenbrough, Gentlemen Justices.

Anderson Bound to his Behaviour

Edward Anderson of North Farnham parish haveing been summoned to answer the presentment of the Grandjury against him for a Common and Notorious swearer, and this Day Appearing but offering nothing materiall to Excuse himself it is the oppinion of this Court and accordingly Ordered that for the said Offence he give good and sufficient security for his good Behaviour During the Tearm of one year.

Whereupon the said Edward Anderson Together with Thomas Osborne his Security in Open Court acknowledged themselves Indebted unto Our sovereign Lord the King his heirs and successors in the sum of Twenty pounds sterling to be Levyed on their Lands and Tenements goods and Chattles with Condition that if the said Edward Anderson shall be of good behaviour as well towards his Majestie as all his Leige people That Then this Recognizance to be Void and of none Effect or Else to remain in full Force.

Williams bound to his Behaviour

Henry Williams son of John Williams of North Farnham parish haveing been summoned to Answer the presentment of the Grand jury against him for being a Common disturber of the peace, and this day Appearing but offering Nothing Materiall to Excuse himselfe. It is [132] the oppinion of this Court and accordingly ordered that for the said offence he give good and sufficient security for his good Behaviour During the Tearm of one Year.

Whereupon the said Henry Williams son of John Williams Together with John Tarpley Jr. Gentleman his Security in Open Court acknowledged themselves Indebted unto our Sovereign Lord the King his heirs and Successors in the sum of Twenty pounds sterling to be Levyed on their Lands and Tenements goods and Chattles with Condition that if the said Henry Williams shall be of good Behaviour as well towards his Majestie as all his Leige people. That then this Recognizance to be Void and of none Effect, or Else to remaine in full Force.

[Henderson bound to his behaviour]

John Henderson of Sittenburn Parish having been Summoned to answer the presentment of the Grandjury against him for being a Common Swearer and Drunkard, and this Day Appearing, but offering nothing Materiall to Excuse himselfe; It is the Oppinion of this Court and Accordingly Ordered that for the said Offence he Give good and Sufficient Security for his good Behaviour During the Tearm of one year.

Whereupon the said John Henderson Together with Alvin Mountjoy his Security in Open Court Acknowledged themselves Indebted unto our Sovereign Lord the King his heirs and Successors in the sum of Twenty pounds sterling to be Levyed on their Lands and Tenements goods and Chattles, with Condition that if the said John Henderson shall be of good behaviour as well towards his Majestie as all his Leige people, That then this Recognizance to be Void and of None Effect or Else to remaine in full Force.

Gosely bound to his behaviour

Joseph Gosely of Northfarnham parish having been Summoned to Answer the presentment of the Grandjury against him for being a Common Swearer, and this day Appearing, but Offering Nothing Materiall to Excuse [133] himselfe, It is the oppinion of this Court and Accordingly ordered that for the said Offence he Give good and Sufficient Security for his good behaviour During the Tearm of one Year.

Whereupon the said Joseph Gosely Together with John Garzia Clark his Security in open Court acknowledged themselves Indebted unto our sovereign Lord the King his heirs and Successors in the sum of Twenty pounds sterling to be Levyed on their Lands and Tenements goods and Chattles with Condition that if the said Joseph Goseley shall be of good behaviour as well towards his Majestie as all his Leige people, That then this Recognizance to be Void and of None Effect, or Else to Remaine in full Force.

At a Court Continued and held for Richmond County the Fourth day of July 1728.

Present: Thomas Griffin, Charles Grymes, Joseph Belfield, Willoughby Newton and Thomas Wright Belfield, Gentlemen Justices.

Mcmahon bound to his Behaviour

Arthur Mcmahon of North Farnham parish haveing been Summoned to Answer the presentment of the Grandjury against him for a Common Swearer and this day Appearing, but Offering Nothing Materiall to Excuse himselfe. It is the Oppinion of this court and Accordingly Ordered that for the said Offence he Give good and sufficient Security for his good Behaviour during the Term of one year.

Whereupon the said Arthur Mcmahon Together with Thomas Curtis his Security in open court acknowledged themselves Indebted unto our Sovereign Lord the King his heirs and Successors in the sum of Twenty pounds Sterling to be Levyed on their Lands and Tenements goods and Chattles with condition that if the said Arthur Mcmahon shall be of good Behaviour as well [134] towards his Majestie as all his Leige people, That then this Recognizance to be Void and of None Effect, or Else to Remain in full Force.

Milner Bound to his Behaviour

John Milner of North Farnham parish on Farnham Creek haveing been Summoned to Answer the presentment of the Grandjury against him for being a Common and prophane Swearer, and this day Appearing, but offering Nothing Materiall to Excuse himself, It is the Oppinion of his court and accordingly ordered that for the said offence he give good and Sufficient Security for his good Behaviour during the Term of one Year.

Whereupon the said John Milner together with Richard Woolard his Security in Open court Acknowledged themselves Indebted unto our sovereign Lord the King his heirs and Successors in the sum of Twenty pounds Sterling to be Levyed on their Lands and Tenements goods and Chattles with Condition that if the said John Milner shall be of good Behaviour as well towards his Majestie as all his Leige people, That then this Recognizance to be Void and of none Effect, or Else to remain in full Force.

Anderson bound to his Behaviour

Edward Anderson of North Farnham parish haveing been Summoned to Answer the presentment of the Grandjury against him for a Common Swearer and Disturber of the peace, and this Day Appearing, but offering [nothing] materiall to Excuse himself It is the Oppinion of this court and Accordingly ordered that for the said Offence he Give good and Sufficient Security for his good Behaviour during the Terme of one Year.

Whereupon the said Edward Anderson together with William Garland his Security in Open court Acknowledged themselves Indebted unto our sovereign Lord the King his heirs and Successors in the sum of Twenty pounds Sterling to be Levyed [135] on their Lands and Tenements goods and Chattles with condition that if the said Edward Anderson shall be of good Behaviour as well towards his Majestie as all his Leige people, That then this Recognizance to be Void and of none Effect or Else to Remain in full Force.

Thomas bound to his Behaviour

Evan Thomas of North farnham parish haveing been Summoned to answer the presentment of the Grandjury against him, for being a Common Drunkard, and this day Appearing, but Offering nothing Materiall to Excuse himselfe It is the Oppinion of this court and Accordingly ordered that for the said Offence he give good and Sufficient Security for his good behaviour during the Terme of one year.

Whereupon the said Evan Thomas together with Gabriell Parquett Jr. his Security in open court Acknowledged themselves Indebted unto our sovereign Lord the King his heirs and successors in the sum of Twenty pounds sterling to be levyed on their Lands and Tenements Goods and Chattles with Condition that if the said Evan Thomas shall be of good Behaviour as well towards his Majestie as all his Leige people, That then this Recognizance to be Void and of None Effect, or Else to Remain in full Force.

Smith Bound to his Behaviour

William Smith of North Farnham parish haveing been Summoned to Answer the presentment of the Grandjury against him for being a Common Swearer and this day Appearing, but offering nothing Materiall to excuse himselfe it is the oppinion of this court and Accordingly Ordered that for the said Offence he give good and Sufficient Security for his good Behaviour during the Terme of one year.

Whereupon the said William Smith together with William Garland his security in open court Acknowledged themselves Indebted unto Our sovereign Lord the King his heirs and Successors in the sum of Twenty pounds Sterling to be Levyed on their [136] Lands and Tenements Goods and Chattles with Condition that if the said William Smith shall be of good Behaviour as well towards his Majestie as all his Leige people, That then this Recognizance to be Void and of none Effect or Else to Remain in full Force.

Packett Bound to his Behaviour

Gabriell Packett Jr. of North Farnham parish haveing been Summoned to Answer the presentment of the Grandjury against him for being a Common Drunkard, and this day Appearing, but offering Nothing Materiall to Excuse himselfe It is the oppinion of this Court and Accordingly ordered that for the said Offence he give good and Sufficient Security for his good Behaviour during the Terme of one year.

Whereupon the said Gabriell Packett together with Evan Thomas his Security in open court acknowledged themselves Indebted unto our Sovereign Lord the King his heirs and Successors in the sum of Twenty pounds Sterling to be Levyed on their Lands and Tenements Goods and Chattles with Condition that if the said Gabriell Packett shall be of good Behaviour as well Towards his Majestie as all his Leige people, That then this Recognizance to be Void, and of none Effect, or Else to Remain in full Force.

Clarke Bound to his Behaviour

John Clarke of North Farnham Parrish haveing been Summoned to answer the presentment of the Grandjury against him for being a Common Drunkard, and this day Appearing, But Offering Nothing Materiall to Excuse himself, It is the Oppinion of this court and Accordingly ordered that for the said Offence he give good and Sufficient Security for his good Behaviour during the Terme of one year.

Whereupon the said John Clarke together with Robert Smith his Security in Open court acknowledged themselves Indebted unto our sovereign Lord the King his heirs and Successors in the Sum of Twenty pounds Sterling to be Levyed on their Lands and Tenements, goods and Chattles, with Condition that if the said John [137] Clarke shall be of good Behaviour as well towards his Majestie as all his Leige people that then this Recognizance to be Void and of none Effect, or Else to Remain in full Force.

Taylor Bound to his Behaviour

Simon Taylor of North Farnham parish haveing been Summoned to Answer the presentment of the Grandjury against him for being a Common Drunkard, and this day Appearing, But offering Nothing Materiall to Excuse himself, It is the oppinion of this court and Accordingly ordered that for the said Offence he

Give good and Sufficient Security for his good Behaviour during the Terme of one Year.

Whereupon the said Simon Taylor together with Hugh Lambert his Security in Open court Acknowledged themselves Indebted unto our Sovereign Lord the King his heirs and Successors in the sum of Twenty pounds Sterling to be Levyed on their Lands and Tenements goods and Chattles with Condition that If the said Simon Taylor shall be of good Behaviour as well towards his Majestie as all his Leige people, That then this Recognizance to be Void and of None Effect, or Else to Remain in full Force.

At a Court held for Richmond County the Seventh day of August 1728.

Present: John Tayloe, Charles Grymes, Willoughby Newton and Thomas Wright Belfield, Gentlemen Justices.

Black bound to his Behaviour

Doctor James Black of North Farnham parish haveing been Summoned to Answer the presentment of the Grandjury against him for being a Common and Notorious Swearer and this day Appearing but Offering nothing Materiall to Excuse himself It is the Opinion of this court and accordingly Ordered that for the said Offence he give good and Sufficient Security for his good Behaviour during the Terme of One year.

[138] Whereupon the said Doctor James Black Together with Thomas Barber his Security in open court Acknowledged themselves indebted unto our sovereign Lord the King his heirs and Successors in the sum of Twenty pounds Sterling to be Levyed on their Lands and Tenements goods and Chattles with Condition that if the said Doctor James Black shall be of good Behaviour as well towards his Majestie as all his Leige people, That then this Recognizance to be Void and of None Effect or Else to Remain in full Force.

Rooker bound to his Behaviour

Robert Rooker of North Farham parish haveing been Summoned to Answer the presentment of the Grandjury against him for being a Common Drunkard and Swearer and this day Appearing but offering nothing Materiall to Excuse himselfe. It is the Opinion of this court and Accordingly ordered that for the said Offence he give good and Sufficient Security for his good Behaviour during the Terme of one Year.

Whereupon the said Roger Rooker Together with Edward Cornwell his Security in open court Acknowledged themselves Indebted unto our Sovereign Lord the King his heirs and Successors in the sum of Twenty pounds Sterling to be Levyed on their Lands and Tenements goods and Chattles with condition that if the said Roger Rooker shall be of good Behaviour as well Towards his Majestie as all his Leige people, That then this recognizance to be Void and of None Effect or Else to Remain in full Force.

Present: Newman Brockenbrough and John Woodbridge, Gentlemen.

Russell Fined

Joseph Russell Jr. of North Farnham parish this day appearing to Answer the Complaints of John Hamond one of the Under Sherriffs of this County for refuseing to Assist him the said Hamond in Conveying a prisoner to the Goale [**139**] of this County, but haveing nothing Materiall to offer to Excuse him, It is therefore Ordered that the said Joseph Russell be Fined the sume of Tenn Shillings to our Sovereign Lord the King.

At a Court held for Richmond County the Fourth day of September 1728.
Present: John Tayloe, Charles Grymes, Newman Brockenbrough, Willoughby Newton, Thomas Wright Belfield, John Woodbridge Gentlemen Justices.

Sambo Whipt and pillor'd

Whereas Sambo a Negro man Slave belonging to Billington McCarty was by Vertue of a Mittimus from John Woodbridge gentleman one of the Magistrates of this County Committed to the County Goal for strikeing one Thomas Patty, and for stealing two sheep belonging to Daniell Hornby, and for stealing Twelve poultry belonging to one Martin Sherman, which Matter being proved by the Oaths of the said Thomas Patty, Martin Sherman and two Negro Slaves,[84] and the said Negro Sambo offering nothing Materiall to Excuse himselfe, It is therefore ordered that for the said offence the Sherriff take the said Negro Sambo and carry him to the common Whipping post and give him thirty nine Lashes on his bare back well laid on, and then sett him in the pillory and naile both his Ears, therefore to stand one hour and at the Expiration of the same to cut them both off.[85]

Heyles bound to his Behaviour

John Heyles of North Farnham parish haveing been Summoned to Answer the presentment of the Grandjury against him for being a common Swearer and Drunkard and this day Appearing but Offering Nothing Matteriall to Excuse himself, It is the Opinion of this court and accordingly Ordered that for the said Offence he give good and Sufficient Security for his good Behaviour during the Terme of one year.
Whereupon the said John Heyles Together with Thomas White his Security in

---

84. Witnesses for the crown testified under oath. Two were required, or one with "pregnant circumstances," for example, catching the offender in the act; *Statutes at Large*, 3:269–70 (1705). In England, two witnesses were required only in treason cases; other offenses could be prosecuted with a single witness; Blackstone, *Commentaries*, 4:350–51.

85. The statutory penalty for a second conviction upon a charge of stealing hogs; *Statutes at Large*, 3:277 (1705). Sheep and poultry were not mentioned in the statute. The alternative to using the analogy of the hog statute to sentence offenders was to regard the theft as grand larceny, the penalty for which was death, with benefit of clergy for first offenders.

open court Acknowledged themselves Indebted unto our Sovereign Lord the King his heirs and Successors in the sum of Twenty pounds Sterling to be Levyed [140] On their Lands and Tenements Goods and Chattles with Condition that if the said John Heyles shall be of Good Behaviour as well towards his Majestie as all his Leige people, That then this Recognizance to be Void and of None Effect or Else to remain in full Force.

Long bound to his Behaviour

Phillip Long of Sittenborn parish haveing been Summoned to answer the presentment of the Grandjury against him for a Common and Notorious Swearer and this day Appearing but Offering Nothing Matterial to Excuse himself, It is the Opinion of this court and accordingly Ordered that for the said Offence he Give good and Sufficient Security for his good Behaviour during the Terme of one year.

Whereupon the said Phillip Long Together with Joseph Patterson his Security in open court Acknowledged themselves Indebted Unto our Sovereign Lord the King his heirs and Successors in the sum of Twenty pounds Sterling to be Levyed on their Lands and Tenements Goods and Chattles with Condition that if the said Phillip Long shall be of Good Behaviour as well Towards his Majestie as all his Leige People, that then this Recognizance to be Void and of None Effect or Else to remain in full Force.

Russell Fined

Charles Russell of Northfarnham parish this day Appearing to Answer the Complaints of John Hamond one of the Under Sherriffs of this County for refuseing to Assist him the said Hamond in Conveying a prisoner to the Goale of this County, but haveing Nothing Matteriall to offer to Excuse him, It is therefore ordered that the said Charles Russell be Fined the Sum of Tenn Shillings to Our Sovereign Lord the King.

Skelly bound to his Behaviour

James Skelly of North Farnham parish haveing been Summoned to answer the presentment of the Grandjury against him for being a Common Drunkard, and this day Appearing but offering Nothing Matteriall to Excuse himselfe, It is the opinion of this court and accordingly ordered that for the said Offence he give good and Sufficient Security for his good Behaviour during the Terme of one year.

[141] Whereupon the said James Skelly Together with Richard Brown his Security in open court Acknowledged themselves Indebted unto our Sovereign Lord the King his heirs and Successors in the sum of Twenty pounds sterling to be levyed on their Lands and Tenements goods and Chattles with Condition that if the said James Skelly shall be of good Behaviour as well Towards his Majestie

as all his Leige people, That then this Recognizance to be Void and of None Effect or Else to Remain in full Force.

At a Court held for Richmond County the Fifth day of February 1728/9.

Present: John Tayloe, Joseph Belfield, Willouby Newton, Thomas Wright Belfield and John Woodbridge, Gentlemen Justices.

Morgan bound to his Behaviour

Whereas it appearing to this court by the Oaths of Mary Collier, Jane Simonds, and John Hefford and Ann Hefford, That Anthony Morgan doth frequently abuse his wife Ann Morgan, and that he lives in Adultery with one Sarah Ann Simonds, It is Therefore Ordered that the said Anthony Morgan enter into bond with good and Sufficient Security in the Sum of one hundred pounds Sterling for his keeping the peace, and also for his Dismissing the said Sarah Ann Simons from her dwelling and Cohabitation with him in his house, as also for his Refraining himselfe from resorting to or frequenting her Company, and that the sherriff take him into Custody, and him safely keep, intill he shall give such Bond with Security as aforesaid.

At a Court Continued and held for Richmond County the Sixth day of February 1728/9.

Present: John Tayloe, Joseph Belfield, Willouby Newton and John Woodbridge, Gentlemen Justices.

Durham bound to his Behaviour

[142] Thomas Durham of North Farnham parish haveing been Summoned to answer the presentment of the Grandjury against him for a Most Notorious Drunkard and prophane swearer and this day Appearing but offering Nothing Matteriall to Excuse himself it is the Opinion of this court and accordingly ordered that for the said Offence he give good and Sufficient Security for his good Behaviour during the Tearm of one Year.

Whereupon the said Thomas Durham Together with Jeremiah Greenham his Security in open court acknowledged themselves Indebted to our Sovereign Lord the King his heirs and Successors in the Sum of Twenty pounds sterling to be Levyed on their Lands and Tenements goods and Chattles with Condition that if the said Thomas Durham shall be of good Behaviour as well Towards his Majestie as all his Leige people, That then this Recognizance to be Void and of none Effect or else to remain in full force.

[Gaydon bound to his behaviour]

George Gaydon of North Farnham parish haveing been Summoned to Answer the presentment of the Grandjury against him for a Common and prophaine Swearer, and this day Appearing but Offering nothing Matteriall to Excuse himself it is the Opinion of this court, and accordingly Ordered that for the said Offence he give good and Sufficient Security for his good Behaviour during the Tearm of one year.

Whereupon the said George Gaydon Together with John Pursley his Security in open court Acknowledged themselves Indebted to our Sovereign Lord the King his heirs and Successors in the Sum of Twenty pounds sterling to be Levyed on their Lands and Tenements goods and Chattles, with Condition that if the said George Gaydon shall be of good Behaviour as well Towards his Majestie as all [143] his Leige people That then this Recognizance to be Void and of None Effect or else to remaine in full force.

Abshone bound to his Behaviour

William Abshone of North Farnham parish having been Summoned to Answer the presentment of the Grandjury against him for being a Most Notorious Drunkard, prophane Swearer common fighter and Barrettor,[86] and this Day Appearing but offering Nothing Matteriall to Excuse himselfe it is the Opinion of this Court, and Accordingly by Ordered that for the said Offence he give good and Sufficient Security for his good Behaviour during the Tearm of one Year.

Whereupon the said William Abshone Together with Hugh Lambert his Security in Open court Acknowledged themselves indebted to our sovereign Lord the King his heirs and Successors in the sum of Twenty pounds sterling to be Levyed on their Lands and Tenements goods and Chattles, with Condition that if the said William Abshone shall be of good Behaviour as well Towards his Majestie as all his Leige People, That then this Recognizance to be Void and of None Effect, or else to Remaine in full Force.

Floyd bound to Behaviour

Magnus Floyd of North Farnham parrish having been Summoned to Answer the presentment of the Grandjury against him for a Common and prophane Swearer and this day Appearing but offering Nothing Materiall to Excuse himselfe it is the Opinion of this court and Accordingly Ordered that for the said Offence he give good and Sufficient Security for his good Behaviour during the Tearm of one year.

Whereupon the said Magnus Floyd Together with William Walker his Security in open court acknowledged themselves indebted to our Sovereign Lord the King his heirs and Successors in the sum of Twenty [144] Pounds sterling to be Levyed on their Lands and Tenements goods and Chattles with Condition that if

---

86. A barrator was a quarreler, or one who spread false stories, started fights, or brought about frivolous legal suits. "Common" meant frequent or habitual.

the said Magnus Floyd shall be of good Behaviour as well Towards his Majestie as all his Leige people, That then this Recognizance to be Void and of None Effect, or else to remain in full force.

Hughlett bound to his Behaviour

John Hughlett of North Farnham parish having been Summoned to answer the presentment of the Grandjury against him for being a common and prophane swearer and Drunkard and this day Appearing but Offering Nothing Materiall to Excuse himselfe it is the Opinion of this court and Accordingly Ordered that for the said Offence he give good and Sufficient Security for his good Behaviour during the Tearm of one year.

Whereupon the said John Hughlett Together with Anthony Sidnor his Security in Open court acknowledged themselves indebted to our Sovereign Lord the King his heirs and Successors in the Sum of Twenty pounds sterling to be Levyed on their Lands and Tenements goods and Chattles with Condition that if the said Hughlett shall be of good Behaviour as well Towards his Majestie as all his Leige people, That then this Recognizance to be Void and of None Effect, or else to remain in full force.

At a Court held for Richmond County the Fifth day of March 1728/9.

Present: John Tayloe, Charles Grymes, Joseph Belfield, Willoughby Newton and Thomas Wright Belfield, Gentlemen Justices.

White bound to his Behaviour

William White of North Farnham parish haveing been Summoned to Answer the presentment of the Grand jury [145] Against him for a prophane and Common Swearer and this day Appearing but Offering Nothing Materiall to Excuse himselfe it is the Opinion of this court, and Accordingly Ordered that for the said Offence he give good and Sufficient Security for his good Behaviour during the Terme of one Year.

Whereupon the said William White Together with George Smithe his Security in Open court Acknowledged themselves Indebted to our Sovereign Lord the King his heirs and Successors in the Sum of Twenty pounds sterling to be Levyed on their Lands and Tenements goods and Chattles with Condition that if the said William White shall be of good Behaviour as well towards his Majestie as all his Leige people, That then this Recognizance to be Void and of None Effect or else to remaine in full Force.

[McMillion bound to behavior]

Stephen McMillion of North Farnham parish haveing been Summoned to Answer the presentment of the Grandjury against him for a Notorious Drunkard and Common prophane Swearer and this day Appearing but Offering

Nothing Materiall to Excuse himselfe it is the Opinion of this court and Accordingly Ordered that for the said Offence he give good and Sufficient Security for his good Behaviour during the Terme of one Year.

Whereupon the said Stephen McMillion Together with Thomas Suttle his Security in Open court Acknowledged themselves Indebted to our Sovereign Lord the King his heirs and Successors in the Sum of Twenty pounds, sterling to be Levyed on their Lands and Tenements goods and Chattles, with Condition that if the said Stephen McMillion shall be of good Behaviour as well Towards his Majestie as all his Leige people, That then this Recognizance to be Void and of None Effect or else to remaine in full Force.

Procter bound to his Behaviour

Edward Procter late of North Farnham parish haveing been Summoned to Answer the presentment of the Grand jury against him for being a Most Notorious Drunkard and prophane [146] Swearer common fighter and Barretor, and this day Appearing but offering Nothing Matteriall to Excuse himselfe it is the Opinion of this court and Accordingly Ordered that for the said Offence, he give good and Sufficient Security for his good Behaviour Dureing the Tearme of one year and that he be Fined Twenty shillings Current Money to our Sovereign Lord the King.

Whereupon the said Edward Proctor Together with Henry Suttle and Joseph Bragg his Security's in Open court Acknowledged themselves Indebted to our Sovereign Lord the King his heirs and Successors in the Sum of Twenty pounds sterling to be Levyed on their Lands and Tenements goods and Chattles with Condition that if the said Edward Procter shall be of good Behaviour as well Towards his Majestie as all his Leige people, That then this Recognizance to be Void and of None Effect, or else to Remaine in full Force Also the said Henry Suttle and Joseph Bragg in Open court Obliged themselves their heirs etc. for the said Edward Procters payment of the said Twenty shillings as before Ordered.

At a Court held for Richmond County the Second day of Aprill 1729.
Present: Thomas Griffin, John Tayloe, Joseph Belfield, Willoughby Newton, Thomas Wright Belfield and John Woodbridge, Gentlemen Justices.

Dean Bound to his Behaviour

William Dean of Sittenborne parish haveing been Summoned to Answer the presentment of the Grandjury against him for a Common and prophane swearer and this day Appearing, but offering Nothing Materiall to Excuse himselfe it is the Opinion of this court, and Accordingly Ordered that for the said offence he give good and Sufficient Security for his good Behaviour during the Term of one Year.

Whereupon the said William Dean together with Edward Eidson his Security in Open court [147] Acknowledged themselves to be Indebted to Our Sovereign Lord the King his heirs and Successors in the Sum of Twenty pounds Sterling to be Levyed on their Lands and Tenements goods and chattles with Condition that if the said William Deane shall be of good Behaviour as well Towards his Majestie as all his Leige people, That Then this Recognizance to be Void and of none Effect, or Else to remaine in full force.

Pickering whipt and bound to her Behaviour

Whereas Ann Pickering by Vertue of a Mittimus from Thomas Wright Belfield Gentleman one of the Justices of this court was remitted to the county Goale on Suspicion of Stealing from Thomas Thornton a peice of Scotts plad, a peice of Linnen and a Small peice of Cantaloons and other goods, and being Now brought before his Majesties Justices here present, on Examination of Severall Evidences touching the Same, It is the Opinion of this court, that the said Ann Pickering is Guilty of crime Laid to her charge, It is therefore Ordered that the Sherriff take her and carry her to the common Whipping post and give her Twenty five lashes on her bare back well laid on, and then to give Security for her good Behaviour dureing the Tearm of one year.

Whereupon the said Ann Pickering together with Thomas Beckham and Edward Tomlinson her Security's in Open court acknowledged themselves Indebted to our Sovereign Lord the King his heirs and Successors in the Sum of Twenty pounds Sterling to be levyed on their Lands and Tenements goods and Chattles, with Condition that if the said Ann Pickering shall be of good behaviour as Well towards his Majestie as all his Leige people That then this Recognizance to be Void and of None Effect, or Else to remaine in full force.

At a Court held for Richmond County the Fourth day of June 1729.
Present: Thomas Griffin, John Tayloe, Charles Grymes, Willoughby Newton, Thomas Wright Belfield and John Woodbrige, Gentlemen Justices.

[Nicholl's Examination]

[148] Whereas John Nichols by Vertue of the Mittimus from Thomas Griffin Gentleman one of the Justices of this court was committed to the County Goale on Suspicion of takeing a prell[87] of Tobacco out of a Tobacco house belonging to Henry Miskell, and being now brought before his Majesties Justices here present, on Examination of Severall Evidences touching the same it is the Opinion of this court that the said John Nicholls is Guilty of the crime laid to his charge, It is therefore Ordered that the Sherriff take him and carry him to the common whipping post and Give him Thirty Nine Lashes on his bare back well laid on, and then to keep him in safe Custody untill he gives good and Sufficient Security for his good Behaviour Dureing the Terme of one Year.

---

87. Not a standard measure or container of tobacco. Possibly equivalent to a basket.

Edward Anderson of North Farnham parish haveing been Summoned to Answer the presentment of the Grandjury against him for being a Most Notorious Drunkard prophane Swearer common fighter and Barreter, and this day Appearing but Offering Nothing Matteriall to Excuse himself it is the Opinion of this court and Accordingly Ordered that for the said Offence he give good and Sufficient Security for his good Behaviour Dureing the Terme of one Year and that he be fined Twenty shillings Current Money to our Sovereign Lord the King.

Whereupon the said Edward Anderson Together with Richard Branham his Security in open court Acknowledged themselves Indebted to our sovereign Lord the King his heirs and Successors in the Sum of Twenty pounds sterling to be levyed on their Lands and Tenements, goods and Chattles, with Condition that if the said Edward Anderson shall be of good behaviour as well towards his Majestie as all his Leige people That then this Recognizance to be Void and of None Effect, or else to remain in full force also the said Richard Branham in Open Court Oblidged himselfe his heirs etc. for the said Edward Andersons payments of the said Twenty shillings as before ordered.

[**149**] At a Call'd Court held at the Court house of Richmond County the 20th day of June 1729.
[Justices not listed]

Mark Luke's examination

Whereas Mark Luke was by Vertue of a Mittimus from Thomas Wright Belfield Gentleman one of the Justices of this Court remitted to the County Goale for feloniously takeing a Sheep from John Petty and Certain goods from Samuell Cooke, and being now brought before his Majesties Justices here present being Examined Saith[:]

That about the Tenth Instant at Night he went to Thomas Petty's Sheep penn and took out a Sheep, and from thence he went to Charles Spoes Sheep penn to gett another but was taken by the said Spoes Servant man, and that he Designed to carry the said Sheep to Mr. Churchills Negroe Quarter.

That the goods which was found in the hallow tree belong'd to one of Mr. Churchills Negroes.

That he has lived in the Woods near Mr. Churchills Quarter and sometimes in the Quarter along with the Negroes for three or Four months last past and that the said Negroes Supplyed him with Meale and hominy.

It appearing to the Court upon the aforesaid Examination that there is Just cause for Trying the said prisoner at the Generall Court for the Crime aforesaid whereof he is accused, It is therefore Ordered that the said Mark Luke be remanded to the prison of this County under the Custody of the Sherriff and from thence to be convey'd to the publick Goale of Williamsburgh as the Law in such Cases Directs.

Morton's Recognizance

William Morton of Sittenborne parish in Richmond County in Open Court before his Majesties Justices Acknowledged himselfe Indebted to our Sovereign Lord the King his heirs and Successors in the Sum of Tenn pounds Sterling to be Levyed of his Lands and Tenements goods and Chattles with Condition that if the said William Morton shall [150] personally Appear at the Next Generall Court on the Fourth day thereof, and then and there give such Evidence as he knows against Mark Luke who stands committed for felony and Do not Depart thence without leave of that court, That then this Recognizance to be Void, or else remain in full force.

Petty's Recognizance

John Petty of Sittenbourne parish in Richmond County in Open court before his Majesties Justices Acknowledged himselfe Indebted to our Sovereign Lord the King his heirs and Successors in the Sum of Tenn pounds Sterling to be Levyed of his lands and Tenements goods and Chattles with Condition that if the said John Petty shall personally Appear at the next Generall Court on the Fourth day thereof and then and there give such Evidences as he knows against Mark Luke who stands committed for felony and Do Not Depart thence without Leave of that court, That then this Recognizance to be Void, or else to remain in full force.

Cooke's Recognizance

Samuell Cooke of Sittenbourne parish in Richmond County in Open court before his Majesties Justices acknowledged himselfe Indebted to our Sovereign Lord the King his heirs and Successors in the Sum of Tenn pounds sterling to be levyed of his Lands and Tenements goods and Chattles with Condition that if the said Samuell Cooke shall personally Appear at the Next Generall Court on the Fourth Day thereof, and then and there give such Evidence as he knows against Mark Luke who stands commited for felony, and Do not Depart thence without leave of that court, That then this Recognizance to be Void, or else to remaine in full force.

At a Court held for Richmond County the Second day of July 1729.
Present: Thomas Griffin, John Tayloe, Newman Brockenbrough, Willoughby Newton and Thomas Wright Belfield, Gentlemen Justices.

Simon a Negro Whipt

[151] Whereas Simon a Negro man slave belonging to Mr. Armstead Churchill was by Vertue of a Mittimus from Thomas Wright Belfield Gentleman one of the Justices of this court committed to the County Goale on suspicion of felo-

niously stealing certain hoggs from William Morton and Edward Eidson, and being Now brought before his Majesties Justices here present on Examination of the said William Morton and Edward Eidson and severall Negro slaves belonging to the said Armstead Churchill, It is the Opinion of this court that the said Negro Simon is Guilty of stealing one hogg from the said Morton and one hogg from the said Eidson, It is therefore Ordered that for the said Offence the sherriff take him and carry him to the common whipping post and give him thirty nine lashes on his bare back well laid on.[88]

Guy a Negro Whipt

Whereas Guy a Negro Man belonging to Mr. Armstead Churchill was by Vertue of a Mittimus from Thomas Wright Belfield Gentleman one of the Justices of this court committed to the County Goale on Suspicion of feloniously stealing hoggs from William Morton and Edward Eidson, and certaine goods from Samuell Cooke, and being Now brought before his Majesties Justices here present on Examination of the said William Morton, Edward Eidson and Samuell Cooke and Severall Negro slaves belonging to the said Armstead Churchill, It is the Opinion of this court that the said Negro Guy is Guilty of hogg stealing. It is therefore Ordered that for the said Offence the sherriff take him and carry him to the common whipping post and Give him Thirty nine Lashes on his bare back Well laid on.

Tony a Negro Whipt and pillor'd

Whereas Toney a Negro Man slave belonging to Mr. Armstead Chruchill was this day brought before the court as An Evidence against Simon and Guy two Negro men slaves belonging to the said Armstead Churchill on Suspicion of hogg stealing, And it fully Appearing to this court that the said Toney in Giving his Evidence has told Lyes and Given false Testimony, It is therefore Ordered that the Sherriff take him and Naile one of his Ears to the pillory and there to stand for the space of one hour and then cutt the said Ear off, [152] and then to Naile the other Ear to the pillory and at the Expiration of one hour to cutt the said Ear off, and after having so done to carry him to the common Whipping post, And give him thirty nine Lashes on his bare back well laid on.[89]

Jone a Negro whipt and pillored

Whereas Jone a Negro Woman slave belonging to Mr. Armstead Churchill was this day brought before the court as an Evidence against Simon and Guy two Negro Men slaves belonging to the said Armstead Churchill on Suspicion of hogg stealing, And it fully appearing to this court that the said Jone in Giving

---

88. The statutory penalty for a slave's first offense of stealing hogs. Hogs and tobacco were treated at great length in the statutes, suggesting their importance in the economy of colonial Virginia.

89. A statutory penalty; *Statutes at Large*, 4:127 (1723).

her Evidence has told Lyes and Given false Testimony, It is therefore ordered that the Sherriff take her and Naile one of her Ears to the pillory and there to stand for the space of one hour and then to cutt the said Ear off, and then to Naile the other Ear to the pillory and at the Expiration of one hour to cutt the said Ear off and after having soe Done to carry her to the Common whipping post and give her Thirty Nine lashes on her bare back well laid on.

At a Court held for Richmond County the First day of October 1729.

Present: Thomas Griffin, John Tayloe, Charles Grymes, Newman Brocken-brough, William Newton, Thomas Wright Belfield and John Woodbridge, Gentlemen Justices.

Blackmore Bound to his Behaviour

George Blackmore of North Farnham parrish having been Summoned to Answer the Presentment of the Grandjury against him for being a Common and prophane Swearer and this day Appearing but offering nothing Materiall to Excuse himself it is the Opinion of this court and accordingly Ordered that for the said Offence he give good and Sufficient Security for his good Behaviour during the Terme of one Year.

[153] Whereupon the said George Blackmore Together with Solomon Redman his Security in Open court Acknowledged themselves Indebted unto our Sovereign Lord the King his heirs and Successors in the sum of Twenty pounds sterling to be levyed on their lands and Tenements goods and Chattles with condition that if the said George Blackmore shall be of good Behaviour as well towards his Majestie as all his Leige people, That then this Recognizance to be Void and of none Effect, or Else to Remain in full Force and Vertue.

Mcmahon Bound to his Behaviour

Arthur Mcmahon of North Farnham parish having been Summoned to answer the presentment of the Grand Jury against him for being a Common and prophane Swearer and this day Appearing, but offering Nothing Materiall to excuse himselfe it is the opinion of this court, and accordingly ordered that for the said Offence he give good and Sufficient Security for his good Behaviour During the Term of one year.

Whereupon the said Arthur Mcmahon Together with Henry Miskell his Security in Open court acknowledged themselves Indebted unto our Sovereign Lord the King his heirs and Successors in the sum of Twenty pounds sterling to be Levyed on their Lands and Tenements goods and Chattles with Condition that if the said Arthur Mcmahon shall be of good Behaviour as well toward his Majestie as all his Leige people, That then this Recognizance to be void and of none Effect, or Else to Remain in full Force and Vertue.

Packett Bound to his Behaviour

Gabriell Packett Jr. of North Farnham parish having been Summoned to answer the presentment of the Grandjury against him for being a Common Drunkard, and this day Appearing but offering nothing Materiall to Excuse himselfe it is the Opinion of this court, and accordingly ordered that for the said Offence he give good and Sufficient Security for his good Behaviour During the Terme of one year.

[154] Whereupon the said Gabriell Packett Together with Solomon Redman his Security in Open court Acknowledged themselves Indebted unto our Sovereign Lord the King his heirs and Successors in the Sum of Twenty pounds sterling to be Levyed on their Lands and Tenements goods and Chattles with Condition that if the said Gabriell Packett shall be of good Behaviour as Well Towards his Majestie as all his Leige people, That then this Recognizance to be Void and of None Effect, or Else to Remain in full Force and Vertue.

Pecura Bound to his Behaviour

William Pecura of North Farnham parrish having been Summoned to Answer the presentment of the Grandjury against him for a common Drunkard and prophane Swearer, and this day Appearing but Offering nothing materiall to Excuse himself it is the Opinion of this court and accordingly Ordered that for the said Offence he give good and Sufficient Security for his good Behaviour During the Terme of one Year.

Whereupon the said William Pecura Together with Thomas Osborne his Security in Open court Acknowledged themselves Indebted unto our Sovereign Lord the King his heirs and Successors in the Sum of Twenty pounds sterling to be Levyed on their Lands and Tenements goods and Chattles with Condition that if the said William Pecura shall be of good Behaviour as well Towards his Majestie as all his Leige People, That then this Recognizance to be Void and on None Effect, or Else to Remain in full Force and Vertue.

At a Call'd Court held at the Court house of Richmond County the 30th day of December 1729.

Present: Thomas Griffin, John Tayloe, Newman Brockenbrough, Thomas Wright Belfield and John Woodbridge, Gentlemen Justices.

Frost whipt

[155] Whereas Joseph Frost, Hannah Paine, William Bird, Bartholomew Richard Dodson, William Francis and Timothy Harris was by Vertue of a Mittimus from John Woodbridge Gentleman one of the Magistrates of this County committed to this County Goale on Suspicion of Breaking Open a Tobacco house belonging to Robert Harison of Northumberland County and takeing out a certain quantity of Tobacco, and being now brought before this court, and on

Examination of Severall Evidences touching the same. It is the Opinion of this court that the said Joseph Frost is Guilty of the Crime laid to his charge, It is therefore Ordered that the Sherriff take him and carry him to the Common whiping post and give him Thirty Nine lashes on his bare back well laid on, The said Hannah Paine, William Bird, Bartholomew Richard Dodson, William Francis and Timothy Harris are Discharge[d], Nothing Appearing against them.

At a Court held for Richmond County the Fourth Day of February 1729/30.
Present: John Tayloe, Charles Grymes, Joseph Belfield, Newman Brockenbrough, Willoughby Newton, Thomas Wright Belfield, Gentlemen Justices.

Livack Bound to her behaviour

Mary Livack the wife of Thomas Livack according to her Recognizance this day Appearing to Answer the Complaint of her said Husband, for threatening to Shoot him, But offering Nothing Matteriall to Excuse her selfe; It is therefore Ordered that she give good and Sufficient Security for her good Behaviour During the Terme of one Year.[90]

Whereupon the said Mary Livack together with William Walker her Security in Open court Acknowledged themselves Indebted unto our Sovereign Lord the King his heirs and Successors in the Sum of Twenty pounds Sterling to be levyed on their lands and Tenements goods and Chattles with Condition that if the said Mary Livack shall be of good Behaviour as well towards his Majestie as all his Leige people, That Then this Recognizance to be Void and of none Effect, or Else to Remain in full force and Vertue.

Harry a Negro Pillor'd

Whereas Harry a Negro Man Slave belonging to Mr. John Caine of Northumberland County was by Vertue of Mittimus from John Tayloe Gentleman one of the Magistrates of this County Committed to the County Goale for stabbing with a knife in the Belly a Negro Man Call'd Jim Belonging to William Fantleroy Gentleman and the said Negro Harry being now brought before this court, But not Denying [156] What is laid to his charge; It is therefore Ordered that for the Offence the Sherriff take him and sett him in the pillory and Naile both his Ears, therefor to stand one hour, and at the Expiration of the same, to cutt them both off.

At a Call'd Court held at the Court house of Richmond County the 19th day of February 1729/30.
Present: John Tayloe, Joseph Belfield, Thomas Wright Belfield and John Woodbridge, Gentlemen Justices.

---

90. Thomas Livack had already come to the court, see above, pp. 103–4, and would again, p. 126 (1730).

[Branch whipped]

Whereas Ann Branch was by Vertue of a Mittimus from Thomas Wright Belfield Gentleman one of the Magistrates of this County Committed to the County Goale for picking the pockett of one James Ingles and Takeing thereout a handkerchief and Severall Letters, and being now brought before this court and on Examination of severall Evidences touching the same, It is the Opinion of the court that the said Ann Branch is Guilty of what is laid to her charge, It is therefore Ordered that the sherrif take her and carry her to the common Whipping post and give her Thirty nine lashes on her bare back well laid on, And also that she give good and Sufficient Security for her good Behaviour Dureing the Terme of one Yeare, And that she Remain in the Sherrifs Custody untill she gives Such Security.[91]

At a Court Continued and held for Richmond County the Fifth day of March 1729/30.

Present: Thomas Griffin, John Tayloe, Willoughby Newton and John Woodbridge, Genetlemen Justices.

Osborne bound to his Behaviour

Thomas Osborne of North Farnham parish having been Summoned to Answer the presentment of the Grandjury against him for being a Common prophane Swearer and this day Appearing but Offering nothing matteriall to Excuse himself, It is the Opinion of this court and Accordingly Ordered that for the said Offence he give good and Sufficient Security for his good Behaviour dureing the Terme of one Year.

Whereupon the said Thomas Osborne Together with Marmaduke Beckwith his Security in Open court Acknowledged [157] themselves Indebted unto our Sovereign Lord the King his heirs and Successors in the sum of Twenty pounds Sterling to be levyed on their lands and Tenements goods and Chattles with Condition that if the said Thomas Osborne shall be of good Behaviour as well towards his Majestie as all his Leige People That then this Recognizance to be Void and of none Effect, or else to Remain in full force and Vertue.

Hopwood bound to his Behaviour

Moses Hopwood of North Farnham parish having been summoned to Answer the presentment of the Grand jury against him for being a Common prophane Swearer, and this day Appearing but offering Nothing Matteriall to Excuse himselfe it is the Opinion of this court and Accordingly ordered that for the said Offence he give good and Sufficient Security for his good Behaviour Dureing the Terme of one year.

---

91. Picking pockets was larceny, petty if the goods taken did not exceed 12*d.* in value. If violence was threatened against the victim, the act became robbery.

Whereupon the said Moses Hopwood Together with Christopher Pridham his Security in Open court Acknowledged themselves Indebted unto our Sovereign Lord the King his heirs and Successors in the sum of Twenty pounds sterling to be levyed on their lands and Tenements goods and Chattles with Condition that if the said Moses Hopwood shall be of good Behaviour as well towards his Majestie as all his Leige people, That then this Recognizance to be Void and of none Effect, or Else to remaine in full force and Vertue.

Nelson bound to his Behaviour

Alexander Nelson of North Farnham parish having been summoned to Answer the presentment of the Grandjury against him for being a common prophane Swearer, and this day Appear[ing] but offering Nothing Matteriall to Excuse himself it is the Opinion of this court and Accordingly ordered that for the said Offence he give good and Sufficient Security for his good Behaviour Dureing the Terme of one Year.

Whereupon the said Alexander Nelson Together with Thomas Livack his Security in Open court Acknowledged themselves Indebted unto our Sovereign Lord the King his heirs and Successors in the sum of Twenty pounds sterling to be Levyed on their lands and Tenements goods and Chattles with Condition that if the said Alexander Nelson shall be of good Behaviour as well Towards his Majestie as all his Leige people, That then this Recognizance to be Void and of none Effect, or else to Remain in full force and Vertue.

Billings Bound to his Behaviour

Thomas Billings of North Farnham Parish haveing been Summoned to Answer the presentment of the Grandjury [158] against him for being a common prophane Swearer, and this day Appearing but offering Nothing Matteriall to Excuse himselfe it is the Opinion of this court and Accordingly Ordered that for the said Offence he give good and Sufficient Security for his good Behaviour Dureing the Terme of one Year.

Whereupon the said Thomas Billings Together with Tobias Pursley his Security in Open court Acknowledged themselves Indebted unto our Sovereign Lord the King his heirs and Successors in the Sum of Twenty pounds Sterling to be levyed on their lands and Tenements goods and Chattles with Condition that if the said Thomas Billings shall be of good Behaviour as well towards his Majestie as all his Leige people. That then this Recognizance to be Void and of none Effect; or else to Remain in Full force and Vertue.

Mckenny Bound to her Behaviour

Afiah Mckenny of Sittenborne parish haveing been Summoned to Answer the presentment of the Grand jury against her for being a Vagrant Idle person,[92]

---

92. A statutory offense; see *Statutes at Large*, 4:208–14 (1727), and Church, ed., *Laws of Virginia, Supplement*, 253–55 (1723). If the vagrant would not find work, he could be forced to choose between twenty-five lashes or being bound by the court to a year's labor. The statutes had already begun to

and this day Appearing but Offering nothing Matteriall to Excuse herself it is the Opinion of this court and Accordingly Ordered that for the said Offence she give good and Sufficient Security for her good Behaviour Dureing the Term of one Year.

Whereupon the said Afiah Mckenny together with John Ingram her Security in Open court Acknowledged themselves Indebted unto our Sovereign Lord the King his heirs and Successors in the Sum of Twenty pounds sterling to be levyed on their lands and Tenements goods and Chattles with Condition that if the said Afiah Mckenny shall be of good Behaviour as well towards his Majestie as all his leige people, Then this Recognizance to be Void and of none Effect, or Else to Remain in full force and Vertue.

At a Court held for Richmond County the First Day of Aprill 1730.

Present: Charles Grymes, Joseph Belfield, Newman Brockenbrough, Willoughby Newton and Thomas Wright Belfield, Gentlemen Justices.

Dodson Bound to his Behaviour

[159] Whereas Lambert Dodson was bound over to Appear at this Court by Vertue of a Warrant from John Woodbridge Gentleman One of the Magestrates of this County to Answer the Complaint of James Wilson for Assaulting Beating and Bruising him and this day Appearing but offering nothing Materiall to Excuse himself, it is the Opinion of this Court and Accordingly Ordered that for the said Offence he give good and Sufficient Security for his good Behaviour dureing the Terme of one Year, And that he be Fined Twenty Shillings Current money to our Sovereign Lord the King.

Whereupon the said Lambert Dodson Together with Charles Dodson his Security in Open Court Acknowledged Themselves Indebted unto our Sovereign Lord the King his heirs and Successors in the Sum of Twenty pounds Sterling to be levyed on their lands and Tenements goods and Chattles with Condition that if the said Lambert Dodson shall be of good Behaviour as well Towards his Majestie as all his Leige People, That then this Recognizance to be Void And of None Effect, or else to Remain in full force; Also the said Charles Dodson in Open court Obliged himselfe his heirs etc. for the said Lambert Dodsons payment of the said Twenty Shillings as before Ordered.

Livack Fined and Bound to his Behaviour

Whereas Thomas Livack was bound Over to Appear at this Court by John Woodbridge Gentleman one of the Magistrates of this County to Answer the Complaint of Thomas Bryant for Threatening to do some bodily hurt to the said Bryant and this day Appearing but offering Nothing Materiall to Excuse him

---

distinguish between idle vagrants and vagrants of "ill-repute." The problem was not repaired by statute, and later laws show that vagrancy continued to plague the justices; *Statutes at Large*, 6:29–31 (1748).

selfe, it is the Opinion of this Court and Accordingly Ordered that for the said Offence he give good and Sufficient Security for his good Behaviour dureing the Terme of one year, And that he be Fined Fifty Shillings Current Money to our Sovereign Lord the King.

Whereupon the said Thomas Livack together with William Walker his Security in Open Court Acknowledged themselves Indebted unto our Sovereign Lord the King his heirs and Successors in the Sum of Twenty pounds Sterling to be levyed on their lands and Tenements goods and Chattles with Condition that if the said Thomas Livack shall be of good Behaviour as well Towards his Majestie as all his Leige people, That then this Recognizance to be Void and of none Effect, or Else to Remain in full force; Also the said William Walker in Open Court Obliged himselfe his heirs etc. for the said Thomas Livack's payments of the said Fifty shillings as before Orderd.

[**160**] At a Court held for Richmond County the Sixth day of May 1730.

Present: Thomas Griffin, John Tayloe, Joseph Belfield, Willoughby Newton, Thomas Wright Belfield and John Woodbridge, Gentlemen Justices.

Diggs Fined

William Diggs of North Farnham parrish being return'd upon the Pannell of the Grand jury to Attend this Court this day, and not Appearing when Called is hereby Fined Two hundred pounds of Tobacco to our Sovereign Lord the King, which the Sherrif of this County is Ordered to Collect of him Upon refusall of payment by Distress.

At a Call'd Court held at the Courthouse of Richmond County the Sixth day of July 1730.

Present: Thomas Griffin, Joseph Belfield, William Newton, Thomas Wright Belfield and John Woodbridge, Gentlemen Justices.

Jones Discharged

Whereas Ann Jones was by Vertue of a Mittimus from John Woodbridge Gentleman one of the Justices of this Court Committed to the County Goal for being Assesary to a felony Comitted in this county by one William Cook alias Bridges, and being now brought before this Court but noe Sufficient Evidence Appearing against her is Discharged.

Cooks Examination

Whereas William Cook alias Bridges of North Farnham parrish in Richmond County was by Vertue of a Mittimus from John Woodbrige Gentleman one of the Justices of this Court Committed to the County Goale for feloniously takeing out of the house of Thomas Scurlock of the Same Parrish and County in the Night one fine hatt, three yards of Kersey, one Course Shirt etc. and being now brought before his Majesties Justices here present[,] being Examined Saith That on the Twelfth day of June last in the Night he went to the widow Comerons where Ann Jones lived and that he and the said Ann Jones sett off that Night and Travelled Up to the falls of Rappahanock River but Denyes that he took the goods which he is Charged with.

[161] Ann Jones aged Twenty Eight years or thereabouts being Sworn saith that on the Twelfth day of June last in the Night William Cook the prisoner at the Barr came to Ann Comeron's where she lived and brought along with him one Fine hatt a parcell of Kersey and course Linnen, one shirt and Some other odd things, but does not know where he got them, and he asked her to go along with him up the County, and Accordingly they Sett off that Night and Travelled to the falls of Rappanhanock River where they parted[;] That she hired herself to one Thomas Phillips and the said William Cook said he would go up to a place call'd the Marsh about Thirty Miles above the falls and that he left the hatt and other things along with the said Thomas Phillips.

It Appearing to the Court upon the aforesaid Examination that there is Just Cause for Trying the said Prisoner at the General Court for the Crime aforesaid whereof he is Accused, It is therefore Ordered that the said William Cook alias Bridges be remanded to the prison of this County under the Custody of the Sherrif, and from thence to be Conveyed to the publick Goale of Williamsburgh as the Law in such Cases Directs.

Scurlock Recognizance

Thomas Scurlock of North Farnham parrish in Richmond County in Open Court before his Majesties Justices Acknowledged himself Indebted to our Sovereign Lord the King his heirs and Successors in the Sum of Ten pounds Sterling to be levyed of his Lands and Tenements, goods and Chattles with Condition that if the said Thomas Scurlock shall personally Appear at the next General Court on the Fourth day thereof and then and there give such Evidence as he knows against William Cook Alias Bridges who stands Committed for felony, And do not Depart thence without leave of that Court, That then this Recognizance to be Void, or Else to remain in full force.

Jones's Recognizance

Ann Jones of North Farnham Parrish in Richmond County, in Open Court before his Majesties Justices Acknowledged herself Indebted to our Sovereign Lord the King, his heirs and Successors in the Sum of Ten pounds Sterling to be levyed of her lands and Tenements goods and Chattles with Condition that if the said Ann Jones shall personally Appear at the Next Generall Court on the Fourth Day thereof, And then and there give such Evidences as she knows against William Cook alias Bridges who Stands Committed for felony and do not

Depart thence without leave of that Court, That then this Recognizance to be Void, or Else to remain in full force.

[**162**] At a Call'd Court Continued and held at the Court house of Richmond County on Thursday the 13th day of August 1730.

Present: John Tayloe, Joseph Belfield, Thomas Wright Belfield, John Woodbridge, Gentlemen Justices.

Henderson Whipt and bound to her Behaviour

Whereas Mollinder Henderson was by Vertue of a Mittimus from John Tayloe gentleman one of the Justices of the Court Committed to the County Goale for receiving, concealing and feloniously keeping a Gold watch and chain, ten peices of coin'd Gold, a Gold Stone Ring etc. Stolen by Elizabeth Dickenson[93] from Mary McCarty and Delivered to the said Mollinder Henderson and being now brought before this Court and an Examination of Severall Evidences touching the same[,] it is the Opinion of this Court that the said Mollinder Henderson is Guilty of the Crime laid to her Charge, It is Therefore Ordered that the Sherrif take her and Carry her to the Common Whipping post and give her Twenty Lashes on her bare back well laid on and then keep her in his safe Custody till Monday next at which time the said Sherrif is Ordered to Give her Nineteen Lashes More on her bare back as aforesaid and then to keep her in his safe Custody till she Enter into bond with good and sufficient Security for her good Behaviour during the Term of one Year.

At a Call'd Court held at the Court house of Richmond County on Monday the 17th day of August 1730.

Present: John Tayloe, Joseph Belfield, Thomas Wright Belfield, John Woodbridge, Gentlemen Justices.

Newgent Discharged

Whereas Edward Newgent was by Vertue of a Mittimus from John Tayloe Gentleman one of the Justices of this Court Committed to this County Goale for feloniously Robbing and Burning the house of Col. Thomas Lee of Westmoreland County, and being now brought before this Court, but Noe Evidence Appearing against him he is therefore Discharged.

---

93. The May 1730 statute (*Statutes at Large*, 4:271–73), now applied, and Henderson could be tried for the misdemeanor of knowingly "buying or receiving" stolen goods, whether or not the principal was convicted.

McCarty's Examination

Whereas Robert Brooks, John Lewis, Edward Newgent and Mary McCarty was by Vertue of a Mittimus from John Tayloe Gentleman one of the Justices of this Court Committed to this County Goale for feloniously Robbing and Burning the house of Col. Thomas Lee of Westmoreland County and being now brought before his Majesties Justices here present, And being asked by the Court what they had to say concerning what they were Charged with, they Severally Answered they were not Guilty.

[163] Elizabeth Dickenson Aged Thirty years or thereabout being Sworn saith that some Small time before Christmas last she see ten peices of Gold, one Gold watch and Chain, and one Ring in the hands of John Davis, who is now Servant to Thomas Robinson, Robert Brooks and Mary McCarty being present and that the said Davis Gave them to the said Mary McCarty, and told her if she would be a good girle she should never want nothing, the said McCarty asked him where he gott them there, he answered at Col. Lee's, and then asked him how he got them there, he Answered he did the fact which the Sailors suffered for, and then asked him what the Meaning was of what he said[; he] answered Ambrose Howard Beat the Bush and he Kecht [caught] the Bird and being Asked the meaning of that word, he answered Concerning Col. Lee's house and Plate and being Asked about that, he Answered he and Robert Brooks and two more Sett the house a fire, he said he went into the Cherry tree Room, and found Plate and went into Another Room and See a Silver Tankard Upon a Shelfe over a fire place and took it up and Drank out of it, and it vext him because he forgott to hand it out, That he threw out of the window one bed [spread?] and a pair of sheets and that he see a Molatto woman in the Kitchen cleaning Candlesticks and See her come out and goe up a pair of stairs by the Kitchen[;] when he was talking about the Cherry tree Room, he was Asked if Cherrys grew in it, Robert Brooks answered noe, but when he workt at Captain Lee's he was drinking Syder with the Servants and they told him there was Such a Room where the plates lay. Then this deponant, Mary McCarty, Robert Brooks and John Davis went to Patrick Spence's and the said Davis Showed them the Molatto woman that he See at Col. Lee's House, That she and Mary McCarty went to Mr. Barnes's Landing and hid in the Sand the said ten peices of Gold, Gold Watch and Ring which held Seven Stones And about two or three Months After that, the said Mary McCarty went and fetcht them and Carryed them to William Moseley's and hid them in a hallow tree Between two Goards, And After that the said McCarty told her at Mr. Minors Spring that if she would lett them alone till she was free, she would goe Away with her whereupon this deponant told her she would tell on it, Upon which the said McCarty reply'd if she did she would hang her if she had Fifty Necks.

It appearing to the Court upon aforesaid Examination that there is Just Cause for trying the said Robert Brooks, John Davis, and Mary McCarty at the General Court for the Crime aforesaid whereof they Are Accused, It is therefore Ordered that the said Robert Brooks, John Davis and Mary McCarty be [164] remanded to the Prison of this County under the Custody of the Sherrif, and from there to be Conveyed to the Publick Goale of Williamsburgh as the Law in Such Cases Directs.

Dickenson's Recognizance

Elizabeth Dickenson of Sittenbourne Parish in Richmond County in Open Court before his Majesties Justices Acknowledge herself Indebted to our Sovereign Lord the King his heirs and Successors in the Sum of Ten pounds Sterling to be levyed of her Lands and Tenements goods and Chattles, with Condition that if the said Elizabeth Dickenson shall personally Appear at the Next Generall Court on the Fourth Day thereof and then and there give such Evidence as she knows against Robert Brooks, John Davis, and Mary McCarty who stand Committed for felony, and do not Depart thence without leave of that Court, That then this Recognizance to be Void, or else remain in full force.

William's Recognizance

Jane Williams of Sittenbourne Parish in Richmond County in Open Court before his Majesties Justices Acknowledge herself Indebted to our Sovereign Lord the King his heirs and successors in the Sum of Ten Pounds Sterling to be levyed of her lands, and Tenements goods and Chattles with condition that if the said Jane Williams shall personally Appear at the next General Court on the Fourth day thereof, And then and there Give such Evidence as she knows against Robert Brooks, John Davis and Mary McCarty who stand Committed for felony, And do not Depart thence without leave of that Court, That then this Recognizance to be Void, or Else to Remain in full force.

Mosely's Recognizance

Samuel Mosely of Westmoreland County in Open Court before his Majesties Justices Acknowledge himself Indebted to our Sovereign Lord the King his heirs and Successors in the Sum of Ten pounds Sterling to be levyed of his lands and Tenements goods and Chattles, with Conditions of the said Samuel Moseley's wife named Mary Moseley shall Appear at the next General Court on the Fourth day thereof And then and there give such Evidence as she knows against Robert Brooks, John Davis and Mary McCarty, who stand Committed for felony, and do not Depart thence without leave of that Court, That then this Recognizance to be Void, or Else to Remain in full force.

Dickenson to give security for her behavior

[165] Elizabeth Dickenson of Sittenborne Parish in the County Appearing to be a person of very ill Behavior, It is therefore Ordered that she give good and Sufficient Security in the Sum of Ten pounds Sterling for her good Behavior during the Term of one Year. And that she remain in the Sherif's Custody untill she gives Such Security.

Henderson Bound to her behavior

Whereas Mollinder Henderson at the Call'd Court continued and held at the Court house of this County the Thirteenth Instant was Committed to the Sherrifs Custody untill she should give good and Sufficient Security for her good Behavior during the Terme of one year.

Whereupon the said Mollinder Henderson Together with Thomas Turner and John Bowen her Security's Acknowledged themselves Indebted to our Sovereign Lord the King the said Mollinder Henderson the Sum of Twenty pounds Sterling And the said Thomas Turner and John Bowen Each of them in the Sum of Tenn pounds Sterling to be levyed on their lands and Tenements goods and Chattles, with Condition that if the said Mollinder Henderson shall be of good Behaviour as well towards his Majesty as all his leige People, That then this Recognizance to be Void and of none Effect, or Else to remain in full force.

At the Court held for Richmond County The Seventh Day of October 1730.

Present: John Tayloe, William Fantleroy, Joseph Belfield, Willoughby Newton, Thomas Wright Belfield, John Woodbridge and Thomas Barber, Gentlemen Justices.

Mary a White Woman Whipt

Whereas Mary a white woman Servant Belonging to John Samford was by Vertue of a Mittimus from Thomas Wright Belfield Gentleman one of the Magistrates of this County Committed to the County Goale for takeing Upon her by Inchantment, Charm, witchcraft or Conjuration, to tell where Treasure is, or where goods left may be found,[94] And being Now brought before this Court, and on Examination of Severall Evidences touching the Same, It is the Opinion of this Court that the Said Mary is Guilty of what is laid to her Charge, it is therefore ordered that the Sherrif take her and Carry her to the Common Whipping post, and give her thirty nine lashes on her bare back well laid on.

[166] At a Court Continued and held for Richmond County the Fifth day of November 1730.

Present: John Tayloe, William Fantleroy, Willoughby Newton, John Woodbridge, and William Glasscock, Gentlemen Justices.

Baker a Negroe Whipt

Whereas Baker a Negro Man Slave Belonging to Capt. Thomas Wright Belfield was by vertue of a Mittimus from John Woodbridge Gentleman one of the

---

94. In England, 9 George II, c.5 (1736), made it a misdemeanor for any person to pretend to use witchcraft; all other laws on witchcraft were removed from the books. Until this time, using witchcraft to discover hidden treasure was punishable with pillory and imprisonment for a first offense and death for a second offense; 1 James I, c.12 (1603). Conjuring and casting spells were felonies without benefit of clergy. In Virginia, treasure telling was punishable under the Jacobean statute (Webb, *Justice of Peace*, 361–62), but Mary was not charged with a felony. The case was another evidence of the flexibility justices exhibited.

Justices of this Court Committed to the County Goale on Suspition of Stealing one hogg from Mr. James Samford and being now brought before his Majesties Justices here present on hearing the Evidence of two Negro Slaves against him and what he had to Say in his defence are of Opinion that he is Guilty of the Crime laid to his charge, It is therefore Ordered that for the said Offence the Sherrif take him and carry him to the common Whipping post and give him Thirty Nine Lashes on his bare back well laid on.

Abshone fined and Bound to the Peace

Anthony Morgan haveing Sworn the peace against William Abshone before Willoughby Newton Gentleman one of the Magistrates of this County, and the said William Abshone this day Appearing, It is therefore Ordered that he give Security for keeping the Same during the Terme of one Year, And that he be Fined Fifty Shillings Current money to our Sovereign Lord the King.

Whereupon the said William Abshone Together with Hugh Lambert and John Elmore his Securitys in Open Court Acknowledged themselves Indebted Unto our Sovereign Lord the King, his heirs and Successors and the said William Abshone in the Sum of Twenty pounds Sterling and the said Hugh Lambert and John Elmore Each of them in the Sum of Tenn pounds Sterling, to be levyed on their Lands and Tenements goods and Chattles with Condition that if the said William Abshone shall keep the peace of our Sovereign Lord the King towards his said Majestie and all his Leige people, and Espetially towards the said Anthony Morgan, That then this Recognizance to be void and of none Effect or Else to Remain in full force. Also the said Hugh Lambert and John Elmore Obliged themselves their heirs etc. for the said William Abshones payment of the said Fifty shillings as before Ordered.

James a Negro Quartered

[**167**] At a Session of Oyer and Terminer held at Richmond Court house on Tuesday the Third day of November one Thousand Seven hundred and Thirty in the Fourth year of the reign of our Sovereign Lord George the Second by the Grace of God of Great Brittain France and Ireland King Defender of the Faith etc. by Vertue of a Speciall Commission for the Tryall of all Treasons petty Treasons or Misprisions thereof Felonys Murthers or other offences or Crimes whatsoever Committed Within the County of Richmond by a Negro man Slave named James Belonging to Christopher Petty, Directed to Thomas Griffin, John Tayloe, William Fantleroy William Downman, Charles Grymes, Joseph Belfield, Robert Tomlin, Samuell Peachey, Willoughby Newton, Thomas Wright Belfield, John Woodbridge, Thomas Beale, Thomas Barber William Glasscock and Samuell Glasscock Gentlemen.

Present: John Tayloe, William Fantleroy, Willoughby Newton, John Woodbridge and Thomas Barber, Gentlemen Justices.

Whereas James a Negro man Slave belonging to Christopher Petty was by

Vertue of a Warrant from John Woodbridge Gentleman one of the Magistrates of this County Committed to this County Goale the Thirteenth day of October last for Feloniously Murdering Mary Petty Daughter of the Said Christopher Petty and the Sherrif having made return to this Court on the back of the Said Warrant that he found the Said Slave dead in prison, It is therefore Ordered that the Sherrif take the body of the Said Negro James and cutt it into four Quarters and hang and [a] Quarter up at Potoskey Ferry, and [a] Quarter at Captain Newtons Mill, and [a] quarter at Moratico Mill and the other Quarter in William Griffins old Field and Stick his head on a pole at the Court house,[95] and that he be Allowed fore [doing it] the Sume at the Laying the Levy.

At a Court Continued and held for Richmond County the Fourth day of February 1730/1.

Present: John Tayloe, William Fantleroy, William Newton, Thomas Barber and William Glasscock, Gentlemen Justices.

Metcalfe Judgment against him

[168] John Tarpley Jr. Gentleman Attorney of our Lord and King brought an Information in this Court against Gilbert Metcalfe Planter for One Thousand three hundred Seventy Seven pounds of Tobacco due by Writeing [an] Obligatory [note] dated the Eleventh day of October one Thousand Seven hundred Twenty three from the said Gilbert Metcalfe to one Thomas Moverly of Westermoreland County[,] which said Moverely Did lay violent hands on himselfe by hanging himself with a hairhalter as by an Inquisition taken upon the view of the body of the Said Moverley before Henry Ashton Gentleman one of his Majesties Coroners may Appear,[96] the Said Gilbert Metcalfe this day Appear'd and Acknowledged the Debt to be Justly due Except Eighty nine pounds of Tobacco, thereupon the motion of the Said John Tarpley Judgement is Granted our Said Lord the King against the Said Gilbert Metcalfe for Twelve hundred and Eighty Eight pounds of Tobacco being the Ballance[,] which is Ordered to be paid with Costs Also Execution.

Jackson Judgment Against him

John Tarpley Jr. Gentleman Attorney of our Lord the King brought an Information in this Court Against Nathaniel Jackson Planter for one Thousand pounds of Tobacco due by Writing [an] Obligatory [note] dated the Ninth day of

---

95. This is the penalty for petty treason. It does not appear that the court tried James but merely ordered his corpse's dismemberment and display. Slaves in armed conflict with their Virginia masters were executed and displayed in a similar manner; Scott, *Criminal Law*, 162. Dismemberment and display of the bodies of dead traitors attainted for their rebellion by Parliament was a common sight during the Wars of Roses; A. F. Pollard, *The Reign of Henry VII* (New York, 1967), 1:51–53.

96. A coroner's jury found that Moverly had committed the crime of *felo de se*, that is, suicide. *Felo de se* was a voluntary, willful act, from which the victim died within a year; Webb, *Justice of Peace*, 237–38. The penalty was foreiture of goods and chattels to the crown. Moverly's estate included debts owed him by others, in particular by Jackson and the others named in the king's action.

May one Thousand Seven hundred Twenty three from the Said Nathaniel Jackson to one Thomas Moverly of Westmoreland County which said Moverly did lay violent hands on himself by hanging himself with a hair halter as by an Inquisition taken upon the View of the body of the Said Moverley before Henry Ashton Gentleman one of his Majesties Coroners may Appear, the Said Nathaniel Jackson haveing been Summoned to Answer the same, And Being now Called, but not Appearing[,] thereupon on the motion of the Said John Tarpley Judgment is Granted our Said Lord the King against the Said Nathaniel Jackson for the Aforesaid Sum of one Thousand Pounds of Tobacco which is Ordered to be paid with Cost Also Execution.

Richards Judgment Against him

John Tarpley Jr. Gentleman Attorney of our Lord the King brought an Information in this Court against William Richards[,] planter[,] for Five hundred and Thirty pounds of Tobacco due by writeing [an] Obligatory [note] Sealed with his Seal and dated [**169**] the Eighteenth day of January one Thousand Seven hundred Twenty three[/]Four from the said William Richards to one Thomas Moverley of Westmoreland County which Said Moverley did lay violent hands on himself by hanging himself with a hair halter as by an Inquisition taken upon the view of the body of the Said Moverley before Henry Ashton Gentleman one of his Majesties Coroners may Appear the Said William Richards haveing been Summoned to Answer the Same, and being now Called, but not Appearing, thereupon on the Motion of the Said John Tarpley Judgement is Granted our Said Lord the King against the Said William Richards for the aforesaid Sum of Five hundred and Thirty pounds of Tobacco, which is Ordered to be paid with costs Also Execution.

Taylor Bound to his Behaviour

John Taylor of North Farnham parrish haveing been Summoned to answer the presentment of the Grand jury against him for a Common Drunkard and Disturber of the peace and this day Appearing but offering Nothing Materiall to Excuse himself it is the Opinion of this Court and Accordingly Ordered that for the Said Offence he give good and Sufficient Security for his good Behaviour during the Terme of one year.

Whereupon the said John Taylor together with James Suggitt his Security in Open Court before his Majesties Justices Acknowledged themselves Indebted unto our Sovereign Lord the King his heirs and Successors in the Sum of Twenty pounds Sterling to be levyed on their Lands and Tenements goods and Chattles, with Condition that if the Said John Taylor shall be of good Behaviour as well towards his Majestie as all his Leige People, Then this Recognizance to be Void and of none Effect, or Else to Remain in full Force and Vertue.

At a Court Continued and held for Richmond County the 5th Day of August 1731.

Present: John Tayloe, Joseph Belfield, William Newton, John Woodbridge and Thomas Barber, Gentlemen Justices.

Gibbs Bound to her Behaviour

Ann Gibbs according to her recognizance this day Appearing to answer the Complaint of Mary Deakwood (for that she is afraid the Said Ann Gibbs will beat; wound, maim or kill her) but the Said Ann Gibbs offering nothing Materiall to Excuse herself, It is therefore Ordered that she give good and [**170**] Sufficient Security for her good Behaviour dureing the Term of one Year.

Whereupon the said Ann Gibbs together with Charles Dodson her Security in Open Court Acknowledged themselves Indebted unto our Sovereign Lord the King, his heirs and Successors in the Sum of Twenty pounds Sterling to be Levyed on their Lands and Tenements, goods and Chattles with Condition that if the Said Ann Gibbs Shall be of good Behavour as Well towards his Majestie as all his Leige people, Then this Recognizance to be Void and of none Effect. or Else to Remain in full force and Vertue.

At a Court held for Richmond County the First day of September 1731.

Present: John Tayloe, William Fantleroy, Joseph Belfield, Samuell Peachey, William Newton, Thomas Wright Belfield, John Woodbridge, Thomas Barber and William Glascock, Gentlemen Justices.

Pheny Bound to his Behaviour

Thomas Pheny according to his Recognizance this day Appearing to Answer the Complaint of Mary Russell for Assaulting beating and Abuseing her[,] Also a Servant man named George Raven belonging to the said Russell[,] but Offering nothing Materiall to Excuse himself, It is therefore Ordered that he give good and Sufficient Security for his good Behaviour during the Term of one year.

Whereupon the said Thomas Pheny together with Michaell Connell his Security in Open Court Acknowledged themselves Indebted unto our Sovereign Lord the King his heirs and Successors in the Sum of Twenty pounds Sterling to be Levyed on their lands and Tenements, goods and Chattles with Condition that if the Said Thomas Pheny Shall be of good behaviour as well towards his Majestie as all his Leige people, then this Recognizance to be Void and of none Effect, or Else to Remain in full force and vertue.

[**171**] At a Court Continued and held for Richmond County the Second day of September 1731.

Present: John Tayloe, William Fantleroy, Thomas Wright Belfield, and Thomas Barber, Gentlemen Justices.

Stephens Fined

Whereas Joan Stephens last March Court pleaded not guilty to an Information Exhibitted against her by John Tarpley Jr. Gentleman Attorney of our Lord the

King for Tending of Seconds for Tobacco,[97] Whereupon a Jury was this day Impannelled and Sworn to try the matter in Issue by name Alexander Newman, John Bruce, Thomas Beckham, William Smith, Edmund Northern, James Suggitt, Luke Thornton, William Petty, Edward Jones, William Bruce, Dominick Newgent and Richard Branham who haveing heard the Evidence and received their Charge were Sent out, and Soon after returning into Court, and agreed, gave in their Verdict which in these Words "Wee of the Jury doe find Joan Stephens Guilty for Tending Tobacco Seconds and at that time had one Tythable,[98] James Suggitt F.M:,"[99] which Verdict on the Motion of the King's Attorney is Ordered to be Recorded.

Whereupon it is Considered by the Court and the Court doth hereby Order that the Said Joan Stephens doe pay unto our said Sovereign Lord the King Five hundred pounds of Tobacco (pursuant to the Law in that Case made and provided) Together with Costs and One Attorneys Fee Also Execution.

Hinds Fined

Whereas Benjamin Hinds this day pleaded not Guilty to an Information Exhibitted against him by John Tarpley Jr. Gentleman Attorney of our Lord the King for Tending of Seconds for Tobacco, Whereupon a Jury was this day Impannelled and Sworn to Try the Matter in Issue by Name Alexander Newman, John Bruce, Thomas Beckham, William Smith, Edmund Northern, James Suggit, Luke Thornton, William Petty, Edward Jones, William Bruce, Dominick Newgent and Richard Branham[100] who haveing heard the Evidence and received their Charge were Sent out and Soon after returning into Court and Agreed gave in their Verdict which is in these Words, "Wee of the Jury doe find Benjamin Hinds Guilty for Tending Tobacco Seconds by Evidence of John Deane, James Sluggit F. M:" which verdict on the Motion of the Kings [172] Attorney is ordered to be recorded—whereupon it is Considered by the Court and the Court doth hereby Order that the Said Benjamin Hinds doe pay unto our Said Sovereign Lord the King Five hundred pounds of Tobacco (pursuant to the Law in that Case made and provided) Together with Costs and One Attorney's Fee Also Execution.

At a Court held for Richmond County the Sixth day of October 1731.

Present: William Fantleroy, Samuell Peachy, Willoughby Newton, Thomas Wright Belfield, Thomas Barber, William Glasscock, Gentlemen Justices.

---

97. Under one of the tobacco statutes of 1720 (*Statutes at Large*, 4:87–89 [1720]), the mislabeling of the quality of the tobacco during packaging was a serious misdemeanor. Throughout the eighteenth century, the House of Burgesses strove to regulate the production and marketing of this crop.

98. Because the penalty was based upon a formula—multiplication of five hundred pounds of tobacco by the number of tithables who worked in the fields of the defendants that year—the jury included that number in its finding.

99. Foreman of the jury.

100. The same jury sat in Stephens's trial, evidence that a given trial jury sat for more than one case. This was English practice as well. The jury retired to consider its verdict after each case and returned to the courtroom to report its findings to the justices.

Duncan Whipt and Bound to his Behaviour

Whereas John Duncan was by Vertue of a Mittimus from Samuell Peachey, Gentleman one of the Magistrates of this County Committed to the County Goale for feloniously takeing Ten pounds of Wool and Ten pounds of Sheet Lead from Mr. John Tarpley Jr. and being now brought before this Court, and on Examination of Severall Evidences touching the same, It is the Opinion of this Court that the said John Duncan is Guilty of what is laid to his Charge, It is therefore Ordered that the Sherif take him and Carry him to the Common Whipping post and Give him Thirty nine lashes on his bare back well laid on, and then to give Security for his good Behaviour During the Term of one Year.

Whereupon the said John Duncan Together with John Tarpley Jr. Gentleman his Security in Open Court Acknowledged themselves Indebted unto our Sovereign Lord the King his heirs and Successors, The said John Duncan in the Sum of Twenty pounds Sterling and the said John Tarpley in the Sum of Ten pounds Sterling to be Levyed on their Lands and Tenements goods and Chattles, With Condition that if the said John Duncan shall be of good Behaviour as Well Towards his Said Majestie as all his Leige people, That then this recognizance to be Void and of None Effect, or Else to remain in Full force.

[**173**] At a Court held for Richmond County the First day of December 1731. Present: John Tayloe, William Fantleroy, Joseph Belfield, Samuel Peachey and Thomas Wright Belfield, Gentlemen Justices.

Andras Whipt and to give Security for his Behaviour

Whereas Mary Long and Susanah Long her daughter made Oath before Thomas Wright Belfield Gentleman one of the Justices of this Court that they were afraid John Andras would beat would maim or kill them, and therefore prayed Surety of the peace against him, And the said John Andras failing to give Security for his Appearance at this Court to Answer the same, he was there upon Committed to the Goale of this County by the said Thomas Wright Belfield, and being now brought before this Court, on Examination of Severall Evidences against him, It appears to this Court that the said John Andras not only threatened to do Some bodily Hurt to the said Mary and Susanah Long, but that he diverse times endeavoured to abuse the said Susanah Long, It is therefore Ordered that for the said Offences the Sherif take him and Carry him to the Common Whipping post and give Thirty Nine lashes on his bare back well laid on, and also that he Give good and Sufficient Security for his good Behaviour during the Term of one year, And that he remain in the Sherriffs Custody untill he Gives Such Security.

Present Thomas Barber Gentlemen

Humphreys whipt

Whereas Ann Humphreys was by Vertue of a Mittimus from Thomas Barber Gentleman one of the Magistrates of this County Committed to the County Goale for feloniously stealing of one Check lining Womans Apron from Frances Barber, And being now brought before this Court on hearing the Evidence Against her and What She had to Say in her defence, It is the Opinion of this Court that the said Ann Humphreys is Guilty of what is laid to her Charge, It is therefore Ordered that the Sheriff take her and Carry her to the Common Whiping post and give her Thirty Lashes on her bare back well laid on.

[174] At a Court Continued and held for Richmond County the Second day of March 1731/2.

Present: John Tayloe, William Fantleroy, Samuell Peachey Thomas Barber and John Woodbridge, Gentlemen Justices.

Dudley Bound to his Behaviour

William Dudley of North Farnham Parrish haveing been Summoned to Answer the presentment of the Grand jury against him for being a Common notorious Drunkard and this day Appearing but offering nothing matteriall to Excuse himself it is the Opinion of this Court and Accordingly Ordered that for the said Offence he Give good and Sufficient Security for his good Behaviour during the Term of one year.

Whereupon the said William Dudley Together with Alexander Clark his Security in Open Court Acknowledged themselves Indebted unto our Sovereign Lord the King his heirs and Successors in the Sum of Twenty pounds Sterling to be Levyed on their Lands and Tenements Goods and Chattles, with Condition that if the Said William Dudley shall be of good Behaviour as well Towards his Majesty as all his Leige people That then this Recognizance to be void and of no Effect otherwise to remain in full Force and vertue.

At a Court held for Richmond County the Fifth day of April 1732.

Present: John Tayloe, William Fantleroy, Joseph Belfield, John Woodbridge, Gentlemen Justices.

Russell judgment Bound to his Behaviour

It appearing to this Court that Joseph Russell Jr. of North Farnham parrish in this County keeps a disorderly house,[101] It is therefore Ordered that he give good and Sufficient Security for his good Behaviour during the Term of one year.

---

101. A bond for good behavior, for the head of a household was responsible for order in his own house—among his servants, guests, and children—just as he was for his own conduct.

Whereupon the said Joseph Russell Jr. Together with John Brown and Tobias Purcell his Security in Open Court Acknowledged themselves Indebted unto our Sovereign Lord the King his heirs and Successors, The said Joseph Russell in the Sum of Twenty pounds Sterling [175] and the Said John Brown and Tobias Purcell each of them in the Sum of Ten pounds Sterling to be Levyed on their Lands and Tenements, Goods and Chattles, with Condition that if the said Joseph Russell shall be of good Behaviour as well towards his Majesty as all his Leige People, That then this Recognizance to be Void and of none Effect, Otherwise to remain in Full force and Vertue.

At a Court Continued and held for Richmond County the Sixth day of Aprill 1732.

Present John Tayloe, William Fantleroy, Joseph Belfield, Samuel Peachey and Thomas Barber, Gentlemen Justices.

Holland Bound to his Behaviour

Henry Holland of North Farnham Parrish haveing been Summoned to Answer the Presentment of the Grandjury against him for being a Common Drunkard and Common Swearer, And this day Appearing but offering nothing materiall to Excuse himself It is the Opinion of this Court and accordingly Ordered that for the said Offence he give good and Sufficient Security for his good Behaviour during the Term of One year.

Whereupon the said Henry Holland Together with Arthur Mcmahone his Security in Open Court Acknowledged themselves Indebted unto our Sovereign Lord the King his heirs and Successors in the Sum of Twenty pounds Sterling to be Levyed on their Lands and Tenements Goods and Chattles, with Condition that if the said Henry Holland shall be of good Behaviour as well Towards his Majestie as all his Leige People, That then this Recognizance to be Void and of none Effect, Otherwise to remain in full force and Vertue.

Taylor Bound to his Behaviour

John Taylor of North Farnham Parrish haveing been Summoned to answer the presentment of the Grand jury against him for being a Common notorious Drunkard, and this day Appearing but offering nothing materiall to Excuse himself it is the Opinion of this Court, and Accordingly Ordered that for the said Offence he give good and Sufficient Security for his good Behaviour during the Term of one year.

Whereupon the said John Taylor together with William [176] Taylor his Security in Open Court Acknowledged themselves Indebted unto our Sovereign Lord the King his heirs and Successors in the Sum of Twenty Pounds Sterling to be Levyed on their Lands and Tenements goods and Chattles with Condition that if the said John Taylor shall be of good Behaviour as well towards his

Majestie as all his Leige people, That then this Recognizance to be Void and of None Effect, Otherwise to Remain in full force and Vertue.

At a Call'd Court held at the Court house of Richmond County the First day of May 1732.

Present: Joseph Belfield, Thomas Wright Belfield, John Woodbridge, Thomas Barber, Gentlemen Justices.

[*Hall and Lynhain bound to their behaviour*]

Whereas Robert Hall and Christopher Lynhain by Virtue of a Mittimus from Joseph Belfield gentleman one of the Magistrates of this County was Committed to the County Goale for being Guilty of Burglary in Breaking Open the Mansion house of Mr. Edward Barradall and being now brought before this Court and Several Evidences being produced and Examined but not proving the fact yet it Appearing to the Court that the said Robert Hall and Christopher Lynhain are Persons of ill behaviour, It is therefore Ordered that they give Good and Sufficient Security for their good Behaviour.

Jackson's Recognizance

David Jackson of North Farnham Parish this day in Open Court before his Majesties Justices Acknowledged himself Indebted to our Sovereign Lord the King his heirs and Successors in the Sum of forty Pounds Sterling to be Levyed on his Lands and Tenements goods and Chattles on the Condition that if his foresaid Man named Christopher Lynhain (who was Committed to the said County Goale on Suspicion of Breaking Open the house of Mr. Edward Barradall) Shall be of good Behaviour as well towards his Majestie as all his Leige People during the Term of One year, That then this Recognizance to be Void and of none Effect or else to Remain in full force and Vertue.

[*Packett recognizance*]

[177] Gabriel Packett Jr. of North Farnham parish this day in Open Court before his Majestys Justices Acknowledged himself Indebted to our Sovereign Lord the King his heirs and Successors in the Sum of forty Pounds Sterling to be Levyed on his Lands and Tenements goods and Chattles with Condition that if his Servant Man named Robert Hall (who was Committed to this County Goale on Suspicion of breaking Open the house of Mr. Edward Barradall) shall be of good Behaviour as well towards his Majesty as all his Leige people During the Term of One year, That then this Recognizance to be Void and of none Effect or Else to Remain in full force and Vertue.

At a Court held for Richmond County the Sixth day of September 1732.
Present: Joseph Belfield, Samuel Peachey, John Woodbridge, Thomas Barber, Richard Barnes, William Jordan and Anthony Sidnor, Gentlemen Justices.

Jones to give Security for his Behaviour

It appearing to this Court that Richard Jones of North Farnham parish in this County is a person of very ill behaviour: It is therefore ordered that he give good and Sufficient security for his good behaviour, and that he remain in the Sherrifs custody untill he gives such security.

At a Court Continued and held for Richmond County the Seventh day of November 1732.
Present: Joseph Belfield, Samuel Peachey, Richard Barnes, Anthony Sidnor, Gentlemen Justices.

Abshone and others Judgment against them

Judgment upon a Sciere [scire] facias is renewed to our Sovereign Lord the King against William Abshone Hugh Lambert and John Elmore for fifty shillings currency it being a fine laid on said Abshone the fifth day of [178] November MDCCXXX for breaking the peace whereupon it is ordered that they pay the same also Execution.[102]

At a Court held for Richmond County the fifth Day of February 1732/3.
Present: Joseph Belfield, Samuel Peachey, Thomas Barber and William Jordan, Gentlemen Justices.

[Garland and others, judgment against them]

Upon a Sciere [scire] Facias brought by our Sovereign Lord the King against William Garland and William Nash upon a Recognizance entered into by them before John Tayloe Gentleman each of them in twenty pounds sterling to our said Sovereign Lord the King for one Anthony Morgans keeping the peace and good behaviour to which the said William Garland and William Nash by George Eskriege Gentleman their attorney having put in their pleas And John Tarpley Jr. Gentleman Attorney of our said Lord the King haveing demur'd to the said[;] upon arguing of which the said demurr is adjudged good,[103] Therefore it is

---

102. The king's attorney brought a writ of *scire facias* to renew the judgment against Abshone and others. After a year and a day had passed, Abshone had not yet paid his fine. The cost of execution of the writ, due the sheriff, was added to the fine.

103. Garland and Nash demurred to losing their recognizances in Morgan's case until Morgan's guilt or innocence was determined. The court ruled in favor of this plea and forestalled execution of

considered and accordingly ordered that Execution Issue against the said William Garland for the aforesaid sum of twenty pounds sterling, And against the said William Nash for twenty pounds sterling, off their and each of their lands and Chattles respectively to be levyed according to the form and effect of the recognizance aforesaid, but no Execution to Issue till a suit now depending in this Court between our Sovereign Lord the King and the aforesaid Anthony Morgan be determined.

At a Court Continued and held for Richmond County the Sixth day of February 1732 [1733]

Present: Joseph Belfield, Richard Barnes, William Jordan and Anthony Sidnor, Gentlemen Justices.

Jackson bound to his Behaviour

[**179**] It appearing to this Court that Christopher Dominick Jackson is a person of an ill behaviour It is therefore ordered that he give good and Sufficient Security for his good behaviour.

Whereupon the said Christopher Dominick Jackson together with Archibald Mitchell his security in open Court acknowledged themselves Indebted unto our Sovereign Lord the King his heirs and Successors in the sum of twenty pounds sterling to be levyed on their Lands and tenements goods and Chattles with Condition that if the said Christopher Dominick Jackson shall be of good behaviour as well towards his Majesty and all his Leige People That then this Recognizance to be Void and of none Effect Otherwise to remain in full force and Virtue.

At a Court held for Richmond County the Second Day of Aprill 1733.

Present: Joseph Belfield, Samuell Peachey, Thomas Barber, Richard Barnes and Anthony Sydnor, Gentlemen Justices.

William Richards Judgment against him

On the Sciere [scire] Facias at the suit of our Sovereign Lord the King against William Richards on a Judgment obtained by our said Lord the King against the said Richards at a Court held for this County the Fourth Day of February 1730/1 For Five hundred thirty pounds of Tobacco the said William Richards being Duly summoned to show why the said Judgment should not be renewed, and being now called but not appearing, the said Judgment is hereby renewed for the said Sum of Five hundred and thirty pounds of Tobacco and it is ordered

---

the writ until the king's suit against Morgan was settled; see p. 145, below. Eskridge, counsel for Garland and Nash, was also Morgan's counsel and had lately been the king's attorney.

that the said William Richards pay the same to our said Lord the King also Execution.

Jackson judgment Against him

[**180**] On the Sciere [scire] facias at the suit of our Sovereign Lord the King against Nathaniel Jackson on a Judgment obtained by our said Lord the King against the said Jackson at a Court held for this County the Fourth Day of February 1730/1 for One thousand pounds of Tobacco the said Nathaniel Jackson being Duely Summoned to show why the said Judgment should not be renewed, and being now call'd but not appearing, the said Judgment is hereby renewed for the said Sum of One thousand pounds of Tobacco, and it is ordered that the said Nathaniel Jackson pay the same to our said Lord the King also Execution.

At a Called Court held at the Court house of Richmond County on Thursday the Fifth Day of Aprill MDCCxxxiii.
Present: Joseph Belfield, John Woodbridge, Thomas Barber, Richard Barnes, William Jordan, Anthony Sydnor, Gentlemen Justices.

[*Cavernor and others examined*]

Whereas David Cavernor, Hannah Cavernor, William Hambleton, John Lovee and Rebeccah Dance was by Vertue of Two mittimus's from Joseph Belfield Gentleman one of the Justices of this Court Committed to the County Goal on Suspicion of Fellony, and Being now brought before his Majesties Justices here present and together with Several Witnesses being Diligently Examined Touching the said Fact, It appearing to the Court there is Just Cause for trying the said David Cavernor, Hannah Cavernor and William Hamleton at the General Court for the Crime aforesaid, where of they are accused, It is therefore ordered that the said David Cavernor, Hannah Cavernor and William Hambleton, be remanded to the prison of This County under the Custody of the Sherrif and from thence [**181**] to be Conveyed to the Publick Goal of Williamsburgh as the Law in Such Cases Directs.

At a Call'd Court held the Court house of Richmond County on thursday the 5th day of Aprill 1733.
Present: Joseph Belfield, John Woodbridge, Thomas Barber, Richard Barnes, William Jordan, Anthony Sydnor, Gentlemen Justices.

Comings's Recognizance

Samuel Commins of Lunenburg Parish in Richmond County in open Court before his Majesties Justices acknowledged himself Indebted to our Soverign

Lord the King his Heirs and Successors in the Sum of Ten pounds Sterling to be Levyed of his lands and tenements goods and Chattles, with Condition that if the said Samuel Commin's (Servant man named Alexander Jones) shall personally appear at the next Generall Court the Fourth day there of, and then and there give such Evidence as he knows against David Cavernor, Hannah Cavernor and William Hambleton who stands committed for Felony, and do not depart Thence without leave of that Court That then This Recognizance to be void, or else to remain in full force.

Suttle's Recognizance

Henry Suttle of Lunenburgh Parish in Richmond County in open Court before his Majestys Justices acknowledged himself Indebted to our Sovereign Lord the King his Heirs and Successors in the sum of ten pounds Sterling to be levyed of his lands and tenements goods and Chattles, with Condition That if he the said Henry Suttle shall Personally appear at the next Generall Court on the fourth Day there of and then and there give Such Evidences as he Knows against David Cavernor Hanah Cavenor and William Hambleton who Stands Committed for felony, [182] and do not depart thence without Leave of that Court, That then this recognizance to be void, or Else to remain in full force.

Mrs. Garzia's Recognizance

Mrs. Mary Garzia of Lunenburgh Parish in Richmond County in open Court before his Majesties Justices Acknowledged her Self Indebted to our Sovereign Lord the king his Heirs and Successors in the sum of Ten pounds Sterling to Levied of her Lands and Tenements Goods and Chattles, with Condition That if she the said Mary Garzia shall personally appear at the next General Court on the Fourth day Thereof and Then and There give such Evidence as she knows against David Cavernor Hannah Cavernor and William Hambleton who stands Commited for Felony, and doe not Depart thence without Leave of That Court That Then This Recognizance to be void, or Else to remain in full Force.

At a Court held for Richmond County the Third Day of July 1733.
Present: Charles Grymes, Joseph Belfield, Samuel Peachey, Thomas Barber and Leroy Griffin, Gentlemen Justices.

The King against Morgan

Upon a Scire facias brought by our Sovereign Lord the King against Anthony Morgan upon recognizance entered into by him before John Tayloe Gentleman in Forty pounds Sterling to our said Lord the King for to refrain all Cohabitation, Converse or Communication with Sarah Ann Simmons, To which The said Anthony Morgan by George Eskridge his Attorney put in his pleas, and John Tarpley Jr. Gentleman Attorny of our said Lord the King [183] his replication, and agrees it may be Enquired of by a Jury of the vicinage and whereupon a Jury was This Day Impanneled and sworn to try the matter[104] in issue by name Alexander Clark etc. who having heard the evidence, and received their Charge, were sent out, and soon after returning into Court and agreed gave in Their verdict, which is in these words, "Wee of the Jury find the Defendant not guilty.["] Alvin Mountjoy foreman[;] which verdict on motion of the Defendants Attorny is ordered to be Recorded and the suit Dismist.

At a Court held for Richmond County the sixth Day of August MDCCxxxiii.
Present: Charles Grymes, Samuel Peachey, Joseph Belfield, Thomas Barber, William Glascock, Leroy Griffin, William Jordan and Anthony Sydnor, Gentlemen Justices.

Lyell fined

Jonathan Lyell of Northfarnham Parish being Returned summoned as Juryman to attend Court This day, and not appearing when Called, is hereby fined Twenty shillings Currant mony to our Sovereign Lord the King which the Sherrif of this County is ordered to Collect of him upon Refusall of payment by Distress.

At a Call'd Court held at the Court house of Richmond County the 17th day of November 1733.
Present: Samuell Peachey, Leroy Griffin, Daniell Hornby, Richard Barnes and William Jordan, Gentlemen Justices.

Holloway whipt

Whereas William Holloway by vertue of a mittimus from Samuell Peachey Gentlemen one of the Justices [184] of this Court was Committed to the County Goale on Suspicion of Stealing brandy and some other things out of the house of Mary Lewis widow, and being now brought before his Majestys Justices here Present, on Examination of Severall evidences touching the same, It is the opinion of this Court that the said William Holloway is guilty of the Crime laid to his Charge, It is therefore order'd that for the said offence the Sherriff take him and Carry him to the Common whiping post, and give him thirty nine lashes on his bare back well laid on.

At a Call'd Court held at the Court house of Richmond County on Monday the Fourth Day of March 1733/4.

---

104. After Morgan pled to the charge, he put himself upon the country, his right under English and Virginia law; Webb, *Justice of Peace*, 192–93. The plaintiff, the king's attorney, agreed to the jury trial.

Present: Joseph Belfield, Samuel Peachey, John Woodbridge, Thomas Barber, William Glascock, Leroy Griffin, Daniell Hornby, Richard Barnes and William Jordan, Gentlemen Justices.

Faithfull's Examination

Whereas Jonathan Faithfull was by vertue of a Mittimus from John Woodbridge Gentleman one of the Justices of this Court committed to the County Goale on Suspicion of Felony and being now brought before his Majestys Justices here present and Together with several Witnesses being Diligently Examined touching the said Fact, it appearing to this Court that there is Just cause for trying the said prisoner at the next Generall Court for the Crime aforesaid, whereof he is accused, It is therefore ordered that the said Jonathan Faithfull be remanded to the Prison of this County, under the Custody of the Sherriff, and from thence to be Conveyed to the Publick Goale of Williamsburg, as the Law in such Cases directs.

Griffith's Recognizance

[185] William Griffith of Nor[th]farnham Parish in Richmond County in open Court before his Majesties Justices Acknowledged himself Indebted to our Sovereign Lord the King his heirs and Successors in the Sum of Ten pounds Sterling to be Levy'd of his Lands and Tenements goods and Chattells, with Condition that if the said William Griffith shall personally Appear at the next Generall Court on the Fourth day thereof and then and there give Such Evidence as he knows against Jonathan Faithfull who stands Committed for Felony, and do not Depart thence without Leave of that Court that then this recognizance to be void, or Else to remain in full force.

Mason's Recognizance

Nathaniell Mason of Northfarnham Parish in Richmond County in open Court before his Majesties Justices acknowledged himself Indebted to our Sovereign Lord the King his heirs and Successors in the Sum of Ten pounds Sterling to be Levy'd of his Lands and Tenements goods and Chattells, with Condition that if he the said Nathaniel Mason shall Personally Appear at the next Generall Court on the Fourth Day thereof and then and there give such Evidence as he knows against Jonathan Faithfull who stands Committed for Felony and do not Depart thence without leave of that Court that then this Recognizance to be void, or Else to remain in full force.

Hornby's Recognizance

Daniell Hornby Gentleman of Northfarnham Parish in Richmond County in open Court before his Majesties Justices Acknowledged himself Indebted, to our Sovereign Lord the King his heirs and Successors in the sum of Ten Pounds Sterling to be Levy'd of his lands and Tenements [186] goods and Chattells, with Condition if the said Daniel Hornby Gentleman shall personally appear at the next Generall Court on the Fourth day thereof and then and there give such Evidence as he knows against Jonathan Faithfull who stands Committed for felony and do not depart thence without Leave of that Court that then this Recognizance to be void, Else to remain in full Force.

At a Court held for Richmond County the First Day of Aprill 1734.

Present: Joseph Belfield, Samuell Peachey, Thomas Barber, William Glascock, Leroy Griffin, Daniell Hornby, Richard Barnes, Anthoney Sydnor, Gentlemen Justices.

Taylor bound to Behaviour

John Taylor of Northfarnham Parish having been Summon'd to answer the Presentment of the Grandjury against him for being a Common Drunkard, a Common Swearer and a Common Disturber of the Peace and this Day appearing but offering nothing material to Excuse himself, It is the Opinion of this Court and accordingly Ordered that for the said Offence he give good and Sufficient Security for his good behaviour During the Term of one Year.

Whereupon the said John Taylor together with John Williams his Security in open Court Acknowledged themselves Indebted unto our Sovereign Lord the King his heirs and Successors in the Sum of Twenty pounds Sterling to be Levyed on their Lands and tenements goods and chattles with Condition that if the said John Taylor shall be of good behaviour as well towards his Majestie as all his Liege People that then this Recognizance [187] to be void and of none Effect, or else to Rmain in full force and Vertue.

Legg Bound to his Behaviour

Thomas Legg of Northfarnham Parish having been Summoned to answer the Presentment of the Grandjury against him for being a Common Drunkard, a Common Swearer and a Common Disturber of the Peace, and this Day appearing but offering nothing material to Excuse himself, It is the opinion of this Court and Accordingly Ordered that for the said offence he give good and Sufficient Security for his good behaviour During the term of one year.

Whereupon the said Thomas Legg together with Jonathan Lyell his Security in open Court Acknowledged themselves Indebted unto our Sovereign Lord the King his heirs and successors in the Sum of Twenty pounds Sterling to be Levy'd on their Lands and tenements goods and Chattells with Condition that if the said Thomas Legg be of good behaviour as well towards his Majesty as all his Liege People that then this Recognizance to be Void and of none Effect, or Else to Remain in full force and Vertue.

At a Call'd Court held at the Court house of Richmond County on Satturday the 29th day of June 1734.

Present: Joseph Belfeild, Thomas Wright Belfield, John Woodbridge, Daniell Hornby, William Jordan, Anthoney Sydnor, Gentlemen Justices.

Collingwood's Examination

Whereas John Collingwood alias Tanner[,] Richard Smith and Two Negroe Men named Peter and Beshoof was by Vertue of a mittimus From William Jordan gentleman one of the Justices of ths Court Committed to the County Goal on Suspicion of Murdering one [188] John Shaw, by Cutting the Throat of the said Shaw, and then throwing him over board, and being now brought before his Majesties Justices here present, The said John Collingwood Saith[:] That he being skipper of Mr. Humphry Hill's sloop, one John Shaw this day Six weeks [ago], was put on board the said sloop at the bristol mines to look after a Sea Store of Capt. Williams's which was to be put on board a Ship in York River, That the said Shaw had on, one new pair of Shoes, one white Shirt, one pair white Trowsers and one Light Colour'd Jackett, and that about pain's Island, over against the Clifts, a little above the warf, between Sun sett and dark, the said Shaw (he believes) in Coming out of the Flatt into the Sloop Fell into the River and was Drowned, That there was about three people on Shore, and he Fired a Gun at them, and talk't with them, and then went in a Canoo with his Gun towards the shore, That the Flatt was a long side, the Sloop Fast'ned to the timber head before the Change, That when he went to get into the Flat to help the said Shaw the Flatt was shear'd off to the Length of her painter, and that he could not get in till a Negro hal'd her up, that he saved the said Shaw's hat and a paper that was Floating on the water, That when he was in the Sloop he see the said Shaw's Shoulders out of water, his Jacket was on, and he believes his hat was on his head.

JOHN COLLINGWOOD

Smith's Examination

Richard Smith says, that he belong'd to Mr. Humphry Hill's Sloop, and that one John Shaw this day Six weeks, was put on board the said Sloop at the bristol mines, to look after a Sea Store of Capt. Williams's which was to be put on board a Ship in York River, and then the said Shaw [189] was to bring back Capt. William's horse, the said Shaw had on, one Strong new pair of Shoes, one white shirt, and one pair of white linen trousers, That the Skipper Fired a Gun at some people on Shore, and went into a Canoo to goe a Shore to scare the people, That the Flatt was fastned to the Catt head on the Larboard side, all the way down that they Came too about sun sett over against Pain's Island, That he and Negroe Peter went down, he heard the Skipper upon the Deck call hall up the Flatt Quickly, Quickly, upon that he and negro Peter got up, upon Deck, and he heard them say a man was overboard, That the Skipper was alone in the Flatt, That he did not see any blood, nor any Signs of the said Shaw's Destroying himself.

RICHARD SMITH.

It appearing to the court by the Oaths of Richard Fry Martha Fry, Thomas Bragg, Thomas Greenstreet and Thomas Wilmott—that there is Just Cause For

Trying the said John Collingwood and Richard Smith at the generall Court for the Crime aforesaid, whereof they are accused, It is therefore ordered that the said John Collingwood and Richard Smith be remanded to the prison of this County, under the Custody of the Sherriff, and from thence to be Convey'd to the publick Goal of Williamsburg, as the Law in such Cases Directs.

Fry's Recognizance

Richard Fry in open Court before his Majesties Justices acknowledged himself Indebted unto our Sovereign Lord the King his heirs and Successors in the Sum of Ten pounds Sterling to be Levyed of his Lands and Tenements, goods and Chattels with Condition that if the said Richard Fry shall personally appear at the next Generall Court on the Fourth Day thereof and then and there give Such Evidence as he knows against [**190**] John Collingwood alias Tanner and Richard Smith who stands Committed for Felony and does not Depart thence without Leave of that Court, that then this Recognizance to be void, or Else to Remain in Full Force.

Martha Fry's Recognizance

Martha Fry in open Court before his Majestys Justices Acknowledged herself Indebted to our Sovereign Lord the King his Heirs and Successors in the sum of Ten pounds Sterling, to be Levyed of her Lands and tenements goods and Chattles with Condition that if the said Martha Fry shall personally appear at the next Generall Court on the Fourth Day thereof, and then and there give such Evidence as She knows against John Collingwood alias Tanner and Richard Smith, who stands Committed for Felony and do not Depart thence without Leave of that Court that then this Recognizance to be Void, or Else to Remain in Full Force.

Bragg's Recognizance

Thomas Bragg in open Court before his Majesties Justices Acknowledged himself Indebted to our Sovereign Lord the the King his heirs and Successors in the Sum of ten pounds Sterling to be levy'd of his Lands and tenements goods, and Chattles with Condition that if the said Thomas Bragg shall Personally appear at the next Generall Court on the Fourth Day thereof and then and there give Such Evidence as he knows against John Collingwood alias Tanner and Richard Smith, who Stands Committed for Felony and do not Depart thence without Leave of that Court that then this Recognizance to be Void, or Else to Remain in Full Force.

Negroe Peter and Beshoof's Tryal

[**191**] At a Session of Oyer and Terminer Held at Richmond Court house on Thursday the First Day of August, MDCCxxxiv in the Eighth year of the Reign of our Sovereign Lord George the Second by the grace of God King of Great

Britain France and Ireland defender of the Faith etc. by Vertue of a special Commission for the Tryall of Treasons, petty Treasons, or misprisions thereof, Felonys, murthers, or other offences or Crimes whatsoever Committed within the County of Richmond, by two Negroe men Slaves named Peter and beshoof belonging to Mr. Humphry Hill of King William County, Directed to William Fantleroy Charles Grymes, Joseph Belfield, Robert Tomlin, Samuell Peachey, Newman Brockenbrough, Thomas Wright Belfield, John Woodbridge, Thomas Barber William Glascock, Samuell Barber, Daniell Hornby, Richard Barnes, George Glascock, William Jordan and Anthony Sydnor Gentlemen.

Present: Thomas Wright Belfield, John Woodbridge, Daniell Hornby, Richard Barnes and William Jordan, Gentlemen Justices.

Memorandom that on this day being the First day of August MDCCxxxiv an indictment was preferr'd against Two Negro men Slaves Called Peter and Beshoof in these Words—Richmond Ss John Tarpley, Jr. Attorney of our Lord the King, in the name of our said Lord the King doth accuse and arrain Peter and Beshoof Two Negroe Slaves belonging to Humphry Hill Gentleman of the County of King William in the Colony of Virginia For that the said Peter and Beshoof together with other persons unknown on the Eighteenth day of May in the year of our Lord one thousand seven hundred and thirty four in the Parish of Lunenburg in the County of Richmond aforesaid with malice prepensed[105] [**192**] did kill and Murder one John Shaw, then being one of our Lord the King's Liege People, and in the Peace and Whereupon the said Attorney For our Lord the King For and in behalf our Lord the King Prays legal prosecution against the said Negro Peter and Beshoof.

In: TARPLEY JUN: ATTP D R[106]

Whereupon the said Peter & Beshoof was brought to the Bar, and arrain'd for the said Felony, and there pleaded not guilty, and there upon the Court proceed on their Tryal, (After the Hearing the Evidence of Richard Fry, Martha Fry, Thomas Greenstreet Jr. and Thomas Willmott Against them, and what they Had to say in their Defence) are of opinion they are not guilty, of the Felony, For which they stand Indicted, it is therefore ordered that they be acquitted.

Greenstreet's Recognizance

Thomas Greenstreet of Lunenburg Parish in Richmond County in open Court before his Majesties Justices acknowledged himself Indebted to our Sov'reign Lord the King his Heirs and Successors in the Sum of Ten pounds Sterling to be Levyed of his Lands and Tenements goods and Chattles, with Condition that if the said Thomas Greenstreet's Son Nam'd Thomas Greenstreet Jr. shall Personally appear at the next general Court on the Fourth day thereof, and then and there give Such Evidence as he knows against John Collingwood alias Taner and Richard Smith who stands Committed for Felony, and do not depart thence

---

105. A variant of the law French term for "aforethought" and a necessary condition for the prosecution to establish in murder cases.

106. King's attorney; literally, "attorney pro dominus rex," attorney for the king. "In" is an abbreviation for "indorsed." Throughout the run of the *RCP*, abbreviations in these informations changed.

without Leave of that Court that then this Recognizance to be Void, or Else to remain in full Force.

Hunt's Recognizance

[193] William Hunt of Lunenburg Parish in Richmond County in open Court before his Majesties Justices acknowledged himself Indebted unto our Sov'reign Lord the King his Heirs of Successors in the Sum of Ten pounds Sterling to be Levy'd of his Lands and Tenements goods and Chattles with Condition that if the said William Hunt's (Servant Man Named Thomas Willmott) shall Personally appear at the next Generall Court on the Fourth Day thereof and then and there give Such Evidence as he knows against John Collingwood alias Taner and Richard Smith who stands Committed for Felony, and do not depart thense without Leave of that Court that then this Recognizance to be Void, or Else to remain in Full Force.

At a Court Held for Richmond County the Second Day of September MDCCxxxiv.

Present: Samuel Peachey, Thomas Wright Belfield, Richard Barnes, William Jordan, Gentlemen Justices.

Dent bound to his behaviour

It appearing to this Court that Anthony Dent Stole a hat and some other odd things from Charles Nicholls of this County It is therefore Ordered that For the said Offence—the Sherrif take him and Carry him to the Common Whiping Post, and give him Twenty five lashes on His bare back well laid On, and also that He give Security For His good behaviour, during the Term of One Year, Where-upon the said Anthony Dent Together with Michael Connell and Thomas Fenny His Securitys in Open Court Acknowledged themselves Indebted unto our Sov-ereign Lord the King his Heirs and Successors in the Sum Twenty pounds Sterling to be Levy'd on their Lands and Tenements goods and Chattles with Condition that if the said Anthony Dent shall be of good behavior. [194] As well Towards his Majesty as all His Leige People that then this Recognizance to be void or of None Effect, or Else to Remain in full Force and Vertue.

Dent's Recognizance

Anthony Dent in Open Court before his Majestys Justices Acknowledged him-self Indebted unto our Sovereign Lord the King His Heirs and Successors in the Sum of Ten pounds Sterling To be Levy'd of his Lands of Tenements goods and Chattles. With Condition that if the said Anthony Dent shall Personally Appear at the Next Court to be Held for this County, and then and there give Such Evidence as He knows against Charles Nicholls on Suspicion of Stealing Tobacco

From Billington McCarty, and do Not Depart without Leave of this Court, that then this Recognizance to be Void, or Else to Remain in Full Force.

At Court Held for Richmond County the Fourth day of November MDCCxxxiv.

Present: Samuel Peachey, John Woodbridge, Thomas Barber, Daniell Hornby, William Jordan, and Anthoney Sydnor, Gentlemen Justices.

Branham Fined

It appearing to this Court that Richard Branham Constable between Monokin Mill and Totuskey Ferry did not do His Duty Concerning a Warrant directed to Him, Granted to Richard Meeks, It is therefore Ordered that He be Fined one shilling to our Sovereign Lord the King.

At a Court Continued and held for Richmond County the Seventh day of January MDCCxxxiv [1735].

Present: [**195**] William Fantleroy, Landon Carter, Daniel Hornby, William Jordan and Gilbert Hamilton, Gentlemen Justices.

Jones bound to his Behaviour

John Jones of Lunenburgh Parish this Day Appearing to Answer the Presentment of the grandjury Against Him for being a Common Disturber of the Peace, but offering Nothing Material to Excuse Himself, It is the Opinion of this Court and Accordingly Ordered that For the said Offence He Give Good and Sufficient Security for His good behaviour during the Tearm of One Year.

Whereupon the said John Jones Together with Henry Sisson His Security in Open Court Acknowledged themselves Indebted unto our Sovereign Lord the King His Heirs and Successors in the Sum of Twenty Pounds Sterling to be Levyed on their Lands & Tenements goods and Chattles with Condition that If the said John Jones shall be of good behaviour as well Towards His Majesty as all his Leige People that then this Recognizance to be Void and of None Effect, otherwise to Remain in full force and Vertue.

At a Court Continued and held for Richmond County the Eighth Day of January MDCCxxxiv [1735].

Present: Landon Carter, Daniel Hornby, William Jordan, and Gilbert Hamilton, Gentlemen Justices.

Williams Jr. bound to his behaviour

Henry Williams Son of John Williams of Northfarnham Parish this Day Appearing to Answer the Presentment of the grand jury against Him for being a Common Swearer a Disturber of the Peace, but offering Nothing material [**196**] to Excuse Himself, It is the Opinion of this Court and Accordingly Ordered that for the said Offence He give good and Sufficient Security for His good behaviour during the Tearm of one Year.

Whereupon the Said Henry Williams Jr. Together with Luke Millner His Security in open Court Acknowledged themselves Indebted unto our Sovereign Lord the King His Heirs and Successors in the Sum of Twenty Pounds Sterling to be Levy'd on their Lands & Tenements goods and Chattles with Condition that if the said Henry Williams Shall be of good behaviour as Well Towards his Majestie as all His Liege People that then this Recognizance to be Void and of None effect, or Else to Remain in Full Force and Virtue.

Williams Sr. bound to son's behaviour[107]

Henry Williams of Northfarnham Parish Having been Summoned to Answer the Presentment of the grandjury against Him For a Common and Prophane Swearer and this Day Appearing but offering Nothing material to Excuse Himself, It is the Opinion of the Court and Accordingly Ordered that For the said Offence He give good and Sufficient Security for His good behaviour during the Tearm of one Year.

Whereupon the Said Henry Williams together with Richard Branham His Security in Open Court Acknowledged themselves Indebted unto our Sovereign Lord the King His Heirs and Successors in the Sum of Twenty Pounds Sterling to be Levyed on their Lands and Tenements goods and Chattles with Condition that if [**197**] the said Henry Williams shall be of good behaviour as Well Towards His Majesty as all His Leige People that then this Recognizance to be Void and of None Effect or Else to Remain in full Force and Virtue.

At a Court held for Richmond County the Seventh Day of April MDCCxxxv.

Present: William Fantleroy, Samuel Peachey, Newman Brockenbrough, Thomas Wright Belfield, Landon Carter, Daniel Hornby, William Jordan and Gilbert Hamilton, Gentlemen Justices.

Carnon bound to her behaviour

It appearing to this Court that Margrett Carnon of Northfarnham parish is a Person of an ill behaviour, It is therefore Ordered that she give Good and Sufficient Security For Her good behaviour During the Term of one Year.

Whereupon the said Margrett Carnon together with John Sarjeant her Secu-

---

107. This seems to be an error; both father and son were presented for misconduct, and both gave bond for their good behavior.

rity in Open Court Acknowledged themselves Indebted unto our Sovereign Lord the King His Heirs and Successors in the Sum of Twenty Pounds Sterling to be Levyed on their Lands and Tenements goods and Chattles with Condition that If the said Margret Carnon shall be of Good behaviour as well Towards his Majesty as all His Liege People that then this Recognizance to be Void and of None Effect or Else to Remain in Full Force and Virtue.

Duncan and others Whipt

[**198**] It Appearing to this Court that three Servant men Named John Dunkan, Bryan Kelly and———[108] did divers times unlawfully Confederate together, with an Intention to Abscond From their Master's Service,[109] It is therefore Ordered that For the said Offence, the Sherrif take them and Carry them to the Common Whiping Post, and give each of them twenty Lashes on their bare ba'x well laid on.

At a Court held for Richmond County the Second Day of June MDCCxxxv.
Present: Charles Grymes, Samuell Peachey, Thomas Wright Belfield, Daniel Hornby, William Jordan and Gilbert Hamilton, Gentlemen Justices.

Abshone bound to his behaviour

William Abshone of Northfarnham Parish Having been Summoned to answer the Presentment of the grandjury against Him For a Common Drunkard, a Common Prophane Swearer and Disturber of the Peace and this Day appearing but offering Nothing Material to Excuse himself, It is the Opinion of this Court and Accordingly Ordered that For the said Offence He give Good and Sufficient Security for His good behaviour during the Term of one year.

Whereupon the said William Abshone together with Hugh Lambert His Security in open Court acknowledged themselves Indebted unto our Sovereign Lord the King His Heirs and Successors in the Sum of Twenty pounds Sterling to be Levy'd on their Lands and Tenements goods and Chattles with Condition [**199**] that if the said William Abshone shall be of Good behaviour as well towards His Majestie as all His Liege People that then this Recognizance to be Void and of none Effect or Else to Remaine in Full Force and Virtue.

At a Court held for Richmond County the First Day of September MDCCxxxv.
Present: Newman Brockenbrough, John Woodbridge, Thomas Barber, Landon Carter, Daniel Hornby, William Jordan and Anthony Sydnor, Gentlemen Justices.

---

108. The name is erased in the original.

109. Conspiracy to run away was not a statutory offense, though running away was. For unlawful assembly, however, the court could punish Dunkan and his associates: "If Three or more Persons meet, with Intent to do any unlawful Act, this is unlawful Assembly"; Webb, *Justice of Peace*, 272.

Nash bound to the Peace

George Nash this Day appearing before this Court by Virtue of a warrant issued out against Him by John Woodbridge gentleman one of His Majesties Justices of the Peace For this County, For being a Notorious and Common disturber of the Peace, It is therefore Ordered that He give Good and Sufficient Security to Keep the Same.

Whereupon the said George Nash together with Tobias Purcel His Security in open Court acknowledg'd themselves Indebted to our Sovereign Lord the King His Heirs and Successors the said George Nash in the Sum of Forty pounds Sterling, and the said Tobias Purcell in the Sum of Twenty pounds Sterling, to be Levy'd on their Lands and Tenements, goods and Chattles, upon Condition that if the said George Nash shall Keep the Peace of our Sovereign Lord the King towards His said Majesty, as all His Liege People that then this Recognizance to be Void, and of None Effect or Else to Remain in Full Force and Virtue.

McKenny bound to the Peace

John McKenny this Day appearing before this Court [**200**] by Virtue of a warrant issued out against Him by John Woodbridge gentleman one of His Majesties Justices of the Peace For this County, For being a Notorious and Common disturber of the Peace, It is therefore Ordered that He give good & Sufficient Security to Keep the Same.

Whereupon the said John McKenny together with Henry Suttle His Security in Open Court acknowledg'd themselves Indebted to our Sovereign Lord the King His Heirs and Successors the said John McKenny in the sum of Forty Pounds Sterling, and the said Henry Suttle in the Sum of Twenty pounds Sterling, to be Levy'd on their Lands and Tenements Goods and Chattles, upon Condition that if the said John McKenny shall Keep the Peace of our Sovereign Lord the King towards His said Majestie as all His Leige People, that then this Recognizance to be Void, and of none Effect, or Else to Remain in Full Force and Virtue.

George Russell bound to the Peace

George Russell this Day appearing before this Court by Virtue of a Warrant issued out against Him by John Woodbridge gentleman one of His Majesties Justices of the Peace for this County, for being a Notorious and Common Disturber of the Peace, it is therefore Order'd that He give good and Sufficient Security to Keep the Same.

Whereupon the said George Russell together with Joseph Russell jr. His Security in Open Court Acknowledged themselves Indebted to our Sovereign Lord the King His Heirs and Successors the said George Russell in the Sum of Forty Pounds Sterling, and the said Joseph Russell jr. in the Sum of Twenty pounds Sterling to be Levy'd on their Lands and Tenements, Goods and Chattles, upon Condition that if the said [**201**] George Russell shall keep the Peace of our Sovereign Lord the King towards His said Majesty of all His Liege people that then this Recognizance to be Void, and of none Effect, or Else to Remain in Full Force and Vertue.

Russell bound to the Peace

Thomas Russell this day appearing before this Court by Virtue of a warrant issued out against Him by John Woodbridge gentleman one of His Majesties Justices of the Peace For this County, For being a Notorious and Common Disturber of the Peace it is therefore Ordered that He give good and Sufficient Security to Keep the Same.

Whereupon the said Thomas Russell Together with John Russell His Security in Open Court acknowledged themselves Indebted to our Sovereign Lord the King His Heirs and Successors the said Thomas Russell in the Sum of Forty pounds Sterling, the said John Russell in the Sum of Twenty pounds Sterling, To be Levy'd on their Lands and Tenements, goods and Chattles, upon Condition that if the said Thomas Russell shall Keep the Peace of our Sovereign Lord the King Towards His said Majesty and all His Liege People, that then this Recognizance to be Void, and of None Effect, or Else to Remain in Full Force and Virtue.

Serjeant and others Whip't

Whereas William Serjeant, Abraham Moore, James Harrison and Elizabeth Sollare by Virtue of a Mittimus from Anthony Sydnor gentleman one of the Justices of this court was Committed to the County Goal For Felloniously taking Two Virginia Cloth Gowns from William Stone, and one Chect Linen Shirt from William Frazier, and being Now brought before His Majesties Justices Here present, on Examination [202] of Several Evidences touching the Same, It is the Opinion of this Court that they are guilty of the Crimes Laid to their Charge, It is therefore ordered that the Sherrif take the said Elizabeth Sollare and Carry Her to the Common Whiping post and give Her Fourteen Lashes on Her bare back well Laid on, and then take the said Serjeant, Moore and Harrison and give Each of them twenty five Lashes on their bare ba'x well Laid on, and it is Further Ordered that the said Sarjeant, Moore and Harrison give Each of them good and Sufficient Security for their good behaviour during the Term of one year.

Moore bound to his Behaviour

Abraham Moore together with Thomas Nash His Security in Open Court acknowledged themselves Indebted to our Sovereign Lord the King His Heirs and Successors, the said Abraham Moore in the Sum of Twenty pounds Sterling, and the said Thomas Nash in the Sum of Ten pounds Sterling to be Levy'd on their Lands and Tenements, goods and Chattles with Condition that if the said Abraham Moore shall be of good behaviour as well Towards His Majesty, as all His Liege People, that then this Recognizance to be Void, and of None Effect or Else to Remain in Full Force.

Harrison Bound to his Behaviour

James Harrison together with Daniell Hornby His Security in Open Court acknowledged themselves Indebted unto our Sovereign Lord the King His Heirs and Successors, the said James Harrison in the Sum of Twenty pounds Sterling and the said Daniel Hornby in the Sum of Ten pounds [203] Sterling, to be Levy'd on their Lands and Tenements, goods and Chattles with Condition that if the said James Harrison shall be of good behaviour, as well as Towards His Majesty, as all His Liege People, that then this Recognizance to be Void, and of None Effect or Else to Remain in Full Force.

Sarjeant bound to his behaviour

William Sarjeant together with William Creele His Security in Open Court Acknowledged themselves Indebted unto our Sovereign Lord the King His Heirs and Successors, the said William Sarjeant in the Sum of Twenty pounds Sterling, and the said William Creel in the Sum of ten pounds Sterling to be Levy'd on their Lands and Tenements goods and Chattles with Condition that if the said William Sarjeant shall be of good behaviour, as well Towards His said Majesty, as all His Liege People, that then this Recognizance to be Void, or Else to Remain in Full Force.

At a call'd Court Held at the Court house of Richmond County the third day of November 1735.

Present: Samuel Peachey, John Woodbridge, Thomas Barber, William Glascock and Daniel Hornby, Gentlemen Justices.

Lewis to give Security for his behaviour

Whereas Thomas Lewis by Virtue of a Mittimus from John Woodbridge gentleman one of the Majestrates of this County was Committed to the County Goal For [204] Felloniously taking away Christopher Petty's Servant Woman, a Jackett, Petticoat and Apron and being now brought before this Court, and Several Evidences being Produced and Examin'd but not Proving the Fact, yet it appearing to the Court that the said Thomas Lewis is a Person of an ill behaviour, It is therefore Ordered that He give good and Sufficient security For His good behaviour, and that He Remain in the Sherrif's Custody, untill He gives Such Security.

Ordered that the Court be Adjourn'd.

At a call'd Court Court Held at the Courthouse of Richmond County on thursday the Nineteenth day of February MDCCxxxv [1736].

Present: William Fantleroy, Thomas Barber, Landon Carter, William Jordan, Anthony Sydnor, and Gilbert Hamilton, Gentlemen Justices.

Dance Whipt

Whereas Rebeccah Dance by Virtue of a Mittimus from ———[110] Gentleman one of the Justices of this Court was Committed to the County Goal on Suspicion of Stealing a Virginia Cloth Gown etc. from Rachel Redman, and being Now brought before His Majesties Justices Here Present, on Examination of Several Evidences touching the Same, It is the Opinion of this Court, that the said Rebeccah Dance is Guilty of the Crime Laid to Her Charge. [205] It is therefore Ordered that For the said Offence, the Sherrif take Her, and Carry Her to the Common whiping post and give Her thirty Nine Lashes on Her bare back well laid On.

Redman Whipt

It appearing to this Court that Rachel Redman the wife of Richard Redman received Stolen Goods From Rebeccah Dance, the said Rachel Knowing them to be Such,[111] It is therefore Order'd that For the said Offence the Sherrif take Her, and carry Her to the Common whiping post and give Her twenty five Lashes on Her bare back, well Laid On.

At a Court Held For Richmond County the Fifth Day of April MDCCxxxvi. Present: William Fantleroy, Samuel Peachey, John Wright Belfield, Thomas Barber, Landon Carter, William Jordan, Anthony Sydnor and William Fantleroy Jr., Gentlemen Justices.

Oglesby bound to behaviour

It appearing that Edward Ogleby of Northfarnham parish is a Person of an ill behaviour, It is therefore Ordered that He give good and Sufficient Security, for his good behaviour. Whereupon the said Edward Ogleby together with Fortunatus Dodson and John Gibson His Securitys acknowledged themselves Indebted [206] to our Sovereign Lord the King the said Edward Ogleby in the Sum of Forty pounds Sterling and the said Fortunatus Dodson and John Gibson in the Sum of twenty pounds Each Sterling to be Levyed on their Lands & Tenements goods and chattles with Condition that if the said Edward Ogleby shall be of Good behaviour as well towards His Majesty as all Liege People that then this Recognizance to be Void and of non Effect or Else to remain in Full Force.

At a Court continued and Held For Richmond County the Sixth day of Aprill MDCCxxxvi.

---

110. The name of the justice was omitted in the original; the clerk probably intended to fill it in, for he left a space. For another example, see p. 37 above.

111. Showing criminal intent; receiving stolen goods unknowingly was not a crime.

Present: William Fantleroy, Samuel Peachey, Newman Brockenbrough, John Woodbridge, Thomas Barber, Landon Carter, Daniel Hornby, William Jordan, Anthony Sydnor and William Fantleroy Jr., Gentlemen Justices.

Fleming bound to his behaviour

It appearing to this Court that William Fleming is a Person of an Ill behaviour, It is therefore Ordered that He give good and Sufficient Security For His good behaviour.

Whereupon the said William Fleming together with Jonathan Lyell His Security acknowledged themselves Indebted to our Sovereign Lord the King the said William Fleming in the Sum of Forty pounds Sterling and the said Jonathan Lyell in the Sum of twenty pounds Sterling to be Levy'd on their Lands and Tenements Goods and Chattles with Condition that if the said William Fleming shall [207] be of Good behaviour as well towards His Majesty as all His Leige People that then this Recognizance to be Void and of Non Effect or Else to Remain in Full Force.

Linton bound to behaviour

It appearing to this Court that John Linton is a Person of an Ill behaviour, It is therefore Ordered that He give good and Sufficient Security For his good behaviour.

Whereupon the said John Linton together with Jonathan Lyell and Edward Anderson His Securitys acknowledged themselves Indebted to our Sovereign Lord the King the said John Linton in the Sum of forty pounds Sterling and the said Jonathan Lyell and Edward Anderson in the Sum of Twenty pounds Each Sterling to be Levy'd on their Lands and Tenements goods and Chattels with Condition that if the said John Linton shall be of Good behaviour as well towards His Majesty as all His Leige People that then this Recognizance to be Void and of Non Effect or Else to Remain in Full Force.

At a Court continued and Held For Richmond County the Sixth Day of July MDCCxxxvi.

Present: John Woodbridge, Landon Carter, Daniell Hornby, Anthony Sydnor, Gentlemen Justices.

Mathews bound to his behaviour

It appearing to this Court that Baldwin Mathews is a Person of an Ill behaviour, It is therefore Ordered that He give good and Sufficient security, for His good behaviour.

Whereupon the said Baldwin Mathews together with Edward Anderson His Security acknowledged themselves Indebted to our Sovereign Lord the [208] King the said Baldwin Mathews in the Sum of forty pounds Sterling and the said

Edward Anderson in the Sum of twenty pounds Sterling to be Levy'd on their Lands and Tenements goods and Chattells with Condition that if the said Baldwin Mathews shall be of goods behaviour as well towards His Majesty as all His Leige People that then this Recognizance to be Void and of None Effect or Else to Remain in full Force.

Anderson bound to his behaviour

Edward Anderson of Lunenburgh Parish having been Summoned to answer the Presentment of the Grandjury against Him For being a common and Notorious Swearer, and this day appearing but offering Nothing Material to Excuse Himself, It is the opinion of this Court and accordingly Ordered that For the said Offence He give good and Sufficient Security for his good behaviour, during the Term of one year.

Whereupon the said Edward Anderson together with James Morton His Security in Open Court acknowledged themselves Indebted unto our Sovereign Lord the King His Heirs and Successors in the Sum of Twenty pounds Sterling to be Levy'd on their Lands and Tenements goods and Chattels with Condition that if the said Edward Anderson shall be of Good behaviour as well Towards His Majesty as all His Leige People that then this Recognizance to be Void and of non effect or Else to Remain in full Force and Virtue.

Pridham bound to His behaviour

Edward Pridham of Lunenburg Parish having been Summon'd to answer the Presentment of the Grandjury against Him For being a common and Notorious Swearer, and this Day [209] appearing but offering Nothing Material to Excuse Himself, It is the Opinion of this Court and accordingly Ordered that For the said Offence He give good and Sufficient Security For His good behaviour, during the Term of one year.

Whereupon the said Edward Pridham together with Joseph Russell Jr. His Security in open court Acknowledged themselves Indebted unto our Sovereign Lord the King His Heirs and Successors in the Sum of twenty pounds Sterling to be Levy'd on their Lands and Tenements goods and Chattels with Condition that if the said Edward Pridham shall be of good behaviour as well towards His Majesty as all His Leige People that then this Recognizance to be Void and of None Effect or Else to Remain in Full Force and Virtue.

Suggitt Bound to Behaviour

Thomas Suggitt of Northfarnham parish Having been Summoned to answer the Presentment of the Grandjury against Him For being a Common Disturber of the peace, and this Day appearing but offering Nothing Material to Excuse Himself, It is the Opinion of this Court and accordingly Ordered that for the said Offence he give good and Sufficient Security For His good behaviour during the Term of one year.

Whereupon the said Thomas Suggitt together with Luke Millner His Security in Open Court Acknowledged themselves Indebted unto our Sovereign Lord the King his Heirs and Successors in the Sum of twenty pounds Sterling to be Levy'd on their Lands and Tenements goods and Chattels with Condition that if the said Thomas Suggitt shall be of good behaviour as well towards his Majesty as all his Liege People [210] that then this Recognizance to be Void and of non Effect or Else to Remain in full force and Virtue.

At a Court Held For Richmond County the Second Day of August MDCCxxxvi.
Present: Charles Grymes, Samuel Peachey, Newman Brockenbrough, Thomas Wright Belfield, William Glascock, Daniel Hornby and William Jordan, Gentlemen Justices.

Slater bound to his Behaviour

Mr. Jon Slater of Lunenburg Parish having been Summoned to Answer the Presentment of the Grandjury againt Him for being a Common Drunkard, and Notorious Swearer, and this Day appearing, but offering Nothing Material to Excuse Himself It is the Opinion of this Court and accordingly Ordered that For the said Offence, He give Good and Sufficient Security For His Good behaviour, During the Term of one year.

Whereupon the Said John Slater together with Solomon Redman His Security Acknowledged themselves Indebted to our Sovereign Lord the King the said John Slater in the Sum of Forty pounds Sterling and the said Solomon Redman in the Sum of Twenty pounds Sterling to be Levyed on their Lands and Tenements Goods and Chattles with Condition that if the said John Slater shall be of good behaviour as well Towards His Majesty as all His Leige People that then this Recognizance to be Void and of none Effect or Else to Remain in full Force.

Crask bound to His Behaviour

It appearing to this Court that William Crask of Lunenburg parish is a Person of an ill behaviour It is therefore Ordered that He give good and Sufficient Security for His good Behaviour.

[211] Whereupon the said William Crask together with Richard Barnes His Security Acknowledged themselves Indebted to our Sovereign Lord the King the said William Crask in the Sum of Forty pounds Sterling and the said Richard Barnes in the Sum of Twenty pounds Sterling to be Levy'd on their Lands and Tenements Goods and Chattles with Condition that if the said William Crask shall be of Good behaviour as well Towards His Majesty as all His Leige People that then this Recognizance to be Void and of None Effect or Else to Remain in Full Force.

[Bigbie to keep the peace]

George Bigbie of Northfarnam Parish being by Virtue of a Warrant of Samuel Peachey gentleman one of His Majestys Justices of the Peace For this County, bound over to appear at this Court, to answer the Complaint of His wife Mary Bigbie For Assaulting beating and Bruising Her, the said George Bigbie accordingly appear'd this Day in Court, It is therefore Ordered that he give good and Sufficient Security in the Sum of Fifty pounds Sterling For His Keeping the Peace.

Whereupon the said George Bigbie together with Thomas Suggitt and Thomas Nash His Securitys Acknowledged themselves Indebted unto our Sovereign Lord the King His Heirs and Successors in the Sum of One Hundred pounds Sterling to be Levy'd on their Lands and Tenements goods and Chattles with Condition that if the said George Bigbie shall Keep the Peace of our Sovereign Lord the King toward His said Majesty and all His Leige People and Especially towards His said wife Mary Bigbie, that then this Recognizance to be Void, and of None Effect or Else to Remain in Full Force.

[212] At a Court Held Richmond County the Fourth Day of October MDCCxxxvi.

Present: William Fantleroy, Thomas Wright Belfield, John Woodbridge, Landon Carter, Daniel Hornby, William Jordan, Anthony Sydnor and William Fantleroy Jr., Gentlemen Justices.

[McCarty and Southerfield whipt]

It appearing to this Court that John McCarty Servant to Edward Anderson and one Elizabeth Southerfield did Divers times unlawfully Confederate with other Servants belonging to the said Anderson with an Intention to abscond From their Masters Service, It is therefore Ordered that For the said Offence the Sheriff take the said M'Carty, and Carry Him to the Common Whiping post and give Him Thirty Lashes on His bare back well Laid on, and then take the said Southerfield and give Her Twenty Lashes on Her bare back well Laid on.

At a Court Continued and Held For Richmond County the Second Day of November MDCCxxxvi.

Present: Samuel Peachey, Daniel Hornby, William Jordan, Anthony Sydnor, Gentlemen Justices.

Dance bound to behaviour

It appearing to this Court that Rebeccah Dance, is a Person of an Ill behaviour, It is therefore Ordered that she give good and Sufficient Security For Her Good behaviour during the Term of one year.

Whereupon the said Rebeccah Dance together with William Thornton Her Security Acknowledged themselves Indebted to our Sovereign Lord the King in the Sum of Forty pounds Sterling to be Levy'd on [213] their Lands and Tenements goods and Chattles with Condition that if the said Rebeccah Dance shall be of Good behaviour as well towards His Majesty as all His Leige People that then this Recognizance to be Void and of None Effect or Else to Remain in full Force.

At a Court Continued and Held for Richmond County the Sixth day of July MDCCxxxvi.
Present: John Woodbridge, Landon Carter, Daniel Hornby, Anthony Sydnor, Gentlemen Justices.

Tillery Fined

Whereas the Grandjury for the body of this County Last November Court found a bill of Indictment against William Tillery for Assaulting beating and wounding one Edward Obrian, to which the said Tillery Last Aprill Court pleaded Not guilty, Whereupon a Jury was this day Impannelled and Sworn to try the Matter in issue by Name Luke Millner, John Brown, Henry Williams, George Taylor, Richard Meeks, John McKenny, Edward Morris, Edmond Northern, Benjamin Rust, George Spunt, John Smith and Thomas Plummer who Having Heard the Evidence, and Received their charge, were sent out, and Soon after Returning into Court and agreed, gave in their Verdict, which is in these words "We of the Jury find the Defendant guilty" Luke Millner Foreman, which Verdict on the Motion of John Tarpley Junior gentleman the King's Attorney is Ordered to be Recorded And it is Considered by the Court and accordingly Ordered that the said William Tillery for the said Offence be Fined Twenty Shillings to our Sovereign Lord the King, and that He pay the Costs of this Suit.

[214] At a Court Held for Richmond County the third Day of January MDCCxxxvi [1737].
Present: William Fantleroy, Charles Grymes, Thomas Wright Belfield, Landon Carter, Daniel Hornby, Anthony Sydnor, Gentlemen Justices.

Millwood and wife bound to behaviour

It appearing to this Court that Benjamin Millwood and Martha His wife are persons of an ill behaviour, It is therefore ordered that they give good and Sufficient Security for their good behaviour, and that they remain in the Sherriff's Custody untill they give Such Security.

Crowlier's wife bound to Behaviour

It appearing to this Court that Jane Crowlier the wife of William Crowlier is a person of an ill behaviour, It is therefore Ordered that she give good and

Sufficient Security for Her good behaviour, during the Term of one year, and for Paying Fees.

Whereupon the said Jane Crowlier together with Edmond Hazle her Security, acknowledged themselves Indebted to our Sovereign Lord the King in the Sum of forty pounds Sterling, to be Levied on their Lands and Tenements goods and Chattles with Condition that if the said Jane Crowlier shall be of good behaviour, as well towards his Majesty, as all his Liege People, and also pay the Fees, that then this Recognizance to be Void, and of None Effect or Else to Remain in Full Force.

[215] At a Call'd Court Held at the Court House of Richmond County the Fifth Day of Aprill MDCCxxvii.

Present: William Fantleroy, Charles Grymes, Samuel Peachey, Newman Brockenbrough, Daniel Hornby, William Jordan, Anthony Sydnor and William Fantleroy Jr., Gentlemen Justices.

White and others Examinations

Whereas Richard White and William Robinson of Lunenburg Parish in Richmond County, and Thomas Priddell and William Newell of Cople parish in Westmorland County was by Virtue of a Mittimus from William Fantleroy gentleman one of the Justices of this Court remitted to this County Goal for Feloniously stealing out of the House of the Reverend David Morthland of the said Parish of Lunenburg one black broad Cloth Coat, and wastcoat, one pair of Leather Britiches, and one broad Cloth coat trim'd with black, and a black Silk Vest and Leather Britches and Divers other things, and being Now brought before His Majestie's Justices Here Present Richard White says that the black Vest He had on when he was teken belong'd to Mr. Morthland, and a Coat trim'd with black, and that William Newell and Thomas Priddell, Took them out of Mr. Morthland's House, through His sash Window, and gave them to Him by the house over the Fence, and took Some bottles of Cyder out of the Cellar, and also took Mr. Morthland's black Cape cloth Coat and Vest and Leather britches, and Some beef and Pork.

RICHARD WHITE

[216] Thomas Priddell says the black Coat and Jacket Now produced in Court he Had From William Newell.

William Newell says that when He was taken He Had pair of Leather britiches on, but does Not Know where he gott them.

William Robinson Servant to Michael Winder being Sworn saith that Richard White, Thomas Priddell and William Newell came on Tuesday Morning to His Master's House being the twenty ninth of March, about break of Day, that the said Richard White Had a Coat trim'd with black, and black Silk Vest and a Fine shirt on Marked (M) with Red, the said White call'd upon Him to go to Fother[112] Stack, and bid him Make what Hast He could, and when he came there, they Had gott a Wallet of Pork and beef, and a bottle of Cyder, and asking them

---

112. Fodder.

where they gott it, Richard White, Thomas Priddell and William Newell answered they Robb'd Mr. Morthland's House, The said Priddell Had on Mr. Morthland's black coat and Vest and a Fine Shirt with the Same Mark of the other, and a Purse and a book of Poems, The said Newell Had on Mr. Morthland's Leather britches and Slippers[;] Thomas Priddell cut the Mark out of the Shirt and Richard White another Mark.

Richard White told Me He wanted a Betty to break open a Lock, and that He Found Half a shear in the Smith's Shop, and said that would doe, He said He got in the Cellar window, and then Jumpt the Glaze. Meaning [217] they lifted up the Sash, and so got in.

WILLIAM ROBINSON

The Reverend David Morthland being Sworn saith that on Monday Night being the twenty eighth of March His House was Robb'd and He Lost one black Coat and Jacket, one Great Coat, one Pair Leather britches, and some other things.

Henry Settle, Joseph Bragg and Benjamin Bruce of Richmond County being Sworn Saith that on the 31st of March Last they took up as Runaways Richard White, William Robinson, Thomas Priddell and William Newell, That they took From the said White, one Great Coat, one black Silk Vest, and one White Shirt, they took From William Newell one pair Leather Britches, and they took From Thomas Priddell one black Coat and Jackett, one Shirt, one book of Poems and one Purse.

It appearing to this Court Upon the aforesaid Examination that there is Just cause for Trying the said Richard White, Thomas Priddell and William Newell at the General Court for the Crime aforesaid whereof they are accused; It is therefore Ordered that the said Richard White, Thomas Priddell and William Newell be Remanded to the Prison of this County under the Custody of the Sherrif, and From thence to be Conveyed to the Publick Goal of Williamsburg as the Law in such Cases Directs.

Morthland's Recognizance

The Reverend David Morthland of Richmond County in Open Court before His Majestys Justices acknowledg'd [218] Himself Indebted to our Sovereign Lord the King His Heirs and Successors in the Sum of Ten pounds Sterling to be Levy'd of His Lands and Tenements goods and Chattles with Conditions that if the said David Morthland shall Personally appear at the Next General Court on the Fourth Day thereof and then and there give such Evidence as He Knows against Richard White, Thomas Priddell and William Newel who Stands Committed For Fellony and do Not Depart thence without Leave of that Court, That then this Recognizance to be Void or Else to Remain in Full Force.

Settle's Recognizance

Henry Settle of Richmond County in open Court before His Majesty's Justices acknowledged Himself Indebted to our Sovereign Lord the King his Heirs and Successors in the Sum of Ten pounds Sterling to be Levy'd of Lands and Tennements goods and Chattles with Condition that if the said Henry Settle shal Personally appear at the Next General Court on the Fourth Day thereof and then and there give Such Evidence as he Knows against Richard White, Thomas Priddell and William Newell who Stands Committed for Fellony and do Not depart thence without leave of that Court, That then this Recognizance to be Void or Else to Remain in Full Force.

Bragg's Recognizance

Joseph Bragg of Richmond County in Open Court before His Majesty's Justices acknowledged Himself Indebted to our Sovereign Lord the King His Heirs and Successors in the Sum of Ten pounds Sterling to be Levy'd of His Lands and Tenements Goods and Chattels with Condition that if the said [219] Joseph Bragg shall Personally appear at the Next General Court on the Fourth Day thereof and then and there give Such Evidence as He Knows against Richard White, Thomas Priddell and William Newell who stands Committed For Fellony and do not Depart thence without Leave of that Court, That then this Recognizance to be Void or Else to Remain in Full Force.

Bruce's Recognizance

Benjamin Bruce of Richmond County in open Court before His Majesty's Justices acknowledged himself Indebted to our Sovereign Lord the King his Heirs and Successors in the Sum of Ten pounds Sterling to be Levy'd of His Land, Tenements goods and Chattles with Condition that if the said Benjamin Bruce shall Personally appear at the Next General Court on the fourth Day thereof and then and there give Such Evidence as He Knows against Richard White, Thomas Priddell and William Newell who Stands Committed for Fellony and do Not Depart thence without Leave of that Court, That then this Recognizance to be Void or Else to Remain in Full Force.

Winder's Recognizance

Michael Winder of Richmond County in open Court before His Majesty's Justices acknowledged himself Indebted to our Sovereign Lord the King his Heirs and Successors in the sum of Ten pounds Sterling to be Levy'd of His lands and Tenements goods and Chattels with Condition that if the said Michael Winder's (Servant Man Named William Robinson) shall Personally appear at the Next General Court on the Fourth Day thereof and then and there give Such Evidence as He Knows against Richard White, [220] Thomas Priddell and William Newell who Stands Committed For Fellony and do Not Depart thence without Leave of that Court that then this Recognizance to be Void or Else to Remain in ful Force.

At a Call'd Court Held at the Court House of Richmond County on Tuesday the Twelfth day of Aprill MDCCxxxvii.

Present: William Fantleroy, Newman Brockenbrough, Thomas Wright Belfield, John Woobridge, Landon Carter, and William Jordan, Gentlemen Justices.

Millwood's Examination

Whereas on the Complaint of the Reverend David Morthland and William Garland of Lunenburgh Parish Benjamin Millwood of the said Parish in Richmond County, was Committed to the County Goal by Virtue of an Order of this Court the Fifth Instant, on Suspicion of Robbing the House of the said David Morthland and William Garland and being Now brought before His Majesty's Justices Here present, and being asked what He Had to Say to what was Laid to His Charge, He answered, that He would Say Nothing.

The Reverend David Morthland being sworn Saith that in October Last His House was Robb'd, and that He Lost Eight Silver Tea Spoons, which was taken out of a Drawer in a Desk, that was broke open, and also one pair Stockins.

William Garland being Sworn saith that His House [**221**] was Robb'd in October Last and He Lost one Gold Ring, about Eight Shillings in a Purse, and one Coat and Jacket, And in November His House was Robb'd again, and He Lost one Gold Ring, one Felt hat, a parcel of thread Needles etc.

That Benjamin Millwood's wife told Him that the things He Lost in November was brought to their House by His Servant and Her Husband.

That the said Servant and Her Husband went out at Nights to Steel, and brought in at Several times Sheep.

That the said Martha told Him she wonder'd How Rebeccah Dance could say that the Sewett[113] belonged to Mr. Carter when they Had taken as Many other Peoples Sheep.

That the said Martha said that the Silver Spoons Lost by Mr. Morthland was weighed in their House by Robert Thompson and His Servants.

That the Spoons weighed about Fifteen Shillings and Four pence or Sixteen Shillings and Four pence.

That after the Robbery Her Husband carryed away His Servants Named John Plow, Francis Ford and Walter Dawsey.

That the said Martha told Him Her Husband was to Carry Said Servants to North Carolina That He sent His Son William to North Carolina and He took His Servant Walter in Elizabeth Town.

William Garland Jr. of Lunenberg Parish being [**222**] Sworn Saith That His Father's House was Robb'ed in October Last.

That they lost one Gold Ring, Eight Shillings in a Purse, and one Coat and Jacket.

And in November they Lost one Gold Ring, one Hat, and some Needles, Pins, Nutmegs etc.

That Martha Millwood told Him that things was brought to their House by William Garland's Servant Men.

---

113. Suet, that is, animal fat. Most of the testimony is hearsay, gossip among the servants that reached others' ears. Eighteenth-century English and American criminal courts did not bar hearsay; Blackstone, *Commentaries*, 3:368.

That she told Him Her Husband carry'd away His Fathers Servant.[114]

That He pursued them and took Walter in Elizabeth.

That Walter told Him His Mother's Ring was in the Custody of John Wallace's wife who Keeps an Ordinary at the Southern Bridge.

That He went and asked Her for the Rings, she said She Had it of a Taylor that came along with Benjamin Millwood, and He pawn'd it for Liquor.

That she said, the said Millwood Curst the Taylor For so doing; and said She Had the Ring of him, and Had Not satisfy'd Him for It.

That the Taylor answered Her, He Had sold the best Ring in Norfolk Town, and that the other Might go the Same way, and thereupon Call'd for a bowl of Punch.

Walter Dawsey Servant to William Garland being Sworn says that Hee, Benjamin Millwood, Frank Ford [223] and Robert Thompson went on a Sunday about October last to Mr. Morthland's and Frank Ford Help't Him in at the Window, and gave Him a Chizel, to break open the Desk where Robert Thompson told Him He would Find Money, in a secrett drawer.

That with the Chicell He broke open Mr. Morthland's Desk, and took out Eight Silver Tea Spoons and one pair of Stockins.

That Benjamin Millwood the Sunday before Offered to carry Him and Frank Ford away and bid Him be sure to gett money before Hand.

The Deponent Saying He did Not Know where to get money The said Millwood told Him He might get some at the Parson's.

That the Deponent and Benjamin Millwood in October Last went to His Master William Garlands House, And this Deponent went under the House and Lifted up the Scuttle, and went up Stairs, and took out of a Chest one Coat and Jacket.

And in November the Deponent and Benjamin Millwood went to His Master's House, and He Help't Him over the pails, and he went in at the back Door and took out of a box two pair of Knitting Needles, a Quarter of a pound of thread, Two Nutmegs, one paper of pins one Gold Ring, and one Hatt.

That Benjamin Millwood Hearing a Noise went Home before Him and bid Him Follow, and when He came Home He found Benjamin Millwood in bed, and that he Deliver'd what He Stole to him [224] and Benjamin Millwood gave them to His wife.

That Hee, Frank Ford and John Plow lay conceal'd at Benjamin Millwood's about Four or Five Weeks and then took Capt. Tomlin's boat and He Carryed us to Elizabeth, to one Capt. Willson's.

And the Next Day He went to one Wallace's about a Mile and a Half off, at the Sighn of the Red Lyon.

That Benjamin Millwood sold the Ring Hee stole From His Mistris, For Seven shillings and Six pence to the Taylor, and the Taylor to Mrs. Wallace.

The Deponent, Benjamin Millwood, Frank Ford and John Plow Stole a Wether from Colonel Tayloe.

And Kill'd a Sow which Benjamin Millwood said belong'd to Mr. Degges, as they were going with Sails to the boat.

---

114. That is, Millwood carried away William Garland's servant without permission of Garland. This violated section XV of the 1705 Act on servants; *Statutes at Large*, 3:451–52 (1705).

It appearing to this Court upon the aforesaid Examination that there is Just Cause for Trying the said Benjamin Millwood at the Next Court of Oyer and Terminer to be Held at His Majesty's Royal Capitol for the Crime aforesaid whereof He is accused, It is therefore Ordered that the said Benjamin Millwood be Remanded to the Prison of this County under the Custody of the Sherrif, and From thence to be Convey'd to the Publick Goal of Williamsburgh as the Law in Such Cases Directs.

Morthland's Recognizance

The Reverend David Morthland in Open Court before His Majesties Justices acknowledged Himself Indebted to our Sovereign Lord the King [**225**] His Heirs and Successors in the Sum of Ten pounds Sterling to be Levy'd of His Lands and Tenements goods and Chattles with Condition if He the said David Morthland shal appear before the Honorable Court of Oyer and Terminer to be Held at His Majesty's Royall Capitoll on the Second Tuesday in June Next, and so attend From time to time as the said Court shall direct, Then and there to give Evidence For our said Lord the King against Benjamin Millwood who Stands Committed to the Goal of this County on Suspicion of Felloniously Robbing the Houses of the said David Morthland and William Garland then this Recognizance to be Void or Else to Remain in Full Force.

Garland's Recognizance

William Garland in Open Court before His Majesty's Justices acknowledged Himself Indebted to our Sovereign Lord the King His Heirs and Successors in the Sum of Ten pounds Sterling to be Levy'd of His Lands and Tenements goods and Chattels with Condition if he the said William Garland shall appear before the Honourable Court of Oyer and Terminer to be Held at His Majesty's Royal Capitol on the Second Tuesday in June Next and so Attend from time to time as the said Court shall Direct, then and there to give Evidence For our said Lord the King against Benjamin Millwood who Stands Committed to the Goal of this County on Suspicion of Felloniously Robbing the Houses of Reverend David Morthland and the said William Garland then this Recognizance to be Void or Else to Remain Full Force.

Garland's Jr. Recognizance

William Garland Jr. in Open Court before his Majestys Justices acknowledged Himself Indebted to our [**226**] Sovereign Lord the King His Heirs and Successors in the Sum of Ten pounds Sterling to be Levy'd of His Lands and Tenements goods and Chattles with Condition if He the said William Garland Jr. shall appeare before the Honourable Court of Oyer and Terminer to be held at His Majestie's Royal Capitoll on the Second Tuesday in June Next, and so attend From time to time as the said Court shall Direct then and there to give Evidence For our said Lord the King against Benjamin Millwood who Stands Committed in the Goal of this County on Suspicion of Felloniously Robbing the House of

Reverend David Morthland and William Garland then this Recognizance to be Void or else Remain in Full Force.

[*Garland's Recognizance*]

William Garland in Open Court before His Majesty's Justices acknowledged Himself Indebted to our Sovereign Lord the King His Heirs and Successors in the Sum of Ten pounds Sterling to be Levy'd of His Lands and Tenements Goods and Chattles with Condition if the said William Garland's (Servant Man Named Walter Dawsey)[115] shall appear before the Honourable Court of Oyer and Terminer to be Held at his Majesty's Royal Capitoll on the second Tuesday in June Next and so attend From time to time as the said Court shall Direct then and there to give Evidence for our said Lord the King against Benjamin Millwood who Stands Committed to the Goal of this County on Suspicion of Felloniously Robbing the Houses of the Reverend David Morthland and William Garland [**227**] then this Recognizance to be Void or Else to Remain in Full Force.

At a Call'd Court Held at the Courthouse of Richmond County on the Friday the Fifteenth Day of Aprill MDCCxxxvii.

Present: William Fantleroy, John Woodbridge, Landon Carter, Daniel Hornby and Anthony Sydnor, Gentlemen Justices.

Thompson's Examination

Whereas Robert Thompson and Rebecca Dance[116] of King-George County was by Virtue of a Mittimus From William Jordan gentleman one of the Justices of the Court committed to the County Goal on Suspicion of Having Lately Felloniously broke open the House of the Reverend David Morthland of Lunenburg Parish and Stealing from thence Ten Silver Spoons and other things of Value and being Now brought before His Majesty's Justices Here Present and the said Thompson being asked what He Had to say to what was laid to His Charge He answered that He was Innocent.

Walter Dawsey Servant to William Garland of Lunenburg parish being Sworn saith that on a Satturday in October Last, the Deponent, Frank Ford and Robert Thompson Made an Agreement to Robb the Parson's House the Day Following, where Benjamin Millwood was to Meet them.

That the Next Day being Sunday the Deponent and Frank Ford Having an Opportunity went to the Parson's House they being Sent there by [**228**] their Master, For Some Carpenter's Tools, to make a Coffin.

That while the Deponent and Frank Ford was breaking in at the window, Robert Thompson came to them, and bid the Deponent when He was in the House to make Haste and see what He could Gett.

---

115. An example of the master's legal relationship to his servant; Garland bonds himself for his servant's appearance. Masters paid fines for servants and were reimbursed in added time of servitude.

116. In the actual event, only Thompson was examined.

And accordingly the Deponent broke open a Desk, and took out Eight Silver Spoons, also took one pair of Stockins out of the window, and gave them to Frank Ford who gave them to Benjamin Millwood.

And after he came out of the House Robert Thompson bid Him make Haste home, for the People were coming From church and Thereupon Left them and went another way.

WALTER DAWSY

William Garland of Lunenburg Parish being Sworn saith that on the Sunday Mr. Morthland's House was Robb'd, The Deponent and Robert Thompson went to Joseph Russell's at the Court House, to gett some Plank to Make a Coffin.

That Joseph Russell being Just gon' to Church the Deponent staid there till the People were Returning From Church, but Can not remember whether Robert Thompson Staid with Him all the while, or whether He returned Home with Him, but He thinks He did Not.

That some time after the Deponent got home [229] Mrs. Morthland and Some others came to His House, and Charg'd His Servant Walter Dawsey and Frank Ford with the Robbery, because Mrs. Degges said she Saw the said Two Servants going towards the Glebe.[117]

That From the Court house to the Glebe, He takes to be about Half a Mile or three Quarters.

That Martha Millwood saith Her Husband Benjamin Millwood Had Frequently adviz'd Him to Gett Robert Thompson to be apprehended.[118]

And that upon the said Benjamin Millwood's Return From carrying away the Servants[, Millwood] would Hang Him, the said Thompson.

His
WILLIAM GARLAND
Mark

Martha Millwood of Lunenburg parish being Sworn saith that the Said Walter Dawsey, Frank Ford and John Plow, Servants to William Garland, tell Robert Thompson before Her that the said Thompson had Led them, and was the Contriver of Robbing the Parson's House, and told them of the Private Drawer in the Desk, and where the Key was, and the said Servants told the said Thompson that if they were taken or betray'd if He did Not go with them, they would Hang Him, to which the said Thompson Reply'd that if they would be Easy, as Soon as He got one Rebeccah Dance out of Prison, he would goe with them.

That she Heard the said Servants talk Several about the Silver Spoons when Robert Thompson [230] was in Company, and Charged Him with being Concern'd in the Robbery.

That the said Thompson came Frequently to their House, to give the said Servant all the Intelligence He could concerning the Methods that were used to take Them.

That upon the Servants complaint [that] they wanted Victuals, Robert Thompson said that they Might gett good Mutton at Mr. Carter's.

That before the Servants were apprehended the Deponent went Several times

---

117. The minister's land, settled on him for his tenure by the parish.
118. The plan was to cast suspicion upon William Garland.

to Mr. Carter's and Desired Him to take up Robert Thompson, For that she would discover several things which the said Thompson Had been the ring ledr [leader] of if she Durst, because she Had been Threatened Several times by them.

Her
MARTHA MILLWOOD
Mark

It appearing to this Court upon the aforesaid Examination that there is Just cause For Trying the said Robert Thompson at the Next Court of Oyer and Terminer to be held at His Majesties Royall Capitoll For the Crime aforesaid whereof He is accused, It is therefore Ordered that the said Robert Thompson be Remanded to the Prison of this County under the Custody of the Sherrif, and from thence to be Convey'd to the Publick Goal of Williamsburg as the Law in such Cases Directs.

Garland's Recognizance

William Garland in Open Court before His Majestys Justices acknowledged Himself Indebted to our [231] Sovereign Lord the King His Heirs and Successors in the Sum of Ten pounds Sterling to be Levy'd of his Lands and Tenements Goods and Chattles with Condition if the said William Garland shall appear before the Honorable Court of Oyer and Terminer to be Held at His Majesties Royall Capitoll on the second Tuesday in June Next and to attend from time to time as the said Court Shall Direct then and there to give Evidence for our said Lord the King against Robert Thompson who stands Committed to the Goal of this County in Suspicion of Felloniously Robing the House of Reverend David Morthland then this Recognizance to be Void or else to Remaine in full force.

Garland's Recognizance

William Garland in open Court before His Majesty's Justices acknowledged Himself Indebted to our Sovereign Lord the King His Heirs and Successors in the Sum of Ten pounds Sterling to be Levy'd of His Lands and Tennements goods and Chattels with Condition if the said William Garland's (Servant Man Named Walter Dawsey) shall appear before the Honorourable Court of Oyer and Terminer to be Held at His Majesty's Royall Capitoll on the Second tuesday in June Next and attend From time to time as the said Court shall Direct then and there to give Evidence For our said Lord the King against Robert Thompson who Stands Committed to the Goal of this County on Suspicion of Felloniously Robbing the House of the Reverend David Morthland then this Recognizance to be Void or Else to Remain in Full Force.

Carter and Beckwith's Recognizance

Landon Carter and Marmaduke Beckwith gentlemen in Open Court before His Majesty's Justices acknowledged themselves Indebted to our Sovereign Lord

[232] the King His Heirs and Successors in the Sum of Ten pounds Sterling to be Levy'd of their lands and Tennements Goods and Chattles with Condition if (Martha Millwood) shall appear before the Honourable Court of Oyer and Terminer to be Held at His Majesty's Royal Capitoll on the second Tuesday in June Next and to attend from time to time as the said Court shall Direct then and there to Give Evidence For our said Lord the King against Robert Thompson who Stands Committed to the Goal of this County on Suspicion of Felloniously Robing the House of the Reverend David Morthland then this Recognizance to be Void or Else to Remain in Full Force.

At a Call'd Court Held at the Courthouse of Richmond County on Tuesday the Ninth day of August MDCCxxxvii.

Present: John Woodbridge, Daniel Hornby, William Jordan and Anthony Sydnor, Gentlemen Justices.

Kelly's Examination

Whereas Jane Kelly a servant to Elias Fennel of Lunenburg Parish in Richmond County was by virtue of a Mittimus from William Jordan gentleman one of the Justices of this Court committed to this County Goal for Felloniously taking of Sundry fine Shirts, approns, gowns, Stockins, Handkerchiefs and other Goods from the House of the said Elias Fennell and being Now brought before His Majesty's Justices Here present, and being asked what She Had to Say to what was Said to Her charge, she answered that on the **[233]** Thirty first day of July last, she took out of the House of Her Master Elias Fennel seven Shirts and Shifts, two pair of Britches, two Jackets, Two Gowns, one pettycoat, Four aprons, two Hats and Several other things.

Elias Fennel and John Monroe of Lunenburg parish in Richmond County and John Short of Stafford County being sworn saith that on Sunday the last day of July, when Elias Fennel one of the Deponents came Home, He went to bed and soon after John Marks told Him (the other two Deponents being present) He thought Jen'y was going to run away, For that two Servant Men, saw Her with a Pillow bear, upon that the Deponents got up, and the said Elias Fen'el Mist one pettycoat, upon that the Deponents went in pursuit of Her and Found Her set down by the Road, and brought Her in and being Examined what she Had done with the things she had taken, she said she Had not any of them, upon that the Deponents sent two Servants and a Negroe to Look for them, they found the pillowbear under the Fence, and then sent them again, and they found another bundle under the Fence, and when they were brought in, she confest she putt them there, and being asked what she had done with the two Gowns, Caps and other things belonging to Winifred and Frances Davis, she deny'd, that she knew any thing of them, and about an hour and Half after, she went and showed the Depondents where they were, And that there they found, One pair Trousers, in which were two Gowns, two Razors, [234] One Knife and Fork, some Stockins, and other things, and a little Further on, they found two Carolina Hats.

his

ELIAS FENNEL, JOHN MONROE, JOHN SHORT

Mark

It appearing to this Court upon the aforesaid Examination that there is Just cause for Trying the said Jane Kelly at the General Court for the Crime afore-said, whereof she is accused, It is therefore Ordered that the said Jane Kelly be Remanded to the prison of this County under the Custody of the Sherrif, and from thence to be Convey'd to the publick Goal of Williamsburg as the Law in such cases directs.

[Fennel's Recognizance]

Elias Fennel of Richmond County in open Court before His Majesty's Justices acknowledged Himself indebted to our Sovereign Lord the King His Heirs and Successors in the Sum of Ten pounds Sterling to be Levy'd of His Lands and Tennements goods and Chattels with Condition that if the said Elias Fennel shall Personally appear at the Next General Court on the fourth Day thereof and then and there give such evidence as He knows against Jane Kelly who stands Com-mitted For Fellony, and do not Depart thence without leave of that Court, that then this Recognizance to be Void or Else to Remain in Full Force.

Monroe's Recognizance

John Monroe of Richmond County the Same.

Short's Recognizance

John Short of Stafford County the Same.

[235] At a call'd Court held at the Courthouse of Richmond County on Mon-day the Fifteenth day of August 1737.

Present: William Fantleroy, Samuel Peachey, Newman Brockenbrough, John Woodbridge, Landon Carter, Daniel Hornby, Anthony Sydnor, William Fant-leroy Jr., Gentlemen Justices.

Harris's Examination

Whereas John Harris servant to John Short of Stafford County was by Virtue of a Mittimus from William Fantleroy Jr. gentleman one of the Justices of this Court committed to this County Goal For Felloniously taking out of the House of George Wharton one pair of Men's shoes and worsted stockins, one silk Hand-kerchief and a Rool and Divers other things and being Now brought before His

Majesty's Justices Here present and being asked what He Had to say to what was laid to His charge, He answered that as He was Coming along the Road by George Wharton's House He went in Order to get some water but Finding the Door shut He pull'd a Plank From a Hole at one End of the House and Crept in, where he Found one pair of Shoes, one pair of Stockins, one Handkerchief and Sundry other things which He carryed away with Him.

George Wharton of Lunenburg Parish in Richmond County being Sworn saith That the Goods Now Produc'd in Court belongs to Him.

[236] That when He went From Home He left them in a Trunk Lock't up.

That He lock't the Door of His House.

That when He went From Home He Nail'd up a plank at a Hold that was at one End of His House And at His Return He Found it taken away and Likewise found the Lock of His trunk broak and His things Gone.

Thomas Grinstid Jr. of Lunenburg parish in Richmond County being sworn saith that He is an Overseer to Mr. William Brockenbrough.

That on Monday the Eighth Instant some of His Negroes seing John Harris Come out at a Hole of George Wharton's House, they came and told the Deponent of it, Upon that the Deponent and John Horton pursued the said John Harris and over took Him upon the Road with the goods produced in Court, And He own'd that He took them out of the House thereupon they carry'd Him before Mr. William Fantleroy Junior.

John Horton of Lunenburg parish in Richmond County being Swore Deposeth the Same Relating to the Prisoner as Thomas Grinstid hath done.

[237] It appearing to this Court upon the aforesaid Examination that there is Just cause for trying the said John Harris at the Next General Court for the Crime aforesaid where of He is accused It is therefore Ordered that the said John Harris be Remanded to the prison of this County under the Custody of the Sherif and from thence to be Convey'd to the publick Goal of Williamsburg as the Law in such Cases Directs.

Wharton's recognizance

George Wharton of Richmond County in open Court before His Majesty's Justices acknowledged Himself Indebted to our Sovereign Lord the King His Heirs and Successors in the Sum of Ten pounds Sterling to be Levy'd of His Lands and Tennements goods and Chattels with Condition that if the said George Wharton shall Personally appear at the Next General Court on the Fourth day thereof and then and there give such Evidence as He Knows against John Harris who stands Committed For Fellony, and do Not depart thence without Leave of that Court, that then this Recognizance to be Void or Else to Remain in Full Force.

Grinstid Jr. Recognizance

Thomas Grinstid Junior the Same.

Horton's Recognizance

John Horton the Same.

[**238**] At a Call'd Court Held at the Court House of Richmond County on Monday the Twenty sixth Day of September MDCCxxxvii.

Present: Samuel Peachey, Newman Brockenbrough, Landon Carter, Daniel Hornby and Anthony Sydnor, Gentlemen Justices.

[*Sollis's Examination*]

Whereas Elizabeth Sollis Servant to Gabriel Alloway of Northfarnham Parish in Richmond County was by Virtue of a Mittimus From Newman Brockenbrough Gentleman one of the Justices of this Court Committed to this County Goal For opening the Desk of Her said Master and taking thereout on the Eighteenth Day of this Instant Four Gold Rings one pair of Gold Sleve buttons, Two Muzling Handkerchiefs one Silk Do. [ditto] one Cambrick Cap two linen Do. [ditto] and a Silk purse with about Eight shillings Cash in it And being Now brought before His Majesty's Justices Here present and being asked what she had to Say to what was laid to Her Charge she answered that on the Eighteenth day of this Instant she took out of Her Master's Desk, the Key being in the Lock, Four Gold Rings and one brass one, One pair Gold buttons, One purse with Some Money and buttons in itt, Also some Head Cloaths and one Muzling Handkerchief, That she took out of the Trunk, one shirt, one Pillowbear and one Silk Handkerchief.

Gabriel Alloway of Northfarnham parish in Richmond County being Sworn saith that the Goods produced in Court belongs to Him, that the Rings and buttons purse and Muzling Handkerchief and Head Cloaths were taken out of the Drawer of His Desk, and that the other things were taken out of a Trunk [**239**] Thomas Hightower of Northfarnham parish in Richmond County being Sworn saith, that the goods produced in Court also the Rings and purse and what was in it Except Two peices of Silver He took From Elizabeth Sollis.

Henry Williams Jr. of Northfarnham Parish in Richmond County being sworn Saith that Elizabeth Sollis when she was taken she took out of Her bosom one box with Rings in it, and a Purse with one peice of Silver and buttons in it and Gave them to Him.

It appearing to this Court upon the aforesaid Examinac'on that there is Just Cause for Trying the said Elizabeth Sollis at the Next General Court for the Crime aforesaid whereof she is accused, It is therefore Ordered that the said Elizabeth Sollis be Remanded to the prison of this County under the Custody of the Sherrif and From thence to be Conveyed to the Publick Goal of Williamsburg as the Law in Such Cases Directs.

Alloway's Recognizance

Gabriel Alloway of Richmond County in Open Court before His Majesty's Justices acknowledged Himself Indebt'd to our Sovereign Lord the King His Heirs and Successors in the Sum of Ten pounds Sterling to be Levy'd of His Lands and Tenements Goods and Chattels with Condition that if the said Gabriel Alloway shall Personally ap'ear at the Next General Court on the Fourth Day thereof and then and there give such Evidence as He Knows against Elizabeth Sollis who stands Committed for Fellony, and do Not Depart thence without Leave of that Court, that then this Recognizance to be Void or Else to Remain in full Force.

Hightower's Recognizance

[**240**] Thomas Hightower the Same.

Williams Recognizance

Henry Williams Jr. the Same.

At a Call'd Court Held at the Court House of Richmond County on Satturday the Twenty seventh day of August MDCCxxxvii.
Present: William Fantleroy, Newman Brockenbrough, Landon Carter, Daniel Hornby, Anthony Sydnor and William Fantleroy Jr., Gentlemen Justices.

Stewart's Examination

Whereas Alexander Stewart was by Virtue of a Mittimus from William Fantleroy Jr. gentleman one of the Justices of this Court Committed to this County Goal on Suspicion of Stealing one Pistole and a Half From Joseph Russel Junior, and being now brought before His Majesty's Justices Here present, and Having Examined Several Evidences on behalf of the King against the said Alexander Steward, No Sufficient Cause appearing to them upon the said Evidence to remand Him to the Publick Goal of Williamsburgh, It is therefore Ordered that the said Alexander Stewart be Discharged.

At a Court Held for Richmond County the third Day of October MDCCxxxvii.
Present: William Fantleroy, Charles Grymes, Samuel Peachey, Newman Brockenbrough, William Glascock, Landon Carter and Leroy Griffin, Gentleman Justices.

Conner bound to his behaviour

[**241**] Michael Conner of Northfarnham parish having been Summoned to answer the Presentment of the Grandjury against Him for being Drunk the Eleventh day of September Last and a Common Disturber of the Peace and this Day appearing but offering Nothing Material to Excuse Himself, It is the opinion of this Court and accordingly Ordered that for the said Offence He Give good and Sufficient Security for His good behaviour during the term of one year.

Whereupon the said Michel Conner together with Henry Williams Jr. His Security in Open Court acknowledged themselves Indebted unto our Sovereign Lord the King His Heirs and Successors in the Sum of Twenty pounds Sterling to be Levy'd on their Lands and Tenements Goods and Chattels with Condition that if the said Michael Conner shall be of good behavior as well towards His Majesty as all His Liege People that then this Recognizance to be Void and of none Effect or Else to Remain in Full Force and Virtue.

Brady bound to His behaviour

Owen Brady of Northfarnham parish Having been Summoned to answer the Presentment of the Grandjury against Him for being Drunk the Fourteenth September last past and a Common disturber of the peace, and this day appearing but offering Nothing Material to Excuse Himself, It is the Opinion of this Court and accordingly Ordered that for the said Offence He give good and Sufficient Security for His good behaviour during the Term of one Year.

Whereupon the said Owen Brady together with Henry Miskell His Security in Open Court acknowledged [**242**] themselves indebted unto our Sovereign Lord the King His Heirs and Successors in the Sum of Twenty pounds Sterling to be Levied on their Lands and Tennements goods and Chattels with Condition that if the said Owen Brady shall be of Good behaviour as well towards His Majesty as all His leige People that then this Recognizance to be Void and of None Effect or Else to Remain in Full Force and Virtue.

White bound to his behaviour

John White of Northfarnham parish Having been summoned to answer the Presentment of the Grandjury against Him For a Common Drunkard and disturber of the Peace, and this day appearing but offering Nothing Material to Excuse Himself, It is the Opinion of this Court and accordingly Ordered that for the said Offence he Give Good and Sufficient Security for his Good behaviour during the Term of one year.

Whereupon the said John White together with Thomas Suggitt His Security in Open Court acknowledged themselves indebted unto our Sovereign Lord the King His Heirs and Successors in the Sum of Twenty pounds Sterling to be Levied on their Lands and Tenements goods and Chattles with Condition that if the said John White shall be of Good behaviour as well towards His Majesty as all

His Leige People that then this Recognizance to be Void and of None Effect or Else to Remain in Full Force and Virtue.

Davis bound to behaviour

[**243**] It appearing to this Court that Thomas Davis is a Person of an Ill behaviour, It is therefore Ordered that he Give good and Sufficient Security for His good behaviour, and that He Remain in the Sherrif's Custody untill He gives such Security.

Jack Negro Tryall

At a Session of Oyer and Terminer Held at Richmond Court House on Wednesday the Nineteenth Day of October MDCCxxxvii. In the Eleventh year of the Reign of our Sovereign Lord George the Second by the Grace of God of Great Britain France and Ireland King Defender of the Faith etc. by Virtue of a Special Commission For the Tryal of all Treasons Petit Treasons or Misprisions thereof Fellonys Murders or Other Offences or Crimes whatsoever Committed within this County of Richmond by a Negroe Man Slave Named Jack belonging to Dennis M'Carty gentleman of Prince Williams County And Directed to William Fantleroy Charles Grymes Samuell Peachey Newman Brockenbrough Thomas Wright Belfield John Woodbridge William Glascock Landon Carter Leroy Griffin Daniel Hornby William Jordan Anthony Sydnor and William Fantleroy Junior Gentlemen.

Present: William Fantleroy, Samuel Peachey, Newman Brockenbrough, John Woodbridge and William Fantleroy Jr., Gentlemen Justices.

Richmond Ss. Be it Rememb'red for our Sovereign Lord the King that Jack a Negroe Man Slave belonging to Dennis M'Carty of the County of Price William Gentleman stands this day (being the Nineteenth day of October [**244**] MDCCxxxvii And in the Eleventh year of our said Lord George the Second of Great Britain France and Ireland King Defender of the Faith etc. by an Information preferr'd to His Majesty's Commissioners of Oyer and Terminer by William Kennan Deputed Attorney for our said Lord the King) Indicted in these words Richmond Ss. Our Sovereign Lord George the Second of Great Britain etc. Doth Hereby arrain and Indict you Jack a Negro Slave belonging to Dennis M'Carty Gentleman of Fellony and Burglary for that you on the Eighteenth day of September in the year of our Lord MDCCxxxvii At the Parish of Lunenburg in the said County with Force and Arms the Negroe Quarter of Simon Sallard of the County of Westmorland Planter in the Night time did Felloniously break open[,] enter and a pair of Pockets Valued thirteen pounds and Sundry Other Goods being the goods and Chattels of the said Simon there Having Found did Felloniously take and Carry off[;] as also for that you on the Fifteen day of June in the year aforesaid at the Parish and County aforesaid a Drugget Jacket Valued Eight Shillings being the Goods and chattels of Alexander Young of the Parish of Northfarnham in the County aforesaid did Feloniously steal and bear away[;] as Also for that you on the twentyeighth Day of September in the year aforesaid at the parish of Lunenburg in the County aforesaid One Cotton Jacket Value five shillings and one Kersy Cap Value one Shilling being the Goods and Chattles of John Tayloe Esq. of the parish and County aforesaid out of the Negroe Quarter of the said John [Tayloe] did Felloniously steal and Carry off[;] as also For [245] that you at sundry times and from Sundry persons Goods and Chattels to the Value of Twenty shillings at the Parish of Lunenburg and Northfarnham in the County aforesaid did Felloniously Steal and Carry off Against the peace of our said Lord the King His Crown and Dignities and against the Form of Divers Statutes in this Case Made and provided.[119]

WILLIAM KENNAN Domini Rege[120]

Whereupon the said Jack was brought to the Bar and arraigned for the said Fellony and Burglaring and there Pleaded Not Guilty, and thereupon the Court preceding on His Tryall (after Having Heard the Evidence against Him, and what He Had to say in his Defence) are of opinion that He is Guilty of the Felony Mentioned in the said Indictment, within the benefit of Clergy whereupon the said Jacke pray'd the said Benefit and accordingly was burnt in the Hand at the Bar with a Hott Iron, and Ordered that He stand in the Pillory one Hour, and at the Expiration thereof; one Ear to be cut off.

Jacob a Negro's Tryall

[246] At a Session of Oyer and Terminer Held at Richmond Court House on Wednesday the Ninth day of November MDCCxxxvii In the Eleventh year of the Reign of our Sovereign Lord George the Second by the Grace of God of Great Britain France and Ireland King Defender of the Faith etc. by Virtue of a Special Commission For the Tryal of all Treasons Petit Treasons or Misprisions Thereof Felonys Murders or Other offences or Crimes whatsoever Committed within this County of Richmond by a Molato Man Slave Named Jacob belonging to William Fantleroy Gentleman and Directed to Charles Grymes, Samuel Peachey, Newman Brockenbrough, Thomas Wright Belfield, John Woodbridge, William Glascock, Landon Carter, Leroy Griffin, Daniel Hornby, William Jordan, Anthony Sydnor and William Fantleroy Gentlemen.

Present: Charles Grymes, Landon Carter, William Jordan and William Fantleroy Jr., Gentlemen Justices.

Be it Remembered for our Sovereign Lord the King that Jacob a Molato slave belonging to William Fantleroy of the County of Richmond Gentleman Stands this day (being the Ninth day of November MDCCxxxvii and in the Eleventh year of our said Lord George the Second of Great Britain France and Ireland King Defender of the Faith etc. by an Information given to His Majesty's Commissioners of Oyer and Terminer appointed for the tryal of the said Jacob by

119. The concluding phrase "against the form of divers statutes in this case made and provided" appears only in the informations prosecuted by William Kennan, when he was the king's attorney. We have found no statute to which this might refer and conclude that it was pro forma.

120. Missing the "pro" before the "domini." Kennan seems to have made a number of changes in the form of the information.

William Kennan Deputed Attorney for our said Lord the King) Indicted For Felony and Burglary in these Words.

[247] Our Sovereign Lord George the Second of Great Britain etc. doth by William Kennan His Deputed Attorney arrain and Indict you Jacob a Mulato Slave belonging to William Fantleroy of this County Gentleman for that you on the Eighth day of October in the year of our Lord MDCCxxxvii at the Parish of Lunenburg in the said County with Force and Arms the dwelling House of William Fantleroy your said Master in the Night Time with a Felonious intent did break and Enter and two Cloth Jackets value two Shillings and Six pence, One pair of Britches value one Shilling, one Felt Hatt value Eighteen pence, Two Woolen Caps value ten pence, two new Oznabrig Shirts value five Shillings, one New Linen Shirt value two shillings and six pence, One Linen Sheet Value three shillings, One Frying pan Value Eighteen pence, one Rug value three Shillings and Six pence being the Goods and Chattles of your said Master there Having Found did Feloniously take and Carry off. As also for that you on the said Eighth of October in the Year aforesaid the Negroe Quarter of your said Master in the said County and parish with Force and Arms in the Night Time did Feloniously break and Enter and Four Mid'lings of bacon Value Twenty five Shillings and one Narrow Ax value two Shillings there Having Found being likewise the Goods and Chattles of your said Master did feloniously take and Carry off against the peace of our said Lord the King His Crown and Dignity and against the Form of divers Statutes and Act of Assembly in this Case Made and provided.

WILLIAM KENNAN pro D. Rege.

Whereupon the said Jacob was brought to the bar and [248] Arrained for the said Felony and Burglary and there pleaded Not Guilty and thereupon the Court proceeding on His Tryall (after Having Heard the Evidence against Him and what he had to Say in His defence) are of the Opinion that he is Guilty of the Fellony and Burglary Mentioned In the said Indictment.

It is therefore Ordered that the said Molato Jacob Return to the place from whence He came (from thence to the place of Execution) and there to be Hang'd by the Neck, till He be Dead.

Prusuant to an Act of Assembly made in the year 1723 concerning the Tryal of Slaves committing Capital crimes, this court in Pursuance thereof, do Value Jacob a Molato Man Slave belonging to William Fantleroy Gentleman (who was this day Condemend to dye for Fellony and Burglary) to thirty pounds Current Money and Ordered that the Clerk of this Court Certify the Same to the Next Assembly.

At a Court Held for Richmond County the Sixth day of February 1737/8.

Present: William Fantleroy, Samuel Peachey, Thomas Wright Belfield, William Glascock, Daniel Hornby, William Jordan and Anthony Sydnor, Gentlemen Justices.

John Brown bound to behaviour

[**249**] It appearing to this Court that John Brown of Lunenburgh parish in this County threat'ned to do some bodily hurt to Landon Carter, gentleman of the same parish, It is therefore Ordered that He Give Good and Sufficient Security for his Good Behaviour.

Whereupon the said John Brown together with Benjamin Rust and Edward Bates His Securitys in Open Court acknowledged themselves Indebted unto our Sovereign Lord the King His Heirs and Successors in the Sum of one Hundred pounds Sterling to be Levy'd on their Lands and Tenements goods and Chattels with Condition that if the said John Brown shall be of Good Behaviour as well towards His Majesty as all his liege People and more Especially towards the said Landon Carter that then this Recognizance to be Void and of none Effect or Else to Remain in Full Force.

William Brown bound to Behaviour

It appearing to this Court that William Brown of Lunenburgh parish in this County Threatened to do some bodily Hurt to Landon Carter of the Same parish, It is therefore Ordered that He give Good and Sufficient Security for His Good Behaviour.

Whereupon the said William Brown together with Benjamin Rust and Edward Bates His Securitys in Open Court acknowledged themselves indebted unto our Sovereign Lord the King His Heirs and Successors in the Sum of One Hundred pounds Sterling to be Levy'd on their lands and Tennements Goods and Chattels with Condition that if the said William Brown shall be of Good behaviour as well towards His Majesty as all his Liege People [**250**] and More Especially towards the said Landon Carter That then this Recognizance to be Void and of None Effect or Else to Remain in Full Force.

Pridham bound to behaviour

It appearing to this Court that Edward Pridham of Lunenburg Parish is a Person of an ill behaviour, It is therefore Ordered that He give good and Sufficient Security for His good Behaviour.

Whereupon the said Edward Pridham together with Christopher Pridham His Security in Open Court acknowledged themselves Indebted unto Our Sovereign Lord the King His Heirs and Successors in the Sum of Twenty pounds Sterling to be Levy'd on their Lands and Tenements with Condition that if the said Edward Pridham shall be of Good Behaviour as well towards His Majesty as all His liege People That then this Recognizance to be void and of None Effect or Else to Remain in Full Force.

At a Call'd Court Held at the Court House of Richmond County on Satturday the Eighteenth day of March 1737 [1738].

Present: William Fantleroy, Samuel Peachey, Newman Brockenbrough, Landon Carter, Gentlemen Justices.

[*Jenkins's Examination*]

Whereas John Jenkins was bound over to this Court on Suspicion of Killing one James D'Bond, This day the Court having taken the said Matter into Examination and Having Heard Several evidences on behalf of the King against the said Jenkins, No sufficient cause appearing to them upon the said Evidence to [**251**] remove Him to the Public Goal, He is therefore Ordered to be Acquited.

At a Call'd Court Held at the Court house in Richmond County on Monday the First Day of May MDCCxxxviii.
Present: William Fantleroy, Samuel Peachey, Newman Brockenbrough, Daniel Hornby and Anthony Sydnor, Gentlemen Justices.

Dawson's Examination

Whereas Nicholas Dawson was by virtue of a Mittimus from William Fantleroy Gentleman one of the Majestrates of this County Committed to this County Goal on Suspicion of Fellony, This day the Court having taken the said Matter into Examination Having heard Severall Evidences on behalf of the King against the said Dawson No sufficient Cause appearing to them upon the said Evidence to Remove Him to the Public Goal, He is therefore Ordered to be acquited.[121]

At a Court Held for Richmond County the Fifth day of June MDCCxxxviii.
Present: Samuel Peachey, Newman Brockenbrough, Thomas Wright Belfield, Landon Carter and Leroy Griffin, Gentlemen Justices.

Goburn bound to behaviour

Whereas William Goburn of Lunenburgh parish was bound over to appear at that Court on Suspicion of taking some fother and Heves[122] from William Jordan gentlemen and being now brought before this Court, and [**252**] Several Evidences being presented and Examined but not proving the Fact, yet it appearing to the Court that the said William Goburn is a Person of an ill Behaviour, It is therefore Ordered that he give Good and Sufficient security for His good Behaviour.

---

121. Evidence for the king was presented by prosecution witnesses, responding to questions from the justices and, at some sessions, from the king's attorney. The latter official did not prosecute every criminal case; in many, the victim acted as a prosecutor. The defendant could bring or send for his own witnesses. In trials at the General Court, defense witnesses were ordered to appear and were sworn; *Statutes at Large*, 3:391, 298 (1705).

122. Fodder and hay.

Whereupon the said William Goburn together with Nicholas Minor and George Sisson his Securityes in open Court acknowledged themselves Indebted to our Sovereign Lord the King his Heirs and Successors in the Sum of Twenty pounds Sterling to be Levyed on their Lands and Tenements Goods and Chattles with Condition that if the said William Goburn shall be of good Behaviour as wel towards His Majesty as all His Liege People, That then this Recognizance to be Void and of None Effect, or Else to Remain in full Force

At a Court Held for Richmond County the third Day of July MDCCxxxviii.

Present: William Fantleroy, Samuel Peachey, Thomas Wright Belfield, William Glascock, Landon Carter, Leroy Griffin, Daniel Hornby, William Fantleroy, Gentlemen Justices.

Phillyoung bound over to Williamsburg

Charles Phillyoung of Lunenburg parish this day appearing according to His Recognizance Concerning His Forging Two Receits[123] which he produced in discount of a Petition brought against Him in [253] this Court by Mrs. Susanah Metcalf for which an Order was made last Court for the King's Attorney to prosecute Him for the Same, but it is the opinion of This Court that for the aforesaid Crime the said Phillyoung is only Tryable at the General Court,[124] It is therefore Ordered that the said Charles Phillyoung give Good and Sufficient Security for His Personal appearance on the Fourth day of the Next General Court to answer the same.

Whereupon the said Charles Phillyoung together with Thomas Freshwater of Lunenburgh parish His Security acknowledged themselves Indebted unto our Sovereign Lord the King the said Phillyoung in the Sum of Forty Pounds Sterling and the said Thomas Freshwater in the Sum of Twenty pounds Sterling to be Levy'd on their Lands and Tennements Goods and Chattells, with Condition, that if the said Charles Phillyoung shall Personally appear at the Next General Court on the Fourth day thereof, and so attend from time to time as the said Court shall direct, That then this Recognizance to be void and of none Effect or Else to Remain in full Force.

Pally bound to Behaviour

John Pally of Northfarnham parish Having been Summoned to answer the Presentment of the Grandjury against Him for being a Common Swearer and

---

123. Receipts. Phillyoung owed Metcalf money, part of which he tried to remit with two tobacco certificates, or receipts (each giving the weight and value of tobacco supposedly brought to a warehouse); see n. 143, below. These receipts were a common circulating medium of exchange. See ROB No. 10, 620 (1738), for the initial court order.

124. Metcalf complained that the receipts were forged. Virginia statutes made forgery of tobacco receipts a felony; *Statutes at Large*, 4:265–66 (1730). The justices ordered Phillyoung to appear at the General Court.

this day appearing but offering Nothing Material to Excuse Himself It is the opinion of this Court and accordingly Ordered that for the said Offence He give good and Sufficient security for his Good Behaviour during the Term of one year.

Whereupn the said John Pally together with Charles [254] Dobbins His Security in open Court acknowledged themselves Indebted to our Sovereign Lord the King His Heirs and Successors for the sum of Twenty pounds Sterling to be Levy'd on their Lands and Tenements Goods and Chattels with Condition that if the said John Pally shall be of Good behaviour as well towards His Majesty as all His Liege People That then this recognizance to be void and of None Effect or Else to Remain in full Force.

Bonham Bound to Behaviour

Whereas Capt. John Bonham of Lunenburgh Parish was presented by the Grandjury for being a Common Swearer It is therefore Ordered that he Give Security for His good behaviour during the Term of one Year.

Whereupon David Hornby Gentleman in Open Court acknowledged Himself Indebted to our Sovereign Lord the King His Heirs and Successors in the Sum of Twenty pounds Sterling to be Levy'd on His Lands and Tennements Goods and Chattels with Condition that if the said John Bonham shall be of Good behaviour as well towards His said Majesty as all his Leige People That then this Recognizance to be Void and of none Effect or else to Remain in full Force.

At a Call'd Court held at the Court House of Richmond County on Monday the Third day of July MDCCxxxviii.

Present: William Fantleroy, Samuel Peachey, Thomas Wright Belfield, Thomas Barber, Landon Carter, Daniel Hornby and William Fantleroy Jr., Gentlemen Justices.

Wagg Whipt

[255] Whereas Thomas Wagg by Vertue of a Mittimus From Samuell Peachey Gentleman one of the Justices of this Court was Committed to the County Goal on Suspicion of Stealing from Timothy Lary and James Morrison Sundry goods Vizt Four Checkt Linen Shirts 1 pair britches one pair Trousers, Three silk Handkerchiefs, Two worsted Caps and Several other things as pins, needles, Laces, Thimbles, necklaces, shirt buttons, Knives etc. to the Value of Three pounds and being now Brought before His Majesty's Justices Here present on Examination of Severall Evidences touching the same It is the opinion of this Court that the said Thomas Wagg is guilty of the Crimes laid to His Charge It is therefore Ordered that for the said Offence The Sherrif take Him and carry Him to the Common whiping post and give Him Thirtynine Lashes on his bare back well Laid on.

Lary's Recognizance

Timothy Lary in open Court before His Majesties Justices acknowledged Himself indebted to our Sovereign Lord the King his Heirs Lands and Successors in the sum of Ten pounds Sterling to be Levy'd of His Lands and Tenements goods [and] Chattles with Condition that if the said Timothy Lary shall Personally appear on Wednesday the Seventh Next at the Courthouse of this County then and there to give Evidence against a Molato Slave nam'd Harry That then this Recognizance. to be void or Else to Remain in full Force.

Morrison's Recognizance

James Morrison the Same.

Gadon's Recognizance

George Gadon the Same.

Harry a Negro his Tryal

[**256**] At a Session of Oyer and Terminer Held at Richmond Court House on Thursday the thirteenth day of July MDCCxxxviii. In the Twelfth year of the Reign of our Sovereign Lord George the Second by the Grace of God of Great Britain France and Ireland King Defender of the Faith and By Virtue of a Special Commission for the Tryal of all Treasons petit Treasons or Misprisions thereof Fellonys Murders or other offences or Crimes whatsoever Committed within this County of Richmond by a Molato Man Slave named Harry belonging to Edgecomb Sugitt and Directed to William Fantleroy, Charles Grymes, Samuel Peachey, Newman Brockenbrough, Thomas Wright Belfield, John Woodbridge, Thomas Barber, William Glascock, Landon Carter, Leroy Griffin, Daniel Hornby, Anthony Sydnor and William Fantleroy Jr. Gentlemen.

Present: William Fantleroy, Newman Brockenbrough, Thomas Wright Belfield, Leroy Griffin, Anthony Sydnor, and William Fantleroy Jr., Gentlemen Justices.

Memorandom That on this presentment[,] being the the Thirteenth day of July MDCCxxxviii[,] An Indictment was prefer'd against a Negro Man slave Call'd Harry belonging to Edgecomb Suggitt of Richmond County in These words.

Richmond Ss William Robinson for and in behalf of Our Sovereign Lord the King doth present that Harry a Negro Man belonging to the aforesaid Suggitt of the parish of Northfarnham and County aforesaid For that He the said Negro Harry on the 26th day [**257**] of June in the year of our Lord one Thousand Seven Hundred and Thirty eight in the Night of the same day at the parish and County aforesaid in a Certain Long Boat (Belonging to the Martha under the care of Timothy Larry and James Morrison) did Enter and Felloniously take and convey away, Four Check'd Linin shirts, 1 pair of Britches, 1 pair Trousers,

Three Silk Handkerchiefs, two worsted caps and Sundry other things[;] to wit pins, Needles, Lace, Thimbles, Necklaces, Shirt buttons Knives etc. To the Value of Three pounds Sterling Being the proper goods of the said Timothy Larey and James Morrison Contrary to the peace of our Sovereign Lord the King His Crown and Dignity

WILLIAM ROBINSON
Kings Attorney

Whereupon the said Harry was brought to the Barr and arrained for the said Fellony, and He Confessing the Fact, It is the opinion of this Court that He is within the Benefit of Clergy,[125] whereupon the said Harry pray'd the said Benefit, and accordingly was burnt on the Hand at the bar with a Hot iron, and Ordered that He stand in the Pillory one Hour, and at the Expiration thereof, one Ear to be Cut of.

At a Court Held for Richmond County the Seventh day of August MDCCxxxviii.

Present: William Fantleroy, Samuell Peachey, Landon Carter, and Leroy Griffin, Gentleman Justices.

Stone bound to Behaviour

It appearing to this Court that William Stone of Northfarnham parish in this County, Threatened to do some bodily Hurt [258] to Newman Brockenbrough gentleman of the same Parish, It is therefore Ordered that He give good and Sufficient Security for his Good behaviour.

Whereupon the said William Stone together with Jonathan Lyell and Thomas Broom His Securitys acknowledged themselves indebted to our Sovereign Lord the King the said William Stone in the Sume of Forty Pounds and the said Jonathan Lyell and Thomas Broom each of them in the Sum of Twenty pounds to be Levy'd on their Lands and Tennements goods and Chattels with Condition that if the said William Stone shall be be of good behaviour as well towards His Majesty as all His Leige People That then this Recognizance to be void and of none Effect, or Else to Remain in Full Force.

At a Court continued and Held for Richmond County the third Day of October MDCCxxxviii.

Present: John Woodbridge, Thomas Barber, Daniel Hornby, Anthony Sydnor, Gilbert Hamilton and William Fantleroy Jr., Gentlemen Justices.

---

125. It is not clear whether the justices or Suggitt informed Harry of this fact. They were not required by law to assist a defendant in pleading his clergy. The scope of clergyable offenses at this time in the colony was confused and required statutory clarification in 1732. See n. 138 below.

Stone Discharged from His Recognizance

Whereas William Stone of Northfarnham parish at a Court Held for this County the Seventh day of August last was bound to His Good behaviour for threatning to do some bodily Hurt to Newman Brockenbrough Gentleman the said Brockenbrough this Day Moved that the said Stone Might be discharged from His Recognizance by Reason that He believes that the said Stone did not design to do any bodily Hurt to Him which Motion is Granted.

[**259**] At a Call'd Court held at the Court house of Richmond County on Monday the twenty Sixth day of February 1738 [1739].

Present: Samuel Peachey, Newman Brockenbrough, Thomas Wright Belfield, John Woodbridge, Thomas Barber and Anthony Sydnor, Gentlemen Justices.

Dunkin[126] *Whipt*

Whereas Dunkin Montgomery of North Farnham Parish was by vertue of a mittimus From Landon Carter Gentleman one of the Magistrates of this Court Committed to the County Goal on Suspicion of Stealing Tobacco from the Honorable John Carter Esq. out of his Tobacco house, and being Now brought before his Majestys Justices here present, on Examination of Severall Evidences Touching the Same, It is the Opinion of this Court, that the said Dunkin Montgomery is Guilty of the Crime, laid to his Charge, It is therefore Ordered that for the Said offence, the Sherrif take him, and Carry him to the Common Whipping post, and give him thirty nine lashes, on his bare back well laid on, and it is Further ordered that he give good and Sufficient Security for his good behaviour Dureing the terme of one year, and that he remain in the Sherriffs Custody, untill he gives Such Security.

At a Court held for Richmond County the Seventh day of May 1739.

Present: Samuell Peachey, William Glascock, Leroy Griffin, Daniel Hornby and Gilbert Hamilton, Gentlemen Justices.

Wagg bound to his behaviour

[**260**] Thomas Wagg of North Farnham parish this Day appearing according to his Recognizance, on Suspicion of his being an assistant in conveying one of Mr. Daniel Hornbys Servant Men away, and Severall Evidences being produced and Examined, but not proveing the Fact, Yet it appearing to the Court that the

---

126. An unusual marginal note. Ordinarily the last name of the defendant was used.

said Thomas Wagg is a person of an ill behaviour, It is therefore ordered that he give good and Sufficient Security for his good behaviour, During the terme of one Year.

Whereupon the said Thomas Wagg together with Thomas Suggitt his Security in open Court acknowledged themselves Indebted to our Sovereign Lord the King his heirs and Successors in the Sum of twenty pounds Sterling to be Levyed on their Lands and Tenements, goods and Chattles, with Condition, That if the said Thomas Wagge Shall be of good behaviour, as well towards his Majestye, as all his Leige people, that then this Recognizance to be void, and of none Effect or Else to remain in full Force.

At a Court held for Richmond County the Second day of July 1739.

Present: William Fantleroy, Thomas Wright Belfield, Thomas Barber, Landon Carter, Daniel Hornby, Gilbert Hamilton and William Fantleroy Jr., Gentlemen Justices.

Northen, Junior bound to his behaviour

It appearing to this Court that Edmund Northen, Junior of Lunenburg parish is a person of an ill Behaviour, it is therefore orderd that he give good and Sufficient Security for his good Behaviour During the term of one Year.

Whereupon the said Edmund Northen together [261] with Tobias Pursell his Security in Open Court Acknowledged themselves Indebted unto our Sovereign Lord the King his heirs and Successors in the Sum of Twenty pounds sterling, to be Levied on their Lands and Tenements, goods and Chattles with Condition that if the Said Edmund Northen shall be of good Behaviour as well Towards his Majestye as all his Liege people that then this Recognizance to be void, and of none Effect, or Else to Remain in full force and Vertue.

Whereas Edmund Northen Jr. of Lunenburg parish was ordered to be Sett in the Stocks Last Court, but he having Made his Escape from the Sherriff, It is thereupon ordered that the Sherriff should Take him into custody and Safely keep till he Entred into bond, for his appearance at this Court, and the Said, Northen this Day Appearing and submitting himself to the Court, It is ordered that he be fined for the said Contempt Ten Shillings to our Sovereign Lord the King and that he give good and Sufficient Security for his Good behaviour During the Terme of one Year.

At a Call'd Court held at the Court house of Richmond County on Monday the 23d of July 1739.

Present: John Woodbridge, Thomas Barber, Landon Carter, Daniel Hornby and Gilbert Hamilton, Gentlemen Justices.

Taylor's Examination

Whereas Samuell Taylor, a Servant to Thomas Wright Belfield Gentleman of Lunenburg parish in this County was by Virtue of a mittimus from Landon Carter Gentleman one of the Justices of this Court, Committed to the County Goale for Felloniously Breaking and Entering the Dwelling house of Mr. William Kennan on Monday the Ninth of this Instant July Between the hours of Twelve and five in the after Noon in Company with one Thomas Cox, not Yet Taken and Being now brought before his Majestys Justices now present and Being asked what he had to say to what was Laid His Charge, he Answered [**262**] That on Monday the Ninth of the Instant July he went in Company with one Thomas Cox his Fellow Servant from their master Belfield's mill to the house of one Thomas Lewis for A tenant Saw and Stay'd about a Quarter of an hour and as they Returned the said Cox Took the path Leading to Docter Kennans and when they had gone a pretty way on that road, the said Cox told him that he had a Jobb to Doe and asked him, if he would be Concern'd[,] where upon he asked the said Cox what Jobb, who answered to break open Docter Kennans house and that he must Doe it Now, for that their was money in the house, and he knew where it was, and Must have it[;] whereupon he told the said Cox he would Not be concern'd, but asked him how he knew it, who reply'd the Girle (meaning Doctor Kennan's Servant Woman) had Told him it was in a Green purse, and he would Soon gett it[,] for if their was Tenn Locks to open he would gett too it, in tenn minutes and then the said Cox said if you dont care to be Concern'd, at Least goe Down with me to the house and wait till I return, whereupon he and the Said Cox went down the road Together, Till they Came in Sight of the house and he Satt Down in the path by the pasture Gate that Leads to the House, and Saw the Said Cox goe to the House and Break Open the Door that facith the Gate and See him goe in, and after he had been in the house some Short time he heard a Noise like the Crack of a gun which he Took to be Noise of his Breaking open the Chamber Door or Some Great Lock, at which his heart Leapt for fear and he thereupon gott up, and walkt up the path[,] stopt a little while and heard Cox holler [shout] after him who presently came up to him[;] upon that he asked the Said Cox, if he had gott any thing who answered Dam the Bitch, She has Deceived me, for I have broak Open Every Lock in the house and have got a penny of money, nor any thing at all, have I taken, then he Said to the said Cox, Tom you'l be hang'd if any body has seen You, to which Cox answered, that Noe body had [**263**] Seen him doe it, and that noe body could hang him but him, Soe they went to the mill from whence they sett off.

It appears to the Court by the Oaths of William Kennan John Gorden Robert Head, Ann Lewis John Gregory and Elinor Gorman and that there is Just Cause for Trying the Said Samuell Taylor at the Generall Court for the Crime aforesaid whereof he is accused, It is therefore ordered that the Said Samuell Taylor be Remanded to the prison of this County under the Custody of the Sheriff, and from Thence to be conveyed to the Publick Goal of Williamsburg, as the Law in Such Cases Directs.

[Gordon's recognizance]

John Gordon of Richmond County in open Court before his Majestys Justices acknowledged him Self Indebted to our Sovereign Lord the King his heirs and Successors in the Sum of Ten pounds Sterling to be Levyed of his Lands and Tenements, goods and Chattles, with condition that if the Said John Gordon shall personally appear at the Next Generall Court in the forth day thereof and then and there give Such Evidence as he Knows against Samuell Taylor who Stands Committed for Fellony and doe not Depart thence without Leave of that Court then this Recognizance to be void or Else Remain in full force.

[Head's recognizance]

Robert Head of Richmond County in open Court before his Majestys Justices Acknowledged him Selfe Indebted to our Sovereign Lord the King his heirs and Successors in the Sum of Tenn pounds Sterling to be Levyed of his Lands and Tenements goods and Chattles with Condition that if the Said Robert Head shall personally appear at the Next Generall Court on the fourth day thereof and then and there give Such Evidence as he knows against Samuell Taylor Who Stands [**264**] Committed for Fellony and doe not Depart thence without Leave of that court that then this Recognizance to be Void, or Else to Remain in full force.

[Kennan's recognizances]

Mr. William Kennan of Richmond County in open Court before his Majestys Justices Acknowledged him Self Indebted to our Sovereign Lord the King his heirs and successors in the Sum of Tenn Pounds sterling to be Levyed of his Lands and Tennements Goods and Chattles with Condition that if the said William Kennan Shall personally appear at the Next Generall Court on the fourth Day thereof and then and there give Such Evidence as he knows against Samuell Taylor who Stands Committed for Fellony and Doe not Depart thence without leave of that Court, that then this Recognizance to be Void, or Else to Remain in full force.

Mr. William Kennan of Richmond County in Open Court before His Majestys Justices Acknowledged him Selfe Indebted to our Sovereign Lord the King his heirs and Successors in the Sum of Tenn pounds Sterling to be Levyed of his Lands and Tenements Goods and Chattles, with Condition that if the Said William Kennans Servants Name John Gregory and Elinor Gorman Shall personally Appear at the Next General Court, on the fourth day thereof, and then and there give Such Evidence as they know against Samuell Taylor who Stands Committed for Fellony, and doe not Depart thence without Leave of that Court that then this Recognizance to be Void or Else to Remain in full force.

The within Named Samuell Taylor Acknowledged in open Court that he was Convicted in Great Britain for Stealing Two game Cocks that he was Sentenced to be [**265**] Transported for the Same for Seven Years, and was Imported in the

Ship Dorchester Capt. Thomas Whiteing Comander, and Arrived in Virginia last March was Twelve months which is ordered to be Certifyed by

MARMADUKE BECKWITH

CC Cur[127]

At a Court held for Richmond County the Sixth day of August 1739.

Present: William Fantleroy, Thomas Wright Belfield, John Woodbridge, William Glascock, Daniel Hornby, Anthony Sydnor and William Fantleroy Jr., Gentlemen Justices.

Rairdon bound to his behaviour

It appearing to this Court that Timothy Rairdon is a person of an ill Behaviour, It is therefore Ordered that he give good and Sufficient Security for his good Behaviour during the Term of one Year.

Whereupon the said Timothy Rairdon together with Travers Tarpley his Security in open court Acknowledged them Selves Indebted unto our Sovereign Lord the King his heir and Successors in the Sum of Twenty pounds Sterling, to be Levied on their Lands and Tenements goods and Chattles with Condition, that if the Said Timothy Rairdon Shall be of Good Behaviour, as well towards his Majestye as all his Leige people, that then this Recognizance to be Void, and of None Effect, or Else to Remain in full force and virtue.

Roney bound to his behaviour

It appearing to this Court that Patrick Roney is a person of an ill Behaviour, It is Therefore Ordered that he give good and Sufficient Security for his Good Behaviour, During the Term of one Year.

[266] Whereupon the Said Patrick Roney together with John Jonson his Security in Open Court Acknowledged Themselves Indebted unto our Sovereign Lord the King his heirs and Successors in the Sum of Twenty pounds Sterling to be Levied on their Lands and Tenements goods and Chattles with Condition that if the Said Patrick Roney shall be of Good Behaviour as well towards his Majesty, as all his Leige People that then this Recognizance to be Void and of None Effect or Else to Remain in full force and Vertue.

Penny bound to his behaviour

John Penny of Northfarnham parish having Been Summoned to answer the present Ment of the Grandjury against him for being a Common Drunkard and Notorious Swearer and this day Appearing, but offering Nothing Materiall to Excuse himself, it is the Opinion of this Court, and Accordingly Ordered, that

---

127. Clerk of the county court.

for the Said Offence, he Give Good and Sufficient Security for his Good Behaviour, during the Term of one Year.

Whereupon the Said John Penny Together with Thomas Suggitt and Thomas Nash his Securitys in Open Court Acknowledged themselves Indebted unto our Sovereign Lord the King his heirs and Successors in the Sum of Twenty pounds Sterling to be levied on their Land and Tenements Goods and Chattles, with Condition that if the Said John Penny Shall be of Good Behaviour as well Towards his Majestye, as all his Leige people; that then this Recognizance to be Void and of None Effect, other Wise to Remain in full force and Vertue.

Rough bound to his behaviour

John Ruff of Northfarnham parish having been Summoned to Answer the presentment of the Grand [267] jury against him for being a Common Swearer, and this day Appearing but offering Nothing matteriall to Excuse himself it is the Opinion of this Court and Accordingly Ordered that for the Said Offence he Give Good and Sufficient Security for his Good Behaviour, during the Term of one Year.

Whereupon the said John Ruff Together with John Span Webb and Thomas Plummer his Securitys in Open Court Acknowledged them Selfes Indebted unto our Sovereign Lord the King his heirs and Successors in the Sum of Twenty pounds Sterling to be Levied on their Lands and Tenements Goods and Chattles, with Condition, that if the said John Ruff Shall be of Good Behaviour as well Towards his Majesty, as all his Leige people, that then this Recognizance to be Void, and of None Effect, other wise to Remaine in full Force and Vertue.

At a Court Continued and held for Richmond County the Seventh day of August 1739.

Present: William Fantleroy, Thomas Wright Belfield, Thomas Barber, Daniell Hornby, Gentlemen Justices.

Johnson release from his Recognizance

Whereas John Johnson of Westmorland County Yesterday before this Court Entered into a Recognizance to the King in the Sum of Twenty pounds Sterling for one Patrick Roneys Good Behaviour and the said Johnson now appearing and Moveing to be Releast from his Securityship and Giving Sufficient Reasons for the Same, he is therefore here by Releast from his Said Recognizance.

Maynard bound to his behaviour

[268] It appearing to this Court That Samuell Maynard of Lunenburg Parish is a person of an ill Behaviour It is therefore Ordered that he Give Good and Sufficient Security for his Good Behaviour during the Term of one Year.

Whereupon the said Samuell Maynard Together with Edward Tomlinson and William Dixon his Securitys in Open Court Acknowledged themselves indebted unto our Sovereign Lord the King his heirs and Successors in the Sum of Twenty pounds Sterling to be Levied on their Lands and Tenements Goods and Chattles with Condition that if the Said Samuell Maynard Shall be of Good Behaviour as well Towards his Majestye as all his Leige people that then this Recognizance to be Void and of None Effect or Else to Remain in full force and Vertue.

Butler to give Security for his behaviour

It appearing to this Court that William Butler of Lunenburge Parish is a person of an ill behaviour, It is therefore ordered that he give Good and Sufficient Security for his Good behaviour and that he Remain in the Sherrifs Custody, untill he gives Such Security.

Medford bound to his behaviour

It appearing to this Court That Henry Medford of Lunenburg Parish is a person of an ill Behaviour It is therefore ordered that he give Good and Sufficient Security for his Good Behaviour during the Term of one Year.

Whereupon the said Henry Medford Together with Thomas Taylor his Security in Open Court Acknowledged themselves Indebted unto our Sovereign Lord the King his heirs and Successors in the Sum of Twenty pounds. [**269**] Sterling to be Levied on their Lands and Tenements goods and Chattles with Condition That if the Said Henry Medford Shall be of Good behaviour as well Towards his Majestye as all his Leige people That then this Recognizance to be void and of None Effect or Else to Remain in full force and Virtue.

At a Call'd Court held at the Court House of Richmond County On Tuesday the Sixth Day of November 1739.

Present: William Fantleroy, Samuell Peachey, Newman Brockenbrough, Thomas Barber, Landon Carter, Anthony Sidnor, Gilbert Hamilton and William Fantleroy Junior, Gentlemen Justices.

Oldhams Examination

Whereas John Oldham of Northfarnham Parish in this County was by vertue of a Mittimus from Samuell Peachey Gentleman one of the Justices of this Court committed to this County Goale for Feloniously killing one John Hutchins, and being Now brought before his Majestys Justices here present, the Severall Evidences on Behalf of the King were Examined as Follows.

Merryman Thorn of Northfarnham Parish in this County aged 26 Years or thereabouts being Sworn Says, that on the 30th of Last Month in Dews Race Ground, people was Quarrelling and he went up to them and he See John Oldham and John Hutchins Fighting on the Ground and William Creele was Stript Standing over them, and Crying well done Oldham[;] upon that the Deponent puld Creele away and Oldham and Hutchings was up, and then Hutchins

Threw Oldham Down again and Creel went up again and Cryed well done Oldham and then the Deponent puld Creele away again and Soon after they were parted and presently [270] after the Said Hutchins Died and he Verily believes that he Died with That Fighting.

MERRYMAN THORNE

William Toone of Northfarnham Parish in this County aged 38 Years or their about being Sworn Says That on the 30th of Last Month in Dews Race Ground John Oldham and John Hutchins gott to fighting and William Creele was Stript Standing by them, and When they were Down the Said Creele helped Them up, two or Three Times, and the Deponent heard Sombody Say Severall Times, well done Oldham, and Soon after the Said Hutchins Died, and Verily Believes that he Died with that Fighting.

WILLIAM TOONE

William Stone of Northfarnham parish in this County Aged 50 years or there-abouts being Sworn Says that on the 30th of Last Month in Dews Race Ground Mr. Smith Came to him and Told him that John Oldham and John Hutchins was Fighting and that Hutchins would be kill'd if he Did not goe and part Them upon which the Deponent went but before he Could gett to Them he was pull'd Down but Gott up again and Then Somebody Struck him with a Stick over the Face and before he Could gett to them the persons Fighting was parted, and he See Some person putting on the Said Hutchins Cloaths but Before they were on he believes the Said Hutchins was Dead and This Deponent believes the Said Hutchins dyed of the beating he received.

WILLIAM STONE

Reubin Young Aged 25 years or their abouts being Sworn Says that on the 30th of Last Month in Dews Race Ground John Oldham and John Hutchins Gott to [271] Fighting, and they Fought a Considerable Time, that Mr. Smith Came upto the Deponent and Desired him to goe in and part them upon that the Deponent and John Hightower was going to part them But William Stone pusht them both off, and said Hutchins Could Beat him, Soon after they gott in and Helpt them up Twice but were pull'd away before they Could gett them asunder and in a Short time the Said Hutchins Died and this Deponent believes it was occasioned by that fight and this Deponent heard John Oldham Say before the Fight[:] what does Hutchins believe him Self the best man in the Field.

REUBEN R. YOUNG

Harris Toone of Northfarnham parish in the County aged 18 Years or there abouts being Sworn Says, That on the 30th of Last Month in Dews Race Ground he See John Oldham and John Hutchins Stript, and Soon after the Deponent See the Said Hutchins Strik him the Said Oldham a blow, upon that they went to Fighting and the Deponent heard Some people Say well Done Oldham, well Done Hutchins, and after The Fight was over the Deponent with Others helpt to put on the Said Hutchins Cloaths, but ... Before they were on he Believes the Said Hutchins was Dead and this Deponent believes he died of that Fighting.

HARRIS TOONE

Thomas Heart of Northfarnham Parish in this County aged Seventeen Years or thereabouts being Sworn Says That on the 30th of Last Month, in Dews Race

Ground John Hightower and John Hutchins had Some words upon that John Oldham Came up Stript, and presently the Said Hutchins and Oldham Gott to fighting, but Dont know which Struck first, and after they Had fought a Considerable Time Some body said Lett us part them, upon that Two people went in and did part them, and Soon after the Deponent and others was putting on his the Said Hutchin's Cloaths, but before they were on, he believes [**272**] the Said Hutchins was Dead and he Believes he dyed of the Fight.

THOMAS HEART

Joseph Magee of Northfarnham parish in this County aged 26 Years or there abouts being Sworn Says That on the 30th of Last Month, in Dews Race Ground he See people a quarrelling, upon that the Deponent went up and heard Several people cry out well Done Oldham, upon that the Deponent Stript him selfe, and went in to part them, upon that John Hightower Struck the Deponent Two or Three blows Soe the Deponent gott out again and Soon after they were parted and presently after the Deponent and Others were putting on his the Said Hutchins Cloaths Hutchins was Dead, and the Deponent believes he dyed with the Blows he Received in that fight.

JOSEPH MAGEE

John Smith of Northfarnham parish in this County aged 25 Years or thereabouts being Sworn Says That on the 30th of Last Month in Dews race Ground John Hightower and John Hutchins had Some words upon that John Oldham Came up behind Hutchins Stript and asked whether Hutchins Thought him Selfe the best man upon this race ground upon that they gott to Fighting, thereupon the Deponent Desired Severall people to part them and at Last they were parted, then The Deponent asked him the Said Hutchins to put on his Cloaths, but before they were on the Deponent believes he dyed with Blows received in that fight.

JOHN SMITH

[**273**] It Appearing to this Court upon the Aforesaid Examination That There is Just Cause for Trying the Said John Oldham at the Next Court of Oyer and Terminer to be Held at his Majesty's Royal Capitol for the Crime aforesaid whereof he is Accused,[128] It is therefore Ordered that the Said John Oldham be Remanded to the prison of this County under the Custody of the Sherif, and from thence to be Convey'd to the Publick Goal of Williamsburg, as the Law in Such Cases Directs.

[*Thorn's recognizance*]

Merriman Thorn of Richmond County in Open Court before his Majestys Justices Acknowledged himself Indebted to our Sovereign Lord the King his heirs and Successors in the Sum to Tenn pounds Sterling to be levyed of his Lands and Tenements Goods and Chattles with Condition That if the Said Merriman Thorn Shall appear before the honourable Court of Oyer and Ter-

---

128. Though Oldham did not have specific intent to kill Hutchins (specific intent is required for a murder charge), felonious killing was charged because Oldham did start and continue fighting in order to harm Hutchins. Death resulted from blows struck in the fight (an *actus reus*), for which the defendant was responsible. General intent was sufficient for a charge of manslaughter.

miner to be held at his Majestys Royall Capitol on the Second Tuesday in December Next and So Attend From time to time as the Said Court Shall Direct, Then and There to give Evidence for our Said Lord the King Against John Oldham who Stands Committed to the Goal of this County for felony Then this Recognizance to be Void or Else to Remain in Full Force.

William Toone the Same.
William Stone the Same.
Reubin Young the Same.
Harris Toone the Same.
Thomas Heart the Same.
Joseph Magee the Same.
[274] John Smith the Same.

At a Calld Court held at the Court house of Richmond County on Saturday the 24th November 1739.

Present: John Woodbridge, Thomas Barber, Anthony Sidnor, Gilbert Hamilton and William Fantleroy Junior, Gentlemen Justices.

Faithfull Examination

Whereas Jonathan Faithfull of Northfarnham Parish in this County was by Vertue of a mittimus from John Woodbridge Gentleman one of the Justices of this Court Commited to this County Goal for Feloniously Breaking and Entering the Meat house and another house called the Lane house Belonging to Daniel Hornby Gentleman and being now Brought before his Majestys Justices here present, and being asked what he had to Say to what was Laid to his Charge Answered he was not Guilty.

Thomas Plummer of Northfarnham parish in this County aged 30 Years or thereabouts being Sworn Says That being at Mr. Hornbys on the 17th of this Instant and about four of the Clock Next Morning hearing an uproar without Amongst the People, Got up and Mr. Hornby['s] Negroes had Jonathan Faithfull in hold, and Said they had taken him in the Meat house and that he had broke Open and had Got Meat in his Bagg and after Jonathan [Faithfull] was Brought into the Dwelling house we Left him with the people and went to the Meathouse where we found two baggs, I Cannot Say whether in the House or at the Door and one of them was Several peices of Meat and Several peices were Lying out of the Barrils and on Looking about the Meat house Some of the people found a key on the floor, and Trying it with the Lock [275] It Open'd and Shut it as being Fitted for that Purpose, and there was a key found in the Said Door but Would Not So well Open it as the Other both the Said keys the Said Jonathan Owned to be his and being Returned to to Jonathan. Mr. Hornby Or Some of the Company ask'd where he Got the Meat that was in the bagg for he Did not think it his, he Said he had Taken no Meat from anywhere Else but that the Meat in the Bagg was Mr. Hornby's, Mr. Hornby Ask'd the Said Jonathan Liberty to have his pockets Searched to which he Agreed, on which the Deponent Searched[129] them and Took out four Keys then with the other Two found at the Meat house I open'd the Shed wherein Mr. Hornby keeps his Wine and Several Other things, and a house on the River Side out of Which Mr. Hornby Says he Lost a piece of Nunns holland and other things.

Daniel Hornby of Northfarnham parish in this County aged Forty nine Years or thereabout being Sworn Says that very late on Saturday in the Night on the 17th of the Instant hearing the Negro's Calling out that they had Gott Jonathan Faithfull in the Meat house, and that he would get away if Some body did Not Come; upon which this Deponent got up and alsoe desired Mr. Plummer to get up and Secure him and after having put on his Cloaths he went out and Saw that the Meat house Door had been Opened with one of the Keys which the Said Jonathan owned was his and going into [the] Meathouse found that there had been Several peices of Meat Taken out[;] Some of which this Deponent Verily believes was in a bagg by the Door and that one of the Negroes who had then hold of him Told this Deponent that he found and Took the Said Faithfull in the Said House[;] Some Small time after the Deponent asked the prisoner how he had that Meat in the Bagg[;] he Said he had got none from any Body Else but himselfe Meaning the Deponent, The Deponent further Sayeth that he found Several keys in the prisoners possession which he owned, and that he [Hornsby] [276] had Some Goods Landed which he put into a Small house by the River Side among which was Some pieces of Nuns holland which he pack'd about the midle of a Cath with other goods and after it was Carry'd to the Shore he Opened it a miss'd one piece of the Said holland which he Verily believes as near as he Can Judg of Linnen to be the Same which Mr. Nash found in the possession of the said Jonathan.

Henry Williams of Northfarnham Parish in this County aged 30 Years or there about being Sworn Says, that he went to John Taylors who Told him there was Some people at John Deans that he had Some Suspition of, and That he would advise him to goe there and See, and Accordingly he did, but was denyed Admittance, Upon which he sayd he would goe to a Justice and Complain and there upon the Door was Opened after Some people were conceald, and he see Jonathan Faithfull there and ask'd him if it was Not time to goe home the Answere he made was, that he believed it was, upon which he went away to goe home, The Deponent further Sayeth that being down at, Mr. Hornby's after Jonathan Faithfull was apprehended he heard the Said Faithfull Say that all the Meat found in the Bag belong'd to Mr. Hornby, and the Deponent was present when Two of the keys were Tryed which unLock'd one the house by the River Side and the other the Room at the end of the old Store which Said Keys he heard the Said Faithfull Say did Belong to him with the rest that were in the

---

129. Distinct from a search warrant issued by a justice to an officer of the court (Webb, *Justice of Peace*, 137), a search during a field investigation immediately after a felony was reported did not require a warrant. The evidence produced by the search could be used against the suspect to substantiate other charges as well as gain evidence of the crime under investigation. The justices had great discretion in search for evidence of crime in England and her colonies. See William Cuddihy and B. Carmon Hardy, "A Man's House Was Not His Castle: Origins of the Fourth Amendment to the United States Constitution," *William and Mary Quarterly*, 3d ser. 37 (July 1980): 387–91.

Bunch, The Deponent also See one of the keys[,] which the Said Faithfull allow'd to be his[,] unlock the Meat house Door.

John Taylor of Northfarnham parish in this County [277] Aged 35 Years or there abouts, being Sworn Says, That Mr. Nash the Constable Came with a Search Warrant,[130] that he went with him over to John Deans[;] first he Make Sarch there but after came back to the Said Deponents house where the Constable broken Open Jonathan Faithfull's Chest and took there out a piece of Nuns holland Some of it being Cut up at the time, he Farther Sayth that on Saturday past in the Afternoon the Said Faithfull Caught up his horse to ride out but did Not goe till Some Small time in the Night and Did Not return home that Night, The Deponent further Sayth, that Sundry times he did See the Said Faithfull Drinking wine, Some time Mull'd, at the other times Not, and Sometimes did ask'd the Deponent to Drink thereof, and by his Going out at unseasonably hours of the Night and Carrying out Baggs and wallets with him, and by Concealing what he had Brought home, did Occasion Suspition in this Deponent Concerning the said Jonathans Behaviour.

The Deponent seeing the Bag that had the Meat in it, at Mr. Hornbys Meat house[,] Sayeth he verily believeth it Does belong to the Said Faithfull[;] the Empty bag he Says belongs to John Dean, The Deponent further Says that he Never knew any thing of the said Jonathans Buying the pieces of Linnen which he bought of the Dorchester Saylors.

Thomas Nash of Northfarnham Parish in this County Aged 38 Years or there abouts being Sworn Says That on the 8th of November 1739 there Came a search warrant from Daniell Hornby Gentleman Complainant Directed from Capt. Samuel Peachey to him the Said Nash as Constable and he went to the House of John Taylor and after a Search he found a peice of Nuns holland in the Chest Called Jonathan Faithfull's Chest and after a further Search Severall other goods was found Viz wine etc. [278] And further the Deponent Sayeth that on the 18th of this Instant he Came to Mr. Hornby's where he Tried one key which opened the Door Where in Mr. Hornby Keep's his wine.

It Appearing to this Court upon the Aforesaid Examination that there is Just Cause for Trying the Said Jonathan Faithfull at the Next Court of Oyer and Terminer to be Held at his Majestys Royall Capitoll for the Crime, aforesaid whereof he is Accused, It is therefore Ordered that the Said Jonathan Faithfull to be Remanded to the prison of this County and in the Custody of the Sherrif and from thence to be conveyed to the Publick Goal of Williamsburg, as the Law in Such Cases Directs.

[Plummer's recognizance]

Thomas Plummer of Richmond County in Open court before his Majestys Justices Acknowledged him Self Indebted to our Sovereign Lord the King his

---

130. A single justice might issue the warrant upon a complaint. The constable was to carry out the search and bring evidence to the court. The warrant did not have to spell out the exact nature of the evidence sought, and evidence of other crimes gained through the search was admissible in court. The warrant did have to be under the justice's seal and name the offender, criminal cause, and date of issue.

heirs and Successors in the Sum of Tenn pounds Sterling to be Levyed of his Lands and Tenements good and Chattles, with Condition that if the Said Thomas Plummer Shall appear before the Honourable Court of Oyer and Terminer to be Held at his Majesties Royall Capitoll on the Second Tuesday in December Next and attend from time to time as the Said Court Shall Direct Then and there to Give Evidence for our Said Lord the King Against Jonathan Faithfull who Stands Committed to the Goal of this County for felony Then this Recognizance to be Void or Else to Remain in full Force.

Daniel Hornby the Same.

Henry Williams Junior the Same.

John Taylor the Same.

Thomas Nash the Same.

[279] At a Call'd Court held at the Court house of Richmond County on Saturday the 16th Day of February 1739/40.

Present: Thomas Wright Belfield, John Woodbridge, Anthony Sydnor and John Smith, Gentlemen Justices.

Jones Examination

Whereas John Jones of Lunenburg Parish in Richmond County was by vertue of a mittimus from Thomas Wright Belfield gentleman one of the Justices of this Court was Committed to the County Goal, for Feloniously Stealing a horse from William Lewis, and being now Brought before his Majesties Justices here present, and being asked what He had to Say to What was Laid to his Charge, Answered he was Not Guilty.

John Gregory of Lunenburg parish Richmond County Servant to Mr. William Kennan being Sworn Says that on Saturday being the 29th of December 1739 in the afternoon he went away from his Masters house in Company with his fellow Servant John Jones the Prisoner, with a design to Runaway together, and that Night they went to the House of one William Lewis for Quarters[; he] living upon the County Road[,] where they told the Negroes about the house that their master Mr. Kennan had Set them to[—]one Mr. Jordans who lived a little way off[—]for Earthen Ware and Next morning they got up before day and Seeing a Black horse belong to the Said William Lewis Standing at the Corner of the House in a Small piece of Tobacco ground within a fence[,] the prisoner John Jones Told the Deponent that he would have that horse and there upon went into the house and asked one of the Negroes if they could lend them a piece of rope to Sling the Earthen Ware, they Told him they had None then he asked the Negroes if they Could lend them a bridle and when he returned with the Earthen ware he'd leave the Bridle whereupon they let him have a Bridle and he went directly and Catched the Said horse and meanwhile he bid this Deponent go along and he'd Overtake him, the prisoner[;] So Soon as he had Catch'd the horse pulld down the fence and Came leading the horse to this Deponent Who [280] waited for him on the road and Said to the Deponent Come damn You get up, who thereupon got up behind the prisoner and away they Rode up the Road together and they kept the road up the Country in Company Together with the horse till the Tuesday following when the Deponent being galled with riding bare back'd and behind lighted down to walk and when the Prisoner asked him to get up again the Deponent replied that he could ride no farther and that he'd rather chuse to walk to which the Prisoner Replied then damn You Ill Bid you fare well and So rode off, after which this Deponent Never Saw the prisoner till he was brought back to his Masters house by the Constable, and this Deponent farther Saith that the Prisoner and he Intended to have Got to Philadelphia and there the Prisoner told him he design'd to Sell the horse and farther Saith not.

JOHN X GREGORY
mark

William Kennan of Lunnenburg Parish in Richmond County being Sworn Sayth, that on the Saturday after Christmas day being the 29th of December 1739 in the Afternoon he miss'd two of his Servants Viz John Gregory and the Prisoner at the Bar, and when they did not Come home in a little time, he Suspected they were run away[,] having Sent them No where, but Some time after they were Brought home to him at Different times in the Constables hands[,] the Prisoner having been taken by a Hue and Cry Sent by William Lewis after them in Prince William County and When the prisoner was Brought home he Confessed to this Deponent upon his Examination that John Gregory and he went that Night[;] they run away to the House of William Lewis for Quarters the Next morning[;] having Borrowed a Bridle from the Negroes [281] They carried off Lewis's horse, and when this Deponent asked the Prisoner how the horse got away from him, the Prisoner told the Deponent that in Orange County after he had Left John Gregory his fellow Servant being tired with Riding and very much Galled[;] he alighted to walk and as he was leading the Horse by the Bridle along the road the bridle Slipt off the Horses head and thereupon the Horse got away from him and he could Never after catch him wherefore he kept on his way to Sherrando afoot and this Deponent farther Saith that he was present at Mr. Belfields when the Prisoner Made the Confession by him[,] the deponent[,] Attestd but Refused to Sign the Same and farther saith Not.

WILLIAM KENNAN

William Lewis [of] Lunenburg Parish in Richmond County being Sworn Says that on Saturday the 29th of December 1739 he was from home and did not Return till Tuesday Night following when he heard his Black horse was Stolen and it was Suspected to be done by Mr. Kennans Servants who were then Run-away[;] whereupon this Deponent went to the house of Mr. Kennan and got from him, three Hue and Crys[131] and on the Friday morning thereafter this Deponent Set of[f] in Quest of his horse and the said Runaways, but when he got to Duffs Ordinary he met the Constable with one of the Said Runaways Viz John Gregory Returning to his Masters which Said Gregory upon this Deponents Enquiring of him what was become of his fellow Servant the prisoner he told this Deponent that he was gone along Towards Sherando with his[,] the Deponents[,] horse upon which the Deponent made all the Dispatch he could to Over take the

_____

131. Three men to assist Lewis in capturing the runaways.

prisoner and heard when he had got into Orange County that the prisoner was Seen going a foot towards Sherrando where upon, this Deponent Turnd back and Enquiring after the horse he heard of him in the Great Fork in the County of Orange [282] and there he found him and was Told by the people that helpt this Deponent to get his horse again that a boy whom they discribed to be Exactly resembling the prisoner was seen [to] Ride that horse a day or two before and this Deponent father Saith that he was present at Mr. Belfields when the Prisoner made the Confession by him[,] this Deponent[,] attested and farther saith Not.

WILLIAM LEWIS

It appearing to the Court upon the Aforesaid Examination that there is Just Cause for Trying the Said John Jones at the Generall Court for the crime aforesaid where he is accused It is there for Ordered that the Said John Jones be Remanded to the prison of this County under the Custody of the Sherrif and from thence to be Conveyed to the publick Goal of Williamsberg as the Law in Such Cases Directs. The within Named John Jones acknowledged in open Court that he was Convicted in Great Britain, that he was Sentenced to be Transported for Seven Years and was Imported in the Ship Dorchester Captain William Loney Commander and Came into Rappahanock River the Sixth day of February 1736 which is Orderd to be Certifyed by Marmaduke Beckwith Clerk [of] Court.

[Kennan's recognizance]

William Kennan of Richmond County in Open Court before his Majestys Justices Acknowleded himself Indebted to our Sovereign Lord the King his heirs and Successors in the Sum of Ten pounds Sterling to be levyed of his Lands and Tenements Goods and Chattles with Condition that if the Said William Kennan Shall personally appear at the Next Generall Court on the fourth Day there of and then and there [283] Give Such Evidence as he Knows against John Jones who Stands Committed for Fellony and Doe not Depart thence without leave of that Court that then this Recognize to be Void or Else to Remain in Full Force.

William Lewis the Same.

Mr. William Kennan for his Servant Man (John Gregory) the Same.

At a Court for Richmond County the Third Day of March 1739/40.

Present: William Fantleroy, Thomas Wright Belfield, John Woodbridge, Thomas Barber, Landon Carter, Leroy Griffin, Daniel Hornby, Anthony Sydnor, Gentleman Justices.

Creele bound to his behaviour

It appearing to this Court that William Creele of Northfarnham Parish is a person of an ill Behaviour it is therefore Orderd that he Give Good and Sufficient Security for his Good Behaviour During the Term of one Year.

Whereupon the Said William Creele Together with Richard Brown his Security in Open Court Acknowledged themselves Indebted unto our Sovereign Lord the King his heirs and Successors in the Sum of Twenty pounds Sterling to be levied of their Lands and Tenements Good[s] and Chattles with Condition that if the Said William Creele shall be of Good Behavour as well towards his Majesty as all his Leige people, that then this Recognizance to be Void and of None Effect, or Else to Remain in full Force and Vertue.

Hightower bound to his behaviour

It appearing to this Court that John Hightower of Northfarnham Parish is a person of an ill Behaviour, it is therefore ordered that he Give Good and Sufficient Security for [284] his good behaviour During the Term of one Year.

Whereupon the Said John Hightower Together with John Williams his Security in open Court Acknowledged them Selves Indebted unto our Sovereign Lord the King his heirs and Successors in the Sum of Twenty Pounds Sterling to be Levid on their Lands and Tenements Goods and Chattles, with Condition, that if the Said John Hightower Shall be of Good Behaviour, as well towards his Majestye as all his Leige People, that then this Recognizance to be Void and of None Effect or Else to Remain in full force and Virtue.

At a Court Continued and held for Richmond County the 7th Day of March 1739/40.

Present: John Woodbridge, Thomas Barber, Leroy Griffin, Daniel Hornby, Anthony Sydnor, John Smith, Gentlemen Justices.

Pally bound to his behavior

John Pally of Northfarnham parish having been Summoned to Answer the presentment of the Grandjury against him for being a prophane Swearer and this Day appearing but Offering Nothing Material to Excuse himself it is the Oppinion of this Court, and Accordingly Ordered that for the Said Offence he Give Good and Sufficient Security for his Good Behaviour During the Term of one Year.

Whereupon the Said John Pally Together with Billington McCarty his Security in Open Court Acknowledged themselves Indebted unto our Sovereign Lord the King his heirs and Successors in the Sum of Twenty pounds Sterling, to be Levied on their Lands and Tenements Goods and Chattles, with Condition that if the Said John Pally Shall be of Good [285] Behaviour as well Toward his Majestie as all his Leige people That then this Recognizance to be Void and of None Effect or Else to remain in full Force and Virtue.

Tillery bound to his behavior

William Tillery of Northfarnham parish having been Summoned to Answer the presentment of the Grandjury Against him for being a Common Drunkard and Disturber of the peace And this Day appearing but Offering Nothing Materiall to Excuse him Self it is the Oppinion of this Court and Accordingly Ordered that for the Said Offence he Give Good and Sufficient Security for his Good Behaviour During the Term of one Year.

Whereupon the Said William Tillery Together with Thomas Suggitt His Security in Open Court Acknowledged them Selves Indebted unto our Sovereign Lord the King his heirs and Successors in the Sum of Twenty Pounds Sterling to be Levyed on their Lands and Tenements Goods and Chattles with Condition, that if the said William Tillery Shall be of Good Behaviour as well Towards his Majesty as all his Leige People, That then this Recognizance to be Void, and of none Effect or Else to Remain in full Force and Vertue.

Tillery bound to his behavior

Henry Tillery of Northfarnham parish haveing been Summoned to Answer the presentment of the Grandjury against him for being a Common Drunkard and Disturber of the piece and this day Appearing but Offering Nothing material to Excuse him Self it is the Opinion of this Court and Accordingly Ordered that for the Said Offence he Give Good and Sufficient Security for his Good Behaviour During the Term of one Year.

Whereupon the said Henry Tillery Together with Thomas Suggitt and Henry Williams his Securitys in Open Court Acknowledged them Selves Indebted unto our Sovereign Lord the King his heirs and Successors in the Sum of Twenty pounds Sterling, to be Levied on their Lands and Tenements Goods and [**286**] Chattles with Condition that if the Said Henry Tillery Shall be of Good Behaviour as well towards his Majestie as all his Leige people, That then this Recognizance to be void and of None Effect or Else to remain in full force and Virtue.

Brady Bound to his behaviour

Owen Brady of Northfarnham parish having been Summoned to answer the presentment of the Grandjury against him for being a Common Disturber of the peace And this day appearing but Offering Nothing Materiall to Excuse himself it is the Opinion of this Court and Accordingly Ordered that for the Said offence he Give Good and Sufficient Security for his Good Behaviour, During the Term of one Year.

Whereupon the Said Owen Brady Together with Henry Williams his Security in open Court Acknowledged themselves Indebted to our Sovereign Lord the King his heirs and Successors in the Sum of Twenty pounds Sterling, to be Levied on their Lands and Tenements Goods and Chattles, with Condition that if the Said Owen Brady Shall be of Good Behaviour as well towards his Majestie as All his Leige people, That then this Recognizance to be Void and of None Effect or Else to Remain in full force and Vertue.

At a Court held for Richmond County the Seventh Day of Aprill 1740.

Present: William Fantleroy, Thomas Wright Belfield, Landon Carter, Daniel Hornby, Gentlemen Justices.

Medford to give Security for his Behaviour

It appearing to this Court that Henry Medford of Lunenburg parish, is a person of an ill Behaviour [287] It is therefore ordered that he Give Good and Sufficient Security for his Good Behaviour in the Sum of Twenty pounds Sterling and his Security in the Sum of Twenty pounds sterling And that he Remain in the Sherifs Custody until he gives Such Security.

Dawson bound to his behaviour

It appearing to this Court that Nicholas Dawson of Lunenburg parish is a person of an ill Behaviour, it is therefore Ordered that he give Good and Sufficient Security for his Good Behaviour, During the Term of one Year.

Whereupon the Said Nicholas Dawson Together with Wilson Holmes his Security, in Open Court Acknowledged themselves Indebted unto our Sovereign Lord the King his heirs and Successors in the Sum of Twenty pounds Sterling to be Levied on their Lands and Tenements Goods and Chattles, with Condition, That if the said Nicholas Dawson Shall be of Good Behaviour, as well Towards his Majestie, as all his Leige people, that then this Recognizance to be Void and of none Effect, or Else Remain in full Force and Virtue.

At a Court held for Richmond County the Second Day of June 1740.

Present: Thomas Wright Belfield, Thomas Barber, Leroy Griffin, Daniel Hornby, Anthony Sydnor, John Smith, Gentlemen Justices.

Freshwater bound to his Behaviour

It appearing to this Court that John Freshwater of Lunenburg parish is a person of an ill Behaviour, it is therefore Ordered that he Give Good and Sufficient Security for his Good Behaviour During the Term of one Year.

Whereupon the Said John Freshwater Together with Thomas Freshwater his Security in Open Court Acknowledged them [288] Selves Indebted unto our Sovereign Lord the King his heirs and Successors in the Sum of Twenty pounds Sterling to be Levied on their Lands and Tenements Goods and Chattles with Condition that if the Said John Freshwater Shall be of Good Behaviour as well Towards his Majestie as all his leige people, that then this Recognizance to be Void, and of None Effect or Else to Remain in full Force and Virtue.

At a Call'd Court held at the Court house of Richmond County on tuesday the eight day of July 1740.

Present: Thomas Wright Belfield, John Woodbridge, Thomas Barber and Gilbert Hamilton, Gentlemen Justices.

[*Gregory and Gorman's Examination*]

Whereas John Gregory and Ellinor Gorman of Lunenburg parish in Richmond County was by vertue of a Mittimus from Thomas Wright Belfield Gentleman one of the Justices of this court committed to this County Goale for feloniously breaking open the house of William Kennan the 25th June last and also for breaking open a Large Seal Skin trunk in an upper room of the said dwelling house and Stealing and carrying out of the said house the following Goods Viz: a Silver hilted Sword and leather Sword belt, one pair of fine holland Sheets, two pair of Course linnen Sheets, a Mans Coat and breeches, a German Serge Waiscoat two holland waiscoats, a pair of Mens Shoes etc. And being now brought before his Majestys Justices here present, and being asked what they had to say to what was laid to their charge, the said John Gregory answerd, that he was guilty, the said Ellinor Gorman said, it did not Signifye, to say anything.[132]

It is the opinion of this Court that there [**289**] is Just cause for trying the said John Gregory and Ellinor Gorman at the Generall court for the crime aforesaid where of they are accused. It is there fore ordered that the said John Gregory and Ellinor Gorman be remanded to the prison of this county under the Custody of the Sherriff, and from thence to conveyed to the public Goale of Williamsburg, as the Law in Such cases directs.

It appearing to this Court that Ellinor Gorman with in Named is a Convict, and was Imported in the Ship Dorchester Capt. Thomas Whiteing commander, and arrived in Rappanhanock River in the year 1739 which is ordered to be certified by

M. BECKWITH CC Cur. [Clerk of County Court]

[*Kennan's recognizance*]

William Kennan of Richmond County in open Court before his Majestys Justices Acknowledged him Self Indebted to our Sovereign Lord the King his heirs and Successors in the Sum of tenn pound[s] Sterling to be levyed of his Lands and Tenements Goods and Chattles with Condition that if the said William Kennan Shall personally appear at the Next Generall Court on the fourth day thereof and then and there Give Such Evidence as he Knows against John Gregory and Ellinor Gorman who stands Committed for Felony and doe not

---

132. Her refusal to plead did not require any action by the examining court, although if she remained mute at the General Court, she would be recorded as pleading guilty. Rankin, *Criminal Trial Proceedings*, 59, n. 28, finds no one "pressed" to death for standing mute, but under an arson statute (*Statutes at Large*, 4:271–73 [1730]), a person standing mute to an indictment "shall be adjudged a felon." In England judges were to record a person standing "obstinately" mute or refusing to plead to a felony indictment as guilty, but those who were mute for want of reason were to be regarded as pleading not guilty; Blackstone, *Commentaries*, 4:319–20.

Depart thence without Leave of that Court that this Recognizance to be Void or Else to Remain in full force.

William Dixon the Same.

Edward Eidson the Same.

[**290**] At a court continued and held for Richmond County the 3d day of March 1740/1.

Present: Thomas Wright Belfield, Landon Carter, Daniell Hornby, Gilbert Hamilton, Gentlemen Justices.

Pridham bound to his behaviour

Edward Pridham of Lunenburg parish having been Summoned to Answer the presentment of the Grandjury against him for being a common disturber of the Peace and this day Appearing but offering nothing Material to Excuse himself It is the Opinion of this court and Accordingly ordered that for the said Offence he give good and Sufficient Security in the sum of Twenty pounds Sterling for his keeping the same dureing the terme of one Year.

Whereupon the said Edward Pridham together with Joseph Russell Jr. his Security in open court Acknowledged themselves Indebted unto our Sovereign Lord the King his heirs and Successors in the sum of Twenty Pounds sterling to be Levyed on their Lands and Tenements Goods and Chattles with Condition That if the said Edward Pridham shall Keep the Peace of our Sovereign Lord the King as well towards his said Majestye and all his leige people That then, This Recognizance to be Void and of None Effect or Else to Remain in Full force.

Haise bound to his behaviour

Whereas Henry Hays of Lunenburg parish This day Appearing to answer the Presentment of the Grandjury against him for being a common Swearer but Offering Nothing Material to Excuse himselfe It is the Opinion of this Court and According[ly] Ordered that for the said Offence he Give Good and Sufficient Security [**291**] for his Good Behaviour during the terme of one Year.

Whereupon the said Henry Hayes Together with Tobias Pursell his Security in Open Court Acknowledged themselves Indebted unto Our Soverain Lord Lord the King his heirs And Successors in the sum of Twenty Pounds Sterling to be Levyed on their Lands and Tenements Goods and Chattles with condition that if the said Henry Hayes Shall be of good Behaviour as well toward his Majesty as all his Lege People That then this Recognisance to be Void and of None Effect or Else to Remain in full Force.

At a Court held for Richmond County the Sixth Day of July 1741.

Present: Thomas Wright Belfield, Thomas Barber, Landon Carter, Leroy Griffin and William Jordan, Gentlemen Justices.

Dew fined

At a Court held for This County the Fourth Day of May Last Thomas Dew of Northfarnham parish was presented by the Grandjury for Keeping a Tipling house[133] and the said Dew this Day apearing and Confessing the Fact Thereupon on the motion of Charles Beale Gentleman the Kings Attorney Judgement is Granted our said Lord the King against the said Thomas Dew For Two Thousand pounds of Tobacco pursuant To the Law in That Case made and provided Together With Costs.

White bound to his behaviour

It appearing to this Court that John White of Northfarnham Parish is a person of an ill Behaviour it is Therefore ordered that he Give Good and Sufficient Security for his Good Behaviour Dureing the Terme of one year.

Whereupon the said John White Together With John Morgan and Andrew Morgan his Securitys in open Court acknowledged Themselves Indebted to our Sovereign Lord the King in the [**292**] Sum of Ten pounds Sterling to be Levied on Their Lands and Tenements Good and Chattles with Condition that if the said John White Shall be of Good Behaviour as well Towards his said Majestye as all his Leige People that Then This Recognizance to be Void and of None Effect or Else to remain in Full Force.

At a Court held for Richmond County the Third Day of August 1741.

Present: Thomas Wright Belfield, John Woodbridge, Thomas Barber, Landon Carter, William Jordan, William Brockenbrough, Gentlemen Justices.

[Hobbs bound to his behaviour]

It appearing to This court That James Hobbs of Northfarnham parish is a person of an Ill Behaviour it is Therefore Ordered That he give Good and Sufficient Security for his Good behaviour, During the Terme of one year. Whereupon the said James Hobbs Together with Charles Jones and Michael Connell his Securitys in Open Court acknowledged Themselves Indebted to our Sovereign Lord The King in The sum of Ten pounds Sterling to be Levyed on Their Lands and Tenements Goods and Chattles with Condition That if the said James Hobbs Shall be of Good Behaviour as well Towards his said Majesty, as all his Leige people, That then This recognizance to be Void and of None Effect, or Else to remain in Full force.

[**293**] At a Call'd Court held at the Court house of Richmond County the 2d Day of September 1741.

---

133. Selling liquor without a license in one's home was still an offense; Webb, *Justice of Peace*, 242. Dew's presentment is recorded in ROB, No. 11, 174 (1741).

Present: Landon Carter, Leroy Griffin, Gilbert Hamilton, John Smith and William Brockenbrough, Gentlemen Justices.

Hobbs's Examination

Whereas James Hobbs was by Virtue of a Mittimus from Leroy Griffin Gentleman one of the Justices of this County Committed to the County Goale on Suspition of Felony[134] and being now Brought before his Majestys Justices now present and Together with Several Wittnesses being Diligently Examined Touching the said Fact, it appearing to this Court that there is Just Cause for Trying the said prisoner at the Next Generall Court for the Crime aforesaid Where of he is accused, it is Therefore ordered that the said James Hobbs be Remanded to the prison of This County under the Custody of the Sherrif, and from Thence to be Conveyed to the publick Goale of Williams Burg as the Law in Such Cases Directs.

[Luill's recognizance]

Mathew Luill Gentleman of Northumberland County in Open Court before his Majestys Justices Acknowledged himself Indebted to our Sovereign Lord the King his heirs and Successors in The Sum of Ten pounds Sterling to be Levyed of his Lands and Tenements Goods and Chattles with Condition That if he the said Mathew Luill, Shall personally appear at the Next Generall Court, on the Sixth Day There of, and Then and There Give Such Evidence as he Knows against James Hobbs who Stands Committed for Felony, and Doe Not Depart Thence without Leave of that Court, that then this Recognizance to be Void, or Else to Remain in Full Force.

Edward Bates of Richmond County the Same.

Edward Bates for his Two Servants the Same.

[**294**] At a Call'd Court held at the Court house of Richmond County on Thursday the 12th [14th or 21st] Day of January 1741/2.

Present: John Woodbridge, Thomas Barber, Daniell Hornby, Gilbert Hamilton and John Smith, Gentlemen Justices.

Toole and others Whipt

Whereas James Toole Ann Toole alias Pratt and Owin Carnon by Vertue of a mittimus from John Woodbridge and Gilbert Hamilton Gentlemen Two of the Justices of this Court was Committed to the County Goale on Suspition of Steal-

---

134. The word "felony" was occasionally used as a substitute for a felonious theft in criminal court records. In Virginia, the generic term "felony" denoted a crime serious enough to require trial at the General Court.

ing one Red Rugg From Willoughby Newton Gentleman and being Now Brought before Majestys Justices here Present on Examination of Severall Evidences Touching the same, It is the Opinion of This Court that They are Guilty of the Crime Laid to Their Charge, it is Therefore Ordered that the Sherrif Take Them and Carry Them to the Common Whipping post and Give Each of Them Thirty Nine Lashes on their Bare Backs Well Laid on.

At a Called Court held at the Court house of Richmond County on Fryday the 22d Day of January 1741/2.

Present: William Fantleroy, Thomas Wright Belfield, John Woodbridge, Thomas Barber, Daniell Hornby, Gilbert Hamilton, William Brockenbrough, Gentlemen Justices.

Carnons Examination

Whereas Owin Carnon of Lunenburg parish in this County was by Vertue of a mittimus From John Woodbridge Gentleman one of the Magistrates of this County Committed to this County Goale For haveing Taken from one Dominick Newgent one New Coat and Vest and Other Things to the Vallue of Forty Shillings Current Money and being Now Brought before his Majestys Justices here present, and being asked [295] What he had to Say, to What was Laid to his Charge, Answered that on the Twelfth Day of November Last past in the Evening he found The Coat and Jackett (produced in court) Near the prison of this County Near the Main Road and That he Carryed them from thence that Night to Mr. Landon Carters, and Sometime afterwards Carryed them Home and hid them in his Masters (James Tooles) Fodder house, and there concealed them Till the Monday after Christmas, when he Gave them to Michaell Ferrill to Dispose of for him.

This Examination was offered to the prisoner to be Signed, which he Refused.

The Deposition of Dominick Newgent of Northfarnham Parish in this County Taken upon the Examination of Owin Carnon a prisoner Committed for the Felonious Taking his (the said Newgent['s] Coat and Vest) being Sworn in Court Saith That on the 12th Day of November Last past in the Evening, he upon Some provocation offered him, Stript of[f] his Coat Jackett and Shirt[135] and Laid Them and his hat Down about Twenty Five yards Below the Prison, and That Within about Three minutes after Going to put Them on, he missed them, and Verily Believes that the Coat and Jackett produced in Court, are his, and are the same, That he Then Lost.

D. Newgent

The Deposition of James Leith of Lunenburg parish in this County Taken upon the Examination of Owin Carnon a prisoner Committed for Feloniously Taking a Coat and Vest from one Dominick Newgent, being Sworn in Court Sayth, That on Sunday the 15th Day of November Last he Saw a Coat and

---

135. In order to fight, possibly.

Jackett in the Room at Mr. Landon Carters Where James Toole And Owin Carnon Lay, Which Owin Carnon Said Belonged to him, That the Night after the said Carnon, put the same into This Deponents chest Where they Lay till Wednesday morning and Then This Deponent Threw them out, and the Next Saturday the said Carnon Came and Cary'd them away.

JAMES LEITH

[**296**] It appearing to this Court upon the aforesaid Examination That There is Just Cause for Trying the said Owin Carnon at the Next Generall Court For the Crime aofresaid Whereof he is accused It Is Therefore Ordered that the said Owin Carnon be Remanded to the prison of this County under the Custody of the Sherrif and From Thence to be Conveyed to the publick Goale of Williams Burgh as the Law in Such Cases Directs.

[*Newgent's recognizance*]

Dominick Newgent of Richmond County in Open Court Before his Majestys Justices acknowledged himself Indebted to our Sovereign Lord the King his heirs and Successors in the Sum of Tenn pounds Sterling to be Levied of his Lands and Tenements Goods and Chattles with Condition that if the said Dominck Newgent Shall personally appear at The Next Generall Court on the Fourth Day Thereof and Then and There Give Such Evidence as he knows against Owin Carnon Who Stands Committed For Felony and Doe Not Depart Thence Without Leave of that Court That Then This Recognizance to be Void or Else to Remain in Full Force.

Mr. Gilbert Hamilton of Richmond County For George Leith the same.

Ferrill Whipt

It appearing to this Court that Michaell Ferrill Received Stolen Goods[136] from Owin Carnon it is Therefor Ordered That For the said Offence the Sherrif Take him and Carry him to the Common Whipping post and Give him Thirty Nine Lashes on his Bare Back Well Laid on.

[**297**] At a Court Continued and held for Richmond County the Second Day of February 1741/42.

Present: John Woodbridge, Thomas Barber, Daniell Hornby, Gilbert Hamilton and William Brockenbrough, Gentlemen Justices.

Toole bound to his Behaviour

James Toole and Benjamin Rust both of Lunenburg Parish in this County in Open Court acknowledged Themselves Indebted to our Sovereign Lord the King the said James Toole in the sum of Twenty pounds Sterling and the said

---

136. The court has decided that Ferrill knew the goods were stolen.

Benjamin Rust in the Sum of Ten pounds Sterling to be Levied on their Lands and Tenements Goods and Chattles with Condition that if the said James Toole Shall be of Good Behaviour Dureing the Terme of one year, as Well Towards his said Majesty as all his Leige people that, then This Recognizance to be Void and of None Effect Else to Remain in Full force.

At a Court held for Richmond County the 5th day of Aprill 1742.

Present: William Fantleroy, Thomas Wright Belfield, John Woodbridge, William Jordan, and John Smith, Gentlemen Justices.

Thomas bound to his Behaviour

It appearing to this Court that Joshua Thomas of Lunenburg parish is a person of an ill behaviour, it is therefore ordered that he give good and sufficient security for his good behavour, Dureing the Terme of one year.

Whereupon the said Joshua Thomas Together with Benjamin Rust Simon Sallard and George Taylor his Securitys in open Court acknowledged themselves Indebted to our sovereign Lord the King in the sum of Twenty pounds Sterling to be Levied on their Lands and Tenements, goods and Chattles with Condition that if the said Joshua Thomas shall be of good Behaviour as well Towards his said Majestye as all his Leige people, that then this Recognizance to be void, and of None Effect or Else to Remain in Full Force.

Samson a Negro his Tryall

[298] At a Session of Oyer and Terminer held at Richmond, Courthouse on Monday the Third Day of May 1742, in the Fifteenth year of the Reign of our sovereign Lord George the second by the grace of god of Great Britain France and Ireland King Defender of the Faith etc. by Vertue of a special Commission For the Tryall of all Treasons petit Treasons or misprisions thereof Felonys Murders or other offences or Crimes Whatsoever Committed within this County of Richmond by a negro man Slave Named samson Belonging to James Carter of this County and Directed William Fauntleroy Charles Grimes Samuel Peachy Newman Brockenbrough Thomas Wright Belfield John Woodbridge Thomas Barber William Glascock Landon Carter Leroy Griffin Daniel Hornby William Jordan Gilbert Hamilton William Fantleroy Jr. John Smith and William Brockenbrough Gentlemen.

Present: Thomas Wright Belfield, Thomas Barber, Landon Carter, Daniell Hornby, William Jordan, Gilbert Hamilton, John Smith, William Brockenbrough, Gentlemen Justices.

Memorandum—That on this present Day being the Third Day of May 1742, an Indictment was prefer'd against a Negro man Slave Called samson Belonging to James Carter of this County in this words. "Richmond Ss. Memorandum that

William Kennan Gentleman attorney Deputed of our Lord the King in the County aforesaid for this purpose Especially appointed comes here into Court in his proper person[137] this Third Day of May in the year of our Lord one Thousand seven hundred Forty Two and gives the Court hereto understand and be Informed That Sampson, a Negro man Slave Belonging to James Carter of the said County of Richmond on the Twenty Second Day of Aprill in the Fifteenth year of the Reign of our Lord George the second by the grace of God now King of Great Britain France and Ireland Defender of the Faith with force and armes the Kitchen of one Maurice Lynn of the parish of Lunenburg in [**299**] the County aforesaid feloniously did Break and enter in the Night Time[,] Eighty pounds of Bacon of the Vallue of Thirty shillings Currant Money the proper goods and Chattles of the said Maurice Lynn in the said Kitchen then Found then and there Feloniously did Take Steal and Carry away against the peace of our said Now Lord the King his Crown and Dignity etc.["]

Whereupon the said Sampson was brought to the barr and arraigned for the said Fellony and there Pleaded not Guilty and Thereupon the Court Proceeding on his Tryall (after having heard Evidence against him and what he had to say in his Defence) are of opinion that he is Guilty of the Felony mentioned in the said Indictment within the Benefit of Clergy whereupon the said Sampson Pray'd the said Benefit[138] and accordingly was burnt in the Hand at the barr with a hot Iron and ordered that the Sherif Carry him to the Comon whipping Post and give him Twenty Five Lashes on his bare back well Laid on.

At a Court held for Richmond County held 3d Day of May 1742.

Present: Thomas Barber, Gilbert Hamilton, John Smith, William Brockenbrough, Gentlemen Justices.

Deacons bound to his Behaviour

It appearing to this Court that William Deacons of Lunenburg Parish is a person of an Ill Behaviour it is therefore ordered that he give good and sufficient security for his Good Behaviour Dureing the Term of one year.

Whereupon the said William Deacons Together with Henry Williams and Archibald Mitchell his securitys in open Court acknowledged themselves Indebted to our sovereign Lord the King his heirs and successors in the sum of Twenty pounds Sterling to be Levyed on their Lands and Tenements, goods and Chattles, with Condition that if the said William Deacons, shall be of Good

---

137. Kennan was specially appointed to act as the king's attorney for this oyer and terminer court. The phrase was to become a permanent part of the document.

138. To clear up a confusing area of the law, benefit of clergy was assured to slaves convicted of felonies (*Statutes at Large*, 4:325–27 [1732]), except for manslaughter and breaking and entering with theft of more than 5s. worth of goods (crimes which were clergyable when committed by a free person), murder, treason, burglary, and robbery.

Behaviour as well Towards his said Majestye, as all his Leige people, That then this Recognizance to be Void and of None Effect or Else to Remain in Full Force.

Samson a Negro his Tryall

[**300**] At a Session of Oyer and Terminer held at Richmond Court house on saturday the Twenty Ninth day of May 1742, in the Fifteenth year of the Reign of our sovereign Lord George the second by the grace of God of great Britain France and Ireland King Defender of the Faith etc. by Virtue of a special comission For the Tryall of all Treasons petit Treasons, or misprisions thereof Felonys Murders or other Offences or Crimes Whatsoever Committed within this County of Richmond, by a Negro man Slave named Samson Belonging to James Carter of this County and Directed to William Fantleroy Charles Grymes Samuell Peachey Newman Brockenbrough Thomas Wright Belfield John Woodbridge Thomas Barber William Glascock Landon Carter Leroy Griffin Daniel Hornby William Jordan Gilbert Hamilton William Fantleroy Jr. John Smith and William Brockenbrough Gentlemen.

Present: Thomas Barber, Leroy Griffin, Daniell Hornby, Gilbert Hamilton, William Brockenbrough, Gentlemen Justices.

Memorandum That on this present day being the Twenty Ninth Day of May 1742 An Indictment was preferred against a Negro man Slave Called Samson Belonging to James Carter of this County in these words. "Richmond Ss. Be it Remembered that William Kennan Deputed attorney of our Lord the now King for that purpose Specially appointed comes here in to the Court of our said Lord the King in his proper person and gives the Justices of the said Court to understand and be informed that samson a Negro Slave in the Eight day of may 1742 at the parish of Lunenburg in the said County of Richmond with force and armes the Inclosure of a Certain Landon Carter Gentleman did Break and Enter and one Gelding of a grey color of the price of Ten pounds Sterling[,] the proper Gelding of one Henry Hays of the said County and parish[,] there haveing found did Feloniously Take and Lead away against the peace of our said Lord the King his Crown and Dignity etc. Whereupon the said attorney of our Lord the King prays the advice of the Justices of the said court and poscess [process] of Law etc. against the said Samson according to due Course

WILLIAM KENNAN

[**301**] Whereupon the said Samson was Brought to the Barr and arraigned for the said Felony and there pleaded Not Guilty, and thereupon the Court proceeding in his Tryall (after the Hearing the Evidence of Henry Haise against him, and what he had to say in his Defence) are of opinion that he is Not guilty of the Felony for which he stands Indicted, it is therefore ordered that he be acquitted.

At a Court held for Richmond County The Third day of January 1742/3.
Present: Thomas Wright Belfield, John Woodbridge, Thomas Barber, Daniell Hornby, William Jordan, Gentlemen Justices.

Feegins bounds to his behaviour

It appearing to this Court that George Feegins of North Farnham Parish is a Person of an Ill behaviour it is therefore ordered that he give good and Sufficient Security for his good Behaviour dureing the terme of one whole year Whereupon the said George Feegins together with John Oldham his Security in open Court Acknowledged Themselves Indebted unto our Sovereign Lord the King his heirs and Successors in the sum of Twenty Pounds Sterling to be levyed on their Lands and Tenements goods and Chattles with condition that if the said George Feegins Shall be of good Behaviour as well towards his said Majestye and all his Liege People that then this Recognizance to be Void and of none Effect or Else to Remain in Full force.

At a Court held for Richmond County the Seventh day of February 1742/3.
Present: Thomas Wright Belfield, Thomas Barber, William Jordan, Anthony Sydnor and William Fantleroy Jr., Gentlemen Justices.

Efford Bound to his Behaviour

[302] It appearing to this Court that John Efford of North Farnham Parish is a Person of Ill Behaviour It is therefore ordered that he give good and Sufficient Security for his good Behaviour Whereupon the said John Efford Together with Thomas Jesper Jr. and William Lyell his Securitys in open court Acknowledged Themselves Indebted to our Sovereign Lord the King his heirs and Successors in the Sum of Twenty Pounds Sterling to be Levyed on their Lands and Tenements Good and Chattles With Condition that if the said John Efford Shall be of good Behaviour as well Toward his said Majestye as towards his Liege People that then This Recognisance to be void and of none Effect or else to Remain in Full force and Virtue.

At a Call'd Court held at the Court house of Richmond County on Wednesday the 30th day of March 1743.
Present: Thomas Wright Belfield, Thomas Barber, William Fantleroy Jr., and Travers Tarpley, Gentlemen Justices.

Dogaty's Examination

Whereas Mathew Dogaty of North Farnham parish in this County was by Virtue of a mittimus From Travers Tarpley Gentleman one of the Majestrates of this Country committed to this County Goal for Feloniously breaking and Entering the Chest of the James Hinds of the said Parish and Stealing thereout Sundry Peices of Silver of the Value of Forty Shillings Currant Money[139]—And Being Now Brought before his Majestyes Justices here Present and being asked what he had to say to what was Laid to his Charge Answered he was Not Guilty.

[303] James Hinds of North Farnham Parish in this County being Sworn says That on Monday Last was Five Weaks[140] he Went and opened his Chest and see some money that he had in it and on Monday Following in the Evening he went again; the lock was broke and the Money was gone and to the Best of his knowledge he Lost one French Crown, one Spanish Crown two Peices of eight two Mill'd half Crowns Four Pistreens and some bills all in a Dear Skin Purse.

William Tune of Northfarnham Parish in this County being sworn says that on monday was seven night[141] Mr. Sydnor Negroes brought Mathew Dogaty the Prisoner to Christopher Lawsons, and upon Searching him he found a Peice of Eight in his bosome and upon Searching further found in the Knee of his breeches a ragg with some money in it and gave it to Christoper Lawson.

Christoper Lawson of North Farnham Parish in the County being sworn says that on Monday was seven Night being at his own house[,] Thomas Dews Servant man told him to search Mathew Dogaty and he would Find Money about him upon which William Tune searcht the said Dogaty and found one Peice of Eight and some other money in the knee of his Breeches.

It appearing to this Court upon the aforesaid Examination that their is Just Cause for trying the said Mathew Dogaty at the Generall Court for the Crime aforesaid Whereof he is accused. It is therefore ordered that the said Mathew Dogaty be Remainded to the Prison of this County under the Custody of the Sherrif and from Thence to be conveyed to the Publick Goale of Williamsburg as the law in Such Cases Directs.

[Hind's recognizance]

[304] James Hinds of Richmond County in Open Court before his Majestys Justices Acknowledged himself indebted to our Sovereign Lord the King his heirs and Successors in the Sum of Ten Pounds Sterling to be Levyed of his Lands and Tenements Goods and Chattels with Condition that if the said Thomas Hinds shall Personally appear at the Next General Court on the Fourth Day thereof and then and There Give Such Evidence as he knows against Mathew Dogaty who stands Committed for Felony and do not Depart thence without Leave of that Court That then this Recognizance to be Void or Else to Remain in full force.

William Tune of Richmond County the same.
Christopher Lawson of Richmond County the same.

---

139. Coins equivalent in value to 40s. of Virginia paper currency.
140. Five weeks before his testimony in court.
141. One week before.

At a call'd Court held at the Court House of Richmond County on Wednesday the 18th day of May 1742.

Present: Samuell Peachey, John Woodbridge, Daniell Hornby, John Taylor Jr., John Smith, Thomas Plummer, Alvin Mountjoy, Gentlemen Justices.

Lee's Examination

Whereas William Lee of Lunenburg parish in this County was by Virtue of a Mittimus from Samuell Peachey Gentleman one of the Justices of this Court Committed to this County Goale for Feloniously Killing Will a Man Slave Belonging [305] To Thomas Barber Gentleman and being Now Brought before his Majestys Justices here Present the Severall Evidences on behalf of the King were Examined as follows.

William Lyell of North Farnham Parish being First Sworn Saith that on The Second day of May in the Night in Company with William Tillery, went to the Quarter of Mr. Edgecomb Suggit and Took Will a Negro Man belonging to Capt. Thomas Barber who was Runaway and then[,] under an Out Lawry[,] that they Carried the said Negro Home to his Master that Night, And the Next Morning as soon as it was Light Capt. Barber tied him up and Whipt him a Considerable time and Then Sent for his Overseer who Came and by the said Barbers Order whipt him with a catt of Nine tails and Cowskin whip, And Believes that the said Negro Under the Whipping of his Master and Overseer Received about Two hundred Lashes, That dureing the Whiping the said Negro behaved himself Very Sullenly and stubbornly and he[,] often Requested by the Standersby to Submit and beg his Masters Pardon[,] he could Hardly be Prevaled to ask it, and further this deponent saith not.

WILLIAM LYELL

William Dobbins of North Farnham parish being sworn Saith, that on the Fourth day of this Instant May he Went to Capt. Barbers and Heard William Lee Threatning the Negroe will[;] that He went to the Kitchin Where they were and heard the said Lee order the Negroe to Pull off his Jackett[,] who answered that he was so Sore that he Could Not and would Not Pull it off, Upon Which Lee damn'd him and Swore he would have his Hearts Blood out but that he would have it off, And gave him Severall Licks with an Hickory Switch and Sent a Negroe Girl out for a Switch he had at [306] the End of the ditch[;] That while the Girl was gone the Negro Run off and Endeavoured to Escape but that this Deponent and the said Lee caught him Before he got far off; that when he was Taken the said Lee stamp upon his Eye and Kicked him on the Mouth and Carried him Back and Stript And tied up the Negroe and Whipt him and Washed him in Brine, And further this Deponent Saith not.

WILLIAM DOBBINS

George Freshwater of Lunenburg parish being Sworn saith on the Third of May, Instant he this Deponent was at Work near the Road and Saw William Lee come up with the Negro Will, That the said Negro was very Stubborn and would not go along as the said Lee would Have him[;] upon which Lee gave him Eight or ten licks with his Cowskin Whip[;] That the Next Morning he was at work at the same Place and over against it were Capt. Barbers Negros and the said Lee[;]

That upon the Negroe (Will) not working as he would have him he Saw Lee give him a couple of Licks, And further this deponent Saith not.

his
GEORGE FRESHWATER
mark

Thomas Barber gentleman of Lunenburg parish being Sworn saith that after the Negroe Will was Brought home and Whipt as above is related, he ordered his Overseer William Lee to Carry Him to the Smiths and get him Ironed to Prevent his Running away, That the said Lee did not Return till Late at Night and When he Came in this Deponent Heard the [**307**] said Lee tell this Deponents Wife that he was oblidged to Beat Will in Carrying him to the Smiths five Times as Much as he had done Before[,] for that he could not Get him a long without it[;] That the said Negro on the Sixth of May began to Complain of a Pain in his Belly and Stomack and in his Shoulders and afterward of a Pain all over him in Which Condition he Continued till the Tenth in the Night When he died.

THOMAS BARBER

It appearing to this court by the coroners Inquest as also by the depositions of the Evidences that their is Just Cause for trying the said William Lee at the Next Court of Oyer and Terminer to be held at his Majestys Royall Capitol for the Crime aforesaid Whereof he is Accused, upon Which the said William Lee Prayed that he might be admitted to Baile, which is Granted.[142]

[Lee's recognizance]

Whereupon the said William Lee together with John Dozer of Lunenburg parish his Security, in open Court acknowledged themselves Indebted unto our Sovereign lord the King, the said Lee in the sum 200 pounds Sterling and the said Dozier in the sum of one Hundred Pounds Sterling to be levyed on their Lands and Tenements, goods and Chattles, With condition, that if the Said William Lee Shall Personally appear at the Next Court of Oyer and Terminer to be held at his Majestys Royall Capitol in the Citty of Williamsburg and so attend from time to time as the said Court Shall Direct that then this Recognisance to be Void and of None Effect, or Else to Remain in full force.

[**308**] At a Court held for Richmond County the Third day of August 1743.
Present: John Woodbridge, Thomas Barber, John Smith, Travers Tarpley, and Alvin Mountjoy, Gentlemen Justices.

Freshwater fined

It being Proved to this Court that John Freshwater of North Farnham parish Refused to assist Owin Brady one of the under Sherrifs of the County in Keep-

---

142. Lee's offense must have been manslaughter, for murder was not bailable. If the justices found that the blows which killed the slave were meant only to correct or discipline him, there was no crime; *Statutes at Large*, 4:133 (1723).

ing the Peace, It is therefore Ordered that for the said offence he be fined one Shilling to our Sovereign Lord the King.

At a call'd Court held at the Court House of Richmond County on Monday the 24th day of October 1743.

Present: Samuell Peachey, John Woodbridge, Anthony Sydnor, William Brockenbrough, John Tarpley and Thomas Plummer, Gentlemen Justices.

McCoy's Examination

Whereas James McCoy of this County was by Vertue of a Mittimus from John Woodbridge Gentleman one of the Majestrates of this County Committed to this County Goale on Suspicion of Haveing feloniously taken from Travers Colston of Northumberland County Gentleman one Crop Note Marked WE No. 1 Granted to William Hames Jr. and being Now Brought before his Majestys Justices here Present and being Asked what he had to Say to what was Laid to His Charge answered that he found the said Note in the Road Near Metcalfe Dickensons.

[**309**] The deposition of Patrick Cheap Gentleman Taken upon the Examination of James McCoy Charged With the Felonious taking of an Inspectors Note[143] from Travers Colston of the county of Northumberland. This Deponent being Sworn in Court Saith that on the Twenty Ninth Day of June Last the Prisoner at the Barr Came to this Deponent's Store at Nurbana in the County of Middlesex and Laid out With him[,] by the Name of James Stewart[,] a Crop Note from Tososkey Warehouse Mark't W E No. 1 Weighing 980.93.887 Paiable Williams Jr. for which he Received goods and Money to the Value thereof according to their Agreement[;] That upon the Prisoners going out of his Store this Deponent was asked by Mr. John Walker[,] whom he met[,] if he this Deponent Knew the Prisoner and upon his answering in the Negative the said Walker told him the Prisoners Name was James McCoy Whom he Suspected to Have Stolen his Plate Some Time Before, and Further this Deponent Saith Not.

PATRICK CHEAP

The Deposition of Henry Miskell taken upon the above Examination.

This Deponent being Sworn in Court Saith, That upon the Eleventh Day of March last, he with the other Inspector gave out one Inspectors Note for a Hodghead of Tobacco Mark't WE No. 1 Weighing 930: 93: 887[144] Payable to William Hames Jr. that some time afterwards there was a Certificate obtained by Travers Colston from Samuell Peachey Gentleman for the said Note as Lost or Mislaid upon which this Deponent gave him out another Note for the said

---

143. At every public tobacco warehouse, two men appointed by the governor served as inspectors. They opened hogsheads of tobacco, certified that the quality was first rate (or ordered the removal of seconds), then weighed and priced the tobacco. This information was written on the receipt; Webb, *Justice of Peace,* 332.

144. A hogshead of tobacco was a large cask, with capacity for about thirty pounds of the crop, or about sixty-three gallons of fluid.

Hogshead Since Which the said First Mentioned Note has been Presented to Him this Deponent by the order of John Harvey Gentleman and further this Deponent Saith not.

HENRY MISKELL

[**310**] It appearing to this Court upon the aforesaid Examination that there is Just Cause for Trying the said James McCoy at the Next Court of Oyer and Terminer to be Held at his Majestys Royall Capitoll for the crime aforesaid whereof he is accused, It is therefore ordered That the said James McCoy be Remanded to the Prison of this County under the Custody of the Sherrif and from thence to be Conveyed to the Publick Goal of Williamsburg as the law in Such Cases Directs.

[*Cheap's recognizance*]

Mr. Patrick Cheap of Middlesex County in open Court before his Majestys Justices Acknowledged himselfe Indebted to our Sovereign Lord the King his heirs and Successors in the Sum of Tenn Pounds Sterling, to be levyed of his Lands and Tenements Goods and Chattles with Condition, That if the above said Patrick Cheap Shall appear before the Honorable Court of Oyer and Terminer to be held at his Majestys Royall Capitoll, on the Second Tuesday in December Next, and attend From time to time as the said Court Shall Direct, then and there to Give Evidence for our said Lord the King against James McCoy who Stands Committed to the Goal of this County for Felony, Then this Recognisance to be Void, or Else to Remain in Full force.

Henry Miskell of Richmond County the Same.

[**311**] At a call'd Court held at the Court House of Richmond County on fryday the 13th day of January 1743/4.

Present: Samuell Peachey, John Woodbridge, Thomas Peachey, John Tayloe, Jr., Anthony Sydnor, Travors Tarpley, and John Tarpley, Gentlemen Justices.

Vass Examination

Vincint Vass according to his Recognizance this day appearing to Answer the complaint of Daniell Hornby Gentleman on Suspicion of Stealing from the said Hornby one Pistole, one pair of Mens Cotton Hoes Mark[ed] T.C. one pair of Silk Do. [ditto] light pair of Thread and worsted D. [ditto] Some Duroys and Other Goods. This day the Court having Taken the said Matter into Examination, and having hear Severall Evidences, on Behalf of the King against the said Vass, No Sufficient Cause appearing to them Upon the said Evidence to Remove him to Public Goale, he is Therefore ordered to be Acquited.

At a court Continued and held for Richmond County the Fifth day of June 1744.

Present: Samuell Peachey, John Woodbridge, William Brockenbrough, William Fantleroy, Jr., Travers Tarpley, John Tarpley, Gentlemen Justices.

[Schofield bound to his behaviour]

It appearing to this court that Robert Schofield of North Farnham Parish is a person of an ill Behaviour It is therefore ordered That he give good and Sufficient Security for his Good behaviour Dureing the Terme of one Year.

Whereupon the said Robert Schofield Together with Jonathan Lyell and Joshua Hightower, his Securitys acknowledged Themselves Indebted to our Sovereign Lord the King the said Schofield in the Sum of Ten pounds Sterling and the said [312] Lyell and Hightower in the Sum of Five pounds Sterling Each to be Levyed on their Lands and Tenements goods and Chattles With Condition that if the said Robert Schofield Shall be of Good behaviour as well Towards his Majesty as all his Leige people that then this Recognisance to be Void and of None Effect or Else to Remain in full force.

At a court held for Richmond County this Sixth day of August 1744.

Present: Samuell Peachey, Thomas Barber, Daniell Hornby, Anthony Sydnor, Travers Tarpley, Thomas Plumer, Gentlemen Justices.

Polly bound to her behaviour

It appearing to this Court that Frances Polly widow is a person of an Ill Behaviour, It is therefore Ordered that She give Good and Sufficient Security for her Good Behaviour, Dureing the Terme of one Year.

Whereupon the said Frances Polly Widow together with Gregory Glascock and Luke Milner her Securitys Acknowledged themselves Indebted to our Soverign Lord the King, the said polly in the Sum of Ten pounds Sterling and the said Glascock and Milnor in the Sum of Five pounds Sterling Each, to be Levied on their Lands and Tenements Goods and Chattles with Condition, that if the said Frances Polly Widow Shall be of Good behaviour as well Towards his Majesty as all his Leige People, that then this Recognisance to be Void and of None Effect or Else to Remain in Full Force.

Allemond a Negro his Tryall

[313] At a Session of Oyer and Terminer held at Richmond Court house on Monday the 1st day of October 1744 in the Eighteenth Year of the Reign of our Sovereign Lord George the Second by the Grace of god of Great Britain France and Ireland King Defender of the Faith etc. by Virtue of a Special Commission for the Tryall All Treasons petti Treasons or Misprisions thereof Felonys Murders or Other Offences or Crymes Whatsoever Committed Within This

County of Richmond by a Negro Man Slave Named Allemond Belonging to Capt. William Beale of this County and Directed to William Fantleroy, Samuell Peachey, John Woodbridge, Thomas Barber, William Glascock, Landon Carter, Leroy Griffin, Daniell Hornby, William Jordan, John Tayloe Jr., Anthony Sydnor, Gilbert Hamilton, William Fantleroy Jr., William Brockenbrough, Travers Tarpley, John Tarpley, Thomas Plumer, Moore Fantleroy, Alvin Mountjoy, and Nicholas Flood Gentlemen.

Present: Samuell Peachey, Thomas Barber, Daniell Hornby, William Jordan, Anthony Sydnor, William Fantleroy Jr., William Brockenbrough, Travers Tarpley and Thomas Plumer, Gentlemen Justices.

Memorandum that on this present Day being the First day of October 1744 an Indictment was Preferd Against a Negro man Slave Called Allemond, belonging to Capt. William Beale of this County, in these words.

Richmond Ss. Memorandum that William Kennan Gentleman Deputed Attorney for our Lord the King in the county Aforesaid for this Purpose Especially appointed comes hereinto Court in his proper person the first Day of October in the Year of our Lord one Thousand Seven hundred and Forty Four and Gives the court hereto understand and being informed That Allemond a Negro Man Slave belonging to William Beale of the said County of Richmond Gentleman on [314] the 27th day of August in the Eighteenth Year of the Reign of our Lord George the Second by the grace of God Now King of Great Britain France and Ireland Defender of the Faith with force and Arms the Quarter of one William Hodgkinson at the Parish of Lunenburg in the said County of Richmond feloniously did Break and Enter and three Hatts of the Value of Eighteen Pence Each Four Ozaburg Shirts of the Value of two Shillings Each twenty Yards of Course Linnen of the Value of Thirty Shillings Five Yards of Check'd Linnen of the Value of Six Shillings one pair of Long Breaches of the value of Six pence and Sixteen Shillings Current Money amounting in All to the Value of three pounds two Shillings the Proper Goods and Chattles of the said William Hodgkinson in the said Quarter having then Found then and there feloniously did Steal take and Carry away Against the Peace of aforesaid Lord the King his Crown and Dignity etc.

Whereupon the said Allemond was brought to the Barr and Arraigned for the said Felony and there pleaded not Guilty and Thereupon the court Proceeded on his Tryall[;] after having heard the Evidence against him, and What he had to Say in his Defence, are of Opinion that he is Guilty of Receiving Stolen Good[s], Knowing them to be Such, It is therefore ordered that he Stand in the pillery half an hour, and then the Sherrif Take him and Carry him to the common Whipping Post and Give him Thirty Nine Lashes on his bare back Well Laid on.

At a court held for Richmond County the Fourth day of February 1744/5.

[315] Present: Samuell Peachey, John Woodbridge, Daniell Hornby, Travers Tarpley, John Tarpley, Thomas Plumer, Gentlemen Justices.

Connell bound to his behaviour

It appearing to this Court that Michael Connell is a Person of an Ill behaviour It is therefore ordered that he give good and Sufficient Security for his Good behaviour Dureing the terme of one Year.

Whereupon the said Michaell Connell Together with Henry Miskell and James Booth his Securitys acknowledged themselves Indebted to our Sovereign Lord the King the said Connell in the Sum of Twenty Pounds Sterling and the said Miskell and Booth in the Sum of Ten pounds Sterling Each to be Levyed on their Lands and Tenements Goods and Chattles with Condition that if the said Connell Shall be of Good behaviour as well towards his Majestys as all his Leige people that then this Recognisance to be Void and of None Effect or Else to Remain in full Force.

At a court held for Richmond County the 4th day of March 1744/5.

Present: Samuell Peachey, John Woodbridge, Thomas Barber, Daniell Hornby, John Tayloe Jr., Anthony Sydnor, William Brockenbrough, John Tarpley and Thomas Plumer, Gentlemen Justices.

Hamond fined

It being Proved to this court that Samuell Hamond of North Farnham Parish Refused to Assist Michaell Connell Constable Concerning a Runaway, It is Therefore ordered that he be Fined for the said Offence Fifty Pounds of Tobacco to our Sovereign Lord the King.

Hamond bound to his Behaviour

It appearing to this Court that Samuell Hamond is a Person of an Ill behaviour It is therefore ordered that [316] he Give Good and Sufficient Security for his Good behaviour Dureing the Terme of one Year.

Whereupon the said Samuell Hamond together with Daniell Hornby Gentleman his Security Acknowledged themselves Indebted to our Sovereign Lord the King the said Hamond in the sum of Ten pounds Sterling and the said Hornby in the Sum of Five pounds Sterling to be Levied on their Lands and Tenements Goods and Chattles with Condition that if the said Hamond Shall be of Good behaviour as well towards his Majestye as all his Leige people then this Recognisance to be Void and of none Effect or Else to Remain in Full Force.

At a call'd Court held at the Court House of Richmond County on Monday the 1st Day of Aprill 1745.

Present: Thomas Barber, William Jordan, Anthony Sydnor, Thomas Plumer, Gentlemen Justices.

Granger Whipt

Whereas James Granger by Vertue of a Mittimus from Anthony Sydnor Gentleman one of the Justices of this Court was Committed to this County Goale on Suspicion of Stealing a hilling hoe from one Edward Bates and being now Brought before his Majestys Justices here present on Examination of Severall Evidences Thouching the Same it is the Opinion of this Court that he is Guilty of the Crime Laid to his Charge It is therefore ordered that the Sherrif Take him and Carry him to the Common Whiping post and Give him Ten Lashes on his Bare Back Well Laid on.

[**317**] At a court held for Richmond County the 1st Day of April 1745
Present: Thomas Barber, Daniell Hornby, William Jordan, Anthony Syndor, and Thomas Plumer, Gentlemen Justices.

Williams Jr. bound to his Behaviour

It appearing to this Court that Henry Williams Jr. is a Person of An Ill Behaviour It is therefore ordered that he give Good and Sufficient Security for his good behaviour Dureing the Terme of one Year.

Whereupon the said Henry Williams Jr. Together with Thomas Plumer his Security Acknowledged themselves Indebted to our Sovereign Lord the King the said Williams in the Sum of Ten pounds Sterling and the said Plumer in the Sum of Five pounds Sterling to be Levied on their Lands and Tenements Goods and Chattles With Condition that if the said Williams Shall be of Good behaviour as well Towards his Majesty as all his Leige people that then this Recognisance to be Void and of None Effect or Else to Remain in Full Force.

Scipio and Janeys Tryall

At a session of Oyer and Terminer held at Richmond Court House on Wednesday the Twenty Second day of May 1745 in the Eighteenth Year of the Reign of our Sovereign Lord George the second by the grace of god of great Britain France and Ireland, King Defender of the Faith etc. by Virtue of a Speciall Commission for the Tryall of all Treasons petti Treasons or Misprisions thereof Felonys Murders or Other Offences or Crymes Whatsoever Committed within this County of Richmond by two Negroes Names Scipio and Janey Belonging to James Ball of Lancaster County and Directed to William Fantleroy Samuell Peachey, John Woodbridge Thomas Barber, William Glascock, Landon Carter Leroy Griffon, Daniell Hornby, [**318**] William Jordan, John Tayloe Jr. Anthony Sydnor Gilbert Hamilton, William Fantleroy Jr. William Brockenbrough, Travers Tarpley, John Tarpley, Thomas Plumer, William Beale, Moore Fantleroy, Alvin Mountjoy, and Nicholas Flood Gentlemen.

Present: Samuell Peachey, Daniell Hornby, Anthony Sydnor, William Fantleroy Jr., Travers Tarpley, Alvin Mountjoy, and Nicholas Flood, Gentlemen Justices.

Memorandum that on this present day being the Twenty Second day of May 1745 an Indictment was Preferd against Negroes Scipio and Janey Belonging to James Ball of Lancaster County in these words.

Richmond Ss.: Memorandum That Charles Beale Attorney of our Lord the King in the county aforesaid for this purpose Especially Appointed comes into Court in his proper person the Twenty Second day of May in the Year of our Lord one Thousand Seven hundred and Forty Five and Gives the court hereto understand and be Informed That Scipio a Negro man Slave and Janey a Negro woman Slave belonging to one James Ball late of the Parish of Lunenburg in the said County of Richmond on the Twentieth day of Aprill and Sundry other times in the Seventeenth Year of the Reign of our Sovereign Lord George the Second by the Grace of God Now King of Great Britain France and Ireland Defender of the Faith with Force and Arms the store house of one William Jordan Gentleman at the parish and County aforesaid feloniously did Break and Enter and Forty Gallons of Rum of the Value Ten pounds of Lawfull Money of Great [319] Britain and Fifty pounds of Sugar of the Value of Twenty Five Shillings of Like lawful Money of Great Britain[,] the proper Goods and Chattles of the said William Jordan[,] in the said Store house then found then and There feloniously did steal take and Carry away Against the Peace of our said Now Lord the King his Crown and Dignity.

Whereupon the said Scipio and Janey was Brought to the Barr and Arraigned for the said felony and There Pleaded not Guilty. And Thereupon the court proceeding on their tryall (after hereing the Evidence against them and What they had to Say in their Defence) Are of Opinion that they are Not Guilty of the Felony for which they Stand Indicted[;] it is Therefore ordered that they be Acquited But the said Scipio having Broke prison and Refuseing to tell Who assisted him, in getting out[,] it is therefore ordered that the Sherrif Take him and Carry him to the Common Whipping post, and Give him Thirty Nine Lashes on his bare Back well Laid on.

At a court held for Richmond County the First day of July 1745.
Present: Samuell Peachey, John Woodbridge, Thomas Barber, Daniell Hornby, and Alvin Mountjoy, Gentlemen Justices.

Brown bound to his behaviour

John Brown the Younger this day Appearing to Answer the Complaint of the Reverend Mr. Kay for Stopping him on the Kings Highway and Putting him in Bodily Fear it is Therefore ordered that for the said Offence he Give Good and Sufficient Security for his Good Behaviour Dureing the Terme of one Year.

[320] Whereupon the said John Brown together with William Brown and Jeremiah Brown his Securitys acknowledged themselves Indebted to our Sovereign Lord the King the said John Brown in the Sum of Forty Pounds Sterling

and the said William Brown and Jeremiah Brown Each of them in the Sum of twenty Pounds Sterling to be Levyed on their Lands and Tenements Goods and Chattles with Condition that if the said John Brown Shall be of Good Behaviour as well towards his Majesty as all his Leige People then this Recognisance to be Void and of None Effect or Else to Remain in Full Force.

Gower bound to her behaviour

Ann Gower the wife of John Gower this day appearing to answer the complaint of Robert Tomlin Gentleman for Abusing him, it is Therefore ordered that for the said Offence She Give Good and Sufficient Security for her good Behaviour dureing the Terme of one Year.

Whereupon the said Ann Gower together with John Gower her Husband and William Thrift her Securitys Acknowledged themselves Indebted to our Sovereign Lord the King the said John Gower and his wife in the Sum of twenty Pounds Sterling and the said William Thrift in the Sum of Ten pounds Sterling to be Levyed on their Lands and Tenements Goods and Chattles with Condition that if the said Ann Gower Shall be of Good behaviour as well towards his Majesty as all his Liege People then this Recognisance to be Void and of None Effect or Else to Remain in full force.

Jack a Negro Tryall

At a Session of Oyer and Terminer held at Richmond Court house on Fryday the 26th day of July 1745 in the Nineteenth year of the Reign of our Sovereign Lord George the Second by the Grace of God of Great [321] Britain France and Ireland King Defender of the Faith by vertue of a Speciall Commission for the tryall of all treasons Petit Treasons or Misprisons thereof Felonys Murders or Other Offences or Crymes Whatsoever Committed within this County of Richmond by a Negro Man Named Jack belonging to Simon Sallard and Directed to William Fantleroy, Samuell Peachey, John Woodbridge, Thomas Barber, William Glascock, Landon Carter, Leroy Griffin, Daniell Hornby, William Jordan, John Tayloe, Jr., Anthony Sydnor, Gilbert Hamilton, William Fantleroy Jr. William Brockenbrough, Travers Tarpley, John Tarpley, Thomas Plummer, William Beale, Moore Fantleroy, Alvin Mountjoy, and Nicholas Flood, Gentlemen.

Present: Thomas Barber, Daniell Hornby, John Tayloe, Jr., William Brockenbrough, and Travers Tarpley, Gentlemen Justices.

Memorandum that on this Present Day being the 26th day of July 1745 an Indictment was Prefer'd against a Negro Man named Jack belonging to Simon Sallard in these words. . . . . .

Richmond Ss.: Memorandum That Charles Beale Attorney of our Lord the King in the county aforesaid for this purpose Appointed comes into Court in his proper Person this twenty Sixth day of July in the year of our Lord one Thousand Seven Hundred and Forty five and Gives the court Here to understand and be informed That Jack a Negro Man Slave Belonging to one Simon Sallard on the fifteenth day of this Instant Month July about the Eleventh hour in the Night of the Same day with force and Arms at the Parish of Lunenburg in the said County of Richmond the Dwelling House of one Edmund Northern there Situate[d] feloniously and burglariously did Break and Enter and Five [   ] Sterling one Fishing Line of the Value of Six pence [**322**] one Ring of the Value of Six pence Sterling and one bottle with Brandy of the Value of Six pence Sterling of the money goods and Chattles of the said Edmund Northern in the said Dwelling House then and there being found feloniously did Steal take and Carry away aginst the Peace of our now Lord the King his Crown and Dignity.

Whereupon the said Jack was Brought to the Barr and Arrained for the said Burglary and Felony and there Pleaded not Guilty and thereupon the court proceeding on his Tryall after having heard the Evidence against him and what he had to Say in his Defence are of Opinion that he is Guilty of the Burglary and Felony Mentioned in the said Indictment.

It is therefore Ordered that the said Jack Return to the place from whence he came from thence to the Place of Execution and There to be hanged by the Neck till he be dead.

Pursuant to an act of Assembly made in the Year 1723 concerning the Tryall of Slaves Committing Capital Crimes[,] this court[145] in pursuance Thereof Do Value Jack a Negro Man Slave belonging to Mr. Simon Sallard (who was this day Condemed to Dye for Burglary and Felony) to Thirty Five pounds current Money and ordered that the Clerk of this County Certyfy the same to the Next Assembly.

But it appearing to this court that it is the First Offence of this Kind by him Committed and Seeming to them for the circumstances of the case Doubtfull Whether he was Sensible of the crime for which he is Sentenced they Therefore Recomend[146] the said Jack to the Mercy of his honour the Governor.

[**323**] At a court held for Richmond County the Fifth day of August 1745.

Present: Samuell Peachey, John Woodbridge, Thomas Barber, Daniell Hornby, John Tayloe Jr., William Fantleroy Jr., William Brockenbrough, Alvin Mountjoy, Gentlemen Justices.

Pridham bound to his Behaviour

Martin Hughs of Lunenburg parish having Sworn the Peace Against Edward Pridham, before Thomas Barber, Gentleman one of the Majestrates of this

---

145. *Statutes at Large*, 4:128 (1723), and subsequent repassage of the slave trial act directed the court to establish the value of a condemned slave. The statute implied but did not require the House of Burgesses to use this estimate to recompense an owner for his or her loss when the slave was executed.

146. "Sensible" meant *compos mentis;* idiots or a madmen could not be held to have intended to commit a felony because they could not control their own acts. Governors could pardon insane persons for lesser felonies; the king pardoned, upon the governor's application, in murders and treasons; Rankin, *Criminal Trial Proceedings*, 68; Scott, *Criminal Law*, 119–20.

Court And the said Pridham this day Appearing it is ordered that he Give Good and Sufficient Security for his Good behaviour and his Keeping the Peace Dureing the terme of one year.

Whereupon the said Edward Pridham together with Daniell Lawson, and, Thomas Freshwater, his Securitys Acknowledged them selves Indebted to our Sovereign Lord the King the said Edward Pridham, in the Sum of twenty Pounds Sterling and the said Daniell Lawson, and Thomas Freshwater, Each of them in the Sum of Ten pounds Sterling to be Levyed on their Lands and Tenements Goods and Chattles with Condition that if the said Edward Pridham, Shall be of Good behaviour and Keep the Peace as well towards his Majesty as all his Liege People then this Recognisance to be Void and of None Effect or Else to Remain in full force.

At a court Continued and held for Richmond County the Sixth day of August 1745.

Present: Thomas Barber, Daniell Hornby, William Jordan, Anthony Sydnor, Travers Tarpley, William Brockenbrough, Gentlemen Justices.

Spence Fined

[324] Whereas the Grandjury for the Body of this County Last May Court found a bill of Inditment against Robert Spence of Lunenburg Parish for Assaulting Owin Brady one of the Under Sherrifs of this County, and the said Spence this day appearing, and Submitting himself to the court, it is Therefore ordered that he be fined for the Same, twenty Shillings Current Money to our Sovereign Lord the King.

At a court held for Richmond County the third day of March 1745 [1746].

Present: Samuell Peachey, Thomas Barber, Daniell Hornby, John Tayloe Jr., Anthony Sydnor, William Fantleroy Jr., William Brockenbrough, Travers Tarpley, Thomas Plumer, Nicholas Flood, Gentlemen Justices.

Manning Bound to his Behaviour

It appearing that Andrew Manning is a person of Ill Behaviour It is therefore ordered that he give good and Sufficient Security for his good Behaviour dureing the Terme of one Year.

Whereupon the said Andrew Manning together with John Smith Gentleman his Security Acknowledged them selves Indebted to our Sovereign Lord the King the said Mannings in the sum of Ten pounds Sterling and the said Smith in the sum of Five pounds Sterling to be Levied on their Lands and Tenements Goods and Chattles with Condition that if the said Manning shall be of Good behaviour as well towards his Majestye as all his Leige people that then this Recognisance to be Void and of none Effect or Else to Remain in full force.

[**325**] At a court held for Richmond County the Fifth day of May 1746.
Present: John Woodbridge, Thomas Barber, Daniell Hornby, Anthony Sydnor and Alvin Mountjoy, Gentleman Justices.

Williams Bound to his Behaviour

Henry Williams of North Farnham Parish, having been summoned to Answer the presentment of the grandjury against him, for being a Disturber of the peace and this day appearing but Offering nothing Materiall to Excuse himselfe, it is ordered that for the said Offence he give Good and Sufficient Security for his good Behaviour, dureing the Terme of one Year.

Whereupon the said Henry Williams together with Henry Miskell and Roger Williams his Securitys in open Court Acknowledged themselves Indebted unto our Sovereign Lord the King his heirs and Successors in the sum of Twenty Pounds Sterling to be Levied on their Lands and Tenements goods and Chattles with Condition, that if the said Henry Williams Shall be of good Behaviour, as well Towards his Majestys as all his Liege people, that then this Recognisance to be Void and of none Effect or Else to Remain in full force and Virtue.

At a call'd Court held at the Court house of Richmond County on Wednesday the 18th day of June 1746.
Present: John Woodbridge, Thomas Barber, William Brockenbrough, Nicholas Flood, Gentlemen Justices.

Fichling Discharged

Whereas John Fichling of North Farham Parish was by Virtue of a Mittemas from John Woodbridge Gentleman one of the Justices of this court Committed to the County Goal on Suspicion of felony, and being now Brought Before this Court, but noe Sufficient Evidence appearing against him, He is therefore Discharged.

[**326**] At a court held for Richmond County the 7th Day of July 1746.
Present: Samuell Peachey, Thomas Barber, Leroy Griffin, Travers Tarpley and Thomas Plumer, Gentlemen Justices.

Welch Bound to his Behaviour

It appearing to this Court that Patrick Welch is a person of ill Behaviour It is therefore ordered that he give good and Sufficient Security for his Good Behaviour Dureing The Terme of one Year.

Whereupon the said Patrick Welch Together with Jeremiah Greenham and Charles Smith his Securitys Acknowledged themselves Indebted to our Sovereign Lord their King the said Welch in the sum of Forty Pounds and the said Greenham and Smith in the sum twenty pounds to be Levyed on their Lands and Tenements Goods and Chattles With Condition that if the said Welch Shall be of Good Behaviour as well Towards his Majesty as all his Leige People that then this Recognisance to be Void and of None Effect, or Else to Remain in full force.

At a court held for Richmond County the 4th day of August 1746.

Present: Samuell Peachey, John Woodbridge, Thomas Barber, Leroy Griffin, Daniell Hornby, John Tayloe Jr., and Anthony Sydnor, Gentlemen Justices.

Kay Bound to his Behaviour

Sarah Kay the wife of William Kay Clerk having sworn the Peace against her said Husband, it is therefore ordered that he give Security for keeping the same.

Whereupon the said William Kay Together with William Mackay Clerk his Security acknowledged themselves indebted to our Sovereign [327] Lord the king, the said William Kay in the sum of Forty Pounds and the said William Mackay in the sum of twenty pounds, To be Levied on their Lands and Tenements goods and Chattles with Condition, that if the said William Kay Shall keep the peace of our Sovereign Lord the King as well towards his said Majesty and all his Leige People And Especially toward his said Wife Sarah Kay, that then this Recognisance to be Void and of None Effect or Else to Remain in full force.

At a Call'd Court held at the Court house of Richmond County on fryday the 24th day of October 1746.

Present: Samuell Peachey, John Woodbridge, Thomas Barber, Leroy Griffin, Alvin Mountjoy, Nicholas Flood, Gentlemen Justices.

Pain and Rimer Discharged

Rose Paine and Margaret Rimer being Brought before this Court on Suspicion of Stealing wool from Mr. Samford but noe Sufficient Evidence Appearing against them, they are therefore Discharged.

At a called Court held at the Court house of Richmond County on Monday the 24th day of November 1746.

Present: Thomas Barber, Daniell Hornby, William Jordan, John Tayloe Jr., Travers Tarpley, Nicholas Flood, Gentlemen Justices.

Lynes Discharged

Thomas Lynes of Lunenburg Parish having been Committed prisoner to the Goal of this County by Virtue of a Mittimus from William Fantleroy Jr. Gentleman one of his Majestys Justices of the Peace for the County on Suspicion of Vending false Money knowing it to be Such, and for Being aiding on Counterfeiting the Current Coin of this Dominion.

This day the Court having Taken the said Matter into Examination and having heard Several Evidences on behalfe of the King against [**328**] the prisoner, noe Sufficient Cause appearing to them upon the said Evidence to Remove him to the Publick Goal he is therefore ordered to be Acquited.

Grinney a Negroes Tryall

At a Session of Oyer and Terminer Held at Richmond County Court house on Monday the Fifth day of January 1746 [1747] in the twentieth Year of the Reign of our Sovereign Lord George the Second by the grace of God of Great Britian France and Ireland king Defender of the Faith etc. by Virtue of a Speciall Commission for the Tryall of all Treasons Petit treasons or Misprisions thereof Felonys Murders or other offences or Crimes Whatsoever Committed within this County of Richmond by a Negro Man Slave Named Grinney Belonging to Edgecomb Suggit of this County and Directed to William Fantleroy Samuell Peachey John Woodbridge Thomas Barber William Glasscock Landon Carter Leroy Griffin Daniell Hornby William Jordon John Tayloe Jr. Anthony Sydnor Gilbert Hamilton William Fantleroy Jr. John Smith Travers Tarpley John Tarpley Thomas Plummer William Beale Moore Fantleroy Alvin Mountjoy and Nicholas Flood Gentlemen.

Present: John Woodbridge, Thomas Barber, Anthony Sydnor, Travers Tarpley and Alvin Mounjoy, Gentlemen Justices.

Memorandum that on this present day Being the Fifth day of January 1746 [1747] an indictment was preferred against a Negro Man Slave Called Grinney Belonging to Edgecomb Suggitt in this County in these words.

Richmond Ss: Be it Remembered That Charles Beale Gentleman Attorney of our Lord the King in the County aforesaid for this purpose especially appointed comes into Court in his proper person this Fifth day of January in the Year of our Lord one thousand [**329**] Seven hundred and Forty Six [1747] and Gives the Court here to understand and be Informed that Grinny a Negro Slave belonging to Edgecomb Suggitt of the said County on the Last day of July in the XXth Year of the Reign of our Sovereign Lord George the Second by the grace of God of Great Britain France and Ireland, King Defender of the Faith etc. With Force and Arms the Dwelling house of Sarah Hill widow at the parish of the North-Farnham in the County aforesaid feloniously did Break and Enter and Twenty

Pieces of Bacon of the value of Twenty Shillings of Lawful Money of the Currency of this Colony the proper Goods and Chattles of the said Sarah Hill in the said Dwelling House then found then and there feloniously Did Steal take and Carry away against the peace of our said Lord the king his Crown and Dignity.

Whereupon the said Grinney was Brought to the Barr and Arrained for the said Felony and there pleaded not Guilty and thereupon the Court Proceeded on his Tryall (after having heard the Evidence against him and What he had to Say in his Defence) are of the Oppinion that he is Guilty of the Felony Mentioned in the said Indictment with the Benefitt of the Clergy.[147] Whereupon the said Grinny Prayed the said Benefitt and Accordingly was Burnt in the hand at the Barr with a Hot Iron.

At a Called Court held at the Court house of Richmond County on Wednesday the 7th day of January 1746 [1747]

Present: John Woodbridge, Thomas Barber, Anthony Sydnor, John Tarpley and Alvin Mountjoy, Gentlemen Justices.

Thomas Discharged

Margaret Thomas the late wife of Moses Thomas of North Farnham parish in this County, being this day Brought Before this Court for the killing of her said Husband, it appearing to the Court by the Verdict of the Coroners Inquest that the Misfortune Happened by the said Margaret Thomas's Casting a certain Firelock out of the House of the said Moses Thomas [**330**] which was Charged with Powder and Drop Shot[,] was thereby fired and discharged as it fell on the ground and did Casually, and by accident, kill the said Moses Thomas,[148] It is therefore, ordered that the said Margarett Thomas be Discharged.

At a Court held for Richmond County the Fourth day of May 1747.

Present: Samuall Peachey, John Woodbridge, Daniell Hornby, John Tayloe Jr. and Anthony Sydnor, Gentlemen Justices.

Pridham Fined

Whereas a Bill of Inditement was Found by the grandjury against Edward Pridham of Lunenburg Parish for assaulting one William Foster and the said Pridham haveing been summoned to answer the same but not appearing Judg-

---

147. Under the 1732 benefit of clergy statutes, theft of goods in excess of 5s. after breaking and entering should not have been clergyable. The judges told Grinney the opposite and granted his prayer for clergy. Here was another example of the great discretion that was assumed by (not granted to) the justices.

148. In a "casual" homicide, the cause of death was the weapon itself, not its wielder. Webb regards the term as synonymous with "accidental," *Justice of Peace*, 175.

ment was therefore granted against him Last Court by Default and on hearing this day the Evidence on Behalfe of the king against him [the court] are of Oppinion That he is Guilty of What is Laid to his Charge[;] it is Therefore ordered that he be fined for the same twenty Shillings Current Money to our said Lord the king.

At a court held for Richmond County the First day of June 1747.

Present: John Woodbrige, Thomas Barber, Leroy Griffin, Daniell Hornby, William Jordan, John Tarpley and Nicholas Flood, Gentlemen Justices.

Robertson Fined

[**331**] Whereas a Bill of Inditement was found against William Robertson of North Farnham parish for assaulting one John Smith And he having pleaded not Guilty a Jury was Last Court Impannelled and Sworn to try the issue Joyn'd and they having this Day Brought in their Verdict, Which is in these Words: we of the Jury Find the said Robertson Guilty of Ill Behaviour to the said Smith. William Thrift [foreman;] Which Verdict on the Motion of the Kings attorney is ordered to be Recorded And That the said Robertson be fined Two Shillings to our Sovereign Lord the King.

Russell[s] Bound to [their] Behaviour

The Reverend William Kay of Lunenburg parish having sworn the Peace against Thomas Russell it is therefore ordered that he Give Good and Sufficient Security Dureing the Terme of one Year for the keeping the same. Whereupon the said Thomas Russell together with William Dogge his Security Acknowledged themselves Indebted to our Sovereign Lord the King the said Thomas Russell in the sum of Forty Pounds and the said William Dogge in the sum of twenty pounds to be Levyed on their Lands and Tenements Goods and Chattles with Condition that if the said Thomas Russell shall keep the peace of our Severeign Lord the King as well towards his said Majesty and all his Leige people and Especially towards the said William Kay that then this Recognisance to be Void and of None Effect or Else to Remain in full force.

The Reverend William Kay of Lunenburg parish having Sworn the Peace Against George Russell it is therefore ordered that he give Good and Sufficient Security Dureing the Terme of one Year for Keeping the same. Whereupon the said George Russell together with Joseph Russell Jr. his Security Acknowledged themselves Indebted to our Sovereign Lord King the said George Russell in the Sum of Forty pounds and the said Joseph Russell Jr. in the sum of twenty Pounds to be Levyed on their Lands and Tenements Goods and Chattles with Condition that if the said George Russell shall keep the Peace of our Sovereign Lord the king as well towards his said Majesty and all his Leige People and Especially towards the said William Kay that then this Recognisance to be Void and of None Effect or Else to Remain in Full Force.

Belfield bound to his Behaviour

[**332**] Thomas Newman having sworn the peace against Joseph Belfield it is therefore ordered that he Give Good and Sufficient Security Dureing the Terme of one year for keeping the same Whereupon the said Joseph Belfield Together with John Belfield his Security Acknowledged themselves Indebted to our sovereign Lord the king the said Joseph Belfield in Sum of Forty Pounds and the said John Belfield in the sum of twenty Pounds to be levied on their Lands and Tenements Goods and Chattles with Condition that if the said Joseph Belfield Shall keep the Peace of our Sovereign Lord the king as well towards his said Majesty and all his Leige People and Especially Towards the said Thomas Newman that then his Recognisance to be Void and of None Effect or Else to Remain in Full Force.

Chin Bound to his Behaviour

Charles Chinn of NorthFarnham Parish having been summoned to answer the presentment of the grandjury against him for being a Common Swearer and this Day Appearing But offering Nothing Materiall to Excuse him selfe it is the oppinion of this Court and Accordingly ordered That for the said Offence he give good and Sufficient Security for his Good Behaviour Dureing the Terme of one Year.

Whereupon the said Charles Chinn Together with John Span Webb his Security in Open Court acknowledged them selves indebted to our Sovereign Lord the King his heirs and Successors in the sum of Twenty Pounds Sterling to be Levied on their Lands and Tenements Goods and Chattles With Condition that if the said Charles Chinn Shall be of Good Behaviour as well towards his Majesty as all his Leige people that then this Recognisance to be Void and of none Effect otherwise to Remain in Full Force power and Virtue.

[**333**] At a court held for Richmond County the Third day of August 1747.

Present: Samuell Peachey, John Woodbridge, Leroy Griffin, Anthony Sydnor, William Fantleroy Jr., John Tarpley, Nicholas Plumer, Alvin Mountjoy, Gentlemen Justices.

Lyell Bound to his Behaviour

On the Complaint of Elizabeth Brady the wife of Owen Brady She being afraid That William Lyell would Beat wound Main or kill her it is therefore ordered that the said William Lyell give good and Sufficient Security for keeping the Peace.

Whereupon the said William Lyell Together with Richard Brown and William Hamond his Securitys in open Court acknowledged themselves Indebted to our Sovereign Lord the King his heirs and Successors the said William Lyell in the sum of Forty Pounds Sterling and the said Richard Brown and William Hamond in the sum of Twenty pounds Sterling to be Levied on their Lands and Tenements Goods and Chattles upon Condition that if the said William Lyell Shall keep the Peace of our Sovereign Lord the King as well towards his Majesty as all his Leige People that then this Recognisance to be Void and of None Effect or Else to Remain in Full Force and Virtue.

At a court Continued and Held for Richmond County the 4th day of August 1747.

Present: Thomas Barber, Leroy Griffin, Daniell Hornby, William Jordan, John Tayloe Jr., Travers Tarpley, Alvin Mountjoy, Nicholas Flood, Gentlemen Justices.

Pridham Bound to his Behaviour

Edward Pridham of Lunenburg Parish having been summoned to Answer the presentment of the Grandjury against him for being a Common Swearer and this day appearing but offering Nothing Materiall to Excuse himself it is the oppinion of this Court and accordingly ordered that for the said Offence he give good and Sufficient Security for his good behaviour Dureing the Terme of one Year.

[334] Whereupon the said Edward Pridham Together with Burgess Longworth his Security in Open Court acknowledged themselves Indebted unto our Sovereign Lord the King his heirs and Successors in the sum of Twenty Pounds Sterling to be Levied on their Lands and Tenements Goods and Chattles with Condition that if the said Edward Pridham Shall be of Good behaviour as well towards his Majesty as all his Leage People that then this Recognisance to be Void and of None Effect or Else to Remain in Full Force and Virtue.

At a court held for Richmond County the 7th day of September 1747.

Present: Samuell Peachey, Thomas Barber, Leroy Griffin, William Jordan, John Tayloe, Anthony Sydnor and John Tarpley, Gentlemen Justices.

Freshwater to give Security for his Behaviour

It appearing to this court that John Freshwater assaulted Mr. William Kennan it is therefore ordered that he give Security for his good Behaviour Dureing the Terme of one year and that he Remain in the Sherrifs Custody until he give such Security.

Manuell a Negro his Tryall

At a Session of Oyer and Terminer held at Richmond Court house on Tuesday the 6th day of October 1747 in the 21st year of the Reign of our Sovereign

Lord George the Second by the Grace of God of Great Britain France and Ireland King Defender of the Faith etc. by Virtue of a Special Commission for the tryall of all treasons petit treasons or Misprisions thereof Felonys Murders or Other Offences or Crymes whatsoever Committed within this County of Richmond by two Negro men Slaves Names Ralph and Imanuell Belonging [335] to Landon Carter Esq. of this County and Directed to William Fantleroy Samuell Peachey John Woodbridge Thomas Barber William Glascock Leroy Griffin Daniell Hornby William Jordan John Tayloe Anthony Sydnor Gilbert Hamilton William Fantleroy Jr. John Smith Travers Tarpley John Tarpley Thomas Plumer William Beal Moore Fantleroy Alvin Mounjoy and Nicholas Flood of the County of Richmond Gentlemen Greeting.

Present: Samuell Peachey, John Woodbridge, Daniell Hornby, William Jordan and Alvin Mountjoy, Gentlemen Justices.

Memorandum that on this present Day being the Sixth day of October 1747 an Indictment was preferd against two Negroe Men slaves Called Ralph and Manuell Belonging to Landon Carter Esq. of this County in these words. . . .

Richmond [Ss.] To wit: Memorandum that Charles Beale attorney of our Lord the King in the county aforesaid for this purpose especially appointed comes into Court in his proper person the Sixth day of October in the year of our Lord one thousand Seven hundred and Forth Seven and Gives the court hereto understand and be Informed That Manuell and Ralph two Negro Slaves Belonging to Landon Carter of the said County Esq. on the Fourth day of September in the night of the same day in the year of our Lord one thousand Seven hundred and Forty Seven with Force and Arms the Mansion House of the said Landon Carter at the parish of Lunenburg in the aforesaid County of Richmond Felloniously and Burglariously did Break and Enter and two hundred and thirty three Ells of Dreheda Canvas of the Value of Eight pounds Sterling Four Torinton Rugs of the Value of Twenty Shillings Sterling Four suits of Cotton Cloath of the Value of twenty Eight Shillings Sterling, Ten yards of Half Thicks of the Value of twenty Shillings Sterling Four Sides of Leather of the Value of Twenty Shillings Sterling Five files of the Value of Five Shillings Two Dozen of Hose of the Value of thirty Shillings Sterling of the proper goods and Chattles of the said Landon Carter, in the [336] Mansion House then and there found and Feloniously and Burglariously did Steal Take and Carry away against the peace of our now Lord the King his Crown and Dignity.

Whereupon the said Manuell was brought to the Barr and Arraigned for the said Felony and Burglary and there pleaded not Guilty and thereupon the Court proceeded on his tryall after havng heard the Evidence against him and what he had to Say in his Defence are of Oppinion that he is Guilty of the Felony and Burglary Mentioned In the Inditement.[149]

It is therefore ordered that the said Manuell Return to the place From when he came, from thence to the place of Execution, and there to be Hanged by the Neck, till he be Dead.

Pursuant to an act of Assembly made in the year 1723 concerning the Tryall of Slaves committing Capitall Crymes, this Court in pursuance there of, due Value

---

149. Ralph's fate is not recorded.

Manuell a Negro Man Slave Belonging to Landon Carter Esq. (who was this day Condemned to Dye for Felony and Burglary) to Sixty pounds Current Money and ordered That the Clerk of this Court Certifye the same to the Next assembly.

At a call'ed Court held at the Court house of Richmond County the 18th day of November 1747.

Present: Thomas Barber, Daniell Hornby, John Tayloe, Travers Tarpley, Gentlemen Justices.

Lucas Discharged

Thomas Lucas by Virtue of a Mittimus from Travers Tarpley Gentleman one of the Majestrates of this county was Committed to this County Goal for Severall Misdemeaners in aiding and assisting Entertaining and Receiving stolen Goods[150] of a Runaway Servant Man belonging to John Smith Gentleman and being Now Brought before this Court but noe Evidence appearing against him he is therefore Discharged.

[**337**] At a Court Held for Richmond County the 4th day of July 1748.

Present: John Woodbridge, Thomas Barber, Leroy Griffin, Daniel Hornby, John Tayloe, Gentlemen Justices.

Kay bound to the Peace

Sarah Kay Wife of William Kay Clerik Coming into Court and Making Oath That she was afraid of her Life or Some bodily hurt to be done or perceived to be done her by her said Husband, It is Considered and Ordered by the Court, that the said William Kay give Sufficient Security for his good Behaviour for the Term of one Year. Whereupon the said William Kay, with William Fauntleroy Jr. and John Ford his securities Came into Court and Acknowledg'd themselves indebted to our Sovereign Lord the King his heirs and successors To wit: The said William Kay in in the Sum of forty pounds, And the said William Fauntleroy Jr. and John Ford in the Sum of Twenty pounds each, To be Levied on their Goods and Chattles Lands and Tenements, Respectively. Upon Condition that if the said William Kay Clerik Shall be of good Behaviour and Keep the Peace As well Towards his Majesty as towards all his Liege People, and more Especially,

---

150. The criminal cause was receiving stolen goods. Entertaining a runaway was a civil matter. Under the 1705 law (*Statutes at Large*, 3:454–55), a harborer or entertainer of a runaway could be brought to court in an action of debt by the master, for sixty pounds of tobacco for each day that the defendant harbored the servant. If the fact was proven, there was no defense against the charge, but the master had to bring the action; the crown would not do it.

Towards the said Sarah Kay for the Terme of one Year, otherwise this Recognizance be Void or otherwise to Remain in force and Power.

At a Court Held for Richmond County the first day of August 1748.

Pridham Continued in Custody

Edward Pridham being Taken in Custody by an Order of Last Court and Brought before this Court to Answer for being a Common Disturber of the Peace and offering Nothing Material in his Excuse, It is Considered and ordered by the Court that he give Good Security for his Good Behaviour for the Term of one Year And that he Remain in Custody until he give Such Security.

At a Court Continued and held for Richmond County the 2d day of August 1748.
Present: John Peachey, John Woodbridge, Landon Carter, Anthony Sydnor, Gentlemen Justices.

Pridham recognizance

Edward Pridham being Continued in Custody Till he gave Security for his good behaviour Came into Court with William Hammond and Thomas Russell his Securities and Acknowledged Themselves indebted to our Sovereign Lord the King his heirs and Successors, Vizt The Principal in the sum of forty pounds and the Securities in the Sum of Twenty pounds Each; To be Levied on their goods and Chattles, [338] Lands and Tenements Respectively. Upon Condition That if the said Edward Pridham Shall keep the peace and be of the good behaviour As well Towards his Majesty as towards all his Leige People for the Term of one Year as aforesaid Then this Recognizance to be Void; otherwise to Remain in Force and Power.

Henry and Aron's Tryall

At a Session of Oyer and Terminer held at The Court house of Richmond County on the first day of December 1748. By Virtue of a Special Commission for the Tryall of all Treasons petit Treason or Misprisions thereof, Felonys, Murders or other Offences or Crimes Whatsoever Committed or done within Richmond County by Two Negro Man Slaves Named Harry and Aron, Belonging to Joseph Morton Gentleman of King George County And Directed to William Fauntleroy, Samuell Peachey, John Woodbridge, Thomas Barber, William Glascock, Landon Carter, Leroy Griffin, Daniell Hornby, William Jordan, John Tayloe Jr., Anthony Sydnor, Gilbert Hamilton, William Fauntleroy Jr., John

Smith, William Brockenbrough, Travers Tarpley, John Tarpley, Thomas Plummer, William Beale, Moore Fauntleroy, Alvin Mountjoy and Nicholas Flood Gentlemen.

Present: Thomas Barber, Landon Carter, Daniel Hornby, William Beale, Gentlemen Justices.

Memorandum that on the first day of December 1748 and in the xxii Year of the Reign of King George the Second etc. An Indictment was Preferrd Against Two Negro Men Slaves Named Harry and Aron Belonging to Joseph Morton Gentleman of King George County in these Words.

Richmond Ss: Harry and You Aron do Now Stand Severally Indicted by the Name of Harry and by the Name of Aaron for that on the Twenty Seventh day of October Last Past Not having the fear of God before your Eyes but moved and instigated by the Devil, you and each of You joyntly with forces and armes, Entered the Cowpen of Mr. William Jordan in the parish of Lunenburgh County aforesaid and then and there did Feloniously kill and Carry Away one yearling Beef the Property of the said William Jordan of the Value of fifteen Shillings Lawfull Money of Great Brittain, Contrary to the Peace of our Sovereign Lord the King etc. And to the form of the Statutes therein Made and Provided Whereupon the said Harry and Aaron Were brought to the Barr and Arraignd for the said Felony and there Plead Not Guilty Whereupon the Court Proceeded on their Tryall And after hearing the Evidence Against them, And What they had to Say in their Defence, Are of Opinion that they are Guilty of Larceny[,] for which They were burnt in the hand at the Barr with a hott iron and Received 39 Lashes on Their Bare Backs at the Common Whipping Post. And were then Discharged

Dick a Negro his Tryall

[**339**] At a Session of Oyer and Terminer held at the Court house of Richmond County the Seventh day of August 1749 in the xxiii Year of the Reign of our Sovereign Lord George the Second by the Grace of God of great Brittian France and Ireland King Defender of the faith etc. By virtue of a Special Commission for the Tryall of all Treasons petit Treasons of misprisions there of felonies, murders or other Offences or Crimes Whatsoever Committed or perpetratted within the said County of Richmond by Dick a negro Slave the proper Slave of Phillip Ludwell of the County of James City Esq. Directed to William Fauntleroy, Samuell Peachey John Woodbridge Thomas Barber William Glascock Landon Carter Leroy Griffin Daniel Hornby William Jordan John Tayloe Anthony Sydnor Gilbert Hamilton William Fauntleroy Jr. John Smith William Brockenbough Thomas Plummer William Beale Alvin Mountjoy, and Nicholas Flood Gentlemen.

Present: Thomas Barber, John Woodbridge, Leroy Griffin, Daniel Hornby, John Tayloe, William Fauntleroy Jr., Thomas Plummer, and Alvin Mountjoy, Gentlemen Justices.

Memorandum that on the Seventh day of August in the year of our Lord 1749 Charles Beale Gentleman Attorney of our Lord the King in the County aforesaid for this purpose particularly deputed and Appointd Comes into Court here in his proper person and Gives the Court here to Understand and be informed that Dick a Negro Slave the proper Slave of Phillip Ludwell of the County of James City Esq. on the fifteenth day of July in the twenty third year of the Reign of our Sovereign Lord George the Second by the grace of God of great Brittian France and Ireland King Defender of the Faith etc. with force and Armes the Dwelling house of one John Stonum at the parish of Northfarnham in the County Aforesaid feloniously did break and enter and one dark brown drug get which was of the value of thirty Shillings, one Pair of Shoes of the value of three Shillings one Cotton Sheet of the value of Ten Shillings, one pairs of Long Breeches of the Value of two Shillings two Shirts of the Value of three Shillings [**340**] the the proper goods and Chattles of the said John Stonum in the said dwelling house then and there found then and there feloniously did steal take and Carry Away Against the Peace of our Said now Lord the King his Crowne and Dignity.

Whereupon the said Dick was instantly Led to the Bar and being Arraigned of the Premises he Confessed that he was thereof Guilty and thereof did put himself Upon the Court[;] Whereupon it Seems to the Court here that the said Dick is Guilty of the felony aforesaid in manner and form as above against him is Alledged and it being Demanded of him if any thing for himself he had or knew to say Why the Court to Judgement and Execution Against him of and upon the Premises should not Proceed he said he had nothing to say beside what he had before said. Therefore It is Considered by the Court that the said Dick be hangd by the Neck Till he be Dead.

Pursuant to an Act of Assembly in such case made and Provided this Court do Value the said Dick to forty pounds current money and Orderd the Clerk Certify the same to the Next Assembly.

[*Newman and Sam, Negroes, Trial*]

At a Session of Oyer and Terminer held at the Court house of Richmond County on the fifth day of September 1749 in the xxiii Year of the Reign of our Sovereign Lord George the second by the grace of God of Great Brittain France and Ireland King Defender of the faith etc. By Virtue of a Special Commission Under the Seale of this Colony bearing Date the Twenth ninth day of August in the Year aforesaid for the hearing and Determining of All Treasons, Petit Treasons or misprisions thereof felonies, murders or other Offences or Crimes Whatsoever Committed or perpetrated within this county of Richmond by Newman a Negro Slave belonging to Mrs. Elizabeth Griffin and Sam a negro Slave belonging to Ann Mccarty Widdows both of the County Aforesaid Directed to William Fauntleroy Samuell Peachey John Woodbridge Thomas Barber William Glascock Landon Carter Leroy Griffin William Jordan John Tayloe Anthony Sydnor [**341**] Gilbert Hamilton William Fauntleroy Jr., John Smith William Brockenbrough William Beale Moore Fauntleroy Alvin Mountjoy and Nicholas Flood Gentlemen.

Present: Landon Carter, William Jordan, John Taylor, William Brocken-brough, Gentlemen Justices.

Memorandum: That on the fourth day of September in the Year of our Lord one thousand seven hundred and forty nine Charles Beale Gentleman and Attorney of our Lord the King for the County aforesaid for this Purpose particularly appointed and deputed came here into Court and gave the Court here to Understand and be informed That Newman a negro male Slave the proper Slave of Elizabeth Griffin Widdow and Sam a negro male Slave the proper Slave of Ann McCarty Widdow on the Eighteenth day of August in the Year of our Lord One thousand Seven hundred and forty nine the Mansion house of Daniel Hornby Gentleman at the parish of Northfarnham in the County Aforesaid feloniously and burglariously did break and Enter and four Linnen Shirts of the Value of Twenty Shillings One half of the value of two Shillings, two Jacketts of the value of five Shillings, half a pound of thread of the Value of two Shillings, two neck bands of the value of Six pense and Twelve dunghill fowls of the Value of four Shillings[,] the proper goods and Chattles of the said Daniel Hornby[,] in the said Mansion house then and there found then and there feloniously and Burglariously did Steal take and Carry Away Against the Peace of our now Lord the King his Crown and Dignity.

Whereupon the said Newman and Sam were instantly Led to the Barr and being Arraignd of the Premisses Confessed that they were in some part guilty of the said felony and burglary but not of the Whole And thereof did put themselves Upon the Court Upon which divers Witnesses were produced and Examnd Against them and They fully heard in their own Defence, Whereupon it Seems to the Court here that the said Newman and Sam are Guilty of the felony and Burglary aforesaid in Manner and form as Against them is Alledged and it Demanded of them if any thing for themselves they had or knew to Say Why the Court to Judgement and Execution Against them of and upon the prisoners Should not proceed they Answered that they [had] nothing to say beside What [342] they had before said. Therefore It is Considerd by the Court that the said Newman and Sam be hangd by the Neck Till they be Dead.

Pursuant to an Act of Assembly in Such case made and Provided This Court do Value the said Newman to forty Pounds current money And the said Sam to fifty pounds Current money And Ordered the Clerk Certify the same to the Next Assembly.

Powell Examination

At a court Held at Richmond County Court house the Tenth day of October, in the XXVI Year of the Reign of our Sovereign Lord George the Second by the grace of God, King of great Britain etc. And in the year of our Lord 1752 for the Examination of Mathew Powell charged with Felony in Stealing horses from Joseph Simpson clerk of this County.

Present: Thomas Barber, John Tayloe, William Brockenbrough, Alvin Mount-joy, Gentlemen Justices.

The above named Mathew Powell being commited to the Goal of this County charged with the felony Aforesaid, was Led to the Barr and Examined, And thereupon the said Joseph Simpson clerk a Witness was sworn and Examined upon the Premises, And the Prisoner heard in his own defense and upon Consideration of the Evidence of the said Witness and the Circumstances of the Case, It is the Opinion of the Court that the Prisoner ought not to be tryed for the said Supposed fact, by the General Court but ought to be Discharged from his Imprisonment aforesaid, And he is Discharged Accordingly. [343] The Examination of Mathew Powell charged with felony in Stealing horses from the Reverend Joseph Simpson Taken before the Court on Tuesday the 10th of October 1752.

This Examinent Sayth that he never took any horse Belonging to the said Joseph Simpson When he ran away from him, Nor was any such horse found in his possession when he was taken up at Sherando river, Nor is he guilty in any manner of the felony with which he stands charged. And further this Examinent sayth not. Signed in presence of the Court.

MATHEW POWELL

Test. T. TARPLEY DEX[151]

The Deposition of the Reverend Joseph Simpson aged thirty years or there abouts being sworn and Examined deposeth and saith That on the Eighteenth of September last in the morning he Missed the Prisoner at the Bar then his Servant, And upon Enquiring Missed his riding horse which he supposed was taken by the prisoner or one Peter Halppen another Servant of this Desponents who ran away at the same time[,] And afterwards this same Morning he went over to Mr. John Beales and upon Enquiry if any of his horses were Missing found that a grey horse in his possession had been taken away as he supposed by the said Servants[;] Whereupon he immediately Advertised their Running away with a reward of Eight hundred pounds of Tobacco for the taking up of each of the said Servants besides what the Law allowed, and on the Thursday night afterwards he[,] the Prisoner[,] was brot [brought] home by the Constable having been taken up at Sherando River by one Thomas Ashby, Ferryman, And that his the said Simpsons horse which had been so taken away was brot home by his brother from Leeds Town, who received him from the waitingman of Col. Charles Carter who as [344] This deponent was Informed brot him from Shernado ferry where the said Prisoner was taken up, And that this deponent afterwards At a Court held for the said County the 2d day of October instant brot the prisoner before the Court where he Obtained an order for Service for the Lost time and for Charges in Taking up, Where he was also punished According to Law for Altering his Name and forging [a] Pass and that the Prisoner before his running Away had the care of working feeding and riding his horses, And farther this deponent sayth not. Sworn to and Signed in Court.

JOSEPH SIMPSON

Test T. TARPLEY DEX

Gorf and Morgan's Examination

At a Court Held at Richmond County Courthouse 13th day of November in the XXVII Year [1753] of the reign of our Lord George the Second by the grace

---

151. Tarpley was the king's attorney and the letters DEX might have been his abbreviation for [pro] D [ominus] [RE]x.

of God King of Great Britain etc. for the Examination of Robert Gorf and Patrick Morgan Charged with Felony in Stealing Money from Alexander Alloway of this County.

Present: Thomas Barber, William Brockenbrough, John Tarpley, Alvin Mountjoy, Gentlemen Justices.

The above Named Robert Gorf and Patrick Morgan being Committed to the goal of this County charged with the Felony aforesaid were led to the Bar, And thereupon Divers Witnesses to wit, Roger Williams, John Thomas, George Spragg and Alexander Alloway were sworn and Examined upon the premises and the Prisoner's heard in their own defence and Upon Consideration of the Evidence of the said Witnesses, And the circumstances of the Case It was the Opinion of the Court that the said Robert Gorf ought not to be [345] Tryed for the said Supposed fact by the General Court but ought to be Discharged from his Imprisonment aforesaid. And he was according Discharged. Also It is the Opinion of the said Court as the Case appears to them that the said Patrick Morgan ought to be tryed for the said Supposed fact at the next Court of Oyer and Terminer to be held in the City of Williamsburgh on the Second Tuesday in December next, And thereupon he is remanded to Goal.

[Williams's and others' recognizances]

Be it Remembered that on this 13th day of November in the XXVII Year of the reign of our Sovereign Lord George the second by the grace of God of great Britain Franes [France] and Ireland King Defender of the faith etc. before the Justices of the County Court of Richmond of our lord the King at the Court house comes Roger Williams John Thomas and Alexander Alloway of the said County and Acknowledged themselves Severally indebted unto our said Lord the King in the sum of Twenty pounds each of their Respective goods and Chattles land and Tenements to be levied and to our said lord the King his heirs and Successors render'd; Yet upon this condition that if the said Roger Williams, John Thomas and Alexander Alloway shall make their Personal Appearance at the Capitol in the City of Williamsburgh on the Second Tuesday in December next then and there to give Evidence on behalf of our said lord the King against Patrick Morgan touching a Certain Felony whereof he stands accused, And shall not Depart thence without the leave of the said Court then this Recognizance to be void.

Daniel a Negroe his Trial

[346] Memorandum That at the Courthouse of Richmond County on Thursday the 15th day of November In the XXVII Year of the reign of our Sovereign Lord King George the second Anno Domini, 1753, His Majesties Commission under the seale of this his Colony and Dominion of Virginia bearing date the 12th day of November Directed to John Woodbridge, Thomas Barber, Landon Carter, Jonathon Beckwith, Gilbert Hamilton, John Smith, William Brocken-

brough, John Tarpley and Alvin Mountjoy Gentlemen or any four or more of them whereof the said John Woodbridge, Thomas Barber, Landon Carter or Jonathon Beckwith should be one To here and Determine all Treasons Petty treasons misprisions thereof Felonies Murder or other Offences or Crime whatsoever Committed or Perpetrated withtin the County aforesaid by Daniel a Negro Man Slave belonging to Charles Beale Gentleman was openly read, as was in like manner his Majesties Dedimus Potestatem[152] under the said Seale and of the same date for Administering the Oaths etc. to the said Commissioners by Virtue of which the said Thomas Barber and William Brockenbrough administred the Oaths appointed by act of Parliment to be taken instead of the Oaths of Allegiance and Supremacy the Abjuration Oath and test[153] unto the said Jonathon Beckwith and Alvin Mountjoy who subscribed the said Abjuration Oath and test, And then the said Thomas Barber and William Brockenbrough likewise Administered to them the Oath of a Justice of Oyer and Terminer,[154] And the said Jonathan Beckwith and Alvin Mountjoy thereupon Administered the said Oaths Appointed by Act of Parliament to be taken instead of the Oaths of Allegiance and Supremacy the said Abjuration Oath and test unto the said Thomas Barber and William Brockenbrough who also Subscribed the said last mentioned Oath and test. And then the said [347] Jonathan Beckwith and Alvin Mountjoy administered to them the said Oath of a Justice of Oyer and Terminer.

Charles Beale attorney of our Lord the King who for our Lord the King in this part Prosecutes comes into Court in his proper person on Thursday the 15th day of November Aforesaid at the Courthouse Aforesaid Before the said Thomas Barber, Jonathan Beckwith, William Brockenbrough and Alvin Mountjoy Justices as Aforesaid And gives the Court to understand and be informed that Daniel a Negro Man Slave belonging to the said Charles Beale of the County Aforesaid on Monday the fifth of this Instant about the ninth hour in the night of the same day a Dwelling house of John Taylor Esq. in the Parish of Lunenburgh in the County aforesaid with force and arms feloniously and burglariously did break and enter and one coat two jackets one pair of breaches one pair of Stockings one Shirt, one handkerchief and one hat of the Value of Twenty Shillings Sterling and four bits and an half of foreign coined Silver of the proper Goods Chattles and Money of Harry a Negro Man Slave belonging to the said John Tayloe in the said dwelling house then and there found then and there

---

152. The *dedimus* used here authorized the giving of the oaths. The oaths the justices swore pledged loyalty to the royal household, its heirs, and the Protestant succession, and originated in 1690, with 1 Wm. and Mary, sess 1, c.8.

153. This "Declaration of Abjuration," passed in 1713, 1 George I, stat. 2, c.13, pledged the justices not to aid the forces of the pretender. The oath was updated with the accession of each Hanoverian. When the heir to George II, Frederick, Prince of Wales, died, provision was made for an oath of abjuration to ensure that his son, George II's grandson, would be regarded as the lawful king when George II died. The oath of abjuration was required in Virginia in the period 1715–68 in various forms. See Leonard Woods Labaree, ed., *Royal Instructions to British Colonial Governors, 1670–1776*, 2 vols. (New York, 1935), 1:40–41, 431–432.

154. An oath to try cases without favor. Although there were commissions of oyer and terminer and oaths for justices at the oyer and terminer courts that met twice a year in Williamsburg (alternating with the General Court sessions—*Statutes at Large*, 3:288:89 [1705]), there were no additional oaths specified in the statues for oyer and terminer justices at slaves' trials in the county.

feloniously and burglariously did steal take and carry away against the peace of our said now Lord King his Crown and Dignity.

Whereupon the said Daniel was Instantly led to the Bar under the Custody of Nicholas Flood Gentleman Sherif of this County Aforesaid to whose Custody before[,] for the Causes Aforesaid[,] he was Committed, And being Arraigned of the Premises he said he was thereof Guilty, Whereupon it seems to the Court here that the said Daniel is Guilty of the felony and Burglary aforesaid in [**348**] Manner and form as above against him is alleged, And it being Demanded of him if any thing for himself he had or knew to say why the Court to Judgment and Execution against him of and upon the premises should not proceed, he said he had nothing to say besides what he had before said. Therefore it is Considered by the Court that the said Daniel be Hanged by the Neck until he be dead; And it is said to the Sherrif that Execution thereof be done on Fryday the 30th day of this Instant.

Be it Remembered that the Court Valued the said Daniel at Forty five pounds Current Money And order'd the Clerk Certify the same to the Next Assembly.

Bryan et als. Examination

At a Court Held at Richmond County Court house the 22nd day of December in the xxvii Year of the reign of our Sovereign Lord George the second etc. Anno Domini 1753 for the Examination of Thomas Bryan Thomas Penly [and] Ishmael Dew charged with Killing and Destroying James Harriot.

Present: Thomas Barber, Landon Carter, John Tayloe, William Brockenbrough, Gentlemen Justices.

The said Thomas Bryan, Thomas Penley and Ishmael Dew being brot to the bar, Divers Witnesses to wit, Henry Miskell, Daniel Lightfoot, John Williams, Henry Williams, William Harper, John Algood, Isaac Procter, George Sanders, Thomas Williams Sanders and William Barber, were sworn and Examined upon the Premises and the [**349**] Prisoners heard in their own Defence, And upon Consideration of the Evidence of the said Witnesses And the Circumstance of the Case. It is the Opinion of the Court that the Prisoners ought to be tryed for the said Supposed Fact at the next Court of Oyer and Terminer to be held in the City of Williamsburgh on the 6th day of the next General Court And thereupon they are remanded to Goal.

[Miskell's and others' recognizances]

Be it remember'd that on the 22nd day of December in the xxvii Year of the reign of our Sovereign Lord George the second by the grace of God of great Brittain France and Ireland King Defender of the faith etc. before the Justices of the Couty Court of Richmond of our lord the King, at the Court house comes Henry Miskell Daniel Lightfoot, William Harper, John Algood, Isaac Procter, George Sanders and Thomas Williams Sanders of the said County and Acknowledge Themselves severally indebted unto our said Lord the King in the sum of Twenty pounds each of their Respective Goods and Chattles lands and Tenements to be levied. And to our said lord the King his heirs and Successors render'd. Yet upon this Condition that if the said Henry Miskell, Daniel Light-foot, William Harper, John Algood, Isaac Procter, George Sanders and Thomas Williams Sanders shall make their Personal appearance at the Capitol in the City of Williamsburgh on the 6th[155] of the next General Court then and there to give Evidences on behalf of our said Lord the King against Thomas Bryan, Thomas Penley and Ishmael Dew touching a certain Murder whereof they stand accused, And Shall not depart thence without leave of the said Court, then this Recognizance to be Void.

Ridgways Examination

[350] At a Court Held at Richmond County Courthouse the first day of April in the xxvii Year of the reign of our Lord George the second etc. Anno Domini 1754 for the Examination of Peter Ridgway alias Hansna a Convict Charged with felony in Breaking and Entring the Warehouse of William Payne and Stealing his horse and Saddle and sundry goods.

Present: John Woodbridge, Landon Carter, John Tayloe, William Brocken-brough, Alvin Mountjoy, Gentlemen Justices.

The above named Peter Ridgway alias Hansna being Committed to the goal of this County charged with the felony Aforesaid was led to the Bar and thereupon divers witnesses to wit, William Payne and Francis Randall were sworn and Examined upon the premises and the Prisoner heard in his own defence, And upon consideration of the Evidences of the said Witnesses and the Circumstance of the Case It was the Opinion of the Court that the Prisoner ought to be tryed for the said Supposed fact at the next Court of Oyer and Terminer to be held in the City of Williamsburgh on the Second Tuesday in June next . . . . . And thereupon he is Remanded to Goal.

The Deposition of William Payne Commander of the ship Hodgson taken upon the Examination of Peter Ridgway alias Hansna a Convict brought in by the said Payne charged with feloniously Stealing a Gelding belonging to the said Payne And Sundry other goods.

This Deponent being first sworn saith that on Saturday morning [351] The 12th day of January last, when he got up[,] the mate of the ship informed him that the Yaul was loose from the ship And that the Prisoner was missing from among the Servants[;] Upon which one of the men swam ashore and went to the Warehouse, where this Deponent had lodged sundry Parcels of goods and kept his horse. And upon his return to the ship [he] told the Deponent that both his horses were taken out of the said house[;] whereupon he this Deponent went ashore and was Informed by the Overseer of Col. Fauntleroy that the Prisoner had rode away at break of day. That the Deponent then emploied Francis Randall to Pursue the prisoner and disperse advertisements, who some time afterwards returned with his horse[,] the said Prisoner being taken up and afterwards ran away from the said Randall, And also Sundry goods, A pair of Womens Stays two plain hatts one silver lais'd hatt one pair silver spurrs two pair of silk Stock-

---

155. The sixth day of the session, reserved for judicial functions.

ings two Caps two pair of Ruffles and two tuckers Which the Prisoner confess'd to this Deponent he had stolen out of a box lodged in the warehouse and carried off with him, And that he had nailed and lashed the box again. And further this Deponent saith not.

WILLIAM PAYNE

Memorandum, It appears to the Court that the within named Peter Ridgway alias Hansna has been Convicted in great Brittain of Felony and there Sentenced to be Transported for the same, And that the term of transportation is not Expired, And Ordered the same be Certified.[156]

Test T: TARPLEY DEX.

Sherrings Examination

[352] At a Court Held at Richmond County Courthouse the 20th day of May in the xxvii Year of the reign of our Lord George the second etc. Anno 1754 for the Examination of William Sherring Charged with breaking and Entring the lower Church in Lunenburgh Parish in the said County and Stealing the Surplice.

Present: John Woodbridge, Landon Carter, William Brockenbrough, John Smith, Gentlemen Justices.

The above Named William Sherring being committed to the goal of this County charg'd with the felony Aforesaid was led to the barr And being Examined and Questioned if he was thereof guilty of the said felony or not guilty, Answered that he was thereof Guilty, And his Confession being taken and signed in Open Court, It was the Opinion of the Court that the Prisoner ought to be tryed for the said Supposed fact at the next Court of Oyer and Terminer to be held in the City of Williamsburgh on the Second Tuesday in June Next And thereupon he is remanded to goal.

The Examination of William Sherring taken at an Examining Court held in the County of Richmond Aforesaid the 20th day of May 1754. The said Examinent saith that on Tuesday Morning the 30th of April last he broke the lower Church of Lunenburgh Parish and took from thence the greatest part of the Surplice with design to sell it for Victuals, which having offerr'd to sale to Several people But no body buying he threw away upon the road side below Farnham Church and farther this Examinent saith not. The said William Sherring sign'd this Confession in open Court.

his
WILLIAM X SHERRING
mark

Test T: TARPLEY DEX.

[353] May it please your honour—At the Examination of the above Criminal it appearing to us who set in Court both by his Confession and the Information of Others That he Committed the fact wherewith he was Charg'd Rather from an

---

156. The examining court certified Ridgway's previous conviction and his transportation to the colony, under the 1748 law; *Statutes at Large*, 5:545. When the General Court learned this, they would not have to bring half of the trial jury from Richmond, should Ridgway be indicted and put himself upon the country. The new law provided for a jury from Williamsburg and its immediate environs in felony trials of transported felons.

impaired Understanding and dispair Occasional[157] by the Dread of returning to his masters Service than from any Surreptitious or theivish Intention, We thought it proper to Represent the same to your honour and to recommend him as a fit object of mercy to your Honour.

JOHN WOODBRIDGE
LANDON CARTER
JOHN SMITH
WILLIAM BROCKENBROUGH.

Memorandum, It appearing to the Court that the within Named William Sherring has been Convicted in great Brittain of felony and there Sentenced to be Transported for the same, And that the term of Transportation is not Expired, And order'd the same be Certified.

Test T: TARPLEY DEX:

---

157. Probably "occasioned." Another appeal to the governor for a pardon. Compare p. 228 above.

PROPER NAME INDEX

This is an index to proper names. Names with variant spellings are listed in the form in which they appear most frequently in the text.

SUBJECT INDEX